Acclaim for Robert Farris Thompson's

TANGO

"A fascinating meditation on the history of the dance—and all aspects of the music, poetry, and myth it has inspired. Be prepared to sign up for lessons." —*Chicago Sun-Times*

"Robert Farris Thompson's *Tango* indeed is an aesthetic history of that dance of heterosexual passion. The book has gusto and its own deep song of eloquent erotic ecstasy and sorrow. It will inform readers until they are wild with all regret."
—Harold Bloom

"I was startled to find how interesting this subject can be. What a fine book." —Norman Mailer

"The best written book about *any* music or dance in the past decade." —Norman C. Weinstein,
author of *A Night in Tunisia: Imaginings of Africa in Jazz*

ROBERT FARRIS THOMPSON
TANGO

Robert Farris Thompson is the author of, among other works, *Black Gods and Kings*, *African Art in Motion*, and *Flash of the Spirit*. He has been a Ford Foundation Fellow and has mounted major exhibitions of African art at the National Gallery in Washington, D.C. He is Colonel John Trumbull Professor of the History of Art at Yale University, where he is also Master of Timothy Dwight College. He lives in New Haven, Connecticut.

TANGO

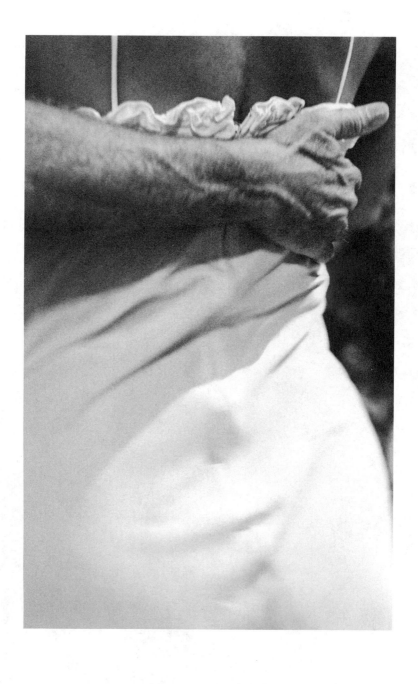

TANGO

The Art History of Love

ROBERT FARRIS THOMPSON

VINTAGE BOOKS
A Division of Random House, Inc.
New York

FIRST VINTAGE BOOKS EDITION, DECEMBER 2006

Owing to limitations of space, permissions acknowledgments can be found on page 363.

The Library of Congress has cataloged the Pantheon edition as follows:
Thompson, Robert Farris.
Tango : the art history of love / Robert Farris Thompson.
p. cm.
1. Tango (Dance). 2. Tangos—History and criticism. I. Title.
GV1796.T3T46 2005
793.3'3—dc22
2005042969

Vintage ISBN-10: 1-4000-9579-4
Vintage ISBN-13: 978-1-4000-9579-7

Author photograph © Yale University
Book design by Iris Weinstein

www.vintagebooks.com

Printed in the United States of America
10 9 8 7 6 5 4 3 2 1

This book is for Alejandro Frigerio and María Julia Carozzi, Alicia and Ian

Churchill, Clark August Hood Thompson and Laura Watt, C. Daniel Dawson,

Pat Kennedy Lawford, and Christopher Munnelly. I also dedicate it to the memory

of four amazing tangueros whom I was privileged to know—Antonio Agri,

José "Lampazo" Vásquez, Pablo Gorcés, and "Rodo" Cieri—and to the

ethnomusicologist who helped change my life, Richard Alan Waterman.

CONTENTS

FOREWORD: SAUNTERING MEANINGFULLY

Who is Robert Farris Thompson? Why do you need to know this? Why do you need to know about tango?

Well, I think some orientation might be of help in order to approach his book in the right frame of mind.

I first stumbled upon RFT in 1974 through his book *African Art in Motion*. As the title suggests, he places objects that we may have seen in museums in the context of the dances, music, and rituals in which they are currently, and have traditionally been, used. They "become activated," to use a favorite phrase of his. His writing, I noticed, is incredibly knowledgeable, but more important to me—wildly enthusiastic. It reads as if Jack Kerouac were still alive and somehow morphed into a professor at Yale. Bob's style, like JK's, resembles jazz, be-bop . . . though he would probably prefer that I said it's like mambo. Whatever. It's poetry, musical. I sought out the videos that accompanied the book, and there I heard the man's voice, which confirmed my impressions.

Like JK, Bob is showing us a new America (north *and* south) that speaks through the vernacular, lawn decorations, hairstyles, gestures, clothing, art, and popular song and dance. It's an America that has been thoroughly Africanized, colonized by beats and attitude rather than by armies and the Church. He calls this Creole hybrid culture Afro-Atlantic, and it's everywhere. I believe it's the cultural story of the twentieth century, but that's another subject.

Some years after coming across his book, I met Bob, dressed at that time to fit the role he plays—Yale professor–Brooks Brothers buttoned-down. It all belies the energetic subversion that are his lectures, which to me are more like performances. If he's talking in your area, go. Even if you think you have little interest in whatever the subject happens to be, just go.

I agreed to write some notes here, though I am far from an expert on tango. So I've been working hard. Last night I fell asleep in a hotel room amongst yesterday's newspapers, pages with scribbled notes, instruction manuals—and a tango playing on the laptop. It's snowing outside.

I wrote down some of my own tango connections. For three years now, I've been touring with The Tosca Strings, primarily a tango group, and fellow Austinite Glover Gil. Some years ago they all began playing tangos at the Continental Club—an unlikely venue for tango some might think, as it's home to a lot of local rock bands. But after a bit they drew dancers, and tango became a regular thing as well as part of the Austin music scene.

Likewise, my friend Toni Basil, a collaborator with many innovative dance groups, such as The Lockers and The Electric Boogaloos, has fallen for tango. We crossed paths recently at a New York *milonga* where I went with JC Herz, a writer on computer gaming. And when the band and I were touring recently in Buenos Aires, I was introduced to members of El Arranque, a "new" tango group that is reviving older amazing arrangements. Many of these were "lost," disregarded, as more "modern" approaches became dominant. But the past is never over, "it's not even past," as Faulkner said.

The tango is making inroads in some pretty unexpected places. There's a kind of explosion going on, with little epicenters and pockets of intensity here and there. In a New York loft I saw dancers "freezing"—one of my favorite dance moves, which consists of no movement. Herz asserted that one of the surprising things she discovered in dancing the tango was the freedom she felt in being led. A seeming contradiction one would think, coming from a modern woman . . . but maybe not.

Robert Farris Thompson makes a case here for African influence on tango, something that will surely not go down easily with eurocentric porteños. But Bob builds his case slowly, methodically piling up evidence, etymological roots or words, gesture, dance. He points out the taste for innovation—something European dance and music was not known for. He names names and references, and in the end it's hard to dispute, though no doubt some will try.

Other porteños will deny that tango has any Afro roots whatsoever—supposedly there are no blacks to be seen on the present-day streets of Buenos Aires. But as Bob points out, this was not always the case, and the crazy mixture of European, African and gaucho (often Andalusian) influences helped create a form that is still evolving today. The writing transcends the subject. What Bob says about the way spiritual attitudes are held, secured, transported, transposed, and morphed into life and tango applies to any number of aspects of our culture. It tells us that if we look around with fresh eyes we might see who we are in a new light. There are myriad versions of our history—this idea is becoming accepted now—and here is a new history not just of Argentine dance and music but also of the whole New World and where it came from and what it is.

DAVID BYRNE
16 March 2005

A mural of a man in a fedora, seven stories high, dominates Avenida Libertador in downtown Buenos Aires (Plate 1). The artist is Carlos Páez Vilaró, a distinguished Uruguayan painter who was born in Montevideo on November 1, 1923. He finished this mural in 1989. It honors the great tango singer Carlos Gardel, the hero of Argentina, the inventor of tango song, who died in a plane crash in Medellín, Colombia, on June 2, 1935.

PLATE 1

Páez painted Gardel blue, the color of heaven. His lips are black. His Cheshire-cat smile lights up the street with the flash of his teeth. He has just finished singing—that's what his smile means. Curved tracks descend, through his face and his shoulders. They represent the River Plate.[1] Along these curved lines Irineo Leguisamo, Gardel's jockey friend, pulls ahead in a race.[2] Diego Maradona plays soccer. A man sells the news of the day.

Gardel's tie is the obelisk that rises at the intersection of Avenida Corrientes, the former great tango way, with 9 de Julio, said to be the widest avenue in the world.

Gardel's broad chest supports signs of industry (a bridge, a factory, a cathedral, an avenue lined with buildings) and pleasure (a couple dancing tango, the male dressed in blue, like Gardel). A ship, emblem of Buenos Aires as a major world port, anchors in space to the left of his face. A blue bird soars toward the sun.

Matching the blue of the singer, the bird adds an element "of friendship and peace," in the words of the artist. To me it represents the soul of Gardel, returning to his city, fulfilling a promise made at the end of the 1945 tango "Adiós pampa mía":

> *I'll return to your land*
> *When I feel my soul rise*
> *Like a dove going to heaven.*[3]

Gardel's back. This is his message: heaven is tucked away, somewhere in Buenos Aires. Quest for its glamour, as when Boca Juniors win a soccer match and fill the streets with honking cars blazing with blue and yellow banners and gesturing, bare-chested, high-spirited guys; or when a horse named Sin Rumbo (No Particular Destination) comes in first and suddenly men and women have the money to start a tango club; or when a woman meets the love of her life and he meets the love of his on the floor of an old tango ballroom.

The smile of Gardel is a challenge: if you want to understand me, master the message of my city. Not just its songs but its streets, not just its music but its dance, not just its dance but its diamond-patterned dance floors, and the red-diamond tablecloths that mirror those patterns, while supporting our creole cuisine: *asado, matambre, empanadas, locro, humitas, pastelitos, alfajores.* Our food and our dance, our literature and our music, our Jorge Luis Borges and our Eladia Blázquez, form one single challenge: you don't reach ten million without a big dream. And what is that dream? Tango. Find out.

TANGO

PREFACE: MOVING WITH AN ARM AROUND LIFE

Convert the outrage of the years into a music.

— JORGE LUIS BORGES, *Antología personal* (1961)

The dance is the thing with which we are
concerned and contains within itself its own
arrangement and and history and finale.

— CORMAC McCARTHY, *Blood Meridian* (1985)

Tango is self-transformation.

— SALLY SOMMER, dance historian (summer 2000)

Tango spanned the twentieth century. It was *the* fabulous dance of
the past hundred years—and the most beautiful, in the opinion of
Martha Graham. Jorge Luis Borges, early on, divined one of the
reasons for its staying power: tango translates outrage into music.

All this and more was evident in 1934, when Enrique Santos Discépolo, in the depths of the Depression, wrote his classic tango lyric
"Cambalache" (Shop Where One Sells Stolen Goods), for the film *The
Soul of the Bandoneón*. "Cambalache" blasted its way into Argentine consciousness with words about time, immortality, and stoicism. The song is
in your face. Today it adorns the back of the menu of the Bar Plaza

Dorrego, in the heart of old Buenos Aires. *Tangueros* know it cold. It's a song that's never out of date, particularly in Argentina's recent crisis.

In January 1999 I found a fragment from "Cambalache" graffitied on a Buenos Aires billboard at the corner of Callao and Sante Fe, in the heart of the Barrio Norte:

> *20th century,*
> *feverish and problematic,*
> *[you're] a shop where they sell stolen goods.*
> *You don't cry,*
> *you get no milk.*
> *You don't cop it, you become a square.*
> *But who the hell cares!*[1]

Danger and violence confronted the world across the whole of the twentieth century. The women and men of tango kept going, turning outrage into song. The brave made abstractions of vicissitude. Small wonder that "Cambalache" became an anthem of the *tangueros,* women and men who organize their lives around the music, and *milongueros,* women and men who organize their lives around the dance. Strong in stance, sure in their motion, they gave the century a set of moves that spanned the whole globe and that are with us forever.

Numerous books describe tango. Most are by Argentine authors, though works by Julie Taylor, Simon Collier, and Nicole Nau-Klapwijk richly deserve mention as well. The best establish the passion of the form. Some are nostalgic, freezing time around the early twentieth century, the era of the *compadritos,* the famous "tango hipsters," with their fedoras and cravats (*funyis y lengues*) (Plate 2), their Victrolas with wide flaring horns, their kisses on street corners under a lamplight or the moon.

Who cares if we are living in the aughts of the twenty-first century? Who cares if Victrolas and compadritos are impossibly remote to Argentine youth living *rock en castellano,* hip-hop, and blue jeans? As with Hugh Grant's character in the movie *Notting Hill,* who had never heard of *Gilda*—Rita Hayworth's greatest role, in which she played a Buenos Aires songstress—the loss is theirs. Tango is timeless, mixing love and action in the motion of the people.

Tango has had its ups and downs, but its strength and elegance outlast negation. Like classic African dance music, one distant cousin, the motion and music defy life's brevity.[2]

In the 1980s Buenos Aires barrio dancers sparked the strongest tango renaissance of the twentieth century, through their performance in the

stage extravaganza *Tango Argentino.* It
had also been barrio dancers, led by two
masters, Petróleo and his black colleague,
El Negro Lavandina, who had sparked
the earlier upsurge of the 1940s. Today
the dance lives on, on the floors of the
milongas (tango dance halls) of Buenos
Aires. There, in places like Sin Rumbo or
Sunderland Club, milongueros reveal,
night after night, why tango lasts: passion
and style conquer all.

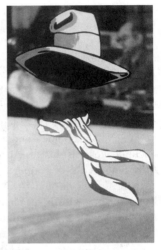

The best tango narratives are strong,
imparting truths and convictions. One
basic message: it is just as important to be
well danced as it is to be well versed or
well read. Equal truths illumine the
music of the tango, where one salutes

PLATE 2

incredible bandleaders, larger than life:
Roberto Firpo, Francisco Canaro, Julio de Caro, Carlos di Sarli, Juan
d'Arienzo, Osvaldo Pugliese, Horacio Salgán, Aníbal "Pichuco" Troilo,
and Astor Piazzolla.

More than music is involved: each master has written a signature
sound, demanding moves that are equally singular. Dancers like Lampazo
or Roberto Tonet translated d'Arienzo's virile rhythm into strong, vivid figures. Di Sarli's sonic parsimony, by contrast, led to elegant refinement, in
relatively few figures.

Juan Carlos Copes was strong enough to dance all of the above, and
also the jazz-inflected, classically tinged "new tango" of Piazzolla, built on
the early modernism of Salgán and Pugliese.

Tango texts are the authentic poetry of Buenos Aires. They create
moods of humor, valor, and longing, only the last of which overlaps a
stereotype of tango as a song of anguish. Above all, tango poets make us
aware of the passing of time. They *live* this awareness, which may well
turn out to be, *au fond,* the very essence of human consciousness.

One especially honors Carlos Gardel, the inventor of the tango song.
His voice and looks are iconic in Argentina. Gardel is the smile in the air
of Buenos Aires. With the blessing of his spirit, we wander the contemporary city, visiting Bar El Chino in the Pompeya barrio, where one hears
tango singing, or going to the Club del Vino in Palermo on a night when
Nelly Omar, *cantante nacional,* is performing onstage.

The great tango dance masters of the first half of the twentieth century included El Cachafaz and Carmencita Calderón, El Vasco Aín, El Negro Santillán, José Méndez, Félix Luján (El Negro Lavandina), and Petróleo. They lit up the nights of the Argentine capital. But later dancers were equally important: Juan Carlos Copes and María Nieves, Ester and Mingo Pugliese, Elsa María and Héctor Mayoral, Suzuki and Pepito Avellaneda, Gloria Darraud and Eduardo Arquimbaud, Elvira Santamaría and Virulazo, Norma and El Pibe Palermo, Nélida and Nelson, Gloria and Rodolfo, "Los Dinzel," Milena Plebs and Miguel Ángel Zotto, Pablo Verón, Natalia Games and Gabriel Angió, Roberto Tonet, Kely and Facundo Posadas, Carlos Anzuate and Margarita de Guillé, and those incredible stylists of *canyengue,* María Cieri and the late Rodolfo Cieri.

In a piece on tango in *The New York Times,* Janny Scott found that "followers" (a euphemism for females) were told not to move until the "leaders" indicated it was time. But she also discovered that tango women do not necessarily mirror what men are doing: "They often do different steps."[3] How to comprehend the contradiction? Study the figures. In the *ocho,* a figure-eight pattern with mirroring pivots, the woman moves back and forth in a sinous sequence that is wholly her own. At its best the ocho becomes a bouquet of motion, tossed like eight roses, at the feet of the partner. One stands still while the other does ocho. This was the step Madonna performed in *Evita.* Ocho is a womanist original, set in motion by men. It is call-and-response on the dance floor. Women's legs are never more beautiful, never more their own, than when sheened in this step.

Gardel is world famous. But so is Libertad Lamarque, the top tango film star, who died in Mexico City on December 12, 2000, while performing in a *telenovela.* Her reputation swept the hemisphere with movies made in Mexico City in the 1940s and 1950s. She left for Mexico just before Juan Domingo Perón came to power, in 1945; according to legend her Argentine film rival, Perón's wife, Evita, forced her into exile.

Women were singing tango before Gardel. The voices of Linda Thelma, Andrée Viviane, and Flora Gobbi are present on the the earliest recorded tangos, from about 1909, 1909, and 1911 respectively. Their work leads on to the incredible Ada Falcón, "the Garbo of tango," to Eladia Blázquez, and finally to *cantantes* of the twenty-first century: Susana Rinaldi, Adriana Varela, Amelita Baltar, Lidia Borda, and María Cieri. In a macho country, to be a tango songstress was one of the ways a woman could "defend herself from hunger, the asphalt jungle—and men."[4]

One of the distinctions between tango and Argentine folk dances, such as *pericón* or *gato,* is improvisation. Milongueros, like jazzmen, prize reshifting figures in reminted transitions each time around.

The comparison with the black music called jazz leads us to the major theme of this book: African and Afro-Argentine influences are continuous in the rise, development, and achievement of the tango. Recognition of this has been rendered problematic, however, by the alleged "disappearance" of the blacks of Buenos Aires. The number of persons of African descent in Buenos Aires went from 34 percent in 1810 to less than 2 percent in 1887, when immigrants from Spain, Italy, and elsewhere flooded the city. By the turn of the century European-oriented citizens in Buenos Aires decided that African elements had disappeared from their population. Even in Carnival street dancing, they believed, African participation had evaporated. Until recently historians accepted and cited this assumption uncritically.[5]

But although the presence of Afro-Argentines may have dwindled, they were culturally critical in music and dance. Their contribution to tango is continuous. As soon as one starts digging into the origins of the tango, its black creole roots emerge. Even if Afro-Argentines did shrink to a mere two thousand by the mid–twentieth century, members of that group were creating moves and composing tango dance tunes out of proportion to their numbers.

This book documents Afro-Argentines working at the center of the tango not just in 1880 but in 2005. That will be news for the elite of Buenos Aires, who will perhaps be surprised to learn that a descendant of the Posadases—a distinguished black family in early tango music— Facundo Posadas, plays a major role in Buenos Aires milonga and tango today. Facundo and his wife, Kely, performed, for instance, with two other great masters, Juan Carlos Copes and Miguel Ángel Zotto, in Miami Beach at the Fontainebleau Hotel in May 2001. Fluent in both tango and jazz dance, Facundo Posadas is a living refutation of the total-disappearance-of-the-blacks-of-Argentina theory, as are his colleagues on the dance floor Carlos "El Negro" Anzuate and Margarita "La Negra" de Guillé.

The fact that Anzuate and Posadas are equally conversant in jazz dance and tango alerts us to the fact that their inspiration is various. As Ricardo Rodríguez Molas points out, black impact on tango entails more than one single line of influence, from the civilizations of Central Africa to the *candombes* of Buenos Aires to tango.[6] The sources are multiple and sometimes indirect, ranging from the coming of the beat of the Afro-Cuban *habanera* to Argentina after 1850, to the integration of key solo moves from candombe in milonga couple dancing in the Buenos Aires of the mid–twentieth century and earlier.

In addition, cakewalk and ragtime arrived in Buenos Aires in 1903, as documented by Sergio Pujol.[7]

As if a triple black dosage—candombe, habanera, and jazz—were not enough, North African–related qualities factor in, too: Andalusian syncopation and percussive heel-stamping (*taconeo*), which trace back to the Moorish era in Spain, also enhance the tradition.

Parenthetically, a brilliant example of how cosmopolitan black Argentine creativity can be, in the range of its influences, is the career of Oscar Alemán (February 20, 1909–October 14, 1980). As Walter Thiers recounts in his book *El Jazz Criollo* (Argentine Creole Jazz), Oscar Alemán was an Afro-Argentine genius who started out as a dancer of black gaucho *malambo*, picked up Afro-Brazilian *cavaquinho* guitar technique in Brazil, became friends with a black North American tap dancer, and ultimately synthesized all of these influences, and more, to become one of Argentina's most famous jazz stars.

Tango culture and tango humanism are Buenos Aires phenomena. They emerged from the encounter of dance concepts from Kongo with the city's cultural and social situation, involving African-born blacks, blacks born in Argentina, European migrants from Spain and Italy come to *hacer la América* (seek their fortune in the Americas), and Europeans born in Argentina, including ex-cattlemen, some of them black, in from the pampas, looking for work.

In telling this history, we consider the artistic contributions not only of Africans on the soil of Argentina but also of Andalusian-influenced gauchos who brought stamping patterns in the dance and Andalusian trilling patterns to song. The habanera arrived, in part, with black Cuban sailors, some settling on the other side of the River Plate in Montevideo, Uruguay, in the late nineteenth century. They inspired the names of black marching groups like Pobres Negros Cubanos (Poor Black Cubans, 1898), Esclavos de La Habana (Slaves from Havana, 1908), and Los Hijos de La Habana (The Sons of Havana, 1912).[8]

Habanera proved critical to the dance history of both Montevideo and Buenos Aires, where it became the beat of the milonga and of the earliest tangos.

All of these elements came together in late-nineteenth-century Buenos Aires. But the strongest root is pure Afro-Argentine, a development of Kongo-style dancing, as elaborated in black dancing groups called candombes that also existed in black Uruguay. Later, in the twentieth century, black social clubs kept up candombe-style dancing. Key candombe steps were inserted into the milonga. Or perhaps it would be truer to say that key candombe steps were inserted into the habanera and that the result of this was the milonga. All of this brought pleasure and joy, inspiring white dancers like El Pibe Palermo.

Paintings, photographs, films, and videos further document this presence. We will consider the Afro-Argentine percussive *malambo* dance and the famous black dueling composers (*payadores*) like the incomparable black lyricist Gabino Ezeiza, who wrote more than five hundred songs. Such presences and episodes, when all brought together, establish the depth of African-influenced aesthetic action today in the capital of Argentina.

As intimated, the roots of the tango intersect with a world-popular Afro-Cuban rhythm, the habanera. The reader will want to know more about this popular beat, its history and nature, and so an entire chapter will examine its impact. It was originally a Central African rhythm, a "call to the dance" (*mbila a makinu*) that in fusing with Iberian and other elements in Cuba took on a life of its own. W. C. Handy heard it in New Orleans, played it in St. Louis, and termed it "the call of the blood."[9]

The global diffusion of habanera is amazing: the mambo of the 1850s, it came to Argentina through no fewer than three sources: Spaniards who had danced it in Madrid, imported sheet music, and later black Cuban sailors, some of whom settled in the late nineteenth century in Montevideo. A transnational phenomenon long before the term was coined, habanera invaded the bars and dives and brothels of Buenos Aires no later than the 1860s, later to be reinforced by black Cuban sailors. It was already there, in some form, before they arrived on the River Plate scene.

Habanera challenged local black dancers and their comrades, sparking competition among the barrio dancers, as we learn from an observer named Fotheringham. The virtuosi of the working-class neighborhoods were culturally prepared to receive and vary the basic Afro-Cuban beat. They looked for style. They played with rhythm. They flaunted newness. When the smoke cleared, the tempo of habanera had quickened. It was now a new dance, the milonga, a purely African word meaning "argument" or "issue" in Kimbundu and "lines of dancers" in Ki-Kongo.

Eventually young black dancers, and the whites and mulattoes who copied them, achieved the culturally impossible when they put together the early tango move, *canyengue*. This was a combination of "position one" in the classic dance of Central Africa—feet flat on the ground, bottom out, torso bent forward, face frozen—with the cheek-to-cheek, arms-around-the-partner romanticism of European embrace dancing.

Canyengue became the name not only of a step but of a mode of being on the dance floor. When Afro-Argentines and their Euro-Argentine comrades departed from this early fusion, they kept the core elements, *cortes* (rhythmized stops) and *quebradas* (torsions of the hips combined with sudden bending of the knees). These "cuts" and "breaks" live on in the tango.

Still danced by a coterie of special experts, canyengue reconnects us to the past. It gives us a measure for establishing the innovations in the subsequent forms of the dance.

The name *canyengue* perfectly fits the dissolution of two styles into one. This word too comes from Central Africa: the imperative of the Ki-Kongo verb "to be liquefied by heat," *kanienge*—to *melt* into the music—reinforced by Kimbundu terms for "dance." Melting, obviously, means getting hot, as when in Kongo an elder cries out *Twisa ndungu!* (Put hot pepper on it!) when he or she feels the dancing is becoming desultory.

Afro-Cuban music, very Kongo-dominated, shares this aesthetic. A telling example: "Échale salsita" (Put Hot Pepper Sauce on It), a Cuban hit *son* of the 1920s. And then there is New York's own Latino music, salsa, a word originally meaning, once again, hot pepper sauce, applied and burning, an ultimate metaphor for swing, drive, and feeling. Thus worlds of cognation, with the Cuban son and mambo and New York salsa, nuance the meaning of *canyengue* on the River Plate.

The dance history part of this book is the longest. The reason is: tango is action. That's what the world loves, more than the text or the sound. We concentrate, accordingly, on great tango dancers, a number of whom we have mentioned. Many were involved with black colleagues. A black dancer, Carlos "El Negro" Anzuate, taught Juan Carlos Copes his first spins or *giros* and other moves, too. El Pibe Palermo hung out with black masters like Arturo Núñez and danced so black that his father was amazed. We especially honor Afro-Argentine dancers of today: tangoists Carlos Anzuate, Margarita de Guillé, Kely and Facundo Posadas, and candombe dancers Tete Salas and Pocha da Madrid. They are the guardians of black incandescence. They are the inheritors of a tradition that goes back to El Negro Agapito, black star of the first tango film, *Tango Argentino,* a short directed by Eugenio Py in Buenos Aires around 1900–06.

That most tangueros today are white no more hides the original—and continuing—black presence than Elvis Presley conceals the heritage of Robert Johnson, or Benny Goodman masks the contributions of Fletcher "Smack" Henderson and Count Basie.

Original works by Argentine visual artists sharpen our sense of tango in motion. The tango art of Hermenegildo Sábat, Carlos Alonso, Rafael de la Fuente, Guillermo Kuitca, Abel Bruno Versacci, Juan Carlos Liberti, Antonio Berni, Juan Batalla, and Dany Barreto, plus Uruguayan artists Coca Ocampo and Carlos Páez Vilaró, crystallize the precision of the tradition, like a Polaroid developing in the palm of one's hand.

In the section on tango as literature, emphasis falls on great lyricists like Ángel Villoldo, Celedonio Flores, Homero Manzi, Enrique Santos Discépolo, Enrique Cadícamo (who literally transposed writing lyrics to novels), and Eladia Blázquez. Flores was black, and Blázquez is a woman. Women emerge strongly as songsters. We honor as well a woman bandleader, Beba Pugliese. Estela dos Santos has written of women who shaped tango dance as richly as the men they danced with: Carmencita Calderón, María Nieves, Ester Pugliese, Gloria Barraud, Elvira Santamaría, Elsa María Mayoral, Nélida Rodríguez, Gloria Dinzel, Natalia Games, and Milena Plebs.

The history of tango music traces a tumultuous sequence, from the earliest recordings to masters of the 1940s (Carlos di Sarli, Juan d'Arienzo, Aníbal "Pichuco" Troilo, Horacio Salgán, Osvaldo Pugliese) and of the 1980s (Astor Piazzolla). Then come the players of today: Néstor Marconi, Pablo Ziegler, Pablo Aslán, and Ignacio Varchausky, and the men of El Arranque.

Salgán and Pugliese are world-class composers. It is our aim to put their works in a more deserving position as against that of their more aggressive colleague, Piazzolla. There is certainly room for more than one person to represent Argentine musical reality to the world. Salgán's "La llamo silbando" and Pugliese's "Malandraca" will hopefully become as famous as Piazzolla's "Adiós Nonino" and "Tanguedia III." The music chapter ends with El Nuevo Quinteto Real, led by Salgán, and El Arranque. These two groups, in differing ways, lead tango music into the future.

Meanwhile Gabriel Angió and Natalia Games, working with Argentina's number one b-boy, a black Argentine youth named Lucas Álvarez, have three times had the audacity to blend hip-hop downrock (break dancing) with traditional tango. As they pull off this incredible blend, lucky the Bethlehem toward which they slouch.

During the early years of tango, in the late nineteenth and early twentieth centuries, young workers from Italy and Spain and elsewhere in Europe flooded the streets of Buenos Aires. But just as the Manchu invaders of the seventeenth century were transformed into avatars of Chinese culture, so the newcomers found their their *argentinidad* in tango. Hence that immortal immigrant-turned-icon-of-Argentina, Carlos Gardel. Hence the descendants of Italian immigrants, the great composers Pugliese and Piazzolla, and the virtuoso player of *bandoneón*, Néstor Marconi.

Tango today is a sea of white faces, but Brazil's *samba*, Colombia's *cumbia*, Peru's *lando*, and Suriname's *kasiko* are not the only black beats on the continent. Tango started black, and milonga, the dance preceding it, even more so. Contemporary tango performers like Copes know this to be true and perform accordingly. From time to time, in reserved little passages, he stamps out a milonga, playing the floor as an instrument of percussion the way a jazzman like Wynton Marsalis might switch to the blues to remind himself where he came from and who he is and why. Milonga, in short, is the conscience of tango. Like blues next to jazz, or *son montuno* with salsa, it keeps tango honest, being close to the roots. In New York the better instructors know this: when teaching the milonga, they stress the rhythmic difference.

Tango as dance, in the phrasing of Cormac McCarthy, contains within itself its own arrangement, history, and finale. The experts we honor, from whom we take counsel, are Argentine. In this book we go back to Buenos Aires and follow women and men to their milongas, their schools of being, where the prose of human action becomes a poetry of valor, pleasure, and precision.

TANGO IN HOLLYWOOD

*I hear the echo of those tangos
of Arolas and Greco
danced upon the sidewalk,
an instant distilled that remains
without before, or hereafter, an anti-oblivion,
having the taste of everything lost,
and everything regained.*

—JORGE LUIS BORGES, "El tango," in *El otro, el mismo* (1969)

In order to recognize a symbol by its sign observe
how it is used with a sense.

—LUDWIG WITTGENSTEIN, *Tractatus Logico-Philosophicus* (1921)

The history of tango tangles with Hollywood. Tango on film is a chronicle of its own, lurid and strange, mixing dreams and deceptions. Often a tango augments a star—Rudolph Valentino, Marlon Brando, Madonna, Al Pacino—not for its sake but for theirs. And the accord with the tango is always with stereotype: sadness, sex, violence, and doom.

This sounds ridiculous and was. But thankfully, in the 1990s, with

Adam Boucher's *Tango, the Obsession* (1998) and Carlos Saura's *Tango, no me dejes nunca* (Tango, Never Leave Me, 1998), truer versions have appeared on the screen. By then the authenticity of Claudio Segovia and Héctor Orezzoli's stage extravaganza, *Tango Argentino,* had cleared the way for genuine footwork, sizzling like a Pollock on the floor.

The trend toward the real article includes the conversion of a major star of film, Robert Duvall, who makes pilgrimages to Buenos Aires and frequents traditional dance halls. He takes lessons from masters like the late Lampazo, Danel and Maria Bastone of New York, and Juan Carlos Copes, the latter described by Duvall as a "Rolls-Royce without a speedometer."[1]

A Buenos Aires television special cuts to a dance floor where Duvall sits enthralled with his girlfriend, studying the moves.[2] Early in 200c Duvall danced tango for President Bill Clinton and the president of Argentina in the White House—at the express request of the Argentine ambassador.[3] On March 28, 2003, Duvall released his own tango film, *Assassination Tango.* It had cameo appearances by major tango dancers like María Nieves, Milena Plebs, Los Hermanos Macana, Pablo Verón, and Gerardo Portalea. We've come a long way from Valentino.

Valentino was the first man to tango on the screens of North America. His tango in *The Four Horsemen of the Apocalypse* (1921) is a celebrated sequence. Measured against Argentine barrio reality, his moves were a travesty, but his charm and self-confidence made people notice him. Rex Ingram, the director of *Horsemen,* tells us why:

> I was attracted at once by Valentino's face. It was obvious that he was *the* exact type for the young tango-hero of the story . . . Rehearsing the tango Rudy did so well I made up my mind to expand this phase of the story. I [used] a sequence in a Universal picture I had made years ago. The sequence showed an adventurous youth going into a Bowery dive and taking the dancer, after he had floored her partner. I transposed this action to South America.[4]

The account is revealing: Ingram was not interested in tango—he just wanted to build up his star.

Valentino was no stranger to tango. He had danced it at Bustanoby's Domino Room, on 39th and Broadway in Manhattan, around 1913.[5] Mirrors around the room magnified his every action. There he learned the style of the "tango pirate"—ostentatious dipping, holding tight, and above all bending the woman back, way back, building an image of conquest.[6]

Valentino was fluent in dips and bends, and that caught the eye of Rex Ingram. *Four Horsemen* was the *Titanic* of its time. Like the Leonardo DiCaprio film, it had an Italianate lead, and a huge cast and budget. Not since *Birth of a Nation* (1915) had Hollywood seen anything like it.[7] But the scene the world remembered was Valentino's tango. John Seitz, the cameraman, photographed the action on a set filled with smoke and tough-looking extras, meant to set off the beauty of the stars.

Valentino appears, you see his face laughing; thin lips, hard eyes, tough jaw. His eyes slit with interest. There is a woman on the dance floor, Beatrice Domínguez, dancing with a man. Rising in his incredible gaucho/flamenco attire, Valentino ambles over. He asks for a dance. Close-up of Domínguez's face: dancing eyes, moist trembling lips. Her partner says no. Valentino sends him flying into a table.

Then Valentino and Domínguez start to dance. Their costumes are so heavy—tassels, shawl, dress, carnations, hat, shirt, chaps, whip, boots, spurs—that initially their motion reads like a ballet between the *Monitor* and the *Merrimack*. Valentino tangos on. Sometimes he holds out a stiff arm in the fashion of the tango of Europe, sometimes not. He looms over Domínguez, bending her back, tango-pirate fashion, with a devastating downward gaze. He is making the world look at *him*. He and Domínguez dip and dip again, in a parody of *quebradas,* Argentine torsions of the hips on bended knees. A black drinks maté and coldly regards them. They sway. Another black sips a beer. They dip. Close-up: their feet in a crossover, Valentino's spurs flashing.

His features ride the motion like a mask. He is dancing his *face,* not the tango. And Domínguez dances her lips and her flowers. Before the finale, when their mouths almost meet, the gaucho vaunts his full strength. He picks up Domínguez bodily and brings her back down to the floor. The bar erupts. They like that. He does it again. Now everyone's standing and shouting. Cut.

Valentino conquered the world with that scene. One tango deserved another: he stalked the floor again in *Blood and Sand* (1922). His faux-tango image would linger in films for some time.

Argentine dancers are bemused. "When we see someone tango, stiff arms and long steps, we laugh and call that dancing *à la* Valentino," Roberto "El Alemán" Tonet, a star of the Broadway stage hit *Tango Forever,* told me in 1998. Still and all, a distinguished Argentine critic, Sergio Pujol, admits that "in spite of the fallacy, Valentino as Buenos Aires type, the success of this dancer-turned-actor is a reality impossible to ignore."[8]

Gilda (1946), a movie about love and gambling in 1940s Buenos Aires, was Rita Hayworth's greatest role. Somewhere in a casino we hear a bandoneón, but that's about it for the tango. In 1946 barrio dancers were creating new steps, but *Gilda* gives no hint of this. Buenos Aires is a stage set, midtown Manhattan with signs in Spanish.

Valentino haunts Billy Wilder's *Sunset Boulevard,* the classic 1950 film. Gloria Swanson, in the role of a passé star of silent film, throws a tango party for just herself and William Holden. The scene is handsome: two dancers and a tango orchestra, in rich black and white. It was shot by John Seitz, the cameraman who had filmed Valentino.

Swanson, keeping Holden under the pretense of hiring him as a writer, hopes to seduce him with the dance music of her era. She will be his Domínguez; he will be her Valentino. She hires a tango orchestra to play, endlessly, just for the two of them, in her Beverly Hills mansion on New Year's Eve.

Holden appears in a tux. The excitement of his looks and the savor of the tango overcome her. She tears off her tiara, like a pirate raising the Jolly Roger, and hurls it to the floor. The camera follows it. Swanson's butler (Eric von Stroheim) retrieves it in white gloves. She rests her head on Holden's shoulder. Getting the point, Holden looks worried.

Swanson tells Holden, "Valentino told me: get rid of my wood floor, replace it with tile." The camera pulls back, revealing a tiled floor in octagonal patterning.

Holden, the hard-boiled screenwriter, abruptly breaks off and heads for another party, where he knows a young girl awaits him. Swanson, irreparably hurt, retires to her bedroom. She slits both her wrists. End of tango.

Nearly half a century later Wilder would tell Curtis Hanson, after the latter's triumphant *L.A. Confidential,* "Now I suppose you'll do a comedy."[9] Hanson did: *Wonder Boys.* Wilder had, too, following *Sunset* nine years later with the hilarious *Some Like It Hot* (1959). Tango in this film is pure slapstick: while Tony Curtis romances Marilyn Monroe on a yacht, using an outrageous Gary Grant accent, the camera cross-cuts to Jack Lemmon, tangoing in drag (to hide from gangsters) with Joe E. Brown. "You're *leading!*" Brown says.

Lemmon and Brown lock hands and move forward, heads in profile, in European stiff-arm tango style. They also mirror Valentino, bending each other backward. Brown has a rose in his mouth. By the end of the scene Lemmon is striking insane gypsy poses. The orchestra is blindfolded— this spares them the travesty.

The misuse of tradition intensified in Bernardo Bertolucci's *Last Tango in Paris* (1972). Forget, if possible, the auteur's ambition to blur art into pornography and vend it as revolution, with a world-class actor, Brando, securing the way. Forget the breakthrough promiscuities that Bertolucci has Brando commit with a smashing ingenue, Maria Schneider. Forget, as well, expectations aroused by the strange, sensual tango danced by Stefania Sandrelli and Dominique Sanda in Bertolucci's earlier film *The Conformist* (1970). Forget, if you can, all of that and cut to a long, famous scene:

Interior: bar, dancing; day
Jeanne is hiding behind dark glasses. Behind them in the room there is
a small tango contest. The jury, in front of a long table, follow with
their eyes the couples dancing with numbers on their backs.
PAUL [BRANDO]: You know the tango is a rite . . . And you must watch the legs of the dancers.[10]

So far so good. Norman Mailer loved it: "[a] near mythical species of tango palace."[11] And the setting *is* beautiful. Vittorio Storaro's camera distills a golden light in colonnaded spaces, a light that illumines intent, moving couples. Gato Barbieri wrote the score. In sum, we savor a tango nirvana.

But not for long. Bertolucci was out to *use* the tango, not to reveal it— to use its fame and its glamour, together with Brando's, to power a dark vision.

He causes the camera to glide like a serpent through the tango contestants, transforming their Eden into hell. Pauline Kael declared the women "bitch-chic mannequin-dancers." Somewhere a compliment to their integrity lies buried in that. To Kael the dancers were "automatons," posing with "wildly fake head-turns."

Bertolucci—and his critics—had misunderstood tango's auteur, which, as the gifted Julie Taylor reminds us, consists of the following: "dancers demonstrate their skill by perform[ing] like somber automatons, providing [themselves with] psychic space."[12] The root of all this is black cool. But by 1972 the Afro-Argentine shaping of the frozen face in tango had long since been forgotten, even among most tangueros.

Bertolucci, in any event, definitely reduced dancers to mannequins. He turned ritual into farce. It gets worse:

PRESIDENT OF THE TANGO JURY: Now gentlemen, ladies, all best wishes for the last tango![13]

Note the last phrase. For some this suggested the end of the tango as a world-class tradition. As if to rub that interpretation in, Brando drunkenly sashays his way across the dance hall, mocking the seriousness of the contestants, mocking their moves, mocking their reason for being. He makes fun of their posture. He falls flat on his back, like a spread-eagled ape.

Then Schneider tells Brando she's leaving him. He chases her, corners her. She pulls out a pistol. She kills him. End of tango.[14]

Critics rose to Bertolucci's faux-revolutionary bait. Pauline Kael pronounced *Last Tango* equal to Stravinsky's *Rite of Spring*—not the best call for someone whose judgments were normally brilliant. Another critic went so far as to denounce the tango judge, as if she were personally responsible for the Vietnam War. It was dangerous to be decent in the 1970s.

Norman Mailer, alone among critics, felt uneasy: "Did [Brando's] defacement of the tango," he asked, "injure some final nerve of . . . deportment."[15]

It did. The damage was not virtual—it was real. Copes remembers, "*Last Tango* was the climax of films that ridiculed tango." People the world over got the impression in the 1970s that tango was "antiquated and comic."[16] Recalling Wittgenstein's famous axiom "The meaning of a symbol is its use," tango had been defined, unfairly, by *mis*-use.

The Argentine military government of 1972 banned *Last Tango*, so Buenos Aires was prevented from making up its own mind at the time. The grim political reality of the *proceso*, the dictatorship of the military junta that ruled Argentina from 1976 to 1983, in many respects put tango—and tango criticism—on ice.

But things started changing in Europe in 1977. That was the year of *Soldier of Orange* (*Soldaat van Oranje*), directed by Paul Verhoeven, one of the best European films of the century. It includes a strong tango, bristling with politics.

This tango was an invention. It does not exist in the memoir of the Dutch hero of the Resistance upon whose life the film is based. As Verhoeven recalls, "We were looking for a situation to bring the hero and the anti-hero of the film together and came up with the tango."[17] One model for their dance was Lemmon's tango with Brown in *Some Like It Hot*.

"I grew up admiring that scene," recalls Verhoeven. The other source was Bertolucci, "but only as a second impression."[18] Verhoeven, in any event, transcended his sources.

Soldaat is the tale of two Dutchmen. Tight friends in school, they separate after the occupation of the Netherlands by Nazi forces in May 1940. One, played by Rutger Hauer, escapes to Great Britain, then returns by submarine in 1943 to spy for the Allies. The other, played by Derek de Lint, joins the German army and becomes an SS officer. (He is eventually shipped to the eastern front, where Soviet partisans assassinate him.) De Lint and Hauer meet at a party in occupied Holland. The scene is a hotel in Noordwijk, a small beach town not far from The Hague. The time is early 1943. There is a swastika on the wall. The room is filled with Nazis. De Lint, as if to extend the aura of Hitler's aggression, suddenly seizes Hauer. He makes him tango with him.

Their dance is war. It returns us, in an odd way, to early days in Buenos Aires, when men tangoed with men, to practice for women. De Lint and Hauer break, however, a fundamental rule of tango dancers: they *talk*.

ALEX [DE LINT]: Quite a disappointment to see you here among these Dutch Nazis and builders of Hitler's bunkers on the coast.

ERIK [HAUER]: Why not? It's war, and it's a nice party, isn't it?

ALEX: I heard you were abroad.

ERIK: That's bullshit!

ALEX: I heard you were in London.

ERIK: You heard wrong. I'm here.

ALEX: Shame we're not fighting on the same side.

ERIK: Yeah . . . a bloody shame.

ALEX: In a couple of years the Germans and English will be fighting together against the Communists.

ERIK: I don't believe that.

ALEX: Well, anyway, we won't be around to see it.[19]

Hidden in this dialogue is an odd prediction of the coming of the cold war. It is clear de Lint is not fooled by Hauer's cover. One senses, correctly, that out of loyalty he will not betray him. So their dance is a mix of friendship and politics, fascism and democracy.

Suddenly the two men break into mirrored head-turns. It puts them in joking relation to their audience—and to tango film history. They're citing *Some Like It Hot* with a dash of *Last Tango*, pure movie faux-tango cool. Hauer and de Lint perform appropriately stone-faced. They are having fun. Beaming, pretty women form a circle around them, giving them space and approval.

They race up and down, high-spirited males in action. One tangoist chose evil and will die. The other will live and become a hero of his nation. But while they are dancing, tango holds back their tarots and gives a full moment.

Tango Argentino, in the mid-1980s, changed the way films depicted tango, but not immediately. Catherine Deneuve and Linh Dan Pham, in Regis Warner's beautiful film *Indochine* (1992), practice tango to the sound of a Victrola on a rubber plantation in colonial Indochina. They dance the European stiff arm. It's all they know. They laugh as they dance, savoring the moment. Dan Pham exclaims, "We'll never get it!"

Woody Allen *did* get it, in terms of tango suggestiveness. Fond of Latino music as an emblem of romance—he once filmed Tito Puente conducting—Allen regales us with the music of the world-famous tango "La cumparsita" (The Carnival Ensemble) in his film *Alice* (1990). Pedro Ochoa, the gifted Argentine film historian, points out that in this film "La cumparsita" becomes a leitmotif of liberation. Every time Alice, a repressed woman, takes charge of her destiny, we hear that tango. Allen, Ochoa concludes, cut through stereotypes to a richer sense of tango: freedom.[20]

Martin Brest's *Scent of a Woman* (1992) and James Cameron's *True Lies* (1992) were similarly enlightening. As Copes recalls, "Before *Tango Argentino* most films made fun of tango dancers. A joke. A clown show. But *Scent of a Woman* saw tango as healing, and in *True Lies* tango demonstrated the culture of the hero. We were witnessing respect for the dance."[21]

In *Scent* Pacino plays the role of a U.S. Army lieutenant colonel, retired after losing his sight. Pacino defies his disability with an amazing tango performed with Gabrielle Anwar.

At first she is shy, but he immediately reassures her: "There are no mistakes in the tango. Not like life. If you get tangled up, you just tango on." This charmingly suggests that sharing an error might lead to a relationship.

Like Swanson and Holden, the pair tango alone to live music. The number is "Por una cabeza," Carlos Gardel's song, one of the noblest of tangos. Anwar slithers one leg around Pacino. She is learning the wiles of the *gancho,* the pattern whose name translates as "hook."

Pacino takes her hand and holds it up high, like a flag of romance. He is miming the style of the twentieth-century master El Cachafaz (The Guy with Attitude). He spins her out, spins her in, in circles of beautiful action.

With *Scent,* movies stopped quoting movies. Argentine motions were appearing at last. The tango in *Scent* was reprised in *True Lies* (1994), where Tia Carrere traps Arnold Schwarzenegger in a tango to the beat of—again—"Por una cabeza." She is an enemy agent. He is a spook. Their tango is sexy. Arnold rubs her bare shoulders with muscular hands. She likes it. Carrere sits for a second on Arnold's massive thigh, performing a *sentada* (a brief seating of the woman on her dancing partner's thigh). Finally, in Steven Spielberg's *Schindler's List* (1993), Liam Neeson dances, once again, to "Por una cabeza."

Then came *Evita* in 1996. The star was Madonna. The Buenos Aires men with whom she tangos in this film (as the young Eva Duarte) are real. They are variously young, old, lonely, and dashing, and she cannot help but surpass them with her beauty. The sound track does not reflect the dance: the music is sped-up and rockized. Madonna nonetheless manages to insert a gancho and an ocho.

Before flying to Buenos Aires, where part of *Evita* was shot on location, Madonna trained in New York with Argentine tango instructors Danel and Maria Bastone. They taught her the ocho she performs in the film.

A fascinating sequence in *Evita*, set in the streets of Buenos Aires, involves a *milonga de la muerte* (milonga of death). The milonga is the fast-paced, syncopated dance that preceded tango. As in Kongo, where grief can be absorbed in a circle of dancers, and New Orleans, the city of Congo Square and jazz funerals, the couples dance milonga to counter the shock of Evita's death.

The sound track betrays us: it does not play milonga, it plays something dirgelike. Nevertheless, the scene is superb: a good-looking young woman collapses in tears on the shoulder of her boyfriend. He holds her tenderly and dances her on. Behind them an older couple tango-milongas, with their eyes closed: life goes on.

Marta Savigliano points out that Sally Potter's *The Tango Lesson* (1998) and Carlos Saura's *Tango* (1998) began a new era of tango in film. Both are completely devoted to tango, unlike prior partial exposures.[22]

The Tango Lesson showcased brilliant dancing by a handsome male lead, Pablo Verón, on location in Paris and Buenos Aires. Riding the success of her distinguished film *Orlando* (1992), Potter starred herself as a screenwriter/aspirant tango performer/lover. Her character becomes obsessed with tango—and with her Argentine dance instructor, Verón. She decides to make a tango film. When she does and starts directing in earnest, her lover complains that she's "changed." Not at all. Potter's narcissism flares incandescently.

One telling example: rather than choosing a moment of real tango, Potter enacts an arty mimesis of Delacroix's painting of Jacob wrestling with an angel. The scene isn't wrestling, let alone tango—she is *goring* Verón with her ego.[23]

Verón, a superb Argentine tanguero, caught Potter's eye in Paris at the Folies-Bergère in 1993. His mentors in Buenos Aires had included Lampazo and other fine dancers in Villa Urquiza. Verón in the film does more than tango: he kicks up his heels dancing jazz on the banks of the Seine and on the moving walkways of Charles de Gaulle airport, recalling Fred Astaire and Gene Kelly.

The reaction of Argentine critics was mixed.[24] But Pedro Ochoa praised the sound track as the most important selection of tangos in a foreign film up to that point.[25] There were classics galore: di Sarli's "Bahía Blanca," "La yumba" by Pugliese, Troilo's "Quejas de bandoneón," and Piazzolla's "Zum" and "Libertango." Potter's taste in tango music was impeccable, and so was her sense of the seriousness of the dance. This she proved with her opening dance scene: Pablo Verón and Carolina Iotti, creating tissues of improvisation and design.

Problems of ego haunt Robert Duvall's long-awaited *Assassination Tango* of 2003. He awarded the key dancing roles to himself and his Argentine girlfriend, Luciana Pedraza. Duvall plays the role of a hired assassin, a hitman, meeting in Buenos Aires with a confused-looking Rubén Blades, plotting to kill an Argentine general.

The hired killer (Duvall), casing the city, stumbles on tango. There is a scene in which Duvall stands, tough-guy bemused, as an attractive young Argentine woman demonstrates the gancho (hook). She shoots her foot in and out of his crotch. He plays this for laughs. Later, at a moment more serious, he asks a man to teach him, in the classic tango manner of male-on-male practice, the fundamental ocho step. In dream sequences Duvall tangos with Pedraza alone.

Duvall takes us to the famous Villa Urquiza tango dance hall, Sin Rumbo, where the superb Milena Plebs unfurls three moves—*salida, giro,* and *sacada*—each danced in perfect definition. "Los Hermanos Macana," Enrique and Guillermo de Fazio, demonstrate male-on-male practice. For a maddeningly brief moment María Nieves uncoils her world-famous legs. The only full tango comes at the end credits. Pablo Verón and a partner pose, gyrate, pose. The film favors tango but not generously so.

The tango in Joel Schumacher's *Flawless* (1999) is brief but resonant.[26] *Flawless* portrays Latina women executing nurturing ochos in the arms of Robert De Niro. He holds them in a pure tango way. He plays a policeman recovering from a stroke; slowly he regains manhood and motion through the steps of the tango. The point of the sequence: tango can heal.

It remained for a brilliant Spanish director to go further, to give us a film completely in love with the tango. This was Carlos Saura's *Tango, no me dejes nunca* (1998). It begins with a view of Buenos Aires, turning gold in the light of a midwinter sunrise. The camera pans in from the river, from the docks and the cranes, to the Torre Monumental in Air Force Square, to stop finally opposite the IRSA building, a modern white skyscraper marking the corner of Juncal and Maipú.

Setting the stage with Buenos Aires itself, Saura, we sense, will develop the tango in its urban humanity, as an act of control to match the fine buildings and streets. And he does. The auteur steps back and shapes many scenes as pretexts for tango. The central male lead, played by Miguel Ángel Solá, is making a movie on tango. He is breaking up with one woman and falling in love with another. Both are tangueras. So their work and their practice keep us within the superbness of tango. We are taken into rehearsals directed by Juan Carlos Copes, one of the main stars of *Tango Argentino*. He counts out his motions to give order to lessons. He takes in his arms a fine woman and guides her through the serpentine glory of the milonga step called *viborita* (little serpent). He performs it with a series of miniature pivots. He teaches his group how to stamp out a beginning to a tango-milonga, like illuminating the first letter of a medieval manuscript.

Music is honored. The camera takes us into an incredible sequence where the great black pianist and tango composer Horacio Salgán plays his own "A fuego lento" (To a Slow Fire). The camera comes up so close to his face, you can actually see—and hear—him "scatting" syllables, under his breath, to coat every note with full energy. He is mouth-drumming music like certain jazz pianists. It's a rare recognition—as is the interview with Facundo Posadas and Margarita de Guillé in Boucher's *Tango, the Obsession* (1998)—of Afro-Argentine presence.

Again and again the film comes alive with silhoutted dancers, stamping and turning, stopping and starting. Saura takes us backstage, then onstage, then backstage again. We come away from his film aware that tango is pride and hard work as well as passion and fire. He establishes forever that tango is the supreme social fact of Buenos Aires.

In sum, tango on film leads from the travesty of Valentino through strange *Sunset Boulevard* and stranger still *Last Tango* to a battle between males in *Soldier of Orange*, to assertion of self in *Scent of a Woman*, to healing in *Flawless*, to women in action in *Indochine*, *Alice*, *Evita*, and *The Tango Lesson*, to tantalizing cameos in *Assassination Tango*, to the ultimate triumph, Saura's *Tango*.

The sequence has shown that the glamour of tango formed its own worst enemy, inspiring directors on the lookout for facile transitions. Characteristically, they quoted tangos from movies rather than citing Buenos Aires directly. Now that is changing, and we are graced with some truths. First, culture is forever. It is politics and ego that fade. Valentino is dead; Evita is gone; but tango *is*. It survived the twentieth century. It took the measure of that era's terror and decorum. At the end Carlos Saura hit the false with the fabulous, sensation with sense, revealing at last real tango couples, moving in love with an arm around life.[27]

2.

TANGO AS TEXT

When we read a poem in translation we want to hand
ourselves over to the given of the poem, to rest in the
authority of its being.

— CYNTHIA OZICK, *Metaphor and Memory* (1991)

Nadie me llama a la mesa de ayer
porque todo es ausencia y adiós.

No one calls me to the table of yesterday
because all is absence and adiós.

— CÁTULO CASTILLO, "Café de los Angelitos" (1944)

If nostalgia is a country, tango is its capital. Tango writes of time, loss,
and love. I ran full tilt into this tradition on a clear winter night in
Buenos Aires in June 1990. The great Roberto Goyeneche was singing
at Café Homero, on Calle Cabrera in Palermo Viejo. In a dark, blue-lit
room filled with smoke and intense couples, Goyeneche stressed a phrase
from Cátulo Castillo's tango "La última curda" (The Last Drink of the
Night): *life is an absurd wound.*

The dark strength of Goyeneche's voice introduced me to a city where lyricists and singers talk back to destiny. The lyricists—Ángel Villoldo, Pascual Contursi, Celedonio Flores, Enrique Santos Discépolo, Homero Manzi, Eladia Blázquez, Mario Árraga, Horacio Ferrer, and others—are strong writers who at their best make abstractions of the bad things that happen, restoring the heart after tears. They establish an alternative literature.

Tango texts, like the blues, hold up a mirror to misfortune. But this will not do as a total description. Discépolo's famous definition of the tango, "a sad thought danced," captures only one of its ruling obsessions. Discépolo was a lyricist; he worked with words. But dancers want music—not words, and not speech—to keep their form and their focus. When sadness comes in, it is a thought to which they *listen*. Tangueros like to move in silence to the music, neither one speaking. Their ecstasies are textless.

In a conflict of impressions, dance rules. The organizers of the stage extravaganza *Tango Argentino* started with equal sections of music, song, and dance, but audience reactions disabused them: overwhelmingly the world wanted dancers. So here we meet one of the internal contradictions of the tango: the portion made of words, the texts of the songs, can be silenced by dancers. But the writing goes on, as does the music. In fact, the texts exist in relation to this tension. In the 1940s the great lyricist Manzi sometimes wrote a kind of blank verse, sometimes literally without verbs; he knew that the music would supply them.

Tango texts change from decade to decade, from writer to writer. What's more, the work of strong writers is temporally translucent, open to both the past and the present. In addition, like poetry over the ages, it deals with matters of both discord and love. There is satire and *amor* in Celedonio Flores. There is sarcasm and jeremiad in Discépolo. A fine nostalgia for a vanished Buenos Aires shapes the work of Homero Manzi, consolidating his attention to desire.

Challenge songs, by black stars like Gabino Ezeiza, influenced the work of Villoldo in the first tangos of the twentieth century. Creole allusiveness exerts a subtle fascination in the work of the remarkable black poet Celedonio Flores; nothing in the barrio escapes that writer's eye. Reminding us of both griots and Andalusian village singers, Flores critiques conceit and pretension. So does Discépolo, but with patented acerbity. Then follows Manzi's geography of desire, Eladia Blázquez's magical realism, and finally the tango modernism of Alejandro Szwarcman, Mario Árraga, and Horacio Ferrer. If Contursi brought narratives of love into tango, Ferrer and Szwarcman opened windows to the world, in a literary equivalent to the musical revolution of Piazzolla.

Argentine critics have produced a veritable literary industry in outlining the contours of tango. Jorge Gottling's *Tango: The Melancholy Witness* spotlights Gardel and the "monotheme"—i.e., *woman*—in three classic poses: absence, presence, and departure.[1] The definition is a tango in itself. Gottling discovers nine themes in the texts of the tango: (1) *skepticism,* as in Discépolo's tango about a man who believes in three things: people, his lover, and his mother, but "the first two betrayed him and Ma went and died"; (2) *the angelic mother,* as in Celedonio Flores's "I'm Afraid" ("leave me with my mother—and by her sainted side I'll build another life and capability); (3) *the break up of a love affair;* (4) *the lovers' reencounter;* (5) *revenge;* (6) *the barrio knife fight;* (7) *the fleeting quality of love;* (8) *retreat into alcohol,* as in Manzi's "Tal vez será tu voz" (Could That Perhaps Be Your Voice, 1943):

> *That cannot be your speech, your anthem,*
> *for I find your voice asleep,*
> *so what I must be hearing*
> *are liquor-generated phantoms.*

Finally, a ninth theme is *gambling,*[2] as in Eladia Blázquez's "La pasión del escolazo" (The Passion for Gambling):

> *If life is a lottery,*
> *It comes with philosophy:*
> *Play the game true.*

Jorge Palacio, in his *Humor in the Tango,* reminds us that around 1900 tango was happy. He refers to the humor of Villoldo and his colleagues, writing in jubilant unison.[3] Borges too was impressed, as he wrote in a poem of 1965:

ALGUIEN LE DICE AL TANGO
(SOMEONE SAYS TO THE TANGO)

> *Tango, once you were happy*
> *As I used to be. . . .*
> *Ever since that yesterday*
> *So many things to the two of us happened*
> *Critical departures and the pain*

Of loving and not being loved back.
I might have died
But you kept extending the Barbary shore of our lives.
Keep in deep memory, O Buenos Aires,
The tango you were and will be.

For the text of the tango *is* Buenos Aires. In search of this truth, some writers turn ethnographic, finding "maté, guitars, and *canción.*" Others become historians of the docksides, restoring to consciousness "a turbulent horizon of tenements, wild dancing, and dives."[4] Still others document the flash of the moves in the later dance halls, mentioning sometimes the masters and their names. At base all are announcing an alternative civilization, where being well danced is just as important as being well read.

Cut through to seven strong writers: Ángel G. Villoldo, Pascual Contursi, Celedonio Flores, Enrique Santos Discépolo, Homero Manzi, Eladia Blázquez, and Horacio Ferrer. They have achieved exemplary status. They cannot, of course, totally represent the tradition, but they will suffice for this chapter. (Other strong writers include Cadícamo, Castillo, Expósito, and Le Pera.) These voices remain present in the esteem of the people. Steeping ourselves in this rich sensibility, we find ourselves wafted toward value and possibility.

It is thrilling to decode the texts. They make you realize that there is this wondrous city far to the south, where the brave and the gifted are battling for love and for livelihood. They share amorous insights, like troubadors. They write us reports from the front. Begin with their earliest tangos.

ÁNGEL G. VILLOLDO (1864–1919)

Ángel G. Villoldo, who wrote "La bicicleta" (The Bicycle), a tango of 1910, was the most esteemed tango lyricist before World War I. "The Bicycle" resembles black "signifying," in its taunts and its humor. A bicycle race sets the stage—cycling was one of the favorite sports in turn-of-the-century Buenos Aires. Villoldo then shifts gears, making fun of technology as if it were a rival guitarist, poised with his instrument and ripe for challenge:

In this day and age
We have this rage

For everything electric,
The microphone,
The telephone
The panpirilintíntophone
Plus cinematography
Biography, caustography,
Pajalacafluchinography,
Not to mention chingatapuchinography.

Villoldo makes up electro-obscenities, humorously inventing technologies and thereby controlling them. He cuts the pretensions of modernism down to size. One can well imagine the fun he would have with the software, cellular, and dot-com phenomena of today. Elsewhere Villoldo tapped a milongalike energy, the energy of youths from the barrios battling for love. In a tango called "Cuerpo de alambre" (Guy with a Wiry Build) of 1910, he wrote:

My girl's got a gift
For the real creole tango,
And all its quick stops.
There's power in her hips,
She's a motor, she's tops.
See her work out,
Doing fours or half-moons
She's tango deluxe.
The perfect woman of my youth.

I'm also hip
To tango and its stops.
Chile and Rodríguez Peña
That's where I bop
With a hard wiry body,
So women say.

Villoldo was a lover, a dancer, a writer. His handsome, mustachioed visage dominated the popular iconography of early-twentieth-century Buenos Aires. Charming to a fault, he said his girlfriend danced better than he did. He celebrated love. He celebrated dance. His tone was invincible.

PASCUAL CONTURSI (1888–1932)

All that changed in 1917. Pascual Contursi brought in the *tango-canción*, tango with romantic argument, tango with a story line, tango with melancholy. Contursi was born in 1888 in Chivilcoy, a small town eighty-odd kilometers west of Buenos Aires. He grew up in the capital, however, in the tough San Cristóbal section, then spent his youth working in a shoe shop. But his heart lay in theater and music, and he salvaged time to mount puppet shows. By his mid-twenties he was living in Montevideo, frequenting cabarets like the Moulin Rouge and the Royal Pigalle. These Parisian names gave hints of pretty women and good times. Like Toulouse-Lautrec, Contursi would come to translate what he saw.

Puppeteering taught Contursi how to dramatize a scene with animated objects. Hanging out put him in touch with street talk (*lunfardo*) on both sides of the River Plate. He witnessed lovers fighting. He heard their tales of anguish. And then of course there were his own misadventures. Drawing on these experiences, Contursi made an emblem of the remnants of the night, in a song that changed the course of tango history, "Mi noche triste" (My Sad Lonely Night), in 1916.

> *Percanta que me amuraste*
> *en lo mejor de mi vida*
> *dejándome el alma herida . . .*
>
> *y el espejo está empañado*
> *y parece que ha llorado*
> *por la ausencia de tu amor . . .*
> *y la lámpara del cuarto*
> *también tu ausencia ha sentido*
> *porque su luz no ha querido*
> *mi noche triste alumbrar.*

> *Woman who ditched me*
> *in the splendor of my youth*
> *searing my soul forever . . .*
>
> *my mirror clouds over*
> *with streaks like tears,*
> *because you're not here . . .*

and the lamp in my room
responds to the gloom
by refusing to light
my sad lonely night.

The song takes up the mood of a man who is desolate. Tears cloud his mirror, a lamp holds back its light; objects turn animate in the hands of a former puppeteer. Contursi peppers the text with terms in lunfardo. Saying *percanta* for "woman," and *me amuraste* for "you ditched me," he challenges Iberian correctness. His tango diction reflects the language in which *porteños* laughed and made love.[5] No one was more aware of the power of the vernacular than Gardel. When he sang this song, nuancing the slang in his own way, the hit was immediate: Gardel's rendering of "Mi noche triste" critics now regard as a decisive moment in porteño art history: the birth of the tango song. Many texts since then have echoed "Mi noche triste." They form a family of melancholy, ultimately linked to the Baroque despair of Francisco de Quevedo, the fatalistic *fados* of Lisbon and Cabo Verde, and the laments of the Cuban bolero.

Some ten years later Contursi was still filling loneliness with personified objects. Here he is, talking to an instrument as a comrade:

BANDONEÓN ARRABALERO
(BANDONÉON FROM THE ROUGH SIDE OF TOWN), 1928

Bandoneón, you see me now, alone and sad,
My singing languished,
You know my soul is filled with anguish.

CELEDONIO ESTEBAN FLORES (1896–1947)

Then came Celedonio Flores, black poet of tango. He was a light-skinned mulatto who hung out with Afro-Argentine colleagues of his era like Manuel and Carlos Posadas, according to the understanding of Facundo Posadas. Carlos Anzuate, the black tangoist, draws our attention to Flores's African hair, even though he was "as light-skinned as I am." In many respects Flores restored satire and celebration, like the black *payadores* he admired in his youth. A boxer in his young manhood, he appropriately fit the battle modes of Afro-Argentine aesthetics. The great tango composer Osvaldo Pugliese praised Flores as "the most progressive writer of the tango, [achieving] a strong and realist form of cultural portraiture."[6] This boxer-poet was born at 48 Talcahuano Street in Buenos Aires, on August 3, 1896. His family moved to Villa Crespo, near Chacarita and Palermo. There, in his late teens, he started writing tango. The people of Buenos Aires would come to see him as the greatest of all tango lyricists. For if the emphasizing beat of black-style milonga had been replaced by the lush harmonic languors of the tango, there were ways to strike back. Flores cut through the fatalism with satire and edged the portraits with affection. One of the truest voices of an alternative literature, he wrote vernacular belles-lettres.

This gave him power. In 1972 the Buenos Aires journal *Estudios de tango* (Tango Studies) polled its readership. Who, they asked, was supreme in tango letters? Answer: Celedonio Flores. In fact, Flores was competitive from the start of his career. In 1914 the Buenos Aires evening journal, *Ultima Hora,* sponsored a contest in vernacular poetry. Celedonio won, with a tango lyric called "Por la pinta." It was printed—and read by Gardel. The text impressed the great singer, who summoned the young poet—Flores was then eighteen—to his recording studio. There "Pinta" was later recorded, with Gardel singing it under a new title, "Margot."

The guitarist at this session, José Ricardo (who also composed the music), and the lyricist, Flores, were both black. Not only that, but the lyrics focused, for a brief telling moment, on one of the core elements of black-influenced dance in Buenos Aires, *canyengue:*

MARGOT, 1919

*Your fine body, currently ruled
by the beat of canyengue, pulsing the tango,
Locked in the embrace of some rich square,
Completes the triumph of your figure in a brilliant dress.
Male compliments, male laughter follow in your wake,
through the cigar smoke, the taste of champagne,
of the nightclub Armenonvil.*

*It hits me: once you hardly had a stitch to wear.
Now your trousseau's silk, embroidered with fine roses.
Your presence so disturbs me, I'd pay money not to see you.
You changed your luck, you changed your name.
You're not my Margarita, now they call you Margot.*

Note a cultural irony: it was her mastering of canyengue, the Afro roots of tango, that propelled this woman into the arms of white society. Behind a straight-faced rejection—I'd rather *pay* than see you—one senses respect for a girl from the tenements who has made it to the big time. The Margot theme continues in the later Flores tangos: "Milonga fina" (Fine Dance-Hall Woman) and "Audacia" (Audacity). In the intriguingly titled "¿*Sos vos? ¡Qué cambiada estás!*" (*Is That You? Boy, Have You Changed!*) (1930), the ending is abrupt:

> So you're ashamed to see me, hey?
> Well, I haven't changed. Ciao, have a nice day.

Throughout these works, a philosophical sympathy for women, including former lovers, distinguishes Flores's hand. This we see in his "Mano a mano" (Working Together) of 1920, which the Argentine novelist Julio Cortázar has declared the finest tango lyric ever written:

> Driven mad by the blues,
> I miss you, and all that you've been.
> You were the sole decent woman in this outcast's life.
> Your fine looks put warmth in my heart.
> You were good, woman, good and consistent.
> I know you loved me
> Like nobody else, like nobody coming.

He recounts his former lover's adventures, affairs with men devious and rich. But he's not judgmental:

> One fine morning
> They may well chuck you out
> Like a used piece of furniture,
> With an all-ravaged heart.
> If you need, then, some aid or counsel,
> Remember this friend,
> Who'll extend you a hand
> Any way that he can,
> Should the occasion arise.

With similar sympathy, Flores's "Viejo smoking" (1930) recounts what an old tuxedo might mean to a gigolo who's seen better days. The device of singing to an object that becomes an icon of loss recalls Contursi. It also throws light on a signature object in the flea markets and antique stores of old Buenos Aires: the ancient Victrolas they sell, as pieces of the voice of Gardel. In any event, Flores portrays dignity like nobody else. He is famous for his social conscience. He is famous for a tango that says that it's hard not to steal when you're starving.

Working in terms of his lived experiences, Flores finds richness in the life of the barrios:

LA MUSA MISTONGA (THE MUSE OF THE POOR), 1926

The muse of the poor in the barrios
Writes in a droll fine vernacular . . .
Unaware of the glories
Of life in Versailles,
She goes out happy, when the night comes,
To watch the boys' street games
To study the smiles of couples sitting down
And the face of heaven, turning dark with the stars
And listen to old tunes.
An organ-grinder plays, inspired by Carriego.
The muse of the barrio is quite unaware
Of the grief of a princess
Who had an affair
With a blond, handsome page boy.
But she will get upset
At a milonguita's misstep
And weep, crying outrage.

Flores's attention to women and their problems is almost womanist. But sexual attraction is a stronger factor—he is transfixed by a beauty, with "bandit eyes and inciting hips," and he loves downtown action:

CORRIENTES Y ESMERALDA (THE CORNER OF CORRIENTES AND ESMERALDA), 1933

This dance hall–loving guy
extends a deep and cordial sigh
before this classic corner. Special heroes,
should one day your luck turn zero,

I'll redeem you, with verse and endeavor,
I'll make you guys live forever.

This was a love poem to the Broadway of Buenos Aires, Corrientes, at a corner where tango was supreme. In 1926, Flores wrote an amazing love song, "Tengo miedo" (I'm Afraid),

> *Please—leave me alone,*
> *I'm afraid of even seeing you*
> *because there's something in my life*
> *I can't forget*
>
> *So, I'm afraid of your eyes*
> *I'm afraid of your lips*
> *I'm afraid of loving you*
> *and starting anew*
> *the whole goddamn blitz.*

Writing straightforwardly of hurt, love, and wisdom, El Negro Cele was a bard of the people. He wrote as he spoke, in street-colored idiom, and so was esteemed as a creole exemplar.

Black elements emerged within his universal themes. Afro-signifying sharpens the exposition of "Margot," about a woman who "outgrew" old friends in favor of big shots, not unlike the Bob Russell and John Benson Brooks black-tinged North American pop hit of fall 1948, "You Came a Long Way from St. Louis" (To Climb the Ladder of Success).

Celedonio wrote a tango titled "The Old African." He also wrote a riposte to Contursi's "Mi noche triste": a tango called "Mi noche alegre" (My Happy Night), recalling the black tradition of the "answer-back" song," a tradition still flourishing in American rap.

Flores lived his experiences and turned them into song. He died in 1947; now we sing them for him. In the Chacarita cemetery in Buenos Aires, tangueros visit another tomb besides the tomb of Gardel, paying homage, leaving presents: someone keeps a red carnation flashing in the lapel of Celedonio's seated stone image. A brass plaque bears an inscription from his "Mano a mano." Set like a subtitle beneath the sculpture, it translates, back into existence, a generous mind and spirit:

> *If you need, then, some aid or some counsel*
> *Remember this friend.*

ENRIQUE SANTOS DISCÉPOLO (1901–51)

El Negro Cele was the poet laureate of the people. Enrique Santos
Discépolo is the darling of the intellectuals. In a first-rate biography,
Sergio Pujol gives reasons why: Discépolo was a blue-ribbon skeptic ("cita
de honor de escepticismo") armed with a reserved moral gaze ("mirada
ética de reserva").[7] The literary elite of Buenos Aires practice their exis-
tentialism, their Marxism, their postmodernism, their whatever, over his
searing language.

Yet the true source of Discépolo's style is popular invention, particularly the writing of Flores. He does not copy Flores; in terms of Harold
Bloom, he "misprisions" him, willfully misinterprets him, achieving a rue-
ful innovation.[8] In famous lines of the tango "Yira, yira" (Hit the Streets,
Hit the Streets, 1930), Discépolo turns a cold shoulder to a woman of the
night, precisely where Flores would commiserate or melt:

> You'll see: all's untrue
> no love is real
> And the world couldn't care less about you
> hit the streets, hit the streets
> should life ever crush you
> adding sadness to savor
> don't expect any rescue
> any hand, any favor.

So the poor woman deserves no alternative destiny. Discépolo is just as
hard on male losers, as in "Quevachache" of 1926:

> Not my fault if you piss life away
> scarfing air, being homeless, being square
> who gives a goddamn
> judgment takes leave,
> making Christ worth no more than a thief!

At his best Discépolo turned betrayal into epigram:

TRES ESPERANZAS (THREE BASIC HOPES), 1933

> Three basic hopes—all turned and fled
> two tinted white, one tinted red

Vanquished by time, first was my mother,
second were people, third was a lover
Three hopes sustained me
But two turned to lies
And Ma went and died!

He invented a tough form of anguish, a refined hurt that fueled continuity. One survives the small deaths, the amorous breakups, and sings out survival:

SIN PALABRAS (WORDS SEEM UNNECESSARY), 1942

Gone blind with amazement was I
amazed that I'd lost you and yet didn't die.

Surviving these shocks brings a mellow elation, the refinement of sadness Buenos Aires calls *mufarse.*

In 1934, in the depths of the Depression, Discépolo gathered all his strengths and took on the twentieth century:

CAMBALACHE
(THE STORE WHERE ONE SELLS STOLEN GOODS)

The world's a coarse mess
and will continue to be so
I hold this true
in 1506, with all of its tricks,
and in 2000, too . . .
Swindlers and machiavels emerge by the hour
guys who are happy and bastards gone sour
Real men and fake men. Give us a break.
The twentieth century's one vast mistake
Unleashing demons.

Try to deny it. One thinks: Hitler, Stalin. But Discépolo had in mind local villains of the 1930s, like Alexander Stavisky, a famous Buenos Aires swindler who killed himself in his jail cell.

"Cambalache" has lines that are legendary:

Twentieth century,
Feverish and problematic,

You're a store where they sell stolen goods
If you don't cry, you don't get to suck
If you can't cop it, you're a square
But who the hell cares.

To read an entire century as a fence for hot goods is brave and brilliant.
A subsequent 1948 tango was straightforwardly tragic:

CAFETÍN DE BUENOS AIRES
(A SMALL CAFÉ IN BUENOS AIRES)

When I was a kid,
I used to stare at you from outside,
There was your world, unreachable
there I was, nozzle pressed against the glass,
looking in,
blue with cold
only afterward, living,
did I come to comprehend.

The world is a school for being.
Since boyhood you taught me
certain marvels
a cigarette held so, belief in one's dreams,
and hope, on the fields of hot love.

The tango ends sadly. Now inside a Buenos Aires café, over "unquestioning tables," the young man weeps, crying out that his lover has left him. But instead of fighting back or getting a new girl, he turns alcoholic.

So intense is despair in Discépolo that a fire of impatience finally takes over us: his critique of melancholy is brilliant and superb, but we yearn for a voice that would cut through urban bad faith to humanity. That voice soon emerged.

HOMERO MANZI (1907–51)

Homero Nicolás Manzione—his original name—was born on November 1, 1907, in Añatuya, southeast of the provincial capital of Santiago del Estero, in north-central Argentina. In 1911, when Homero was four, his father moved the family to Buenos Aires. At sixteen Homero harnessed his hormones and wrote a lyric for an Argentine waltz called "¿Por qué no me besas?" (Why Don't You Kiss Me?). He had the luck, at around this time, of winning the friendship of Sebastián Piana, a great composer, the man behind the renaissance of candombe and milonga in the 1930s. Manzi would write lyrics for Piana half his life.

In an early tango, from his late adolescence in 1925, Manzi gives us a portrait of an old violinist as seen by a lover of tango:

VIEJO CIEGO (THE OLD BLIND VIOLINIST)

Sight-guide at your side, you appear in the night,
laments at the ready in your battered violin.
In the café's smoky haze
your long thin limbs
read like the parts of a puppet.

Your song goes on
Restoring souls,
discovering memories,
a dash of pain, a splash of liquor.

Nostalgia enters, on the wings of your song,
and I think of a girl long since gone
old blind amigo,
play me a tango
make it slow, make it sad,
bring tears to this lad.

At the age of eighteen Manzi had captured one essence of tango: *mufarse*. Julie Taylor, in her book on tango, refines our understanding of this term. Mufarse is bittersweet, like having the blues.[9] It is the momentary overcoming of contingency. One savors one's destiny, bad luck, betrayal, and all—but perhaps one does so in a café, sipping red wine. In 1943 Manzi memorably confronted mufarse, in "Mi taza de café" (My Cup of Black Coffee):

This useless pessimism,
this desire to be sad
to amble around, thinking of yesterday,
brings ghosts from the past

> *who insist that they join me,*
> *when I have my coffee in the afternoon.*

But Manzi was to transcend mufarse, that strange dark elation. He invented a tango that coined a new excellence: the reaffirmation of one's life through a text, that text being Buenos Aires. His 1942 tango becomes a camera:

TANGO

> *Lamplight at the corner, male serenaders, calling out*
> *compliments to good-looking women*
> *dance and song*
> *trick and countertrick*
> *having problems, being broke*
> *hip woman, a broad who's a square*
> *bandoneón, a bad-ass*
> *a neighborhood café . . .*
>
> *Woman of color, caress out of sight*
> *large wooden door, the time is deep night*
> *old woman gossiping,*
> *elegant Las Heras*
> *hocked clothing, silence, fifth edition*
> *memories, marble, flowers, and grief.*

Las Heras is an avenue. Other lines read like streets, filled with color, like Mondrian's *Broadway Boogie-Woogie* (1942–45).

The last line describes a cemetery for the rich, Recoleta, a machine, churning out marble, nostalgia, and yearning—yet somehow its presence makes the city come alive. Recall today the numerous restaurants on Calles Ortiz and Vicente López, facing the walls of Recoleta cemetery, offering drinking and dining at the boundary between worlds.

In the midst of all this a woman of color appears. Is she there to remind us of the black presence in tango? Perhaps, given Manzi's work with the Afro-oriented Piana for whom he wrote tangos in the 1930s about blacks: "Papá Baltasar," for example, about the beloved black wise man and saint from the story of the Nativity. He also wrote milongas like "Pena mulata" (The Pain of a Woman of Color) and "Negra María" (Black Maria).

Manzi's talent for cultural collage matured dramatically in "Sur" (The South Part of Town), a classic text of 1948. In four enigmatic lines images float on their own; verbs are sensed but not seen. The fifth line reveals the preceding four as a compound subject, a subject that finally encounters its predicate:

> *The house of the blacksmith*
> *trouble and pampas*
> *Your house, your path, a deep ditch*
> *sweet smell of herbs and alfalfa*
> *once again fills my heart.*[10]

Manzi here invents a grammar of nostalgia. Only at the end comes the verb, introducing the act of remembering. Then, just like that, the song switches back to conventional diction:

> *Barrios changing, nightmares ringing,*
> *in somebody's head,*
> *bitterness left, when a dream has gone dead.*

The truth of this tango, that nothing is permanent, not even buildings, hit hard in November 1968, when I returned from New Haven to my hometown of El Paso. There I found that the grammar school, Dudley, where I had learned so much—and which I innocently assumed was eternal—was scheduled for demolition. My depression was severe. I hurriedly took photographs of the Dudley auditorium, already in ruins, where once I had watched Sam Donaldson, later a well-known anchorman of American television, declaim on the stage as a child. Fortunately two friends from Dudley, Homer Jacobs and Ralph Lowenfield, took me to dinner with our wives that night. Their humor and banter broke my depression.

In 1949 Manzi's comradeship with the jovial *bandoneonista* Aníbal Troilo triggered a tango where the protagonist counters depression similarly. He avoids the facile melancholy of the she's-left-me-and-I'm-feeling-so-sad kind of song; even in his cups he is slouching his way toward enlightenment:

CHE, BANDONEÓN (HEY, BANDONEÓN)

> *Hey, bandoneón,*
> *the wizard sound of your midnight note*
> *takes mercy on this grieving bloke.*
> *Activate your drowsy bellows*

heal our time, our righteous sorrows.
Hey, bandoneón,
tonight's the night I stomp and roam
confessing the truth,
over numerous drinks,
blur out my pain
over tango.
Then she returns
night after night
in the notes of your melancholy.
Say it ain't so,
bandoneón,
Pounding hard liquor
I'll try to consider:
in playing this game,
did my soul step offsides?

We are in a bar, then suddenly we're in a soccer match: someone's playing offsides (*orsai*). The leap bares a writer responding, not to fashion, but to the loves and imagination of the people. The singer is one step removed from insight. If he sees that the ruin of his love was caused by his own hand, then truth's healing efficacy may be his.

Together with Villoldo's cocky humor, Flores's riddles of gender and class, and Discépolo's dictionary of despair, Manzi affirms the richness of an alternative literature.

And then in the 1960s and 1970s, a woman emerged who commingled their work with her own.

ELADIA BLÁZQUEZ (B. FEBRUARY 1931)

We catch at last the cadences of a woman in the art of Eladia Blázquez. Her presence is remarkable in the macho world of tango. Blázquez has shared some of the secrets behind her rise to destiny in a recent text. Having supportive parents was critical:

> I remember clearly the first manifestations of my passion for music. I tried to convert my [mother's] fire-screen into an instrument, drumming my small fingers against the wood, to match the melodies of [tangos] then in vogue. And I remember the tender patience of my father, building a sup-

port for bottles, each filled with different measures of water, to make a scale, so I could play a concert.[11]

Her mother and father also encouraged her when she took up guitar and piano. Inventing her own instruments led to inventing her own songs, with the whole of Buenos Aires in 1967 as her text:

BUENOS AIRES, IT'S YOU AND ME

Buenos Aires!
I swear on my soul
there's no stronger geography
than your urban landscape.
Here, day after day.
my shoes, dress, and fears
all gently fade
I'd be stripped of pride,
I couldn't exist
under any other sky but yours
even when your tangos hurt
as does, sometimes, a guy's warm hand
even when it's hard
to make a living in this land
Nevertheless, because I am as you are,
be it giving or denying,
I proclaim you, Buenos Aires, my town.

Blázquez allies herself not only with contemporary modes but also with the high-spirited tango-milongas of the past. She feels that "being sad does not necessarily correlate with being profound." Love of Buenos Aires is more important than any mood, and in 1975 became her leitmotif:

EL CORAZÓN AL SUR (POINT THE HEART SOUTH)

My barrio geography
I carry in my mind
that's probably why
it's not all behind—
the grocery, the guys, the corner in action,
I still recognize them, there's still a reaction,
A little of that world remains mine.

Now I know: distance and time
blur away being
you find yourself standing,
on a cardinal point,
returning to childhood
through something in the light,
keeping your heart to the south.

Blázquez and memory defy time's destructiveness. This is victory, but how one achieves it remains elusive: "returning to childhood / through something in the light." Piazzolla was aware of Blázquez's gifts. The great composer commissioned her to write lyrics for his famous "Adiós Nonino," a tango in memory of his father:

I exist! a root in a country
kneaded with your clay
I'm the flesh and blood of an Italian
who gave me my life and my day.
Adiós, Nonino,
your regard lit the skies of my destiny
fearless ardor, credo of love
you became a fine instrument
sowing hope on the road.
I am the honey and salt of your life
the life that I mourn, dear Nonino,
maybe when they cut my life thread
I'll see you and know;
there's no end, there's no dread.

Tango has dealt with bereftness before. But Eladia is a woman, and things are changing. She challenges those earlier songs in which women appear only as mothers or as lovers. She wants tangos where women recapture their intellectual perception, their powers of judgment, "their roads of existence."[12]

She is also acutely aware of what it means to write tangos against globalized rock and jeans. If Manzi were alive now, she says, "I am sure he would write his tangos another way. Because life has changed. Different velocities and urgencies surround us." Her triumph is to stand up and write tangos now, for all Buenos Aires, honoring tradition but on her own terms:

POR QUÉ AMO A BUENOS AIRES (WHY I LOVE BUENOS AIRES)

I'm nourished
thinking my way through the tango . .
because there is a hey!
that stings me awake
because there is a why
that haunts every corner . . .
If you didn't appear, Buenos Aires,
every time I lift my venetian blinds
I would die.
Sometimes, when I get the blues,
and I'm disconcerted
it becomes my pleasure to curse your humid leisure
and share your solitude.

The text is now hers, and she knows it.

HORACIO FERRER (B. JUNE 2, 1933)

Horacio Ferrer, the man who wrote the lyrics for Piazzolla's "new tango," matched wits with the master by fusing the streets of Buenos Aires with a festive surrealism. Unlike lesser tangos that offer no release, this 1969 one was celebratory; this one had a smile that was lifting:

BALADA PARA UN LOCO (BALLAD FOR A CRAZY MAN)

Yes, I know: I'm crazy, crazy, crazy
See the moon rolling down Avenida Callao
With a chorus of children and astronauts
all moving, in waltz-time, surround me.
Come, dance, and fly!

We are in the Barrio Norte, not the suburbs. The street is alive with space-age protagonists—but however surrealistic the scene, we are still in Buenos Aires. The world breaks in. The city remains. Laments for old love affairs melt into air. Carnival takes over.

ENVOI

Tango is the self-assertive song of Buenos Aires. When it is happy, it is happy in the style of black-influenced milonga composers like Villoldo; when it is sad, it makes international the Buenos Aires manner of greeting the blues by taking wine or black coffee on a gray afternoon. (Note the outrageously unattributed mimesis of tango and blues in the title of Françoise Sagan's 1956 novel, *Bonjour, tristesse*.) The assumptions of tango match Buenos Aires. No other city will do. In the discourse about tango and letters, the work of Villoldo is sometimes described as naïve, and "real literature" is said to come in with Contursi. But this seems reflective of old-fashioned ideas about what is serious in literature and what is not. Villoldo and Discépolo are equal in stature but different in approach.

Nor is tango a literary museum, as if nothing new were now being written. In 2004, for instance, Mario Árraga published *Poética del tango* (Tango Poetics) devoted to the steps and dance halls of Buenos Aires.[13] Árraga is charming:

APOSTILLAS DEL TANGO (FOOTNOTES TO TANGO)

Tango . . . is ideal
For passion and argument.
If Freud didn't prescribe it
he just didn't know
that this flower among flowers,
can cure lovesick hours.

Eugenio Mandrini, in his recent anthology *Poetas del tango*, introduces further new writers: Roberto Díaz, Juan Carlos Jara, Miguel Jubany, Gloria Marco, Raúl Héctor de Robles, Raimundo Rosales, and Alejandro Szwarcman.[14] In 1998, Szwarcman, like Manzi, sang of Pompeya:

POMPEYA NO OLVIDA (POMPEYA DOES NOT FORGET)

April just stops
hours don't flow, nor do they die
An aluminum-colored sun
mocks the crest of a house we go by
On Calle Cachi. . . .

I was a shadow, stalking the midafternoon
sometime in April, I seem to recall,
A troubled phantom, passing through Pompeya.

The old nostalgia is felt through new minds. Meanwhile the songs of the tango have internationalized the image of the capital of Argentina in a way rivaled only by the portrait of Rio projected by the bossa nova. The genius of tango is to take down the voices and images of Buenos Aires in a vast heraldic shorthand, lions rampant at the intersection of Corrientes and Esmeralda, heroines and heroes outlined in the glass, when Discépolo peers in or when Blázquez lifts her venetian blinds.

3.

THE CULTURAL PREPARATION

OPEN SUBURBS: THE COUNTRY CONNECTION

Glass skyscrapers sparkling in downtown Buenos Aires make it difficult to imagine that strong rural influences, forming part of the tango, permeate the city. But they do. Country music, country food, country dance, and country forms of religion are popular among the people of Buenos Aires. What the Argentine critic Sergio Pujol discovered in the urban class structure of the Argentine capital—its "undeniable permeability"—is equally applicable to its culture and geography.[1]

Buenos Aires is an extension of the pampas, the vast treeless plains that extend beyond the city. Looking down the broad Avenida 9 de Julio one feels the pampas rolling in, despite the cars, buses, and pedestrians (Plate 3). There is an old saying: "Just scratch [the surface of Buenos Aires] a little and the pampas will appear." The saying has relevance still.

Avenida 9 de Julio, ventilating the city along a north-south axis, symbolizes the openness of Buenos Aires to migrants from the southern pampas and to those from the mountain regions of the north, including Bolivia. Thus Carmen Bernard in her *History of Buenos Aires:*

> Bolivian migrants, who are called *bolitas,* have set themselves up near Nueva Pompeya in lower Flores, in a barrio nicknamed "Boliviatown." Here, as in the region of Lake Titicaca, the Virgin of Candelaria is celebrated the Sunday that precedes the 12th of October. Ensembles of pan-

PLATE 3

pipes and *charangos,* metal-stringed small guitars, sound through the barrio. *Chicha* is drunk, *cochinillo* is eaten, and cigarettes are offered to the
ekeko, mystic beings that incarnate abundance.[2]

Rural patterns of belief continue to collide with materialism in mod-
ern Buenos Aires. From Corrientes in the north has come *chamamé,* a
form of music popular in working-class neighborhoods.[3] Migrants from
Corrientes have also brought the worship of the folk spirit El Gauchito
Gil, a spiritual patron believed to make more miracles happen than even
San Cayetano, the saint whom porteños pray to when they need work.[4]

In August 2000, after paying respects to the tomb of Gardel in the
Chacarita cemetery, my daughter, son-in-law, and I suddenly discovered
an improvised altar set up in honor of Gil in the Parque Los Andes, just
outside the graveyard. A red flag for his spirit was nailed to a tree trunk.
Below, a miniature house enclosing his image was flanked with red flowers (Plate 4). This improvised shrine broadly matches red flag-bearing
shrines to Gil in the town of Empedrado, just to the south of the city of
Corrientes (Plate 5).

Such practices remain largely invisible to upper-class Buenos Aires,
whose gaze is on New York and Europe. But the pampas and the
provinces permeate the city just the same.

The huge sprawling *ombú* and *gomero* trees of inland Argentina are a
case in point. The *ombú* is the national tree of Argentina. On the pampas
it bursts from the earth in multiple trunks, unlike the vertical columns of

PLATE 4   PLATE 5

fir trees or oaks. So does the gomero. Their tangled expressions makes them baobabs of the pampas.

Symbols of up-country ruggedness, ombúes and gomeros have invaded the core of Buenos Aires, complicating the Londonesque feel of some of the barrios. An ombú guards Rodríguez Peña Plaza, near the corner of Paraguay and Pizurno. Another stands in the Parque Los Patricios in western Buenos Aires. Mingo and Ester Pugliese remember dancing tango around a huge old ombú in a large patio in a club called the Chacarita on Calle Teodoro García.[5]

In the Barrio Norte there is a gomero, a gum tree, in front of the La Biela Café, a famous meeting place at the end of Avenida Quintana (Plate 6). Like the ombú at the Chacarita Club, this tree often shelters musicians and dancers. In 2000 I saw Domingo de Marco play tango-bandoneón there (Plate 7), sheltered by the surround of cool branches. He and some dancers, under the gomero, were like gauchos with guitars sheltered by a spreading ombú, hundreds of miles inland.

Who are the gauchos? In his superb book *The Invention of Argentina*, Nicholas Shumway tells us: they are the nomadic inhabitants of the pampas; they are the rural working class in general.[6] The dancing around the ombú at Chacarita and under the gomero by La Biela Café recalls a rural scene painted by Pedro Figari in the 1920s, *Bajo el ombú* (Under the Ombú Tree). It shows two gauchos performing by moonlight, making an ombú their focus. One of them is dancing with a woman. The other, seated on the ground, strums his guitar while a woman seated next to him listens. Their horses are tethered. Three other women are watching and enjoying the music.

PLATE 6   PLATE 7

Cut back to the Chacarita Club patio on the Calle Teodoro García, where people in the 1940s danced tango around an ombú. What Figari painted had invaded Buenos Aires.

The hinterlands also haunt the capital in the "creole cuisine" served throughout the city. *Creole* is a euphemism for "inland traditional." It is a citywide practice to re-create the barbecues (*asados*) of the countryside, in macho events where males come together and follow a grammar that originally came from the country. They carefully inspect the quality of the meats. They use hard woods, not charcoal, for their fires. They follow an order in placing the meats on the rotating spit: first come the thick cuts, progressing through the fine cuts, then innards, then smoked and seasoned sausage, then finally blood pudding.[7] As far back as the 1920s Juan Carlos Copes's father prepared asados for the country's president, Hipólito Irigoyen. The great 1940s tango stylist Petróleo used to throw asados in a public park, bringing country food, urban space, and city dancing together,

The penetration of inland cooking into Buenos Aires restaurants, like El Ceibal in Palermo or El San Juanino in Barrio Norte, is the revenge of the provinces against the urban mimesis of Paris and Rome. The Inca empire strikes back with dishes like *locro* (corn chowder), tamales, *humitas* (small cakes of maize and sugar), and *mote* (another maize-based delicacy).[8] Unsurprisingly, dishes like locro come from cities close to Peru, like Salta. Lima, Peru, was once the center of colonial gravity in Spanish South America, and Buenos Aires a mere outpost. This meant that the glories of Hispano-Peruvian cooking came out of Lima, then traveled south to towns close to Peru, like Salta and Jujuy, in northern Argentina.

The Argentine Northwest, more than any other region, keeps creole cooking alive. From this culinary epicenter come nuanced adaptations of Iberian meat pies (*empanadas*), filled with roast chicken or beef. Each northern town has a signature manner of preparing them.[9]

A. G. Gutiérrez's painting *Vendedora santiaguera* (A Seller of Food in Santiago de Estero) in the Boca Museum in Buenos Aires shows a woman of color selling empanadas in an enormous local style, along with drinks and large plump tomatoes. She displays the plentifulness of the land.

The food served at Buenos Aires tango strongholds like Sunderland Club and Sin Rumbo unfailingly includes empanadas. But king of the country foods is the dish called *matambre,* a cut of beef that a gaucho respects.[10] A lean square sliced from the muscle of the loin and flank of cattle, it is rolled around hard-boiled eggs, shredded carrots, red peppers, spices, olive oil, and other ingredients, wrapped up, and cooked. When ready, matambre is cut into oval slices. The yellow of the egg, the red line of the pepper, and the orange line of the carrots gleam in the circle of the meat. There is a galactic look to each slice.[11]

One of the most dramatic country-to-city incursions seen in Buenos Aires involves tying red ribbons to the rearview mirror (Plate 8) and sometimes back bumper as well (Plate 9) of the city's taxis and cars. Red ribbons guard against envy (*contra la envidia*). Hail several Buenos Aires cabs in a row—at least one will bear ribbons.

Linking the city to the hinterlands, the custom goes back to the days of oxen-led wagons and horse-driven carriages. In the Museum of Fine Arts in Buenos Aires there is a painting, *Un alto en la pulpería* (A Halt by a Country Store) by the nineteenth-century Argentine master Prilidiano Pueyrredón. Led by a road, we follow a transition from a pastoral horizon to a store, before which a covered wagon has stopped. The oxen are standing. Two men are talking. Inside the wagon a piece of red cloth hangs by a thread at the opening. This colored cloth spiritually protects all persons inside from envy and the evil eye.

Cut to porteño horsemen making a living by offering carriage rides, in front of the Museo Eduardo Sivorí, on Avenida Infanta Isabel, or at the entrance to the town zoo on Avenida Libertador. They tie red ribbons to the left-front fetlocks of their horses (Plate 10) to protect them from envy.[12]

The protection of cars with red ribbons (augmented with a rosary in some cases, or an image of San Cayetano, patron saint of the working class) carries a custom associated with horses and oxen into the city and the twenty-first century. In part it derives from an Italian rural tradition: guarding a house from the evil eye by hanging garlic or using red paint on

PLATE 8   PLATE 9

the door. Recall an Argentine folk tradition: tying a newborn baby with a
red ribbon for protection, or the Kongo association of red cloth with
potency, as in the staffs tipped with scarlet noted at an African wedding in
Buenos Aires in the 1820s. In addition, Pedro Figari has painted candombe blacks being protected by the tying-on of red sashes while a person claps ritual accompaniment.[13]

Red ribbons in Buenos Aires cabs likely creolize together such sources
and more, like the inland custom of tying red ribbons to animals to keep
up their spirits and protect them from
disease.[14] But whatever their history,
red ribbons in cars link city to country.
Once there was prejudice against persons from the country, who lived
beyond the western bank or "edge"
(*orilla*) of the Riachuelo (stream) and
were hence known as *orilleros.* Now
cabs with red ribbons have long
since brought outskirts to downtown.
Honking and driving, they are breaking down barriers.

We study this country to city continuum because it is critical to tango
and its origins. With creolized touches
of Andalusian percussion, persons
from the country established in the
city traditions of rhythm that helped
spark the tango.

PLATE 10

THE MOORISH TINGE IN BUENOS AIRES

Traces of Arabized Muslim music and dance inform Andalusia,[15] the southern region of Spain from which migrants brought flamencolike finger-snapping and heel-stamping dance to Argentina. The process began centuries ago with the North African Berber invasion of Spain in the spring of A.D. 711. The seven-hundred-year Moorish presence in southern Iberia left indelible traces in flamenco music and arabesque architecture. Reflections of the Moors prepared Buenos Aires for tango. These traditions filtered in subtly from the country. One of them was a dessert with an Arabic name, a food mentioned by the brilliant twentieth-century Argentine writer and poet Silvina Ocampo in her classic short story, "The Impostor":

> The lady leaned toward me and offered me an alfajor. With a confidential tone she added: —they're laced with *dulce de leche* . . . If I'm not mistaken, you're the son of Jorge Maidana—
> Hesitating, I accepted her alfajor.[16]

What is an alfajor? It is a creole sweet, *típico* Argentine, involving layers of pastry laced with liquid caramelized milk. It is associated especially with the city of Santa Fe, three hundred miles north of Buenos Aires. The word derives from the Arabic *alfahua* (literally, "honeycomb"), for the Moors brought to Spain Islamic traditions of sugar- and honey-based confections. Indeed, the root of the Spanish word *azúcar*, and equally of the English word *sugar*, lies in the Arabic *az-zukkar*.[17]

In Andalusia, alfajores can be made of almonds, walnuts, and honey. But by the time Andalusian migrants reached Santa Fe from colonial Peru, the sweetness remained but the ingredients had changed.

I have tasted alfajores at El Ceibal on Calle Güemes in Palermo. Inside, a wall made of brickwork simulates a ranch on the pampas. The restaurant's owner-chef, Jesús Romero, shared with me some of the basic ingredients of his style of alfajor—*masa de hojaldre* (pastry flour), *azúcar impalpable* (confectioner's sugar), and of course rich, moist layers of *dulce de leche,* just as the woman promises in Ocampo's short story.

This creole dessert, rough and ready, arrived from the provinces. An Afro-Argentine woman who cooked for the nineteenth-century strongman President Juan Manuel Rosas, is said to have invented a rich creole version.

Every time a porteño savors an alfajor, he bites into a history of northerners migrating from Santa Fe, Santiago del Estero, and Catamarca, bringing their food to the capital. These cities in turn inherited the dish from colonial Peru, which in turn adapted it from Andalusian sources. Afro-Argentines in nineteenth-century Buenos Aires specialized in selling alfajores from a tray, suspended from their shoulders. In Montevideo, where black impact is strong, the people named one of the oldest tango steps "los alfajores." This compares with other Afro-American dances named after desserts—Haitian *meringue* and the Dominican *merengue,* both literally referring to the confection made of pounded sugar and egg whites. The alfajor leads us to examine further Andalusianisms in domestic architecture.

LA CASA DEL LIBERTO
(THE HOUSE OF THE LIBERATED SLAVE)

On Pasaje San Lorenzo in the heart of San Telmo, the Soho of Buenos Aires, stands the famous narrow house of a liberated slave (Plate 11). It dates from the nineteenth century.

Labelle Prussin, an authority on Afro-Atlantic architecture, has studied the structure. She first points out that the house itself, vaguely reminiscent of "shotgun" housing among black North Americans, appears to have been built as an infill, in an alley between two elegant residences. The structure on the left is Luso-Baroque, with parapet decoration, crests, and fine scrollwork. The building on the right is Victorian, with a balustrade parapet and simulated masonry scored in the stucco.

The narrow house between them, whitewashed and compact, has green panel doors with strong diamond patterns. High in the Atlas Mountains of Morocco, diamond patterns are cut into doors to ward off the gaze of the envious. Blue or green doors with diamonds are still to be seen in the villages of the Algarve in Portugal and of Andalusia in Spain, where Moors once lived, and they appear, here and there, in old Montevideo.

The outer fabric of the Casa del Liberto in Buenos Aires has broken off in patches, revealing thin brick construction of lintel and arch. The masonry is strikingly similar to brick walling in Morocco, and to doorways published by André Borg in a classic article on the vernacular

PLATE 11

architecture of Tozeur, in south-western Tunisia.[18] This manner of building, brought by migrants from Andalusia to Argentina, led to a wider horizon of style. In Montevideo, in the once largely black quarter known as the Barrio Sur, there are flat-roofed houses topped by ter-races. The word for "terrace" in Arabic is *as-sutayhah*, "the little roof." Flat-roofed structures like these came to the Algarve and Andalusia; they became known as *açoteia* in Portuguese and *azotea* in Spanish, both derived from the same Arabic word.

In Montevideo there is a splendid azotea on Calle Isla de Flores in the Barrio Sur. The door is painted green and has Moorish-like beveled panels. Above the door there is a ribbed stained-glass transom in the pattern of a rising sun with flaring rays. The latter device, which brings light through the door, is the *medio-punto* (fanlight). It traces ultimately back to the sixteenth-century Italian architect Andrea Palladio and took root, in a linear local idiom, in Havana in the nineteenth century. It appears across London as the fanlight.

Rubén Galloza, the late contemporary artist of Uruguay, was famous for his paintings of the streets of the Barrio Sur. He explains that after blacks moved into previously white-owned buildings in the neighborhood in the 1920s and 1930s the medio-punto became a symbol of their culture. They form the backdrop for the *comparsas,* marching bands with African per-cussion that enliven the streets of the Barrio Sur on Epiphany in January.

Why is it important that we know something about Moorish-derived architecture in Uruguay and Argentina? Because it serves as a setting for tango. On Calle Durazno, where Galloza lived, there is a house dating from around 1888 (Plate 12). Not only does it have a blue-painted door with a medio-punto, but the tile floors inside flash with a black-and-white-diamond motif. This is a *piso damero,* a mosaic floor laid down as a checkerboard, a style that derives from the Moors.

Traditional restaurants and tango dance halls in Buenos Aires have pisos dameros. These floors apparently inspired the rise of a symbol of the traditional Buenos Aires restaurant: a white tablecloth covered with a red tablecloth set at an angle to form a strong diamond. When I watched the late, great Lampazo tango at Sin Rumbo in 1997, red-diamond tablecloths behind him echoed the black and white diamonds on the floor. The checkerboard floor read like a challenge: here is the game board, bring on your moves!

Andalusian-derived elements are more than mere backdrop. They play a part in tango motion, in the heel-stamping episodes called *taconeos*. Andalusian influences also permeated the earlier folk dances of the pampas.

Pedro Figari, the Uruguayan painter of local customs, showed traces of this in a painting from the 1920s of a rural dance called *escondido* (the partner is hidden). *Escondido* is a variant of *gato*, "cat," the most important dance of rural Argentina, the gaucho dance par excellence. Figari paints a cat by a door, perhaps punning on the name of the dance.

As in flamenco, couples dance gato apart, flaunting sweeping steps (*escobillaos*) and stamps of their feet (*zapateos*). Escondido dancers alternate in displays of foot-stamping: in Figari's painting the man stamps alone while his partner "hides" behind him, near the drum, in a demonstration of the name of the dance.[19]

Figari is a camera. He documents Iberian castanets and a guitar on the wall. He shows a *bombo* drummer and tambourine player and a harpist whose instrument frames a woman in red, fanning herself and observing.

A door lined in blue frames the gaucho; he is stamping his heels and sounding his spurs while raising his arms and snapping his fingers. Andalusia and the pampas have become one.

Gauchos practiced other Moorish customs on the pampas of Entre Ríos, north of Buenos Aires. Here, during the period 1850 to 1870, they clipped the manes of their horses in sharp sawtooth patterns introduced by the Moors into Spain.[20] The gaucho shown dancing escon-

PLATE 12

dido by Figari wears large star-shaped spurs. Specially shaped and tipped with silver, they derive (according to the Argentine folklorist Luisa J. Cossi) from Iberian spurs of Arabized origin. In any event, flamenco-related heel-stamping and toe-tapping were widely dispersed in the Argentine interior.

At the end of the nineteenth century, gauchos, black and white, came to Buenos Aires looking for work after landowners bought and fenced their cattle ranges. Early forms of tango—like canyengue—accordingly came to include gaucholike sweeps of great beauty. Early tango had moments of sharp heel percussion, as remembered in the 1931 tango "Taconeando" (Striking the Floor with Your Heels):

> The outskirts have vanished,
> with all of their customs . . .
> the outskirts have vanished,
> leaving no trace
> of their songs about love
> or their spirited heel-stamping.

Tango and milonga still include short bursts of heel-stamping, depending on the artist and context. El Pibe Palermo ends phrases with heel-taps, and so at times does Juan Carlos Copes.

Piercing timbres, nasalized delivery, microtonality, and ecstatic trilling—Arabized elements in flamenco singing—do not turn up in the tango, but there is an exception: Carlos Gardel. He listened acutely to everything. In the second line of his famous song "Mi Buenos Aires querido" (My Beloved Buenos Aires) of 1934, he trills two words, a ver (to see), in a light Arabized way. Gardel being Gardel, he hides his sources by keeping them sparing. But there is more, in none other than the work that initiated the tango-canción, "Mi noche triste" of 1917, where he trills the word abrasador (all hot and burning), with the tones of the southern part of Spain. The clincher as to Gardel's sources is a scene in his movie Tango bar (1935), in which he serenades Spanish migrants on a big ocean liner. Aiming to please them with the sound of their own song, he sings with flamencolike trills.

As the distinguished pianist Horacio Salgán reminds us, the dances and percussion of the gauchos do not wholly explain tango. Nevertheless, they formed a part of its climate of emergence. Salgán himself wrote a tango, "Aquellos tangos camperos" (Those Tangos from the Country), "as an homage to the composers of the earliest tangos, a tango with strong rural roots." Salgán also honors tango composers whose melodic ideas were nourished by Argentine country music, artists like Roberto Firpo and Agustín Bardi.[21] He salutes rural/city interactions in his choice of the *bombo,* the drum Figari painted as fueling escondido, as "an authentically national instrument." He used it first in a convention-breaking tango, "Balanceo" (Strong Rocking Motion), in 1963. It was also in this tango that shells came in as percussion.

The point of this section is to note that the percussive sophistication of the music of Andalusia permeated Buenos Aires through several channels: migrants of Andalusian heritage coming in from the pampas, migrants arriving directly from Andalusia, and Spanish dance and Spanish music on the stage of Buenos Aires. Heel-stamping, finger-snapping patterns helped build a city of rhythmic command. When the Afro-Cuban habanera arrived in the 1850s, Buenos Aires was already rich with two main percussion cultures, creolized Kongo and Andalusia. Now there were three.

ITALIAN INFLUENCES

The music of Italy, the nation that gave the West its discourse of music— *crescendo, fortissimo, moderato*—is brilliantly known and scarcely requires an introduction. The popular musicality of Italy is captured by Giacomo Favretto, a Venetian artist, in his painting of 1885, *Strolling Musicians,* now part of the permanent exhibition at the Museum of Fine Arts in Buenos Aires. Three men, a guitarist, a violinist, and a flutist, play on a walkway above a canal in a working-class section of Venice. An aproned shopkeeper comes out to enjoy them. A youth in a gondola stands up in his boat to catch every note. The guitarist pats time, shifting his weight from foot to foot. This strolling trio can be taken as a symbol of the coming of Italian music—opera, tarantella, and canzonette—to Buenos Aires.

The greatest Italian opera singer of them all, Enrico Caruso, was no stranger to Buenos Aires. He sang at the Teatro Colón on June 18, 1914. Gardel, as a youth, used to entertain working-class buddies by singing in the style of Caruso. Later he would actually meet the great man in Montevideo, where Caruso, the story goes, would praise the natural beauty of his voice. Italian music left traces, bel canto refinements, in the art of Gardel. He loved canzonette and learned them by heart. An early composer, Eugenio M. de Alarcón, wrote Italianisms on the score of a composition with a piquant title, *Bite My Left Ear* (1906), indicating how certain passages were to go: *espressivo, legatissimo, scelti, ben ritmato.*

Tango dance too reflected the impact of intense immigration from

Italy. "The Old Tanguero" (Viejo tanguero), a famous anonymous historian of 1913, reports:

> Around 1880 . . . in the barrio of Corrientes . . . tango [dancing] experienced . . . a change, not only of figures but also in terms of the elasticity and swing [contoneos] that were the arresting characteristics displayed at the start. Now it was interpreted by young women who were for the most part Italian. So then it became known as "smooth tango" [tango liso].[22]

Italian opera inspired the black tango pianist Horacio Salgán. Talking about one of his most famous compositions, "A fuego lento" (To a Slow Fire), written in 1950–51, Salgán recalls:

> Since childhood Italian opera had exerted a strong pull. Listening to Rossini's Barber of Seville I found a fascinating passage, a bass part aria called Calumny where the text goes: "[Gossip] keeps on running, running, through the ears of the people." That aria, flowing without a halt to a crescendo, inspired me . . . to write a tango, perhaps the most vanguard of all my tangos, To a Slow Fire.[23]

Salgán was not the only major tango composer inspired by Rossini. There are phrases in Osvaldo Pugliese's first important composition, "Recuerdo" (Fond Memory), written in 1924, that are very interesting in this regard.

FROM CENTRAL AFRICA TO CREOLE ARGENTINA

> African influences became Afro-Argentine and Afro-criollo, finally to be seen simply as Argentine.
>
> —ANA CARA-WALKER,
>   The Art of Creole Expression in Argentina (1983)

> With Afro-American tales . . . immediacy is conveyed by creole language forms.
>
> —ROGER D. ABRAHAMS, African American Folktales (1985)

> Igniting the fire of [Buenos Aires] were people of Kongo descent.
>
> —ENRIQUE CADÍCAMO, Florida y charcas (1945)

Persons from the kingdoms of Kongo and Angola were brought in slave ships to Buenos Aires. Captives also came from West African civilizations like the Yoruba, the Fon, the Nupe (Tapa), and the Hausa. The last burst of the Atlantic slave trade, in the late eighteenth and early nineteenth centuries, involved changes felt in Uruguay and Argentina.

There was, for example, a shift in focus to the Bight of Benin, to modern-day Benin and western Nigeria. This reflected inland events: the disintegration of the Oyo Empire, the Yoruba civil wars, and serious disruptions around Sokoto in the north, involving Hausa and Bornu.[24] This accounts for the presence of Yoruba (Mina Nago), Yorubaized Mahi from the north of Dahomey (Mina Mahi), Dahomeans and others via Ouidah (Fida), Hausa (Auza), and Bornu (Borno) in early-nineteenth-century Buenos Aires.

Sifting sources for the origins of Africans resident in Buenos Aires between 1750 and 1830, George Reid Andrews shows West Africans making up at least a third of sub-Saharan people of known origin.[25]

But in terms of documented impact, numbers, and cultural closeness, the most important were those from Kongo and Angola. They were the ones who gave us the words that named Argentine dances: malambo, milonga, canyengue, tango. Core concepts of their dancing, the "cut" (*nzéngolo*) and the "break" (*tienga ye kanga mu nabyu*), took over tango.

Where precisely did Kongo and Angola blacks come from? In the early nineteenth century 75 percent of them came from a three-hundred-mile strip of coast stretching from Cabinda in Kongo, in the north, to Luanda, in Angola, in the south.

This segment of shoreline directly connects to Buenos Aires slaving. Captives were marshaled on the coast at Loango, Malembe, Cabinda, and Mboma, the latter settlement sited at the mouth of the Kongo. This is essentially North Kongo.[26] The area includes important groups: Yombe, Sundi, and Mboma. These exact Kongo terms reappear in Buenos Aires slave names: Loango, Cabinda, Momboma (Mboma) Umbonia (Mboma), Luumbi (Yombe), Sundi, Kongo itself, and Mondongo (a Kongo term that apparently referred to "upriver mercenaries").[27] The fact that Mboma appears twice is a hint at the number of captives in Buenos Aires who came from the mouth of the Kongo.

Slave-marshaling points in Angola included Luanda, Ambrize, and Kassange, the latter a place on a central route from the interior. The southern Angola route found its principal outlet in Benguela. Through these ports came ethnicities to Buenos Aires whose names reflected either the ports through which they were shipped or their actual points of

cultural origin: Angola, Benguela, Kisanji (Kasanje). There were assort-
ments from the interior of Angola: Ganguela, Ombe (Huombe), Lucango,
Majumbi, Munanda, Kibala (Quipara), Kisama (Quisama), and Umbala.
Grouped ethnically with the Kibala, in northern Angola, was an important Angola group, the Libolo (Lubolo).[28] The name *Lubolo* would
become famous in late-nineteenth-century Afro-Argentine and Afro-
Uruguayan ritual life. Whites picked it up as the name of a marching
group that imitated black styles and black rhythms.

The languages of North Kongo form variants of Ki-Kongo. They are
mutually intelligible. The languages of northern Angola are in some cases
as close to Ki-Kongo as Spanish is to Portuguese. This was not the case
with West African languages like Yoruba (Mina Nago), Nupe (Tacua), and
Hausa (Auza), all mutually unintelligible. Linguistic closeness fostered
bonding and fusion among Kongo and Kongo-related persons in Buenos
Aires. But there were other factors at play that added to the dynamic of
their culture.

First of all, the kingdom of Kongo was a forceful civilization. Luís Vas
de Camões (1524–80), poet laureate of Portugal, lauded Kongo in his
verses of 1556 as "the greatest of all kingdoms" on the coast of Black
Africa.[29] Kongo was indeed a kingdom, like Portugal or Spain, and not a
tribe. Its history was distinguished and urban.

The center of Kongo was Mbanza Kongo, a capital city in what is now
northern Angola. Here there was a famous law court, a currency, and
superb art and ritual. There was a twin capital in the north, Lwangu, the
streets and culture of which impressed a Dutch chronicler of the seventeenth century. The Kongo cluster of ethnicities, as George Peter
Murdock pointed out, "aroused the astonishment of early Portuguese
explorers because of the complexity of their political institutions and their
social life."[30]

Uruguayan and Argentine popular dances were indelibly influenced by
the style of this kingdom. Kongo dances were schools of being. They
taught ethics as well as art, and spirituality and self-defense, too. Unless
we steep ourselves in their nuance and variety, we will never understand
the Central African roots of the tango.

CLASSICAL DANCE IN THE KINGDOM OF KONGO

e, mbari ndumba, bu uwanda disanga
e izola, e yaye

Hey, fine woman, you dance so invitingly.
hey, I'm willing, pretty mama, I'm willing

—J. VAN WING, "Les danses Bakongo," *Congo* (JULY 1937)

What form do you suppose a life would take that
was determined at a decisive moment precisely
by the street song last on everyone's lips?

—WALTER BENJAMIN, "Surrealism: The Last Snapshot
of the European Intelligentsia" (1929)

Many cities have a bearing on the cultural formation of Buenos Aires.
From Genoa came *pizze* and words like *baccan* (boss), creolized into
bacán, the tango word for "big shot." Andalusians from Seville introduced
azoteas (flat-roofed house architecture) and heel-stamping dances. Other
cities—London, Paris, Barcelona, Madrid—were also prominent influences, particularly in town planning and architecture. But two other
cities, albeit never mentioned, are culturally relevant, too: Mbanza Kongo
and Lwangu.

These were the twin capitals of the kingdom of Kongo. Milonga,
canyengue, and tango would not have emerged without their rich dance
culture, a critical antecedent. Neither would they now have their names.

From the founding of the Kongo kingdom in the 1200s, its people
placed dance at the center of their civilization. Fu-Kiau Bunseki, a Mu-
Kongo scholar, remembers elders talking about the glories of dance in
Mbanza Kongo: "They mentioned *makinu ma bakulu* (dances for the
ancestors), *makinu ma mfumu* (dances for the king), the related *makinu
ma nsi* (dances of the nobility), *makinu ma nkisi* (dances in honor of healing spirits), and *makinu ma soonga* (ecstatic dances, climaxed by the
descent of the spirit, from the realm of the ancestors).[31]

Written sources confirm the grandeur of this vision. Giovanni Antonio
Cavazzi da Montecuccolo, writing in about 1670, was impressed with the
makinu mafwete, royal dances performed at the court of the king of
Kongo: "persons of quality" danced for the ruler with "reserve, grace, and
gravity," holding in their left hand a time-keeping rattle.[32] The root term,
mafwete-fwenta, "to dance well," "to dance, twisting the hips," "to set into
motion rich folds of cloth"—pictures this dance glory at the center of
happening.[33] Moving in time, rattle in hand, continues today in Kongo. It
also came to Rio and Buenos Aires.

Sources published over the past four hundred years identify patterns of motion in Kongo. These too relate to black dance in the southern part of our hemisphere. Father Luc de Caltanissetta, writing in May 1698, described a dance at Lemba, in the present-day region of Pool, Congo-Brazzaville. Caltanissetta does not give us a ground plan, but we infer "Kongo lines," one male, the other female, facing each other, or a circle, facing inward, half male and half female. This in any event was what he saw:

> The dance started with handclapping, hands held high. Then each person struck his chest with one hand while extending the other hand or foot towards the person facing him. In this dance one also approached the opposite person with alternating lunges of the shoulder, sometimes the left and sometimes the right.[34]

Fu-Kiau Bunseki saw this same dance performed by a ritual expert, a nganga Lemba, when he was fifteen in North Kongo around 1946. It is part of the Lemba Society repertory. The dance, *makinu ma Lemba,* takes place after initiation. Talking to me in 2001, Fu-Kiau restored Caltanissetta's verbal notice to full body from kinetic memory. He danced with claps held high in the air, followed by alternating left-right kicks, alternating left-right strikings of the chest with his hands (a simplified form of *zuba,* ancestor of *juba* in black United States dancing), and alternately presented shoulders, left-right, right-left.

Clapping high is a sign of alliance and approval (*sinsu kia lusingusunu ye lutambudulu*), like the "high fives" made popular by black American athletes. The combination of slapping (*zuba*) the chest and kicking out (*matambi*) while moving (waving) the shoulders from side to side while bending forward (*níkuna mavembo ku ndambu ye ndambu bu weti yínama*) seals the dance with signs of enthusiasm.

This complex of motion involves spiritual dimensions: kicking close to the earth calls on the ancestors; clapping high and rolling the shoulders, with the body as the boundary between heaven and earth, calls on God. Shoulder activation, *mayembo,* in fact symbolizes the presence of Great God Almighty (*Nzambi Mpungu*). This Lemba motion, then, bears a powerful message: we are moving through worlds, we are not moving alone.

Kongo dancing, ecstatic and transcendent, combines strong designs.

1. *Line (milonga) or circle (lukóngolo) formations* have males on one side, females on the other. Elders insist on this because it avoids problems,

mambu, arising from promiscuous interspersing of the sexes. Of the two formations, elders consider the circle more formal, relating to the noble dances of antiquity, whereas dancing in lines more or less goes with ordinary dancing.

2. *Dancing in the distance (kina mu ntatuki)* is a Bakongo phrase for dancing without touching. Their term is *tatuka,* "to stand apart." This does not mean, however, that there are no couples; no matter how far they stand and move apart, men and women pair up. There is a dramatic moment, called *bumbakana,* where they briefly bump at the thigh or the waist. There can be humor and attitude in apart dancing, as when a woman, confronted by someone she finds unattractive, shout outs *tatuka!* (stay distant, get lost!).

3. Dancing without embracing frees arms, trunk, and legs for full action. This leads to the next characteristic, *total bodily dancing (beti zébuka,* to shake the whole body). Every part of the frame is in action. *Zébuka* translates roughly as "whole lotta shaking going on." Gifted dancers accomplish polycentric levels of expression: they can maintain one drumbeat in their shoulders while playing that off against another drum pattern in their hips.

4. *Multimetric dancing* distributes different time signatures to different parts of the body. Bakongo call this "dancing in harmony with *all* of the beats" (*makumu mawawane*). In other words, a woman may dance to a gong in her feet, taking small steps, while rolling her shoulders to the beat of one drum and weaving her hips to yet a second drum pattern.

5. In the next trait, *embodied percussion,* the dancer not only follows different patterns of meter but *becomes* a percussion instrument. Bakongo call this *kotele mu kumu* (total penetration of the beat). The person is no longer just a dancer—she's a *beat.* Often this means she is dancing and hand-clapping at the same time, the clap being the timepiece, the organizing principle. Or a man may make a percussive stamp on the ground, sealing (*sa sami*) an event with enthusiasm.

   The Kongo body-striking dance *zuba* offers a dramatic transformation of a person into a sounding instrument. Creolized to "juba," it became the famous body-whacking "hambone" dance of black North America. In *zuba,* as in "patting juba" or hambone, the dancer strikes percussion on chest and thighs with both hands. He literally handles the rhythm.

6. The next trait is *overlapping call-and-response dancing.* Call and response supplies the formal structure of Central African song. It

applies to motion because the leader of the song chorus often leads the dance as well. The Ki-Kongo phrase for overlapping antiphony is *yenga ye kumba,* literally "call and response." This phrase almost certainly gave rise to the classical black term for overlapping antiphony in English.

In any event, the lead dancer makes the first move. The chorus—or his partner—overlaps his phrasing and picks it up. "One move calls for another" (*konso n'niku weti bookila n'niku wankaka*).[35] Here is Van Wing's description from 1937: "There are always two persons, or two groups in action, a solo dancer before a group, or a single individual before another individual. They execute periodic movements that are like questions and responses, moving forward and moving back."[36]

As we shall see, that taste for "periodic movement" filtered into tango. It leads to amazing sequences in which the man "calls" with his hand, or his arm, or his body, and the woman "responds" with a gorgeous line of independent action. The blending went far, but the aura remains.

7. Then there is *"hot" dancing (makinu masakidi tiya),* "where fire invades the dance." This includes sexy "winding" of the hips, *tienga* or *makinu ma luketo* (the dance that twists the hips).

8. Also involved is the supreme spiritual expression in Kongo dancing, *mayembo* (ecstatic trembling of the shoulders). *Mayembo* becomes the basic term in Kongo for possession by the spirit. *Tienga,* by contrast, takes the heat and the circular motion of the sun into the hips, sealing life and continuity therein. Also, on an earthier level, *tienga* mimes moving the hips in sexual action. It became "the Kongo grind" in the jazz dance of the United States, "winding" in the Bahamas, "the Kongo" in Trinidad, and *gouyade* in Haiti. In black Cuba, meanwhile, mayembo became a famous move of the rumba.

9. The climax of Kongo dancing between the sexes is *bumbakana.* Man and woman dance forward, approaching each other from their positions in opposed lines, or in opposed segments in a circle, and briefly strike their abdomens together. There are other ways of performing bumbakana, bringing the chest or thighs or even the rump, for example, into momentary collision. This heightened interaction becomes *vacunao* in the Cuban rumba, a word that clearly derives from *bakana,* sexily reinforced by the Spanish verb *vacunar* (to vaccinate). In Argentina bumbakana continues, as a pure element of candombe. It predicts, as we shall see, the various ways of invading the space of one's partner in the tango, which offers a kind of hyper-bakana or baroque vacunao.

In any event, in showing how to enter the life and the rhythm of another person, Kongo dance leaders taught many things. In a small dancing circle they might ask children to jump in the center and dance in formations, to mime constellations in the sky. This taught rudimentary astronomy, for self-navigation when lost in the night. In addition, by insisting that children dance in short bursts, yielding their place to another (*kuvana lisampa*), the elders taught social skills, how to share space and time with one's peers.

Dancing veered into mime. There were animal dances galore, like *kitsusu*, a mime of moving hens and roosters; *kimbwa*, a dog dance; and *kiway*, an essay on the silky motions of cats. Bakongo interwove dance and aspiration, dance and social happening. Dances confirmed key transitions: birth, marriage, initiation, death, and possession by the spirit.

Fu-Kiau adds: "Dancing is the process through which Bakongo manifest approval of important social situations."[37] In other words, dance is chorus, dance is opinion, dance evaluates people's achievements. When, for example, a man has been initiated into the august Lemba society, officiants escort him with dancing to seal their approval (*bafwiti natwa ku nsia makinu*); literally, he must be escorted through the dance.

Dance crowns heightened states of being. It celebrates winning a lawsuit. It celebrates a person recovering from serious illness. The highest level of danced enthusiasm, *mayembo*, trembles the shoulders with the coming of the spirit. But Kongo dance is more than affirmation; spiritually imbued traditions of artistic motion have the power to make you *yíndula mu ntima* (examine your heart) and reflect on life's meaning. Kongo dance can make you face the deepest issues, and sometimes even change your life.[38]

It can turn feisty and combative as well. One jumps in the ring to *sa ntembe* (challenge one's peers) in battles of dance, to test who is best. This develops confidence and agility.

It also links up with the Kongo custom of using dance as an equivalent to close-order drill in the training of young soldiers. Kongo warriors, by means of dance training, were taught to duck (*sanguka*), to twist (*zeka*), and to parry, to avoid being stationary, hence easy targets, in the presence of enemies.

As early as 1491, Duarte López reported from Kongo that "when fighting begins, ordinary soldiers run into the fray in scattered formations, shooting their arrows from afar, turning and dodging, this way and that, darting in all directions to avoid being hit."[39]

Danced military training, as John Thornton shows from a review of his-

torical sources, lies behind this marvel.[40] Danced martial art in Kongo,
with its famous avoidance patterns (*misangi*), clearly influenced the rise
of *esquivas*, patterns of ducking or twisting out of harm's way, in the
defensive moves of capoeira angola, the black martial art of Brazil.[41]

Not all the dances involved athlete-warriors, laughing at arrows, with
hair-trigger twists and quick turns. There were moments when a single
person might cup his chin within his palm. This was a sign of sadness, a
sign of the blues. And when that happened, he might pick up a one-
stringed instrument (*nsiki a lungungu*) or a lamellophone (*nsiki kisanzi*)
and get up and dance to self-performed music. This changed his mood.
This drove the blues away. Compare Willie Ruff, distinguished jazzman:
"Blacks in North America sometimes dealt with the blues with hambone
[*zuba*], striking their chests and finding a bass note, in a deep and strong
frequency, to make themselves tough and rebuild their confidence."[42]

DANCED HIEROGLYPHS: MOTION AND MEANING
IN SEVEN KONGO DANCES

There is a rich system of graphic writing in Kongo: ruler's staffs with ideographic emblems; emblematic pot lids (*mataampha*) for social criticism;
and elaborate cosmographic signs, traced on the earth or on prominent
stones in praise of Kalunga, the world of the ancestors, the ultimate
source of pure power. Writing with signs is a mark of distinction. Its vitality and pertinence spills over into dance.

Some Kongo moves are signs. They bear names and meanings, translating values and cultural aims. This identifies their dance as classical.
The Parthenon, with its named pediments, metopes, capitals, sculptures,
and setting, was an instrument for praising the goddess Athena, tutelary
deity of the city. Similarly, moves in Kongo dance were named and given
meaning. They were used to praise—and embody—ancestral spirit and
insight, the force that gave life meaning.

To sharpen our sense, then, of Kongo impact on dancing in Buenos
Aires, we sample and gloss several dances.

FLAG DANCE AT LWANGU, 1668 (PLATE 13) When someone dies in
Kongo, mourners fashion a special archway (*fumba* or *lukote*). The mourners process through this curved gate. The curve represents the dome of the
sky, domain of God. One goes through this gate to gain power and insight.

The print in Plate 13, depicting a funeral at Lwangu, shows men carry-

PLATE 13

ing a dead person, wrapped in mats (*lwandu*) tied in sections, to the ultimate place where one regains power, the cemetery. This explains the
archway. The pallbearers, and the men around the arch, are all dancing
spiritedly. Each waves a miniature flag (*kimpevula*) in his hand, a sign of
victory (*dimbu kia ndungunu*). They have just won a lawsuit (*mambu*) or
passed through some other ordeal connected with the death of the person. They dance with their flags to show they are happy. Their feathered
bonnets (*mpu a nsala*) translate their rank, as noblemen, and communi-
cate also that they are involved with healing. Their simplified tunics are
signs of their innocence.

In contrast to their jubilation, a person in the archway sits in a position
of sadness, chin cupped in right hand (*fumana*). That person is mourning
either the death of the person, or a loss in a lawsuit, or both. So the men

PLATE 14

with the flags dance through the archway to symbolize their innocence and victory. Black coffee carriers in Brazil, as we shall see, danced with African rattles and a flag in the 1840s (Plate 14). They were proclaiming personal victory on the docksides of Rio.

FUNERAL DANCE FOR A CABINDA DIGNITARY, NORTH COAST OF KONGO, 1780–87 (PLATE 15) Honoring the end of an important man's life and the beginning of his spiritual journey, dancers move around in a circle. The dead ruler, Andris Pukuta, late "minister of commerce" of Cabinda, lies in state on a bier richly decked with striped trade cloths.[44]

Women dance counterclockwise in a circle around the *fwambu,* the covered veranda where the body is resting. Some of the women raise their hands to the sky. This is normally a sign of great joy; here it shows how strongly the women feel about their departed leader. With a sign of ecstasy (*nsindukulu ya mayembo*) they send him off in peace. Others make another send-off sign while wheeling around the bier: wearing long trailing cloths, they deliberately drag them, sweeping the earth, imprinting the sand with a circular track (*nkombila*).

In so doing they clear the area of problems left over from the dead man's life. This grand sweeping of his problems (*komba mambu*) is an aspect of ideal nobility: persons of rank ideally don't accept the debts of a dead man. They sweep them away. They are clearing the name of the late honored ruler with the "broom" of their trailing cloths. He goes to his ancestors free of all debts (*mfuka*) and discrepancies (*mbabani*).

We meet a creolized extension of this funerary rite of ritual cleansing

PLATE 15

PLATE 16

among tradition-minded blacks in Montevideo. Here in the 1920s, the noted *costumbrista* (painter of local customs) Pedro Figari painted black women purifying the way before a funeral procession entering a cemetery (Plate 16). The name of the painting is *Apoteosis* (Apotheosis); Ian Churchill has sketched its essential elements here. They are "sweeping" the path with cloths held before them. The code slightly changes, from dragging cloths to waving them, but the message has remained constant: clear the path for our loved one's departure.[45]

M'TELA DANCE, VILLAGE OF N'ZIETO, BOKO DISTRICT, CONGO-BRAZZAVILLE, JULY 17, 1990 M'tela, a North Kongo dance, takes place at second funerals (*matanga*)—the celebrations that end periods of mourning rather than beginning them—and at rituals of family reconciliation. Its name puns on *telama* (to stand), meaning the steps are performed while the dancer is standing.

Drive and power are packed in this standing. The knees are a blur, moving up, in, and out; up, in, and out; they are miming a paddle (*nkafi*) being rowed (*ntuluza*) with great force. While m'tela is performed, bystanders may shout to the dancer, *Kwabula kulu, mboko diata!* (Trigger your legs and move!). The whole performance is unified by a hand-clap (*nsaala*) that the dancer executes while simultaneously trembling his shoulders (*nikuna mayembo*). He rattles his shoulders "as a sign of pride, sensing great power, coming down from above."[46]

M'tela accompanies the search for agreement and reconciliation. Deep meaning attaches to a dancer who "rows" with his knees across water. He is opening a path to the ancestors. Down this path on the water, so it is prayed, sources of peace will come.

MAKINU MA LUKETO (HIP-GRINDING DANCE), EASTERN KONGO, NORTH BANK OF THE INKISI RIVER, SOUTHWEST OF KINSHASA, LATE 1930S J. Van Wing witnessed a hip-grinding dance in Kongo in the 1930s. It was composed of two lines, one of men, dancing bare-chested with waist-wrappers knotted in front, the other of women, wearing small dance cloths. A lead dancer (*n'tu makinu*) triggers the song and sets the dance beat. When the chorus responds, the dancing begins: everyone starts grinding their hips, moving to a beat called *kiselo*, "an invitation to the dance." The lead dancer then passes in front of the men. As he dances by each male, the male throws his leg out toward a woman. If he looks her in the eye while doing this, the kick is "invitational" (*samba diambookidila*), asking her to partner. If he does this while *not* looking, then it is a "show-off kick" (*samba diamviokila*), meant to attract general attention.

Next the lead dancer starts up a new song, signaling transition. Two couples at a time now dance between the two lines, to a hand-clapping, foot-stamping chorus. At a signal from the leader, the two couples retire, to be replaced by two more. So it goes until everyone has performed.

Finally the leader approaches the women, who, at this sign, advance toward the men, each zeroing in on a partner, pairing up. Then *whack!* they knock their chests together (*bumbakana*). Facing each other, they then dance apart, grinding their hips, until the leader gives the signal to stop. That ends the dance.[47]

N'KWANGA AT DIOSSO, CONGO-BRAZZAVILLE, JULY 5, 1987 As a promise of percussive beauty, the name of the dance *n'kwanga* literally refers to moving to the sound of a basket rattle, called by the same name. N'kwanga is traditionally danced at the coronation of a king and at the funeral of an important person. Witnessed at Diosso near Pointe Noire on July 5, 1987, it was danced to the multimetric richness of two *ngoma* drums, an *nkonko* slit-gong, and a long narrow *ndungu* drum bearing the motif of the monitor lizard (*mbambi a nkakala*). The motif was a proverb: when drumming, don't raise your head as the monitor does, for this is a sign of arrogance.[48]

The dance circle itself, steady and nonrevolving (*lukongolo lwasikila*) is made up of performers facing inward. Women make up one half the circle; the other half is male.

Suddenly a lead dancer leaps into the center. She melts to the ground, on subtly bent knees. "Breaking" to ground level, she "calls" with a gesture, indicating her heart with both hands, then bringing hands forward and out. This means "give from the heart" (*senda tuka mu ntima*). In other words, she jumps into the ring to start life in the circle. She represents the sun. Her gesture spreads healing from the center of life. Echoes of her gesture stream from the circle like the rays of the sun. Fu-Kiau Bunseki completes our understanding with a modernist gloss: "the people in the circle are like cars with dead batteries—she jump-starts them all with her action."[49] Soon everyone is touching their heart, miming the grace that ensures community.

Then she rises and throws her cloth at a man, challenging him to join her. This is *vaana a samba*, "approaching a person and inviting him or her to dance."[50] Her call demands a response: he accepts. He leaps into the ring, turning and moving around her. He leans forward (*yinama*) toward her; he leans back (*yekuka*) away from her. Then he spins and returns to the curve of the ring. Leaning forward says "I follow" (*landa*), meaning "I'll walk where you walk." Leaning back says "I thank you" (*tondwa*), i.e., "I'm grateful for the dance that you shared."

Now the chorus is making another gesture, throwing, in unison, their arms toward the earth (*songa mooko mau mu nsi*). It is a mass invitation. They are saying that the path to the action is now open; enter the dancing court (*wiza mu mbasi*). The leader turns her attention to a talented young man in a white shirt and beige pants. She challenges him, too, with *vaana a samba*. He enters the court fluidly, dancing with slightly curved hands, kept parallel to the earth, lightly carried in front of his body. This is a sign, *lembika mooko,* a gesture of peace and tranquillity. In other words, he greets her while dancing.

He stamps, he turns completely around, then stamps and turns around yet again. This is *zengumuka* (leaping around; showing one's passion for dance).[51] By stamping, he shows he accepts her. He is sealing (*sa sami*) a bond with the stamp of his foot.[52]

TSHIKUMBI SOCIETY DANCE, DIOSSO On the same day in the same area, a dance was performed by members of the traditional Tshikumbi finishing society, which transforms young girls into marriageable women. The society's color is mediatory red.

The initiates dance forward in a flawlessly organized line. Then the grand initiator breaks ranks from this formation and enters the circle, brushing her honorific bracelets with a fly whisk, activating their power. Her shoulders tremble. To the initiated, this communicates that she herself is not dancing. She is *being danced* (*kinuswa*) by unseen high forces. Elderly women surround her, each with a diamond-form rattle (*nsansi*) made of tin. The nsansi are symbols of life held within, seeds in a container that, when shaken, make people move. Outwardly the elders are adding percussion. Inwardly they are challenging the young women: we expect a new life from within all of you, like the stir of the seeds in our rattles. The challenge is answered. Acolytes in the circle begin to vibrate their shoulders, their breasts, and the *kitanda,* the cloth that covers their breasts. They too are being "danced." Their shoulders roll in response to the spirit. Their arms bear raffia ornaments (*mpusu*) like Kongo staffs with mnemonic raffia attachments. The meaning of the mpusu: don't act on your own, remember your vows to be women who heal, not women who curse and cause trouble. With raffia on their arms and in their hair, the acolytes are bound to their ritual responsibilities.

The best dancer "breaks" to the ground. She propels herself forward, opening and closing her heels, scattering dust as she does so. Her litheness and strength impress. Like the m'tela virtuoso at N'zieto, she is "opening a path," inviting her sisters to share in her motion. Then she does somersaults (*ta kinkindu*): being up, in our world, then down, with the ancestors, she rolls the two realms into one. She is showing off athleticism as well, but to the elders her moves signify a search for completeness. When she finishes the sequence, she picks up a whistle and puts it in her mouth. She has succeeded; this gives her the right to blow on the whistle (*bwabu lenda sika nsiba*).

NSUNSA: THE SASS DANCE Dance battles abound in the tango. They are duels on the dance floor, like the night in the 1920s when the famed stylist El Cachafaz took on his black rival, El Negro Santillán. There are precedents galore for tango contests of virtuosity in the Kongo tradition of male-on-male challenge dancing, especially the type called *nsunsa.*

The name *nsunsa* derives from the Ki-Kongo verb *sosa,* "to look for a fight, to malign, to provoke, to sass."[53] In fact, *sosa* seems logical as a source for the American vernacular term *sass,* which has the same valence of defaming and challenging. It was probably reinforced by the English adjective *saucy,* in the sense of "insolent toward superiors."[54]

According to the late Woyo elder Nzau-Balu of the town of Mwanda, nsunsa arose in Cabinda. Elders in Manianga and Yombe contest this, saying it's a virtually pan–North Kongo form, with no known single point of origin. Most sources agree, however, that nsunsa is "old," going back "at least for two centuries," according to Nzau Balu.[55]

An eighteenth-century attestation of this dance in action, across the seas, corroborates this dating. John Gabriel Stedman saw *"soesa"* (note its new creole name) danced among Lwangu (North Kongo) slaves in Suriname, on the north coast of South America, in 1790:

> Soesa [*nsunsa*] consists of [two men] dancing opposite to each other, clapping their hands on their sides to keep time, when each with pleasure throws out one foot. If they meet across, [one person] wins one point, if sides, it is for the other, till one or the other has got twelve, sometimes twenty points, who gets the game. So very eager are they at this play that sometimes six or eight [male] couples are engaged at once.[56]

The same game, with the same rules, goes on today in North Kongo. In Vili country it is called *mbunga,* from *ku bunga,* "to play," for example drawing figures in the sand. I saw it danced on the coast of Woyo country in the summer of 1985 and among Vili near Lwangu (Loango) in the summer of 1987.

The rules of nsunsa and mbunga have stayed the same for more than two hundred years: if I shoot out my right foot at the exact moment my opponent shoots out his left, I win. But if he cancels me with his right, I lose. Each time I win, I get one full point (*kongo dimosi*). With twelve points (*makongo mumputa*), I win the game.

Sharp eyes and lightninglike reflexes rule. The best win with style. Players of mbunga at Diosso in Congo-Brazzaville deliberately shoot out particles of dust with bare feet "to show they are warriors"; the bursts of fine dust (*fundu-fundu*) symbolize smoke from the barrel of a gun.

Although the name and the game, nsunsa, apparently did not emerge in Argentina, as they did in Suriname, a complex of black competitive dances did take root there, like malambo in the country, and tango challenge dances in early-twentieth-century Buenos Aires. Dance combat traditions extended across Kongo and included neighboring civilizations like the Kuyu, which mounted a famous dance contest called *kyebe-kyebe.* All this was probably reinforced by dance duels among captives from Mahi, Yoruba, and Hausa country in early-nineteenth-century Buenos Aires.

TEEZA MAZA, SANGUMUNA, MALAMBO: TESTING, DISPERSING, AND NAILING DOWN PROBLEMS *Teeza maza, sangumuna,* and *malambo* are fascinating dance modes. They deal with problems and symbolically solve them.

Teeza warns people to test the waters of a situation, literally and figuratively, to avoid disaster; sangumuna symbolically disperses (*mwangisa*) and smooths over sources of discord; and malambo metaphorically buries problems, stamping them into the ground.[57] Teeza is popular in Kongo; the dance's full title is *teeza maza* (test the water). The rivers of Kongo are deep, fast-moving, and dangerous, so the dance is a mime of what one must do: test the depth and the speed of the current before entering, to make sure it's safe at that moment. Portraying this, the dancer freezes his right foot "flat on the land." At the same time, he slowly inches the left foot straight forward, "testing the water," while asking, "Do we go with this current or not?" A chorus of onlookers shout out reactions, warning him, with cries like *nsi! nsi!* (dangerous! dangerous!) or *télama! télama!* (stand! stop where you are! don't go any deeper) or encouraging him, with phrases like *dyata! dyata!* (walk in! walk in!) or *tonta! tonta!* (try it! try it!).

Teeza reemerged in the Kongo candombes of Buenos Aires and continues in 2005 among black stars of milonga, but it has apparently lost its original meaning. Kely and Facundo Posadas have improvised a variant of this step, which they learned from observing *candomberos* in action in the 1950s and 1970s in a famous black dancing club in the basement of the Casa Suiza on Calle Rodríguez Peña. They freeze one foot while inching the other foot backward, lowering their knees, going deeper and deeper, and then reversing the slide and rising back up to starting position.

Sangúmuna, dragging the foot across the ground, is important in Kongo. For some, it symbolizes the dispersing (*mwangisa*) of sand, and since there is a saying in Kongo that "problems are like sand" (*mambu mafwanane ye zielo*), dragging the foot over sand and dispersing it symbolically smooths things over. In other words, "dispersing problems" is "putting them on the same smooth level, thus bringing peace" (*mwangisa mambu i sa vo tula mo mu tezo kimosi, vana yenge*).

The drag can be slow or fast—there are verbs that nuance the tempo. *Kwanga*, for example, is a sudden dragging of the foot; *kokela* is dragging the foot either slowly or fast.

Fu-Kiau Bunseki saw an old dance called malambo performed at Kumba in North Kongo around 1951. Malambo is a dance of ritual purification, its aim the solving of social dissension. The dancers stamp their feet vigorously on a prepared portion of ground laden with medicines of peace or reconciliation. Stamping these medicines (*koma bilongo*) into the ground, they "nail" or activate them, for the sake of communal well-being.

The memory of this Kongo stamping dance came to black Argentina and named a rural stamping dance among cowboys, one that absorbed, however, strong influences from heel-stamping traditions (*zapateados*) of

Spain. The name *malambo* and the stamping remain, but Argentine malambo developed as a fast-moving battle dance. It was not "nailing" medicines but a competitive flaunting of stamina and patterns (*mudanzas*) that included tap-dancing, stamping, and brush steps. The man with the most patterns would win. The stiff, erect posture of Argentine malambo came from Spain.

KONGO TO CREOLE TO TANGO

There is more to dance history than reinstatement. Bakongo in South America, in their games and their dances, were seeding the future with a taste for innovation and cultural adaptability.

Recall men dancing with small flags in the Kongo city of Lwangu in 1668 as a sign of victory in a lawsuit or some other matter (Plate 13). Now compare them to Angolan workers, athletically carrying 150-pound sacks of coffee on their heads through the streets of mid-nineteenth-century Rio (Plate 14). At the head of the line two men shake rattles, and one of them also brandishes a flag. The names for their rattles of tin, *ganza* and *kanza,* come from the Kimbundu word for a gourd, *nganza.*

The rattles were "home." They gave the men spirit. The flag stood for victory. Before all Rio they were flaunting translation of work into dance. With their flag, their rattles, and their drive, they were implicitly telling the whites: "You can't destroy us with your work; we're dancing our portage."[58] They also were dramatizing their muscular power: "We're getting stronger, despite our hard labor" (*Twena lendo ye ngolo mpeleko salu biangolo*).

That same cultural confidence characterized the Bakongo who danced before President Rosas in Buenos Aires in 1838. That same self-assertion distinguished the black washerwomen who animated the riverside of downtown Buenos Aires in the nineteenth century. The writer W. H. Hudson saw them as a boy and went away forever impressed. He was struck by their ego strength, by the way they loudly talked back to the rich, spoiled white youths who deliberately trampled their laundry.[59] Then subsequent waves of working-class Italian women replaced them. The riverside went silent. Work was now work. The sass had gone elsewhere, triggering milonga and canyengue.

FIRST WAVE OVER: BEACHHEADS OF KONGO IN
NINETEENTH-CENTURY BUENOS AIRES

Bakongo on the River Plate recalled their distinction, like Jews in Babylon remembering Jerusalem. Confident of their origins, Bakongo in Buenos Aires were noted for cultural assertion.

On October 31, 1795, two chiefs of the Nación Conga (the Kongo nation) in Buenos Aires petitioned the incoming Spanish viceroy, Pedro de Portugal y Yellena, for permission to celebrate his formal entry with their dances. This reflected the Kongo custom of escorting (*natwa*) notables with dance. They were candid about their aim: to preserve the style and culture of their kingdom. They hoped that such dances might continue every Sunday and in the afternoon of every feast day.[60] Between the lines one can read political astuteness: honor the leader, shower him with enthusiasm, then get him to extend your grant.

The dances were sanctioned, and by 1820 there were five major African organizations in Buenos Aires representing Central Africa: Cambunda (Cabinda), Benguela (southern Angola), Lubolo (northern Angola), "Angola," and "Kongo."

Even in captivity persons from the kingdom of Kongo, the most distinguished civilization in Central Africa, exerted an influence that exceeded their numbers and station. Their impact was strong on porteño language, music, and dance, just as it was in Cuba, Haiti, Brazil, and the United States.

Start with speech. Many "African" words in the parlance of Buenos Aires turn out, on close inspection, to derive from Ki-Kongo. With words of the dance, where Bakongo excelled, their presence is especially audible and clear:

CREOLE BUENOS AIRES IDIOM	CLASSICAL KI-KONGO
"¡Ay, güe guí!" Title of a canción composed by José María Palazuelos in Buenos Aires, before 1893, for the Afro-Argentine society of San Benito. It is clear from the "*ay*" that the phrase is meant to be an exclamation, as in Kongo.[61]	**e, ngwe nge!** Ritual exclamation meaning "You, our mother!" or "You, the wonderful thing!"

CREOLE BUENOS AIRES IDIOM

CLASSICAL KI-KONGO

biri-biri
Fake knowledge, pretense, as in *tipos de biri-biri*, "guys who are just messing around," "talking without meaning."

mbiri-mbiri
Idiophone: "leaving a mess behind." Derives from *mbidika*, "heap, pile."

bombo
Large drum mostly used as a bass in Argentine rural folkloric music. Derives from the Spanish *bombo*, "large drum," "player of large drum."

bombo
A twin derivation may be the Ki-Kongo *bombo*, a large Yombe drum used mostly at funerals. Also *bondo*, "a large drum of the ngoma type."

borokotó, borokotó, chás-chás
Dance onomatopoeia among the candombes of Montevideo. It is the rhythm of the chico drum in a candombe drum choir.

borokoto, borokoto, tshia-tshia
Kongo dance onomatopoeia associated with playing on an *nkonko* (a slit-gong), for example to announce the start of a ritual in the forest.

¡Calunga güe!
A candombe ritual exclamation.

Kalunga ngwe!
A Kongo ritual expression meaning "the other world, our mother."

canyengue
Funky, "get-down," old-style kind of tango. But also see Petróleo: " 'Canyengue' means to be 'ungraceful' [by European standards] and 'tired.' "

Kanienge!
Melt! (i.e., into the music).
kiiengu
"Dance" (Kimbundu).
Kanienge means "tired, worn out" in Kongo, as when one's energy *nyenga*—melts—from old age. This second meaning is also present in Kongo-Cuban speech, as in the phrase "*Ya llegó Babá cañengue*" (Ol' Dad just arrived).

carancanfún
Afro-Argentine onomatopoeia word, as in Horacio Salgán's composition "Con bombo legüero."

karankanfu
Dance onomatopoeia, construed to mean "step slowly."

chan-chan
Onomatopeia for the last two notes of a tango; the beat of the tango.

tshia-tshia
Percussive onomatopoeia: "Perform! Perform!" See also *cha-cha-cha*, an Afro-Cuban dance of the 1950s.

chongo
"White person"; "whitey."

zongo
"Gunshot" (Ki-Kongo). Also *muzungu*, "white person" (Ki-Swahili).

CREOLE BUENOS AIRES IDIOM	CLASSICAL KI-KONGO
Cotongo Nickname of a black tango dancer of the 1940s.	**kotongo** "Tall guy." From *tonga*, "height."
Cototo Nickname of a black Buenos Aires musician, c. 1900.	**kototo** "A guy as sharp as an arrow." Also *tooto*, "arrow."
e e e bariló! Dance cry of the Buenos Aires candombes.	**e e e mbadi lo!** "Alas, alas." Cried out on someone's death. See also *e mbadi ona*, "alas" (Ki-Kongo).
fiyingo or fiyinga A very small knife.	**fiya** A small bone hairpin for men. Also *fizye*, "very small, petite."
malambo Argentine rural stamping dance, a duel between two men showing off figures (*mudanzas*) to a six-eight rhythm.	**malambo** Kongo stamping dance, its purpose to "hammer" into the ground specially placed medicines, symbolically burying a serious social issue.
milonga A dance.	**milonga (Ki-Kongo)** Lines of people in a dance, moving single file or revolving in a circle.
milonga A form of song.	**milonga (Kimbundu)** "Words, argument, issue."
mucama "Maid." See Corominas, *Breve Diccionario Etimológico* (1967), p. 406: "Americanism, from Brazil, of uncertain indigenous or African origin."	**mukama** "Royal mistress of a house."
oyeye yumba Candombe ritual phrase.	**Oyeye yumba** "So be it!" "Dance!"
queco "Whorehouse."	**mukeko** "Odor produced by making love." Probably reinforced by the Spanish name Kiko.
quilombo "Whorehouse."	**kilombo** "House or settlement of self-liberated slaves"; militant group. In Brazil *quilombo* means "runaway settlement."

CREOLE BUENOS AIRES IDIOM	CLASSICAL KI-KONGO

taba
A piece of bone used in an Argentine wagering game

taba
A piece of cloth used in a Kongo child's game.

tango
"A dance; a drum; a place of dance."

tanga (plural matanga)
"Fete, festival. Ceremony marking the end of a period of mourning."

tanga dungulu
"To walk showing off, to swagger."

tangala
"To walk heavily and hesitatingly, to stagger, to toddle, to trot, to walk with small steps, to walk like a chameleon, to march with the feet inward, to swagger. A large drum; a small drum."

tangala-tangala
"To walk like a crab."

tangalakana
"To walk zigzag."

tangama
"To take long steps; to leap or bound; to walk seriously or solemnly; to walk like a crab; to be thrown on one's back and be tightly held, as in wrestling."

tangana
"To walk, to move like a chameleon."
W. C. Handy composed "St. Louis Blues" (1912) to a tango rhythm that, intriguingly, he called tangana.

tanganana
"To walk."

yumba
Osvaldo Pugliese's famous rhythmic tango.

yumba
"So be it!" Or, "Dance!" Also *Umba!*, "Dance!" (Ki-Pende).

Shifts in meaning, for example from "royal mistress of a house" to "maid," and from "militant group" to "whorehouse," reflect drastic social change when proud Bakongo became slave laborers in Buenos Aires.

But in spite of the oppression, women and men of Kongo descent planted a flag of words on the soil of Argentina. They unfurled their speech in Montevideo as well. Witness this song, documented by the black Uruguayan writer Lino Suárez Peña:

Chambira, chambire
changombe, chambira.[62]

It derives from a Kongo chant for the dead:

Sambila, sambile
ta ngombe, sambila.

Pray, pray intensely
let us divine [whether this death was the will of God
or caused by witchcraft]
pray [for the departed loved one].[63]

Kongo-derived burial traditions were strong on the River Plate. Figari painted a number of such rituals in black Montevideo. Note that the Kongo word for the celebration that traditionally ends mourning is *tanga* (or *matanga*). The word's semantic range is broad. It means "drum," "second funeral," "festival," or "dance." Variations of the term refer to myriad modes of walking: *tangala,* "to walk with small steps"; *tangalakana,* "to walk making zigzags"; *tanga dungulu,* "to walk in a swaggering way"; *tangala-tangala,* "to walk like a crab."

The semantic range of the Argentine word *tango* is equally broad and covers similar ground. *Tango,* too, means "drum," "place of dance," and "dance motions." Earlier scholars were embarrassed by this, as if the multiple meanings were inherently contradictory. But the very nature of the word's extension planted a clue as to its origin.

Rather than comparing words out of their cultural context, placing one dictionary next to another, we stress the known fact of overlapping funeral customs as a logical site for the rise and continuity of the term *tango.* First, Kongo-style funeral customs were definitely present and strong in nineteenth-century black Buenos Aires and Montevideo. Second, there were two Kongo words for "funeral celebration," *tanga* and *matanga,* referring, as well, to drums, dancing, various styles of motion, and places of celebration.

The creole word *tango* also refers to drums, dance, and place. Semantic overlap here arguably reflects the impact of two very important ritual words, *matanga* and *tangana,* referring to funerals and their rites, and similar roots that refer to sauntering meaningfully and "walking that walk." Note that other creolized Kongo terms of the funeral, like *chambire* (pray) and *bariló* (alas) turn up in Afro-Argentine and Afro-Uruguayan discourse.

The *tanga* continuum, myriad dance terms with myriad nuances, seems a likely source for the name of Argentina's national dance. As the Ki-Kongo term *mambu* was creolized to *mambo* in Cuba, so *tanga* may have changed into *tango* in Argentina.

As blacks fostered this heritage, an Argentine sculptor, Francisco Cafferata, portrayed their humanism. Of Italian descent, he was born in Buenos Aires in 1861. He trained in Italy, but his heart was with the blacks of his nation. They were the subject of many of his works, including heads of mulattoes and an unfinished figure of a legendary Argentine black hero, Falucho.

Cafferata's bronze head and shoulders of a powerfully built male *Slave* (c. 1882), made when he was twenty-one, is an impressive achievement. Now in the Museo de Bellas Artes in Buenos Aires, it is a work of deep sympathy (Plate 17). Intelligence is sensed in the strong pensive face. Though the gaze is downcast and the expression troubled, inner nobility is manifest.

Blacks of this quality guarded their culture in nineteenth-century Buenos Aires. They lived in the Barrio del Tambor (Drum Part of Town), present-day Montserrat and San Telmo, named after the sound of their celebrations. They were the leaders of the meeting houses dedicated to African nations. In 1827 the Cambunda (Cabinda) house was located at 333 Chile Street. The Loango (Lwangu) house was on Córdoba between Montevideo and Uruguay.

In 1830 the famous Kongo dia Ngunga (Kongo of the Royal Bell) house was allegedly located near the present intersection of Avenida Independencia with Calle Santiago del Estero.

Earlier, in 1730, a Jesuit father, Ignacio Chome, struck by the numbers of persons from Kongo and Angola in the city, determined to learn "the language of Angola" (Ki-Kongo), "in use in three kingdoms," in order to preach to and convert them. In 1795 city authorities granted the Kongo nation permission to dance on Sundays and holidays. In 1799 the city granted a similar permit to Cabinda Bakongo.[64]

In 1787 the royal administration of Buenos Aires was startled when a young slave was crowned king of Kongo at a Kongo nation ceremony. The man in question, Pedro Duarte, received as his emblems an umbella and a crown, after which many Bakongo bowed down to him, according to custom. This was too much for colonial authorities. They mounted a case against him, dropping it only after Duarte assured them that the rite made him "greater, not king."[65]

Besides surrogate kingship, there was another reinstatement: martial

PLATE 17

arts. We saw how danced tactics quickened reflexes among the soldiers of Kongo, who were taught how to duck to the ground to avoid being hit by a man or an arrow.

Cut to a poem, by Pantaleón Rivarola, about the English invasion of Buenos Aires in 1806. Horacio Jorge Becco, in his *Negros y morenos en el cancionero rioplatense* (Blacks and Persons of Color in the Songs of the River Plate) notes that Rivarola, with this poem, introduced the theme of the blacks into Argentine literature.[66] The 1807 poem immortalizes an African-born warrior who fought for the city, using Kongo-type tactics of evasion. The relevant section reads:

THE ROMANCE OF THE GLORIOUS DEFENSE OF THE CITY OF BUENOS AIRES

From the Barrio de la Piedad
came a brave, sturdy black.
Armed only with a pike, he went into action,
in the style of his African nation,
by throwing himself down on the ground,
then quickly coming up, to stab an armed Englishman.

He promised his comrades he'd do this.
So, in his own piquant creole,
the black started shouting,
"Shoot! No miss me! No miss me!
Miss me, Brit man, you dead."
So the Brit tried to aim,
and fired his one shot,
but the black, oh so fast,
ducked to the ground,
then ran without fear,
straight through the smoke
and before Brit reloaded
killed him quick with his lance.[67]

"Shouting trash" to the British opponent to disorient him, as Muhammad Ali did to George Foreman in 1974, was part of the plan. But white gratitude for the help of such blacks in the defense of Buenos Aires was short-lived. Less than twenty years later, in fact, in 1822, Buenos Aires banned all black street dancing. (Argentina had thrown off Spanish control a dozen years earlier, in the revolution of 1810.) Public black dancing of any nature was outlawed anew in 1825. This did not stop the Bakongo. In 1830 the superb Franco-Italian draftsman Carlos Pellegrini, who would himself be the father of an Argentine president, documented someone slipping a Kongo dance step into the middle of a Catholic procession (Plate 18).

Pellegrini had trained in Europe as an engineer. Arriving in Argentina in 1828, he found promised engineering projects canceled by politics. Undaunted, he turned to drawing portraits of the aristocracy, in a strong, accurate hand derived from his technical training.

In 1830 he turned these talents to the depiction of a religious procession, *La Procesión de Nuestra Señora del Rosario* (The Procession of Our Lady of the Rosary). Pellegrini shows processioners pouring out of the Iglesia de Santo Domingo (known also as the Iglesia de Nuestra Señora del Rosario), which stands today at the corner of Defensa and Belgrano in San Telmo. The artist records embedded grapeshot clearly visible at the top of the bell tower, left there when Argentines fired on British troops holed up in this church during the invasion of 1806. (When the tower was later reconstructed, replicas of these bullets were inserted in the walls, in the patterns documented by Pellegrini.) Men carry outdoors a massive white statue of the Virgin of the Rosary. Four other men, at the head of the procession, play musical instruments: violin, clarinet, bass viol, and flugelhorn. The African population of Buenos Aires was, at this time, relatively large. Pellegrini gives a sense of this: the clarinetist is black; so are at least eight members of the procession.

Pellegrini reads motion accurately. The musicians all sway to the beat, "dancing" their instruments, in a black creole way. In Kongo terms, the spirit of the music is "waving and swinging them" (*kini biabio bieti nikunswa ye tembuswa*).[68]

An astonishing motion takes place to the left: a black man, carrying a lamp, falls into spirit with deeply bent knees. His dance did not arrive from Europe, any more than fighting an Englishman by falling to the ground did. He is moving in a style that Bakongo call *fukama*, which means "bending the legs like a she-goat," that is, in a knock-kneed way.[69]

PLATE 18

Bending down with knees pressed together is in Kongo an expression of honor. One may curtsy this way before the king, a god, or a spirit, the tomb of an ancestor, a medicine of God (*nkisi*), a magistrate (*mbazi a n'kanu*), or a healer of distinction (*nganga a mbuki*).

Before the image of the Virgin, the black processioner has appropriately manifested a sign of obeisance from the world of his ancestors. In addition, because this gesture is associated also with the image of a knock-kneed bird, he may have also been saying that he felt himself flying, flying with the Virgin toward heaven. (Twelve years later, in 1842, Charles Dickens saw a black dancer performing at Five Points, in New York, "snapping his fingers . . . turning in his knees." Persons from Kongo had been living in the city since 1624.)[70]

A trace of this inflection appears in the tango. Dancers in the early tango style, canyengue, danced close to the earth, inserting "break patterns"—*quebradas*—with knees deeply bent. Compare Natalia Games's and Gabriel Angió's quebrada of 2001 to the quebrada of the partner of Arturo de Navas in 1903 to the fukama of the processioner in 1830. Past informs present. The quebrada from African apart dancing fused with the European couple dance, doubling its panache and effect. This striking transformation led to a widening horizon of Kongo dance impact.

Martín Boneo's painting *A Federal Candombe in the Time of Rosas* shows us a nation within a nation and its idiom of dance. Ian Churchill has copied the essentials of this painting (Plate 19). Members of the Kongo dia Ngunga society perform before President Rosas, the iron-handed ruler of Argentina, in 1838. The precision and authenticity of cultural detail in this painting reflect extended contact between painter and dancers. It was certainly not something Boneo picked up from a single exposure in 1838, particularly since he would have been only nine at the time; he must have painted the event well after that, having frequented Kongo nation dances. Like Figari among candombe dancers in the Barrio

Sur of 1920s Montevideo, Boneo must have kept visiting the nation until he got the moves and the drum structure down. Boneo shows Rosas seated with his daughter, Manuelita. The leader of the Kongo nation sits between the president and Manuelita. The dance took place on Santiago del Estero near San Juan, in or about the present intersection of Santiago del Estero and Avenida Independencia. Two blacks on a bench play harness-tuned Kongo drums (*bangoma yaladukwa mu nsinga*). They are vertically played, as ordinary dance drums are, but another such drum, in the center of the painting, is perambulated horizontally—"so that its power can escape," Fu-Kiau Bunseki points out. This is the *ngoma vudinga,* the "drum with full voice."

The purity of the drum structure that Boneo portrayed betrays the hand of an expert Kongo drum-maker in Buenos Aires. The drum-maker knew his details—the circle of cord (*bese*) around the drum skin, the way the tuning cords (*nsinga*) attach to that circle, and the system of knots (*makolo*) on each cord.

The standing drummer is dancing *sémbuka,* shifting from one foot to the other. He is expressing the sound as he plays it. To the right and behind him, a youth in a green shirt and red pants does a vigorous sembuka, left heel thrust up back, like the tango step *boleo* one hundred years later.

To the right and in front of the standing drummer moves the dance master himself. He curls his palms downward, in front of his body, making the gesture we saw in n'kwanga danced in Diosso: *lembika mooko,* the hands of peace. He is calling with this gesture. He is telling the drummer "*malembe*" (go easy, go easy). We are looking at a gesture that,

PLATE 19

with candombe, would last clear to the 1970s in Buenos Aires and beyond.

The master performs barefoot. Part of his weight is on the ball of his right foot (*n'tu a tambi*, literally "the head of the foot"); his left foot is flat on the ground. A woman with a red ribbon in her hair dances in front of him. She too is barefoot, and she wears a rich wrapper, tied with a knot, like a belt (*mponda*) at the back of her waist.

The spirituality of the moment—they are dancing for their ancestors as well as for Rosas—is communicated by the lifting up of two diamond-form metal rattles (*nsansi*) on towering staffs. The staffs carry raffialike streamers, alluding both to joy and to spirit. These bursts of raffia identify the staffs as *nsungwa,* staffs with tied-on messages.

Nsungwa, when waved, open the door to glory. Their long raffia streamers form mnemonic devices: besides happiness and spirit, they also encode warnings and strong benedictions. Karl Laman talks about them in the second volume of his dictionary: "*mu-sungwa,* herb tied around a handle in order to remember something; *nyanga* leaf knotted to prevent manioc [*nsafu*] theft; knots made from *kimbanzya* leaves, encoding a blessing."[72] Nsungwa are sacred. Wherever they appear, "God passes by." It is taboo to fight in their presence (*ka mosi lenda banda mvita va ntadi a nsungwa*). The peace that they bring reflects in the dance master's gesture. Arming rattles with raffia, the dance has become a matter of morality, like raffia nsungwa attached to Tshikumbi girls, warning them not to argue but to heal. Nsungwa flash high—this means their message is intended for heaven, and for the ancestors as well as for the living (*nsungwa weti natwa mu zulu beni mu songa va wau i nsamu miakangwa evo makolo mieti natwa ku mpemba*).

Long-staff nsungwa with rattles and streamers were still to be seen in the streets of Buenos Aires in the late nineteenth century, as documented by a drawing, "*Negros porteños*" (Blacks of Buenos Aires), in A. Taullard's *Nuestro antiguo Buenos Aires* of 1927 (Plate 20).[73] Small changes are visible. The rattles are now shaped like drumlike small cylinders, not diamond-form nsansi. Raffia streamers have turned into ribbons, but they and the rattles are still carried high, percussion on stilts.

Other strong Kongo elements are visible: the drums; the processioner at the lead leaning back (*yekuka*), like the man dancing n'kwanga at Diosso or children dancing an Nsundi dance (*lungondunga*). The music rolls over his body. It bends his frame back.

Cakewalk, arriving in Buenos Aires from black North America in the early twentieth century, flaunted the same leaning structure and possibly

PLATE 20

reinforced it as it arose in the tango. George Reid Andrews, in any event, takes note in candombe of a cakewalklike step, "bodies alternately thrown forward and back," as a precedent for similar sequences in tango.[74]

In Kongo one interesting meaning of leaning far back and far forward is social defiance: "we are palm trees, bent forward, bent back, but we never break" (*beto tu maba vwenbama ku ntwala ye ku nima kansi ka toluka ko*).[75] Cakewalk, as danced by plantation blacks, was a takeoff on big-house pretensions.[76] One of the original Kongo meanings of leaning, defiance, if remembered in cakewalk, would have deepened its aura of derision.

Kongo curled hands, held in front of the body, reappear in a caricature published on November 30, 1882, in *La ilustración Argentina* in Buenos Aires. The illustration is captioned "Tango." But the black couple pictured dance far apart (*tatuka*). They do not embrace, tango-style. A racist drew this illustration. We are at the mercy of gross, sharp distortions— mouths become snouts; hands become paws—but the truth filters in nonetheless. The gesture of the hands, if ludicrously exaggerated, is clearly based on a creole extension of *lembika mooko* (the hands of peace), known also in Kongo as *yembika mooko* (the hands of discretion). This gesture has been present in Argentina for nearly two centuries. It is impossible to make up the real thing.

Melville J. Herskovits, in his classic text *The Myth of the Negro Past*, reminds us that the funeral is the climax of life in West Africa. Whatever African customs were lost in the Americas, he argues, the honoring of the dead continued, in meticulous rituals cast in the manner of African patterns.[77] Rituals of final leave-taking were famously present among persons of Kongo descent in the capital of Argentina. On March 16, 1867, an article appeared in the local newspaper *La Tribuna* about a Kongo burial (*entierro congo*):

> Day before yesterday we saw something strange in the streets of Buenos Aires. A large company of people were transporting a dead person to the cemetery. . . . There was music, with a strange *chin-chin* beat, played on a tambourine and a guitar. Dancing accompanied the most extravagant and rhythm-led songs imaginable.[78]

This funeral with dancing was a distant cousin of the jazz funeral in the city of Congo Square, New Orleans. Both stem from the Kongo belief that the dead should be sent to the other world with celebration, lest they feel slighted and return to haunt relatives. This Argentine writer was particularly impressed by one aspect of the ritual:

> The funeral procession included carriers of two chairs. At every crossroads they came to a halt and placed the coffin [on these chairs]. Then, after a ritual of sign and countersign, they picked up the box and continued on their way, all singing.[79]

This is pure Kongo. In Central Africa a funeral procession stops where paths cross and also before the gate to the cemetery. This is the reason: at every corner or intersection (*mpamba nzila*) two worlds meet. So one halts at each crossroads so that spirits in all directions may witness (*kala mbangi*) the event, participate, and extend their their full blessing.

One of the basic percussive patterns that back funeral processions in Kongo is rendered in drum syllables this way: *tshia-tshia*. The sound encourages the people in code: *Perform! Perform!* Tshia-tshia relates to another idiophone, also involved with motion and sound: *sya-sya*, "onomatopoeia for the sound of the wash made by the prow of a boat."[80] Apparently both idiophones, creolized together, became the acoustical signature of the tango, *chan-chan*. The *Tribuna* reporter recorded the percussive pattern he *thought* he heard in the procession: "chin-chin." Today *chan-chan* stands for the last two notes of a tango.

Summarizing, Kongo speech, music, instruments, dance, gestures, and even drum syllables were present in Buenos Aires at the birth of the tango. Especially alive were the dance steps, performed in the streets, in the houses of the candombes, and with great passion at funerals. They stemmed from the two tropical cities Mbanza Kongo and Lwangu, not from Naples, Genoa, or Rome. The dance steps persisted in deep cultural memory. Exiled Bakongo kept their moves going, teaching them to succeeding generations. Long after the candombes were officially closed, the steps passed on, now creolized, to black members of dancing clubs in the 1970s and even in the twenty-first century,

This is why Pedro Figari, the famed costumbrista, was able to portray Kongo-derived dance gestures among blacks of the Barrio Sur in the capital of Uruguay with such accuracy and flair.[81] Certain details he painted from memory, having seen enthroned surrogate Kongo kings and queens presiding over the dances of Montevideo candombes in the late nineteenth century, when he was still a child. But the dancing itself stemmed from more recent sources: he sketched black dancers performing candombe in the 1920s, in a basement dancing club in Montevideo. The name of the club was humorous: Los Haraganes Sin Producto (The Bums Without a Product). It was located at the corner of Gaboto and San Salvador in the Harlem of Montevideo, the Barrio Sur. Figari also frequented a Montevideo tenement (conventillo), where he had friends among a community of descendants of black slaves. There he also saw dancing. At Los Haraganes Sin Producto candombe-style dancing continued in the 1920s, as it did at the Shimmy Club in Buenos Aires in the 1970s.

But before traveling to Uruguay to savor Figari, we complete this Argentine section by considering music and dance among black creoles of the country. Here two traditions spectacularly emerged, battles of paired male dancers (malambo), and duels among men making verses on guitar (payada).

MALAMBO AND PAYADA: TAP DUELS AND WORD WARS

"[Cherish] the vigorous rhythms of malambo."

—LUIS F. VILLARROEL, *Tango folklore de Buenos Aires* (1957)

The proud heel-stamping patterns (zapateados) of Andalusian male dancing turn up in rural Argentina. Gato and escondido are cases in point. But the solo male dance called *malambo* consists of nothing but zapateados.[82] This concentration on stamping plus the dance's clear Kongo name indicates a modicum of Central African influence. Black men of Kongo descent must have been reminded of home when they witnessed zapateados, brought to the pampas by migrants from Andalusia.

Blacks named malambo and added some flair to the stamping, but the erect Spanish stance is unmistakable. Hands and arms are not used. The malambo dancer maintains a non-African rigidity of body. Only the feet move. The steps are performed in *mudanzas* (literally "changes," meaning sets of steps grouped in patterns). Malambo virtuosi perform these figures over a rolling six-eight meter, vigorously strummed on guitar. Some Argentines "mouth drum" the beat with the colorful phrase *salchicha con pan, salchicha con pan* (sausage with bread, sausage with bread).[83]

Two men come together to compete in malambo. Each one performs solo his store of mudanzas. Then the next performer moves up and tries to outdo hin. In 1871, in a place called El Bragado, Ventura R. Lynch witnessed a battle of malambo that lasted all night. In the process, each of the contestants showed off seventy-six mudanzas.[84]

Malambo's feistiness relates to *payada,* which pits guitarist against guitarist in battles of strumming and verse. In the United States several noted cowboys were of African descent: Nat Love, Isom Dart, and Bill Pickett. In Argentina so were many gauchos. Ana Cara-Walker reminds us that black workers on the pampas were initally slaves.[85] Their responsibilities included lassoing animals, slaughtering beasts, branding cattle, and breaking in horses.

The last-mentioned task appears in a painting by Cesáreo Bernaldo de Quirós, an Argentine painter who was born in the province of Entre Ríos in 1879 and died in 1968. The name of the painting is *El domador de la encierra* (The Horse Tamer in the Corral) (Plate 21). Now in the Boca Museum in Buenos Aires, it was painted in 1945. De Quirós's study turns a black corral worker into an icon of the pampas, holding a horse by a rein, lowering its head. A strong light strikes his face and his body.

His gaze is oblique—he deliberately avoids the observer. No smile breaks the seal of invincible cool. Similarly "cold" faces will appear in the tango, as they do among singers of payada. I once showed a photograph of the black payador Gabino Ezeiza (Plate 22) to the noted black composer Horacio Salgán and asked his reaction. Salgán studied it for a minute and then said, "*Trasunta dignidad y compostura*" (He radiates dignity and cool).

Cool was imperative in the duels called payada, and blacks were the masters:

> There was an area of musical endeavor in which the Afro-Argentines remained in control throughout the nineteenth century and well into the twentieth. This was the *payada,* a sort of poetic duel in which two guitarist-singers spontaneously compose verses on a given theme or in response to

each other's challenges. A vocal variation on the *tapadas*, the drum duels, the payada was the lineal descendant of the African tradition of musical contests of skill.[86]

Payada descends as well from the challenge songs of Iberia. With this strong dual heritage, it lit up the life of the pampas. There, in 1839–42, Juan Carlos Morel painted *Payada en una pulpería* (Battle of Song in a Pulpería). A *pulpería* is a country store with a bar. Morel shows how these stopping-points, dotting the wagon trails of inland Argentina, doubled as theaters for popular music.

PLATE 21

Etched against shadows, men stand at the bar. A woman walks in from the left. She is white but balances wares on her head in black fashion. At the center of the bar the poets square off. One stands and waits, propping a leg so his thigh can support his guitar. The other is seated. His head falls back slightly. He is singing. Men lean toward his words. Some toast him with grog. A hundred years later, around 1939, a watercolorist named Mario Zavatarro, illustrating a scene from José Hernández's famous epic *El gaucho Martín Fierro,* would show a black payador in action.[87]

At the beginning of the twentieth century Gabino Ezeiza and Higinio Cazón were the two most distinguished payadores dueling (versifiers) in action. Both were of African descent.

So were at least sixteen other payadores: Agapito, Andrés Alfaro, Ramón Barrera, Antonio Cagiano, Andrés Cepeda, Celestino Dorrego, Constantino Ferreti, Valentín Ferreyra, Juan García, Luis García, Pablo Jerez, Felipe Juárez, Pancho Luna, Martín, Ramírez, and Rudecindo Suárez.[88]

Luis García, born in Buenos Aires in 1875, taught payada to the famed white interpreter José Betinotti,[89] who acknowledged this debt with a verse.

Cazón, heavyset with a handlebar

PLATE 22

moustache, was born in the San Telmo barrio in Buenos Aires, in 1866. A triumphal tour of the province of Buenos Aires in 1889 crowned his career. He died in 1914.[90] Cazón lives on, however, in Catulo Castillo's and José Razzano's 1944 tango "Café de Los Angelitos," where he is linked with his black colleague, Gabino Ezeiza.

> *Rivadavia at Rincón*
> *Here friendships flourished*
> *at the Café de los Angelitos,*
> *the bar of Gabino and Cazón.*

Ezeiza was born in San Telmo on February 3, 1858. Payada had come to the city. He started singing it when he was sixteen, in 1874. Mastering the art of composing under fire, he eventually became the grand master.

One of Ezeiza's most brilliant duels took place in 1891 in San Nicolás, a town south of Santiago del Estero. Here he accepted the challenge of Pablo J. Vásquez, a noted payador from Pergamino, a town between Rosario and Buenos Aires.

Ezeiza defeated Vásquez. They met again three years later, in the Florida Theater in Vásquez's hometown of Pergamino. This battle went on for two days, October 13–14, 1894. The following is an excerpt from the finale of the second night:

EZEIZA: *So you're strong and content*
But oh from afar,
I sense things ajar
with your cement—
like the Tower of Pisa.
VÁSQUEZ: *That's what you say,*
but it's easy to see,
the finale's arrived,
and you haven't convinced me.
EZEIZA: *I'll convince you, my man,*
of a strange, droll emergency.
If you can't perceive it
the audience can.
VÁSQUEZ: *My forte is belief*
in such a sanctuary.

I'll find my relief
and come out and beat you.
EZEIZA: *Found your relief?*
Matter of opinion!
You may have found strength,
but you didn't find reason.[91]

That's the way it went that night. Both slugged it out, rhyme for rhyme, verse for verse. In payada, whatever you say gets held against you. Your last thought may pivot your opponent's next line.

Vásquez kept trying, but finally the master dispatched him with this:

EZEIZA: *I see no equality*
in this here rink:
I improvise, simply and quickly,
you have to sit down and think.[92]

Living in verses, Ezeiza would not be matched in this hemisphere until 1940s calypso and 1990s rap. If Ezeiza spoke English and were magically transported to our time, could rappers defeat this brother in rhyme?

Ezeiza took the world's measure in five hundred payadas. He trained first as a newspaperman, which helps explain his cultural breadth, from gaucholike jousting to learned allusions to the Tower of Pisa.

He once sang as three people, dramatizing their differences by accent: he impersonated a badass (*compadrito*) from the southern barrios of Buenos Aires; he became a night watchman from the inland city of Córdoba; and finally he sang as a night watchman who had migrated to Argentina from Spain—all in the same poem. In the voice of the compadrito he taunted the poor dress of the man from the provinces:

> *The heel gets pissed off*
> *when the sock has a hole in it.*

But the Cordoban comes right back with this:

> *Yeah, but the boot even more so*
> *when the pants are too short.*[93]

Read to United States blacks, this droll repartee provokes immediate laughter. They get the message: payada "talks shit," like dozens, like blues, like rap.

Ezeiza made arguments within arguments. No one could touch him. Even death was delayed: near the end of his life, burning with fever, defying his doctor and concerned family members, Ezeiza rose from his bed and sang to an audience in the La Perla Theater, in the Piñeyro district of Avellaneda. The date was September 30, 1916. When the curtain came down, he collapsed on the stage. People helped him to his feet. They took him home, to 97 Azul Street in the Flores barrio. There he died, a week and a half later, on October 12.[94]

Today 97 Azul has a plaque by the door: *Here lived and died Gabino Ezeiza.* The site is a bakery, but it bears his first name: Don Gabino. Inside, the owner, Roberto Heredia, once set up a small shrine, with several framed photographs and Ezeiza's own watch and tall cane.

The tradition lives on today in the work of a black payador, José Curbelo. He was born in 1949 in Canelones, a small Uruguayan town north of Montevideo. There is a photograph from 1966 showing Curbelo at age seventeen, trading verses in Montevideo with Atilio Aníbal Silva, a payador whose youthful nickname was "Pelé" because he resembled the world-famous soccer star.[95] In 1970, at the age of twenty-one, José Curbelo won a prize in Canelones as best payador of the town. Since 1974 he has lived in Buenos Aires, recording payadas. In 2001 Curbelo published an article on black payadores of the River Plate.[96] Curbelo, Silva, and other black improvisers contradict the belief that payada has vanished. That impression was engendered in Argentina by the Ralph Pappier–Homero Manzi film *The Last Payador* (1950).

Many Afro-Argentines living in Buenos Aires in the time of Ezeiza were descendants of Central African civilizations. To that world we will return.

FROM KONGO CANDOMBES TO BLACK DANCING CLUBS

> The truth of worlds, coded in their bodies, and signs of cosmos written on the ground, armed Bakongo captives with a universe within, enabling them to ride across the tragic waters.
>
> — RAMONA AUSTIN, "Body and Cosmos in Kongo Art" (2000)

In the third decade of the nineteenth century, the word *candombe* began to appear in Buenos Aires, referring to self-help dancing societies founded by persons of African descent.[97] The term is Ki-Kongo; it literally means "pertaining to blacks" (*ka* + *ndombe*). Back in Central Africa, Kongo nationalists in the 1940s and 1950s covertly defied Belgian imperialists using, independently, the very same term. To them, *candombe* meant "black culture and self-governance."[98]

So blacks on the River Plate, in calling their gatherings *candombe*, were announcing the whole of their culture, all that they were. Indeed, Ana Cara-Walker points out that the term *candombe* in Buenos Aires meant more than a dance or a music or a congregation.[99] It was all of the above, driven by pride in ethnicity.

There were candombes both in Buenos Aires and in Montevideo. Facundo Posadas says that nuances distinguish the two traditions: Afro-Argentines, he argues, accent the hips when dancing candombe; Afro-Uruguayans accent the shoulders. This places different weights on key dance traits from Kongo, the pelvic grind (*tyenga*) and trembling the shoulders (*mayembo*), a classic sign of the descent of the spirit. In fact, says Kely Posadas, vibrating the shoulders is considered "quite spiritual."

We turn now to candombe in Montevideo and compare its styles to those of black Buenos Aires. Key gestures are shared by both cities. These unities confirm a complex horizon of Kongo-style moves at the birth of the tango in the River Plate region.

Nineteenth-century candombe dancing in black Montevideo, as documented by Reid Andrews (citing Ortiz Oderigo, in turn citing Lauro Ayesterán), followed a set sequence:[100]

First, men and women formed two lines, facing each other. They swayed more or less in place, like the black musicians Pellegrini saw before the Iglesia de Santo Domingo in Buenos Aires in 1830. Occasionally the lines would collide when men and women would strike their bellies together. This was bumbakana.

Bumbakana, to restate, refers in Kongo to a man dancing opposite a woman, then both striking their bodies together. One usually hits with the belly, but hips (*mabunda*) and shoulders (*mavembo*) can also be used. In bringing together the two sexes, the intent is to emphasize life. Buenos Aires and Montevideo know bumbakana as *ombligada*, "to hit with the waist."

Alejandro Frigerio has published a drawing by the late Argentine artist Carybé of Afro-Brazilians performing this move in the twentieth century (Plate 23). The action is deepened by personal flair: the sass of the woman's right hand on her hip, the celebratory hands of the man over his head. Demonstrating at once difference and continuity in the sharing of this Kongo tradition, consider the star contemporary Argentine dance couple, Kely and Facundo (Plate 24), dancing candombe in 2005. Kely lifts up her hands to ward off attack while Facundo moves in, one arm akimbo. He is coming on strong, asserting his presence: "Here I am, baby."

In candombe and samba da roda, as in Kongo, men and women did not normally hold hands in the dance. In Carybé's example, *umbigada,* the man celebrates overcoming this ban: "I can't use my hands, but my belly has caught you!" Disagreements between couples may break out at this point, which is why the dance master brandished his broom when the sequence was over. He was clearing the air of possible resentment, as when, occasionally a woman got "caught" by a man she detested or a man got bumped by a woman he found uncompelling.

Second, the beat got intense. The couples now danced in a circle of hand-clappers, one pair at a time until every couple had danced.

Third, both men and women danced single file in a circle, "melting" their bodies, forward and back, forward and back, while going round and round in a counterclockwise motion.

Finally, the lead dancer suddenly called on the percussionists to make the beat stronger. The circle disintegrated. Everyone now would be dancing apart, soloing, showing off steps, vividly improvising. The dance master then made a final strong shout, ending the dance.

All of this action derived from Bakongo, who guard and remember the meanings of the sequences. The opposition of male and female lines is a sign that the world cannot exist without marriage. That ideal communion is dramatized by bumbakana, the striking of hip against hip, abdomen against abdomen.[101]

PLATE 23

The broom-juggler neutralizes, with passes of his instrument, anything unusual or unwanted. Like black women waving cloths at the head of a funeral procession in early twentieth-century Montevideo, like women in Kongo in the late 1780s trailing long cloths to sweep away envy, he cleanses the road.

The shift to couple dancing extends the motif of social coherence. The cakewalklike sequences were originally danced sayings: leaning forward

PLATE 24

(*yinama*) and leaning back (*yekuka*) refer to the proverb "Don't lean on the future without leaning on the past," as well as to the saying that palm trees spring back when bent down by the wind. In less formal contexts, leaning forward and back just means "hi" and "good-bye."

The final "hot" sequence, when solos break out, is a miniature Mardi Gras. The dancers make hay while the sun still shines. The point is made formally in Kongo: "No matter how noble, no dance is forever" (*Makinu mamfumu ka mazingilanga ko*). The carnival blaze counters the fact that the dance will soon end.

In the paintings of the Uruguayan master Pedro Figari, these four major sequences compact into one. There are no circles, no lines, no broom-wielding master; he is painting a modified candombe, likely based on what he saw in the Barrio Sur in the 1920s. Nevertheless, he brings in the gestures, precise and authentic.

Figari was a genius, a visual Jorge Luis Borges. He knew the power that his right hand possessed: when he painted his self-portrait, he made the end of his paintbrush blaze red, like a lit match or a fuse.[102]

Figari was aggressively liberal. He fought for—and won—primary education for the people of Uruguay. He admired blacks and their culture. They, in turn, trusted him. He defended their cases pro bono in court. His reward was entrée into candombes.[103]

Born in Montevideo on June 29, 1861, Figari trained as a lawyer, practiced journalism, and was elected vice president in the Uruguayan House of Representatives. He continued practicing law until 1919, when he was fifty-eight. Through all these high offices, he never stopped sketching. Visual creativity was the core of his being. Finally, in 1921, when he moved to Buenos Aires, he gave himself over to art. He painted continuously there, from 1921 to 1925. Then he was in Paris for eight years, making art the whole time. Returning to Uruguay in 1933, he became artistic adviser to the Ministry of Public Education. He died in Montevideo on July 24, 1938.

Figari's candombes take and compel us. His sensitive eye captured peaks of excitement. Painting *pericón,* "the national dance of the cowboys," for instance, he cuts to the most telling sequence: when all the men kneel and raise their right hand, and the women, all standing, hold the men's hands and then spin.[104]

He likewise cut to the heart of another gaucho dance, the escondido, when the partner pretends to conceal herself—hence the name *escondido,* "the one who is hidden"—while the man stamps his feet (*zapatea*) and snaps his fingers with castanet flair. He is seeking her presence with sound.[105]

Figari's gift for capturing the high point of pleasure and excitement carries over to his paintings of black dancers. He emphasizes the freestyle finale of the candombes when many are ecstatic and waved by the spirit. He achieved this through various exposures. First, he was taken to candombe as a child. He remembered the presence of the king and the queen of Kongo, seated on their dais, with an altar to black saints behind them. All these appear in his paintings.

Later, in the 1920s, while he was painting full-time in Argentina, he crossed the River Plate to Montevideo to sketch blacks performing in the basement black dance club called Los Haraganes Sin Producto, at the corner of Gaboto and San Salvador in the Barrio Sur.[106]

Around 1940, a couple of years after Figari's death, Silverio Veloz and other black elders shared memories of him in action with a black youth who would grow up to become a distinguished painter himself, Rubén Galloza. They recalled Figari at Los Haraganes in the 1920s, sketchbook in hand.[107] There is a rumor that whitewash there conceals a mural he painted on one of the walls. He also visited black friends in the tenements (*conventillos*): "There Figari could observe the active daily life, rituals and carnivals which were to furnish many of his later subjects."[108]

So Figari, in painting candombe, worked from a mixture of childhood wonder and mature observation.

In *Candombe,* a painting of the 1920s, he brilliantly translated the black royal setting, showing the surrogate king and queen of Kongo on their dais. An altar bears small images of three black saints. On the dais a musican plays an ngoma-derived drum, circled with three lines like many drums in Kongo. Standing beside him, a man cups his hands on his mouth, amplifying sound as he shouts out a song. The king at far right is receiving a present from a black woman. She leans from a window embellished with a blue cloth with white crosses.

Below we see many women dancing. Their hands curl peacefully in front of their bodies. Far to the left a young man and a woman come together in a couple dance. Curled hands are cooling and calling (*lembika ye bokila*). They call as an emblem of well-being. Ecstasy seizes a woman in a green blouse. She lifts up a hand as spirit pervades her.

The theme of possession appears in another candombe painting. Here a man, rhythmizing his shoulders, brings his hands down to the level of his knees, flattens them, and holds them out straight.[109] This gesture is variously known in Kongo as *lembama* (to bring calm), *kuluka* (being cool), and finally *vwembama* (referring to flat hands held low, as if leaning on a low table, meaning "I need support, I am becoming possessed"). His legs form a lozenge, an amorous sign that in this context probably suggests connection with spirit (*sinsu kia mbundani ye nza ya kimpeve*).

Figari's authenticity of detail is better understood when we discover that Veloz and other Haraganes veterans remembered seeing him in the company of a brilliantly versed black confidant named Tingilupi, who drew his attention to what was important.[110] By the 1920s many whites assumed that candombe was dead. Tingilupi and others proved otherwise. And the spirit was with them. The *candomberos* were communicating, with gestures of their hands, the arrival of an intelligence that both challenged the assumptions of unknowing whites and exalted the setting of their basement exile. In the splendor of these signs, curved palms or raised hands, they were signing proximity to heaven, revealing transcendence. Gauchos in action were hearty and festive. But candombe was more: it was not frozen folklore but change and transition, becoming eventually a brand-new world dance form, the tango-milonga.

In another candombe painting of the 1920s, dancers move once again before of the king of Kongo, seated with a medal, and the queen with her fan. A cloth on the wall frames both these figures, announcing their importance, like the raffia velour hangings that backed Kongo kings in Africa.[111] At left a man dances on the ball of his right foot, like the dance master in front of President Rosas, and holds a palm flat in front of his body. Rising on one foot, he makes a winglike hand gesture in Kongo that would mean "I am stealing away [*tilumuka*], I am flying, a spirit has come to my head." Another man makes a lozenge of space with sharp-angled knees, likely communicating amorous availability. All are responding to the beat of an ngoma.

More gestures unfurl in another beautifully detailed painting, reproduced here by Ian Churchill (Plate 25). Two women dance with downward curled palms. In the center moves a woman, palms carried forward, parallel to the ground. Two men kick up their heels, like the youth whom Boneo showed dancing before Rosas, and like a prediction of the rise of a similar tango step, the boleo, in the 1930s and 1940s. Two raise a hand overhead, a sign of excitement. People in Kongo call this gesture *yangalala*, from the verb *ku yannga* (to be joyous). Behind, the queen sits.

Framed by a door, a man makes percussion by clapping his hands in a highly special way, left hand over right, both held horizontally, then right over left, again horizontally. This is ritual applause (*ta mapwo-pwo*). Miming the placing of one world over another, it means that the event is backed by the ancestors.

The woman in the center, dancing with flat hands, seemingly leans on an invisible table. This is *vwembama,* whose meaning is clear: "I need support, I am not in control. I am caught by a force from beyond." The winglike structure of her hands as they form this pattern also suggests flight, from this world to the next. Flat hands are urgent, announcing the spirit. Curved hands are calming, slowing things down.

Comparison of candombe, as documented by Figari in Montevideo, with candombe in Buenos Aires reveals the sharing of a gesture idiom; in both cities we see hands curled, hands flat, and hands held on high as an emblem of happiness. But parallels between Montevideo and Buenos Aires, in dancing candombe, go deeper. What follows is a summary in which we discover black roots of the tango.

CANDOMBE IN TRANSITION: PRIVATE MOVES
IN PUBLIC SPACES

The steps of candombe are noble, aligning with evocations of black royalty. "Kongo," "Angola," and other Central African associations in nineteenth-century Montevideo and Buenos Aires elected kings and queens to lead them. The tradition included rich dress and rich dance, parts of which continue to this day.

Galloza's *Coronación de los reyes Kongo* (Crowning of the Kings of Kongo), dated 1997, documents the last Kongo coronation in Montevideo

PLATE 25

(Plate 26). The ceremony depicted took place around 1905. The scene is a throne room, or *sala* (hall, large room). It was located at the corner of Calle Ibicui and Calle San José in the Barrio Sur.

The king and the queen, splendidly dressed, are seated amid gathered officials. Their twin grandchildren appear at the queen's knee. The *gramillero,* the herbal doctor to the king, stands to their left, next to a matron who sits with a fan.

The king's special mediator, the *bastonero* (holder of the staff), stands at the ruler's side, holding a red-and-white-striped cane in his right hand. Six other dignitaries stand behind the king. Behind them, in a niche, gleams an altar to the Virgin. According to Galloza, the two percussion-ists at far left are playing a drumroll (*introducción*). Their drums bring back the voices of the ancestors. Flags, candelabras, and pennants com-plete a rich setting. Everyone is dressed in European finery, all save one: the bastonero wears a red hat, blue coat, white shirt, and leggings, but over his waist goes a Kongo-derived apron, with painted-on red and white dots. In Kongo such an apron was called an *mbati,* made of the spotted skin of a civet cat (*mbala*). The catskin apron has been a Kongo sign of nobility for centuries. L. Degrandpre in 1787 (Plate 27) and Olfert Dapper in 1668 (Plate 28) depicted important men wearing this item in Lwangu and Cabinda.[112] Mbati symbolized mediation. They stood for ancestral power, brought from forest to town, even as felines are unafraid to prowl the two locations. On the River Plate painted-on dots, or sewn-on sequins, came to symbolize the original spots of the civet cat.

When the last salas in Buenos Aires and Montevideo closed at the

PLATE 26

beginning of the twentieth century, some of their personages reemerged as street maskers during pre-Lenten festivities and holidays. Private figures were invading public spaces. Thus Montevideo street processioners include the "matron" (*mamá vieja*) and the old doctor of herbs (*gramillero*). The bastonero returns as the *escobero,* the broom-twirling dancer. He juggles his broom while he marches, letting it roll down his chest and his thighs without using his hands. But the apron that he inherited from the bastonero remains virtually unchanged.

Alejandro Frigerio brings to our attention a cartoon showing an escobero dancing in the streets of Buenos Aires that was published in *Caras y caretas* on February 16, 1901 (Plate 29). The title is *Bailando con muchas contorsiones* (Dancing with Many Contortions). It shows a black athlete dancing with broom in one hand and duster in the other,

PLATE 27   PLATE 28

doubling his weapons of purity. Both broom and duster have ribbons tied onto them, like the staffs with cloth strips attached to them in Kongo and the staffs with rattles and raffia strips danced before President Rosas in Argentina in 1838. Three whites look on with amazement. The escobero twists his body into an impossible knot while swirling his instruments around him. At the same time, he "breaks" close to the earth.

PLATE 29

Something else is going on, something significant: he dances with an actual catskin. Here is a link between Kongo and creole, between the original mbati and the River Plate equivalent all dotted with sequins or painted-on dots. To Kongo commentators, the contortionist's dance is immediately comprehensible: "I have a power [the catskin] and a message [mnemonic ribbons tied to broom and the duster]—clean up your house!" (*komba nzo aku*).[113]

In Kongo twisted roots are signs of spirit. They stand for the *simbi*, the highest class of the dead. The strange roots in the High John the Conqueror charms of the black American South are influenced by Kongo faith. Incredible contortions like those of the 1901 escobero are also seen by Bakongo as shaped by the spirit.

If the dancer was in touch with the lore of his ancestors, he may have been mocking the whites all around him: "My body is twisted because I am simbi" (*Nitu ami yimeni zekakana kadi mono i simbi*); "because I am simbi [or possessed of their spirit,] I fear no one. I say what I want. Nobody can do anything about it."[114] Whether or not the point was defiance, here was a distinct parallel for tango. The twist of the body, deepened by "breaking," flaunted an ultimate quebrada.

The process is complex and fascinating. It inspires us to revisit, one final time, aspects of Kongo in the dance of candombe.

First we have *lembika mooko* (the hands of peace). This is dancing with hands held flat before the body, parallel to the earth, more or less even with one's chest. Such hands are cool. They stabilize. They radiate well-being.

In 1949 M. Cahen, a former director of the Museum of Central Africa in Tervuren, Belgium, photographed a figurated tomb two kilometers south of Seke Banza, which is north of the Kongo River in Yombe country.

The tomb's decoration unites figural and ideographic dimensions: the top displays pinwheels moving forever, signs of the wheeling of the soul; below, human figures salute us from the other world. Two are women. Both make the calming *lembika mooko* gesture with their right hands. With the left hand one supports her husband at work while the other secures a child in her lap. They call to bring peace (*bokila mu nata twala yenge*).

Hands that float without weapons, that appear without fists, signal a composure that is fluent and deep. Recall the young man in beige pants and white shirt filmed dancing n'kwanga at Diosso in North Kongo. He was calling and responding with this amiable sign, positively accepting an invitation to the dance (Plate 30).

Figari picked up this gesture in Uruguay. In a detail of one of his paintings, three women—one in brown, one in white, and one in orange and white stripes—peacefully dance with their hands curving down. They are echoed exactly by two women of color photographed dancing candombe in the 1970s at the Shimmy Club in Buenos Aires (Plate 31). The photograph was published in 1980 in an issue of the journal *Todo es historia,* dedicated to the blacks of the city. A woman in a dark dress with tiny white spots dances in the direction of the camera. Her face is frozen. Her gaze is distant. She calls with an outward curled hand. A woman in white to her right is smiling. She calls out with pleasure, again with curled hand, to a young man in a white shirt who has focused his dancing on her. Figari could have been painting *them,* the elegant curl of their extended right hands floating before them peacefully.

Other strong gestures, derived from candombe, enlivened the Shimmy Club discourse. One was *kyaadi,* touching the head with the hand as a sign of distress. It came with captives from Kongo to Buenos Aires.

In the art of the motherland, we call attention to a Dondo figurated trumpet collected in 1910 in the Göteborg Museum in Sweden. Here a mourner touches the back of his head with both hands. One hand on the chin can mean the same thing. In yet another variant a hand placed over the eye indicates blacking out images of loss or great pain.

In Buenos Aires the last-mentioned gesture, placing hand over eye, reemerged in candombe. It was originally accompanied by a Kongo cry of lamentation, *e e e mbadi lo* (alas, alas). The latter eventually creolized in Buenos Aires into *e e e baríló.* It became a set pattern in the dance of candombe—one hand brought up over one of the eyes, like a visor, and then the other—but the original meaning was apparently lost.

Figari painted a woman striking this pose. Even a stranger can guess

PLATE 30   PLATE 31

what she means: something has happened that she does not want to see. Her left hand shields her eyes, while her right rests on her thigh.

The Argentine anthropologist Alejandro Frigerio has videotaped Facundo Posadas and Carlos Anzuate, both veterans of the Shimmy Club, dancing this gesture, touching the head with alternating hands and simultaneously singing out "*e e e bariló*."[115] Argentine films of the 1930s and 1940s, those focused on candombe, show black people dancing in the streets of Buenos Aires, making this eye-shielding gesture. In 2004 I photographed the noted black salsa master Tete Salas, who frequented the Shimmy Club in his youth, dancing candombe, covering his eyes, first with his right hand, then with his left (Plate 32).

In the Figari painting, where a woman shields her eyes with her left hand, an amazing human figure in top hat and black coat looms up in space with his right hand held high and his left curved and low. Gustavo Vilela, a black Montevidean, says this gesture is seen on the streets of the city when Carnival is celebrated today: while moving forward, one holds up one's right hand, then the left hand, in continual alternation.[116]

This is a Kongo step, "calling and receiving." The call, understood, salutes the highest power, Great God Almighty (*Nzambi Mpungu*). One seeks to receive His blessing and to share it immediately with the community. Receive with the high hand, give with the low hand. The empty hand rises, the weighted hand falls, hence the continuing alternation. This meaning was apparently lost in Buenos Aires and Montevideo.

We come now to leaning. Recall that in the dance called n'kwanga a young man accepted a dance, leaning forward, and departed, with thanks,

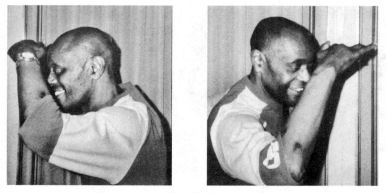

PLATE 32

leaning back. Leaning is also defiance, as when a palm tree bows down to the wind only to spring right back up.

In the black United States this kind of leaning went straight into cakewalk. It was taken to extremes by Afro-American drum majors, who lean back at incredible angles.[117]

In the third stage of candombe, when women and men formed a conga line, they danced leaning backward and forward. In Kongo terms they were "melting" (*kanienge*) to the beat. This kind of motion, as we saw back in Kongo, protects what is new (leaning forward) with the past (leaning back). The latter type of lean appeared in Buenos Aires black street processioners of the late nineteenth century (Plate 24). Lino Suárez Peña saw a similar move in Montevideo in 1924. He talked about dancers "arching their spine, gracefully back."[118]

There was mimesis of this vogue among whites who marched in Carnival *comparsas* around 1900. Acting like Africans, they savored the music, letting its waves roll over their bodies, leaning back while marching.

This move persists in tango, when the male leans forward at a sharp angle and the woman correspondingly leans back, and vice versa. When executed dramatically, with the partner leaned back to the floor, it is known as the "drop." Given the advent of cakewalk in Buenos Aires in 1903, there is probably more than one root to the "drop."

The climax of couple dancing in Kongo is bumbakana. Women and men bump together bellies, or thighs, or chests. There were further variants, as when one danced lifting a leg in the air (*timbula*), then suddenly swung around with the knee at the partner. Yet another way of doing this was to saunter behind one's partner, back to back, then suddenly bump posteriors (*bunda*) together.[119] Figari shows this before an Andalusian-type house with a flat roof (*azotea*): a black woman in pink, hand thoughtfully on chin, and a black man in brown playfully bump derrieres. With forward-curled palms, the man shows his pleasure, his ease.

We have already seen the delightful drawing published by Frigerio showing black Brazilians completing this move.[120] In jubilant unison the male raises both hands over his head: he is celebrating a "catch" without using his hands. This was the step, as we hope to show, that, reinforced by maxixe, launched a score of strong invasive moves in the tango.

Today white Buenos Aires is not supposed to know about such things. But at a birthday party given at the Sunderland Club in 1997 for the late, great Lampazo, someone put on a tape of candombe music. Instantly white tangueros formed a circle, and out jumped a portly white Argentine man who bumped a woman with a whack of his stomach.

Finally, tanguero couples, wherever they be, inexorably cycle counterclockwise. The custom descends from the circle of candombe, possibly reinforced by the waltz, but it ultimately goes back to counterclockwise-cycling dancers in Kongo. The original meaning: we are following the path of the sun, we are following the cycle of life everlasting.

The links between tango and this treasury of motion surprise those who believe that candombe died when the last salas closed. But the rhythms persisted and reemerged in comparsas, in street processions, in the last decade of the nineteenth century. They also continued in basement black dancing clubs like Los Haraganes in Montevideo in the 1920s and the Shimmy Club in the Centro barrio of Buenos Aires in the 1950s through 1970s.

On February 15, 1902, the Buenos Aires illustrated journal *Caras y caretas* published a photograph of the presidential table in the meeting room of the old candombe of the kingdom of Benguela, which was south of the kingdom of Kongo in Angola. The cultures of the Benguela area were broadly cognate with those of Kongo. Now the male leader of the candombe was dead, but his wife had kept the room exactly as he left it, and this was the way it was photographed; Alicia Churchill has sketched the essential elements of the photograph. (Plate 33).[121]

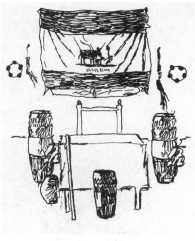

PLATE 33

The flag of the society anchored ancestral spirits. When the leader was speaking, he was backed by the banner of heritage. The flag was flanked by two tambourines and two ritual fly whisks (*nsesa*). In Kongo a fly whisk is a sign of the giving of blessings (*nsesa i sinsu kia lusakumunu*). Two nsesa here implied that the leader had the power to bless across worlds, the living and the dead. Such actions swept (*komba*) evil from the room. Three ngoma drums made a circle around the table of the late president, with his chair at the position of power. The cane of the leader, as if awaiting his return, leaned against the right-hand side of his table. In Kongo a staff (*mvwala*) is always kept to the right of a seated ruler.

To the writer of the article, to judge from his comments, the assembling of these objects meant but one thing—the end of a tradition—but spirit is boundless. The round of the drums comes back in the circle of tango couples today. Purifying images associated with the nsesa, too, were transposed and continued: blessing with these instruments, the king swept out evil. After his death they turned into brooms, nsesa equivalents with which escoberos swept streets of trouble and continue to sweep them today.

Fly whisks and drums, at the old Benguela sala, were signs of an ebullience that was never to end. Whirl without end, as James Joyce might have said. When the beat of the habanera came down from black Cuba, black Buenos Aires inevitably responded.

4.

HABANERA: THE CALL
OF THE BLOOD

An indefinable stylistic quality, *salanc*, is critical to the
Catalunyan habanera, like swing in jazz, duende in flamenco, and canyengue in tango.

—XAVIER FEBRES, *Aixo es l'Havanera* (This Is Habanera, 1995)

I n Trinidad, across the Paraguayan border from Posadas, Argentina, a
sculptor for the local Jesuitic mission carved, around 1760, a frieze of
angel-musicians. One strums a harp, another bows a violin, but one
vivid angel beats time with one foot and shakes a huge bass maraca, as
large as his head. Heaven includes dance percussion.[1]

A century later in southern Buenos Aires, dancers shared similar feel-
ings. Black dance *was* their heaven. When the Afro-Cuban habanera,
words and rhythm in enchanting combination, arrived in Buenos Aires
after 1850, it triggered a sequence that led to three dances: milonga,
canyengue, and tango.

It also assisted in the birth of maxixe, the dance before samba, in late-
nineteenth-century Brazil. Oneyda Alvarenga, in a classic text on
Brazilian popular music, writes: "Polka gave [maxixe] its motion, the Afro-
Cuban habanera gave it its beat, and popular black Brazilian music com-

pleted the fusion with signature syncopations and improvisatory wit."[2] In developing the maxixe, blacks mixed the "Kongo grind," the moving of the hips in a piquant manner, with insertions of a leg between the legs of the partner, just as in tango today. Maxixe was hot, lambada a hundred years before its time.

Meanwhile, in North America, habanera infiltrated jazz. It inspired classical composers in Europe: Georges Bizet, Manuel de Falla, Claude Debussy, Maurice Joseph Ravel, and Erik Satie. Today habanera is the official tavern music of the Catalan coast of northeastern Spain. We are dealing with a music that rounded the world and goes on.

The secret of habanera's longevity is its seductive bass pattern. The habanera bass, still audible in milonga, is outwardly simple: a dotted eighth note followed by a sixteenth and two eighth notes. Every other beat is strong, *da*, ka *ka* kan, *da*, ka *ka* kan. This invites off-beating. In fact, the habanera bass could be characterized as the $E = mc^2$ of Afro-world ballroom. It promises—and delivers—release of energy. *Da*, ka *ka* kan, as tangueros "mouth-drum" it, is more than a riff, a repeated phrase, an ostinato. It is a module, meant to be combined with other modules, making three and two pulses, sounding simultaneously: W. C. Handy, blues composer, referred to the pattern as "the call of the blood," black blood understood.[3]

For the habanera bass speaks in a percussive Esperanto understood from St. Louis to Capetown. It commands us to dance. In working-class Buenos Aires it conjured improvised dance moves among blacks and their friends. Early in the twentieth century a black guitarist named Luciano Ríos would carry it straight into tango.

The original bass beat had simmered in Cuba since the early nineteenth century. In 1798 a local writer, Buenaventura Pascual Ferrer, estimated that in Havana there were around *fifty* public dances a day.[4] Today such intensity amazes. The action included steps that Pascual Ferrer called zapateos, boleros, guarachas, and congos.[5] Mention of "zapateos," together with almost certainly rhythmic "congos," suggests that the creole dancers of Cuba were working with traditions both Iberian and Central African.

The Cuban musicologist Alejo Carpentier identified the bass of the habanera in the 1856 contradanza "Tu madre es Conga" (Your Mama is Kongo). It was the hit of Santiago de Cuba in 1856.[6] "Tu madre es Conga" was considered a contradanza, a Spanish form, but actually the power of the habanera rhythm had produced something new and creole. Describing the structure of something he called *danza,* José García de

Arboleya, a Spanish writer in Cuba in 1859, was referring to the same thing:

> The irresistible creole *danza* [is] a true Cuban specialty. It is the old Spanish contradanza modified by the voluptuous climate of the tropics. The dance consists of two parts, each with eight measures in 2/4. Each measure composes a figure in the dance, like the *paseo* (the walk), the *cadena* [the conga line], the *sostenido* [the continuous motion], and the *cedazo* [dancing as couples to waltz time]. In the first two there is less movement and expression but in the *sostenido* and *cedazo,* couples turn playful [*retozan*] and begin to dance piquantly [*picante*], swinging and swaying in a flirtatious, charming way.[7]

The transition from ease to ebullience compares with moving from *largo* to *montuno,* that is, from set text to hot improvisation, in the later Afro-Cuban son and rumba. African influence, not tropical weather, lies behind this.

Danza existed before de Arboleya documented it. Esteban Pichardo had described Havana blacks dancing it in 1836:

> Black couples excel [*descollan*] in interpreting this dance, adapting it to their ancestral temperament and spirit. [There is] suave foot-tapping (*zapateo*) executed by the young men of this region, and a coming and going, in serpent like lines, in the "chains" [*cadenas*] followed by voluptuous swaying in the *cedazo* [couples in waltz time] . . . all of this happens with an African ear for time and an ingratiating gift for fine style.[8]

Whites were quick to pick up on this Afro-Cuban form. Thus Félix Tanco, an observer of nineteenth-century Cuban life, remarked in a letter, "Who cannot see, in the movements of our young men and women, that when they dance contradanzas and waltzes, they are imitating the gestures of the blacks in their cabildos."[9] *Cabildos* were Afro-Cuban equivalents of the Afro-Argentine candombe societies of Buenos Aires. Musicians of color added fuel to all this. At the time, they virtually monopolized the staffing of Cuba's dance orchestras.

Habanera was to spread beyond dance. It would also develop, around the late nineteenth century, into a concert music composed primarily for piano. As dance, too, it would be codified and formalized. In 1969, over a century after its emergence, Antonio Cisneros Lugones published a standardized way of dancing habanera in Argentina. Set sequences unfolded in four measures each: a holding of hands in a march, a return, a spin to the right, a spin to the left, a habanera step, an Argentine waltz step in eight measures, spins for eight measures, and so forth.[10] This creole development had considerably transformed the original. As danza turned into habanera, it had become a dance of individual couples, locked in embrace position. J. E. Alexander, in Havana in 1830–40, the time of this transformation, suggests how this happened: "The [new form] of danza was invented, without any doubt, with young love in mind. The dance is simple, the movements free and easy, for the principal object is to bring the two sexes together."[11]

In Cuba by 1860 the rhythm that would come to be called habanera was becoming strictly vocal, a song form. But it kept syncopation, it kept the strong bass, its lyrics picked up phrases from black street sellers, and some songs had Afro-Cuban themes: "Your Mama Is Kongo" and "The Bishop of Guinea."

Meanwhile, rhythm with romance, habanera the dance came to Buenos Aires around 1850. Black sailors, arriving in Montevideo from Cuba, were later messengers of habanera. They inspired at the turn of the century the names of black *comparsa* societies in Montevideo, like the Pobres Negros Cubanos (Poor Black Cubans), founded in 1898, Esclavos de La Habana (Slaves from Havana), in 1908, and Los Hijos de La Habana (The Sons of Havana) in 1912.

Another important medium was sheet music—published in Cuba, as Tamara Martín reminds us, since 1803.[12] And the dancing continued. In the bars and the brothels, the styles were direct, earthy, different from the "literary habanera" that Lugones would publish in 1969. Less fancy, more body, was what was happening. Jorge Novati and Inés Cuello show that "broken style dancing" (*bailar quebrado*)—bending the knees and undulating the hips—combined with embracing, in the funkier styles of Buenos Aires habanera.[13] The fusion of styles was sensuous and superb—the Kongo grind, caught in a waltzlike embrace.

Habanera caused a sensation in Madrid simultaneous with its sweep of Buenos Aires. García de Arboleya concluded his report on the danza by observing that in the 1850s it was the hit of the Spanish capital. It was here, in the 1850s, even though de Arboleya would still be calling it "danza" in 1859, that it would become known by the term *habanera*.

Cuba created it. Madrid named it. Then it conquered the world.

Its power emerged in the lines of the bass. They were strong and indelible, and they were African—these were key Kongo riffs. There was an intuition of this in the title of that 1856 contradanza with a habanera beat, "Your Mama Is Kongo." And note that a dance called "congo" had preceded habanera.

Yet because habanera traveled to Spain, there to take root, some writers claimed that it had an Iberian origin. Alejo Carpentier, dean of Cuban ethnomusicologists, would have none of it: "there are too many reasons to lead us to believe that the rhythm of the tango [i.e., the habanera bass] was known in the Americas before it was known in Spain. And it was the blacks who were primarily responsible."[14]

To which one might add: specifically exiles from Kongo. They brought a stylized bass drumbeat to black dancers of Havana and Santiago. Then it turned up in the bass patterns of danza and habanera. This is not too surprising: most of the musicians were black.

MBILA A MAKINU: THE CALL OF THE DANCE FROM BEYOND THE HORIZON

In Kongo there is a bass ngoma-drum pattern identical to the bass of the habanera. Bakongo translate its pulses into syllables: *ka,* ka *ka* kan *ka,* ka *ka* kan. These syllables are close to the ones that tangueros use when verbally notating the beat of the habanera: *da,* ka *ka* kan, *da,* ka *ka* kan. When people are not dancing, and a drummer on the bass or "mother" ngoma drum (the ancestor of the famous conga drum of Cuba) wants to generate action, he repeats this pattern—*ka,* ka *ka* kan, *ka,* ka *ka* kan—on his drum. This is the message: "Now hear this, now hear this. Everyone get out there and dance!"

The name of this beat is, in fact, "the call to the dance" (*mbila a makinu*). *Mbila* puns on *bila* (to cook), meaning "dance with enthusiasm." Other percussionists come in with their lines. A dance is soon under way.[15]

The use of the bass drum, as opposed to the treble, is deliberate: treble voicings represent our world, but bass patterns come from the spirit. "They are the sounds from beneath the horizon. They capture the deep part of what people are thinking."[16] Bass brings transcendence.

This signature call on bass drum went to Cuba. There Bakongo, the majority black musical culture of the island, reestablished the pattern. It would eventually become habanera.

The Afro-Iberian habanera, armed with harmonies and words from Iberia and propelled by a bass that was black and spiritual, became the first world beat. Its wide diffusion, as we have seen, was facilitated by

Cuba's sheet music publishing industry. One powerful messenger was Mexican: Mexico's Eighth Cavalry Military Band, more than sixty performers strong, was the *succès fou* of the New Orleans World's Cotton and Industrial Exposition of 1884–85. The danzas and habaneras they played became a rage through the city.[17] Repercussions were felt in St. Louis. In around 1906, twenty-one years after the exposition, W. C. Handy played habanera to dancers in Dixie Park, a black carnival site in that city. The music called them back to themselves: "When we came to the habanera rhythm, containing the beat of the tango, I observed that there was a sudden proud and graceful reaction [among the black dancers]."[18]

Handy played another habanera, Sebastián Iradier's hemisphere-wide hit, "La paloma" (The Dove), written in 1859. The reaction was identical. And so he concluded: "There was something negroid in that beat, something that quickened the blood of the Dixie Park dancers."[19] Handy was "signifying." He well knew what that "something" was: the swing and the suasion of the bass. *Mbila a makinu* had arrived in North America.

In New Orleans the habanera bass went straight into jazz. Jelly Roll Morton, who almost certainly learned it from Mexican bands in New Orleans, called it the "Latin tinge," and Lil Hardin (later Louis Armstrong's wife) played it. It continued in rhythm and blues. In the 1970s the popular New Orleans pianist Professor Longhair was alternating a habanera bass and a boogie-woogie riff with his left hand while playing triplets with his right.[20] In fact, John Szwed reminds us, the habanera bass line crosses over into the twenty-first century as the basic beat of the "second line," the dancers who follow parading jazz bands.[21] Mbila lives on. How appropriate, then, that Wynton Marsalis, himself from New Orleans, performed an important fusion of tango and jazz at Lincoln Center in May 2001 and titled the concert "The Latin Tinge."

Meanwhile, back in Cuba, Eliseo Grenet, writing on popular music in 1939, lamented the disappearance of habanera as dance. He felt that habanera as song was dying out, too, "due to the lack of the nineteenth-century atmosphere, which it faithfully reflected."[22] Grenet was apparently unaware that habanera as song was very much alive in Spain. Nor had he remembered the classical composers whose habaneras were and are still current.

Masters of symphonic music had sensed the authority of habanera early on. They stole from its fire. First there was the Spaniard Sebastián Iradier, who lived in Cuba in the 1850s and acquired there a taste for habanera. Iradier's song in habanera rhythm, "La paloma," became one of the best-known songs of Latin America. In 1938 Jelly Roll Morton played it to illustrate the "Spanish tinge" in jazz to the musicologist Alan Lomax. Iradier inspired Manuel de Falla and several composers in France: "suddenly Bizet writes an habanera in *Carmen* and the word habanera—music from Havana—from that very moment enters the classical vocabulary of the world. Debussy, in his *Night in Granada,* includes a sequence in habanera time, as does Ravel, in the third movement of his *Spanish Rhapsody.* Eric Satie writes an habanera for his *Sites Auriculaires.*"[23] Debussy and Ravel enveloped habanera in impressionist mists, music for the dancing of elegant ghosts. All of this music is still played today.

Habanera as dance is hard to find in the twenty-first century, though old steps appear in the Argentine instruction book published by Lugones in 1969. As *music,* however, it permeates milonga to this day—though at a much faster tempo than in "La paloma." What's more, early recorded "tangos," like Juan Maglio's version of Alfredo Bevilacqua's "Emancipación" of 1912, are really habaneras. The formula was simple: habanera beat + melody. By the time of Julio de Caro's brilliant "Tierra querida" (Beloved Land) of 1927, tango had absorbed habanera rhythmic structure. De Caro added slide and drag effects on violin and bandoneón, placing them in the melody where you might least expect them; but these rich innovations should not conceal the fact that he had tangoized the habanera.

Aníbal Troilo's "La tablada" (The Slaughterhouse) tango, recorded August 28, 1962, leads to a moment when the guitarist plays habanera in the clear. It's as if he were saying, "This is what we come from, this is what we can recall." Francisco Canaro, in his version of Sebastián Piana's "Milonga sentimental," does more than recall: it's habanera all the way. And consider Troilo's extraordinary milonga "La trampera" (Cheating Woman) of 1962: he starts with a habanera beat at a sizzling tempo, then crosses it with samba, backbeat, and jazz. Habanera still haunts milonga today, drawing attention to moments in the narrative of tango that might otherwise go forgotten.

Milonga restores habanera. So do the taverns of Spain.

Today one of the strongest domains of habanera as song is the coast of Catalonia, to the north of Barcelona. Castor Pérez Diz, himself a distinguished singer and guitarist of contemporary habanera, explains how this happened: he dates the advent of habanera in Catalonia to around 1875–1900.[24] (Madrid, as we have seen, had already received it.)

At the end of the nineteenth century, following the collapse of Iberian authority in the Caribbean in the wake of the Spanish-American War, returning Spanish sailors, soldiers, and displaced colonials (*indianos*) brought the beat with them from Cuba. Habanera took root in Galicia, Asturias, the Basque country, Castille, Catalonia, Valencia, Alicante, Murcia, Cádiz, Seville, Huelva, and the Canary Islands. Each of these areas, Pérez Diz shows, added subtleties of instrumentation and vocal expression.

One of the main centers of contemporary Iberian habanera today is a tiny fishing port on the Costa Brava, northeast of Barcelona: Calella de Palafrugell. Here habanera *cantatas* take place in the summer. The beach, anchored boats, and nearby arcades serve as found bleachers for *habaneristas* who sing from a brilliantly lit dais. A village of three hundred swells with thousands of visitors, all come to hear habanera. In the winter the cognescenti gather in cafés to savor the style more privately.

CALELLA DE PALAFRUGELL, LA BELLA LOLA BAR,
DECEMBER 17, 1999

Francesc "Paco" Cardona is a black-haired, vigorous Catalan who owns a fine tavern in Calella. He named it La Bella Lola, after a famous habanera brought to Catalonia by sailors from Havana:

> *There you go, gorgeous Lola,*
> *a wild flash moving on the land.*
> *Sailors go mad*
> *and you tremble the hand*
> *Of even the pilot.*

Cardona builds his life around the habanera: he sings it, studies it, and invites habaneristas to serenade the clients of his tavern.

A roaring fire warmed his tavern when I visited it on a wintry night in 1999. Couples were drinking shots of whiskey and beer. On one side of the fireplace was a shelf full of pamphlets and books—all on habanera—placed there for browsing. At midnight two men sat down at the table next to the counter. One, gray-haired and debonair, was Castor Pérez Diz. He would sing baritone and play the guitar. The other guitarist, with a thick black moustache, was Alfons Carreras, the tenor and guitarist.

Together they sang of amorous destiny, of Catalan sailors falling in love with black women (*mulatas*) in Havana, then remembering them fondly back home. Sometimes Carreras pointed to the table, breaking up a phrase with a gestural comma. Pérez sang with his chin on his guitar, partnered with his instrument in a tangolike way. He played his guitar as an extension of his chest, finding strings in his heart, strumming bass with his thumb, the bass figuration that defines habanera. There was "second-lining" from the end of the table, apprentice habanera singers responding, harmonizing, repeating the words. They knew them by heart. Dancing thumb against strings, Castor Pérez provided the bass that accompanies any sentiment. They soon sang in Catalan:

> Benvingut pensament
> que perfumes la galta
> i em deixes un vers
>
> *Welcome, philosophy,*
> *perfume my cheek*
> *and leave me a verse*

Truths came to the table in song. One habanera startled a woman in her forties. She blushed, then hid sudden tears behind hands, concealing her reaction. The men sang "Los palmares de Cuba" (The Palm Trees of Cuba), about a mulata capturing men by force of her *bilongo*, the Kongo-Cuban term for medicine and spirit. They even sang a habanera referring to black origins, a traditional composition called "Negrito Congo" (Black Guy from Kongo):

> Yo soy un negrito congo
> que en el África nací
> ay, ay, ay que en en el África nací
> vengo a cantarte unos tangos
> que se bailan allí
> ay, ay, ay
> que se bailan allí.
>
> *I'm a black guy from Kongo*
> *born in Africa*
> ay, ay, ay
> *I said, born in Africa*
> ay, ay, ay
> *I come to sing tangos*

that are danced over there
ay, ay, ay
that are danced over there.

Cuban creole influence enlivened their climax, "Habanera embrujada" (Spell of the Habanera), a habanera-son composed in the last decade of the twentieth century in the Canary Islands. The song tells a story: once upon a time a Canarian woman falls in love with a Canarian man. But she loses him, when he leaves for the Caribbean to *hacer la América*, to make his fortune abroad. So she prepares a Macbeth-like charm to bring back her lover:

Jugo de tuno, ojo de baifo
Cola lagarto y poquito de ron
Tres oraciones a Santa Marta
pa' que nos firme la absolución

Juice from a cactus, eye of baifo
tail of a lizard, a splash of rum
three prayers spoken to Santa Marta
so she will grace it as well and done.[25]

He returns. Time has gone by: he doesn't recognize her. So she gets possession of his handkerchief and "dresses" it with further medicine. They come together.

Carreras and Pérez chanted the refrain in spirited Afro-Cuban fashion. The moment was charged with *salanc,* the Catalan word for "swing." Shoulders started swaying. A man drummed the tabletop. A youth smacked his thighs. The music had once again demonstrated the power of habanera to jump oceans, to jump cultures, and to call, with its beat, distant peoples together.

Catalonia is a time machine. It takes us back to Buenos Aires in the second half of the nineteenth century, when habanera attracted sharp dancers to the floor. Many were Afro-Argentine. They improvised. Some of their steps came direct from candombe. They called the new blend the milonga.

5·

MILONGA: THE GREAT BUENOS AIRES CONVERSATION

Pandikisa: to connect words; to recover oneself.

— W. H. SANDERS AND W. E. FAY, *Vocabulary of the Umbundu Language* (1885)

Milonga, spirited and strong, emerged in Argentina in the 1870s. It was not a mere precursor to tango but a tradition in its own right, with its own sound, its own mode of action. Derived from Kimbundu and Ki-Kongo words meaning, respectively, "argument" and "moving lines of dancers," milonga furthered a tradition of aesthetic dueling: pugnacity as poetry, battling as dance. It was, in short, African-influenced "carving contests" on a scale turned heroic.

When leading tangueros—Juan Carlos and Johanna Copes, Kely and Facundo Posadas, El Pibe Palermo and Norma, Ester and Mingo Pugliese—show off their edge, they often choose milonga as their medium.

Still, we have to be careful to avoid viewing milonga as always a fight or a contest. Early milongas in Spanish and Portuguese vaunt potent songs of nostalgia.

The first milonga songs were coined on the pampas, "the gently rolling pasture stretch[ing] in all directions as far as the eye can see, empty save for herds of grazing cattle, a few traditionally garbed cowboys on horseback, and the occasional tree."[1] The pampas roll across Argentina and Uruguay and continue into southernmost Brazil, the state of Rio Grande do Sul. Brazilians of this region call themselves gauchos. Hence there are milongas in Portuguese as well as in Spanish, and the former are seasoned with nostalgia. Take José Mendes's "Mensagem de saudade" (Message of Yearning), for example, or this short milonga from Rio Grande do Sul:

> Tenho saudosa lembrança
> dos pagos onde nascí
> dos meus tempos de criança
> que tão felices eu vivi.

> *I was born on the pampas*
> *which I miss and remember*
> *happy years of my childhood*
> *which time took as tender.*[2]

So some milongas are tinctured with yearning. But a dominant mode is competition and argument, a mode shared with the combative tradition of payada—of dueling guitarists improvising verses on the pampas. In fact, when payada reached Buenos Aires, the city renamed it milonga. The song turned to dance as well, with a form and ebullience that blaze to this day.

Europe has been aware of *milonga*, as an Angolan word for "argument," since at least 1630. At that time Portuguese officials on the coast of Angola were complaining to Lisbon that Queen Nzinga, an indigenous leader of the interior, was sending out messages—milonga—to persuade local populations to join her. The black queen was also issuing lightly veiled challenges to Portuguese authority.[3] These taunts too were milonga. So in seventeenth-century Angola the term meant "words, speech, or argument." But it also referred to inciting people, talking back to authority, and verbal rebellion.

This rich range of meanings, brought to Argentina by captives from Angola, took root in the River Plate region. Logically, milonga came to name the challenge singing (*payadas*) and drum duels (*tapadas*) of dismounted gauchos (*compadres*) looking for work in Buenos Aires around 1860.

The masters of payada were heavily black. When payadas became milongas, traditions of battling combined with a wallop. It was as if Queen Nzinga were stalking the streets of Buenos Aires around 1860–84, flashing her wit and self-confidence:

> You gentlemen professing milonga,
> let's battle right here.
> Smoke us, milonguero,
> if you dare.[4]

The poets of milonga composed their verses in Iberian lines of eight syllables and sang them to the accompaniment of Spanish guitar. Their melodies descended as they sang. They began on high notes and ended on low notes. This step wise descent shares commonalities with the structure of Central African melody.

But again, not all milongas were boastful. In 1925 Enrique Vicente Arnold penned a melancholy masterpiece, establishing a mood reminiscent of Quevedo, the classic poet who wrote about death:

> La muerte es vida vivida
> la vida es muerte que viene
> ya la vida no es otra cosa
> que muerte que anda luciendo.

> Death is lived life
> life is death on the way
> for life is no more than
> death making hay.[5]

Borges esteemed this lyric. It appealed to his stoicism.

BORGES WRITES MILONGAS: SONGS FOR SIX STRINGS (1965)

Inspired, Borges himself wrote milongas and published them, in 1965, in a volume called Para las seis cuerdas (Songs for Six Strings). Admiring the mixture of battle and art, he decided to join the tradition. What he was resonating to were creole redistillations of African and Andalusian traditions of poetic jousting.

Borges's milongas give perspective on courage—this from a poet who, when verbally assaulted in New York in the late 1960s, apparently as an alleged member of "the establishment," startled his young assailant by challenging him to go outside and settle the matter man to man. It was more than startling: Borges was blind and then in his sixties. So Borges naturally finds:

> *There is one thing about which*
> *no one repents*
> *no one on earth:*
> *having lived bravely.*[6]

Borges wrote about tough guys. He focused on their stern code of courage. Milonga, he felt, reflected their valor. It gave back to the nation "the certainty of having been brave." That element, in addition, traced back to the blacks:

MILONGA FOR PERSONS OF COLOR

> *When our nation was born*
> *one morning in May*
> *the gauchos only knew*
> *how to wage war on horseback,*
> *but someone remembered*
> *how strong the black men were,*
> *men who were no strangers to courage,*
> *so a regiment arose*
> *of blacks and mulattoes.*

None were more valiant. Recalling their heroism, Borges is haunted by a black face that he meets near midcentury, "worked over by time yet serene," like Cafferata's bust of a black man. This causes him to wonder:

> *To what heaven with drums*
> *have they gone?*[7]

That wondering sense, of respect and indebtedness, reappears in another milonga by Borges. This one tells of a young man of color who lit up his barrio with his charm and his dance:

> *I sing of a tough guy,*
> *handsome patron*

of the less saintly houses
of the barrio Triunvirato.

Dancer and player
half-indio or black—who can say which—
everyone favored him
in the tenement we now call the projects.

Always attentive
to black women in the doorways
they loved their brave guy
he gave them all a good time.

But someone got jealous:

a bullet cut him down
at the corner of Thames and Triunvirato
The barrio went mute
the barrio called Quinta del Ñato.[8]

To kill a likable young person was senseless and shocking. Still, Borges found meaning. Bravery and art are not pointless; they serve to instruct us, teach, and exhort us, creating a momentum that lasts to this day:

THE HIPSTERS WHO ARE GONE

What we took as apochrypha lives on
in a manner of walking
in a style of strong strumming
in a face, in a whistle,
simple things masking glory
in an intimate patio with grapevines
where tangos lend rage to guitars.[9]

Thus poets and dancers of milonga built, on their own, a city-sustaining landscape. To Borges milonga was "one of the great conversations of Buenos Aires." His book marked a climax of talk about talk in milonga. He revealed that milonga, both as verse and as action, invests its best followers with valor and drive. To this they respond with all that they have, acquiring the toughness to fight time itself.

CHECK OUT MY BODY AND MY LOOK: MILONGA
TAKES ON BUENOS AIRES

Starting in rural Argentina around 1860, as a song among cowboys,
milonga after 1870 acquired choreography in town and country. In 1872
the word, in the dance sense, entered Argentine literature, in José
Hernández's epic poem, *El gaucho Martín Fierro:*

> *I learned . . .*
> *that there was a dance over there . . .*
> *and so I went . . . to see the milonga.*[10]

Milonga combined voice with hard bodies. It took over the streets of
Buenos Aires. Each barrio had a self-proclaimed leader:

> *I'm from from uptown,*
> *barrio del Retiro,*
> *I don't worry 'bout*
> *who I knock down.*

> *I'm from San Cristóbal and Balvanera,*
> *ready for attack,*
> *with a butt as strong as my chest*
> *and hips as tough as my back.*

> *I'm from Montserrat*
> *where sharp blades collide,*
> *what I say with my mouth*
> *I back up with my hide.*[11]

The youth of the city moved in full consciousness of the joys of clean
combat. Eager to assert themselves and to show up their rivals, they took
on the dances of Europe and Cuba. They remade the mazurka, they
played with the habanera, shaping these styles to their will.

Prudes were shocked, but hot-blooded young men had other ideas.
General Ignacio H. Fotheringham, for example, recalling his youth when

he arrived in Buenos Aires from England around 1864–65, brings back a sense of the action:

The Hotel Oriental, nicknamed the "Tal," was the place. It was crowded with enthusiastic aristocrats, come to view dances with stop-pattern flourishes [*milongas de corte especial*], the mazurkas with "horizontal breaks" [*quebradas horizontales*], and passages with knees deeply bent [*agachadas*]. We "threw dust in the eyes" [i.e., deliberately challenged] of men from Retiro, guys who would counter with "check-out-my-body-and-my-look" [*válgame el cuerpo y la vista*].[12]

Novati and Cuello argue that by "milonga" Fotheringham probably meant popular dances in general, and so I have translated it. But there was no mistaking the fact that by this time "stopping and breaking" (*cortes y quebradas*) were imparting to imported dances a distinct creole flavor.

Toughs from Retiro, like most contenders, made boasts of their bodies. What they were doing seems cognate with hip-hop today: constant dance battles, strong boasting verses, and "breaking" to the floor in the dance (*quebradas horizontales*). This changed the habanera. They turned it into a force that would become the milonga, leading the way with key steps emergent, the cuts (*cortes*) and the breaks (*quebradas*). With these signature motions the youngbloods were actually extending the reach of candombe, the creolized aura of Kongo.

ROGUE COMMAS FOR HOT DANCERS: CORTES AND QUEBRADAS

Dancers in Kongo call sharp, sudden pauses cuts (*nzéngolo*). Cuts symbolize change (*dimbu kia nsóbolo*) in the sense that drummers challenge good dancers with sharp shifts in patterning to test their alertness and ability to improvise. An ngoma drummer, without warning, might confront a dancer with a cut like this: *mbrekete-mbrekete, pa!* or *mbrekete-mbrekete, ta!* The seasoned dancer knows what to do: stop on the *pa* or the *ta*, then immediately start up again, building an improvised sequence.

Returning to Argentina, two final notes—coded as the syllables *chan-chan*—announce the end of a milonga or tango. At this point the best dancers cut (*corte*) with a brilliantly held pose.

The syllables *chan-chan* derive from Ki-Kongo, from a standard dance phrase meaning "step it down" or "perform" (*tshia-tshia*).[13] This was creolized to chan-chan and cha-cha, in Kongo-influenced Cuba,[14] and to "chan-chan" in Argentina. So an idiom for pausing, directly translated from Kongo to the River Plate, from nzengolo to corte, took root in Buenos Aires. But when referring to posing, the concept transcends the Bakongo: it is also a criterion of fine dance among Mande, Akan, Dahomea, and Yoruba peoples in West Africa. Among the Akan of Ghana, "the timing of the last gesture is critical, the hallmark of fine dancers; if the dancer makes a mistake the people will jeer and make fun of him."[15]

Kongo performers sometimes translate a cut in the dance as a "knot" (kolo), uniting different passages of motion. Elders explain that "a halt in the dance ties two phrases together" (kanga i mu vaanga kolo).[16]

Tangueros similarly cut at the chan-chan, the two final notes of a milonga or tango, but they also cut fluently at quick pauses in the middle of a tango—at the internal chan-chans, as it were. Dancing milonga means cutting at the end. Dancing to tango, chock full of pauses, means knowing how to respond to endless rogue commas in the music.[17]

Turn now to quebrada, which means twisting the hips while bending the knees. It is very common in Kongo, where it can be called "weaving the hips and tying knots quickly" (tyenga ye kaanga makolo mu nabyu).[18]

Blacks in Buenos Aires kept up this move in Kongo candombes and later in informal dance clubs. From there it spread out, among working-class dancers, people whom the rich and the snobbish called medio pelo, "would be aristocrats."

But they were aristocrats. They were aristocrats of style. Some of their parents and grandparents had danced before elected kings and queens in the halls (salas) of candombes. There fancy dress matched fancy stepping. And the white toughs who mimed them dressed carefully, too, giving attention to homburgs, cravats, and striped pants.

Cutting and breaking turn up in black Cuba, to be echoed still later in South Bronx hip-hop. There are stops (cierres) and breaks to the floor galore in rumba and mambo. This, in turn, via Latinos in New York, led to freezes (sudden pauses) and breaking (horizontal floor work) in the choreography of hip-hop.

"Breaking" in rumba appears in the film Another Thin Man of 1939. A black rumbero, dancing with a rumbera, spins to the ground, then comes back up. Each time he goes down, his pattern is different. So the mazurkas that Ignacio Fotheringham witnessed in Buenos Aires in around 1865, with their horizontal breaks, relate to a history of black dance in the north.

In the process, the tempo got faster. Offbeats grew stronger. Néstor

Marconi, the gifted bandoneonista, has a phrase for what happened: "Milonga is an excited habanera" (*Milonga es una excitación de la habanera*).[19] How so? The original habanera divided into four pulses, in a standard two-four where every other note was stressed.

In becoming milonga, though, all four notes turned strong, as tempo was doubled. The music was aroused. In the speed of the phrasing, the strength of the first beat weakened the fourth. This gave an almost waltz-like feel to milonga: one-two-three (four), one-two-three (four), as against the explicitly sounding *one,* two, *three*-four of the slower habanera. Pablo Ziegler, the modern tango pianist, believes that the popularity of the polka in late-nineteenth-century Buenos Aires had a bearing in quickening the pace of milonga.

Perhaps in response to the ambiguity of the beat—but also, as we will see, to reconcile milonga to the three-beat rhythms of candombe—milonga dancers started inserting a third step over the first two beats of the measure. This created a cross-rhythm, the *milonga del traspié* (literally "stumble-step milonga"), taking three steps over two beats. Precisely when this happened remains in dispute. Some say early, in the late nineteenth century; others say the 1930s, in the time of Méndez. Mingo Pugliese argues that traspié was the 1940s inspiration of Arturo Intile, "which he worked out very swiftly" in the dance clubs of western Buenos Aires. Since each master would nuance traspié in his own private way, reinventing it again and again, all the above versions may be true.

In any event, whether early or late, offbeat phrasing of the footwork is Afro in bearing and style. It mirrors the black past as a quintessence of candombe. Star candombe dancers, in control of the beat, step both on, and between, the main pulses of the drum.

Ventura Lynch, writing in 1883, was the first to report the candombe-milonga connection. He also marked out the difference between malambo, the rural solo stamping-battle of the gauchos, and milonga, the emerging town couple dance: "If in the malambo the gaucho shows off all his agility, flexibility, and dexterity, in the milonga he glories in genius, sharpness, and quick subtle tricks."[20] In other words, malambo dancers stamp out more or less set figures to show off their stamina and repertoire, but milongueros challenge all comers by *improvised* sequences, extending the feistiness of payada and tapada.

Then Lynch made another distinction between malambo and milonga, one that has been quoted many times:

> Malambo is not sung; milonga is danced only by the tough guys [*compadritos*] of the city, who have created it as a burlesque of the dances that blacks

perform in their places of ritual. It is an extension of movement done to the drums of candombe.[21]

Lynch was contrasting gaucho solo dancers with the toughs of the city, practicing with themselves or moving with women, satirically dancing a mime of black motion. He meant, as the context makes clear, that milonga, as dance, is performed by compadritos as opposed to gauchos. He says, without evidence, that compadritos were the *only* persons who were dancing milonga. But he certainly was not saying that *all* dancers of milonga, at *all* times, were making fun of the blacks in their dancing. For some compadritos *were* black. Others were mulatto. In the competitive spirit that was dominant in dancing—*válgame el cuerpo y la vista,* as Fotheringham wrote—blacks would inevitably have excelled. They lived and inherited battles of aesthetic inspiration. It is absurd to think that only white toughs were capable of aggression and satire—as if Gabino Ezeiza had never existed, as if battles of dance were unknown to candombe.

Better to return to Lynch's critical finding: milonga is linked to candombe. If this were true among enthusiastic white dancers in the early 1880s, imagine the intensity in black situations. Candombe gives milonga its edge: syncopated, staccato, and upbeat. Nothing in the way that milonga is danced in 2005—whether by Afro-Argentine masters like Kely and Facundo Posadas and Carlos Anzuate, or by black-trained virtuosi like El Pibe Palermo, or by first-rate instructors like Livio Javier Catuara and his brother—remotely suggests a burlesque. El Pibe Palermo, while dancing, may make fun of fops or pretenders but never milonga itself.

We can clarify Lynch with one single factor: black people in Buenos Aires; blacks who kept on being black, impervious to white mimesis of their improvisatory splendor. For in the world of white vogue, tango "eclipsed" the milonga around 1906, when the "demise" of the dance was made fun of in a Buenos Aires revue, *Homburgs and High Hats.* That was that, as far as the white elite were concerned; they moved on to the next fad. But milonga *among blacks* just kept on rolling, in selected dancing clubs.

That spirit can surface in all-white situations. The brilliant bandoneonista Néstor Marconi, performing at the Club del Vino in Palermo on a Saturday night in the austral summer of 2000, suddenly drummed milonga on the side of his bandoneón. Women in the audience started swaying their shoulders. So did three men. Playing this beat, Marconi brought back some blackness, in the midst of an art music crowd.

PIANA TO TROILO

Milongas have had an electrifying musical impact. Friction between tradition and change clearly generated part of that current. The habanera beat might be the still turning point of milonga, the core of its music, but it was constantly challenged by forces from without, like changes in the tango, and within, the issue here being the creative restlessness of black innovators for whom dancing to the same steps was anathema.

Twentieth-century Argentine dance orchestras performed both tangos and milongas. They honored the two styles—though clearly favoring tango—when they played or recorded. The development of the milonga thus paralleled that of the tangos: from trios to orchestras, from intuition to training, from playing by ear to reading sheet music. Yet regardless of the changes, milonga stayed relatively black, a study in staccato self-expression. Its pulse stayed fast and its melodic accents stayed off-beat.

Key white composers honored this potency. First and foremost was the remarkable Sebastián Piana, born in Buenos Aires on November 26, 1903. In the 1930s, collaborating with the renowned lyricist Homero Manzi, Piana started composing candombe-milongas. In 1939 he even organized a band called the Orquesta Típica Candombe, using candombe drums. Inspired by—and perhaps envious of—the hemispheric boom in Afro-Cuban rumba and Afro-Brazilian samba in the 1930s and 1940s, he led, in his own words, a return to the "severity and onomatopoetic strength" of Argentina's own black traditions.[22]

Piana and Manzi's stream of compositions was largely responsible for a renaissance of milonga in the Buenos Aires dance world of the 1930s. The enthusiasm was in part a reaction against the tango canon of sadness that had been in circulation since the advent of tango-canción in 1917. Porteños fell in love again with the sass and celerity of milonga. There is a photograph of Piana, playing milonga on piano. Borges sits by his side, absorbed and approving.[23]

Piana was fascinated by 1940s Afro-Cuban "onomatopoeia"—such as *tumba y retumba la tumba, tumba y retumba la rumba* (roughly, "the dancer breaks and gets down, breaks and gets down in the rumba"). The phenomenon in rumba inspired the Argentine composer, who called on Manzi to write in that vein and to weave in strong themes that were local and black. One of these ventures was "Pena mulata" (The Pain of a Mulatto Woman), which Carlos di Sarli played in 1940. Another, from

1942, was "Papá Baltasar," Baltasar being the black wise man at Bethlehem, a favorite saint among Afro-Argentines.

But the real trigger for the milonga renaissance came earlier, from Piana's "Milonga sentimental," with lyrics by Manzi, from 1931:

> Varón, pa'quererte mucho
> varón, pa' desearte el bien
> varón, pa'olvidar agravios
> porque ya te perdoné.
> Tal vez no lo sepas nunca
> tal vez no lo puedas creer
> tal vez te provoque risa
> verme tirao a tus pies.

> *Man, I love you so much*
> *man, I wish you well*
> *man, forget that offense*
> *it's forgiveness I tell.*
> *Perhaps you'll never know*
> *perhaps it won't seem true*
> *perhaps you'll think it's funny*
> *when I throw myself at you.*[24]

This milonga spells out love from a woman's point of view and was, in fact, commissioned by a woman, Rosita Quiroga. Mercedes Simone sang it in 1933, stressing the repetitions of "man" and "perhaps" and making the song ring with tacit antiphony. Meanwhile the beat was straight habanera from beginning to end.

Francisco Canaro's version dates from the 1930s. There is a moment of pizzicati, some muted jazz trumpet, further expressions, then chan-chan, the milonga is over.

Listen to a later Canaro milonga, "Reliquias porteñas" (Things Left Over from Old Buenos Aires), recorded in 1938. The integration of habanera beat with orchestra is smoother. The strings are more active. The bandoneón avoids downbeats. Piano doubles bass, making things collective. In short, the instruments move in an acoustic parade, making time bright and communal.

Aníbal Troilo, grand bandoneonista, culminated this trend with the epochal milonga "La trampera" (Cheating Woman), which he recorded on August 21, 1962. It dates from a period when orchestras were smaller, the time of the *conjuntos reducidos* (reduced combos). Troilo plays in a quartet. The guitarist is the brilliant Roberto Grela. Also present are Héctor Ayala on guitarrón and Quicho Díaz on bass.[25] Troilo was famous for staggering his notes. His suspended accentuation worked a core organizing principle of black musical happening—he made it apply brilliantly in "Trampera." The song's syncopation meets other black stratagems: first, Troilo vividly strikes the side of his bandoneón, drumming a fast habanera. Then a walking bass enters. Troilo begins playing melody, hitting a backbeat, making the music swing even more. His offbeat is an A, the dominant, or V chord, in the key of D. It pushes like a piston, it pulls like a *biela* (connecting rod), like the indispensable parts that make engines run.

Grela, meanwhile, dots all this action with bright, sparing notes.

Troilo mixes several sources: habanera at fast tempo, jazz bass, art guitar, even a phrase from old samba, the accent of which falls on the rest at the end.

"La trampera" is a milonga tour de force. It is both porteño and carioca, retrospective and new. The beat shaking the notes in the kaleidoscope remains habanera. The richness of allusion rivals that of Stan Getz and João Gilberto, who in the very same year were subjecting bossa nova to similar complications. Two leading Buenos Aires tangueros, Kely and Facundo Posadas, often call for this piece when they wish to perform the milonga.

MILONGA IN MOTION: A DANCE MARKED FOR ARGUMENT

> The beat [is] lurking, dancing in all things whether you are conscious of its presence or not.
>
> —JOHN EDGAR WIDEMAN, *Hoop Roots* (2001)

> To dance the milonga, the way that it should be, season it strongly with candombe.
>
> —EL PIBE PALERMO, quoted in Luis Bruni, "El último compadrito"

There is no one step to milonga. Watch it danced, and the style will suggest itself, intimating its identity in rich variations but never reducing to one formula. Milonga emerges in cultural encounters that fuse. It is lived cultural theory, optimistic and amiable. To follow its motions, steps, and offbeats is to learn to connect roots with new voices, as Troilo did musically in "Trampera."

For Juan Carlos Copes, milonga combines "rapidity with marked syncopation" (*rapidez con gran síncopa*). Its runs (*corridas*) are made of figures that are happily repeated (*figuras que se repiten con alegría*).[26] This matches the perception of María Cieri, master of canyengue who independently suggests this for milonga: "a rapid habanera with runs full of figures that are strongly repeated."[27]

But milongas are not always fast, Facundo Posadas counters. There are rare interventions of the slow introspective feel of the tango. What is distinctive, in his opinion—regardless of tempo—is swing and suave feeling, plus a famous momentum that rarely stops. There are pauses in tango, Kely Posadas agrees, but not in milonga.

Milonga is a story in motion that stays in motion. As stated by El Pibe Palermo, one steps it down (*hay que pisar en todos los pasos*). Headlong momentum augments translation of difference into movement. Milonga works with fast-moving riffs and with countertime moments in which couples take three steps to two beats.

In November 2001 I watched Livio Javier Catuara, a genial instructor at Torquato Tasso Cultural Center in Buenos Aires, teach his young wards how to move to a clavelike pattern in milonga: one, two; one-two-three. Stepping was continuous, but Catuara twisted his body on the *two* of the last phrase and shot out his leg on the *three*. The two against three was Afro-Atlantic, as was the twist of the body, but the step on the three seemed balletic and European. This was a microcosm of milonga as mixture, a creole Esperanto of the night. More than speed or syncopation or forthright continuousness, the pleasure of milonga as dance is cultural interaction.

This leads to a third level of the concept milonga. First is milonga in the ancient Angolan sense of "argument" or "issue"—appropriately applied to the duels of payada and early milonga, where guys taunted guys with their strength and their bodies. Second is milonga in the pure Kongo sense, meaning "circling lines of dancers," superbly returned in the candombes of the River Plate. Milonga as circle lived on in the 1970s, when drunken white porteños forming conga lines used to shout out: *conga conga, conga, que siga la milonga* (party, party, party, let's keep the milonga going). They moved counterclockwise, ghosts from candombe.

But the third expression of the concept milonga is nothing less than "an autonomous creole theory for the reconciliation of cultures."

Esmeraldo Emeterio de Santana, black elder of the Nação Kongo-Angola in Bahia, Brazil, gives us a model with which to comprehend how a creole tradition gets on its feet, then exalts us:

"Angola" is a mixture of Cabinda, Mozambique, Munjola [Teke or Tio] and Kongo. It turned into what we ourselves call *milonga.* They mixed what they heard, what they saw, in the slave quarters where you had people of all nations. But whenever possible they worked to honor their ritual obligations. Everybody contributed a fragment and the result was a kind of patchwork. There wasn't a single nation performing these obligations any more but a mixture, a *milonga.*[28]

Milonga in this sense refers to reconciling cultures until the pieces all fit. Ritual common denominators emerge and take hold: build a drum, move the body, sing a song, honor ancestors. Milonga in this sense sees cultural difference not as predicament but as amiable argument, an argument solved by generosity, shared values, and celebratory spirit.

As a danced social tendency, milonga becomes critically intermediate. Witness how it blended solo processioning by candombe street dancers with the ballroom embrace position of the West.

In a drawing of February 1899, a candombe street drummer moves down the streets of Buenos Aires. Wearing a broad-brimmed hat on the back of his head, as well as shirt, pants, and leggings, he crosses one deeply bent leg over a correspondingly bent leg as he ambulates his way through the city (Plate 34). El Pibe Palermo, who was taught candombe by black friends and associates in the 1930s and 1940s, brings the same street idiom into the language of ballroom. A video document of him dancing at the Akarense dance hall in the 1970s shows him bending his knees, with accent and self-awareness and with a sharp little bounce each time he crosses his right foot over his left foot, then left over right, and so on (Plate 35). Palermo has in effect restored the old drawing to three dimensions, but he does this while embracing in Western ballroom style.

Another example: consider a stylish crossover, this time without knee flexion, flaunted by a solo black street candombe dancer with a duster in his hand in 1899. Then see this echoed in the work of the famous black tangueros Kely and Facundo Posadas, dancing milonga in 2000. The free arms of candombe once again lock into ballroom embracing, but the legs remain free, dotting a line with emphatic crossovers. Crossovers, in fact, are signatures in milonga.

PLATE 34

One final example: when dancing milonga, Facundo Posadas creatively vaunts a move that he observed a gifted black candombe stylist, Precinto, perform in the 1950s in the basement of the Casa Suiza: Precinto's step involved freezing one foot while inching the other forward, pushing out both palms to the side of his body as he did this.

In Facundo's milonga candombe, armwork once again vanishes, for his hands are now encircling his partner. But the stepping remains free, a way of weaving virtuosic variety into the ongoing flow of the action. Bending while cross-stepping, favoring crossovers, and freezing one foot while inching the other subtly forward are classic illustrations of the creolized diction of candombe as absorbed in the heavily black dance styles of milonga.

In all three of these instances, African solo dancing is absorbed in the two-person embrace. But certain foot patterns continue right on, regardless of the new contexts of ballroom and salon. Dancers become translators, reconciling styles from two different worlds. The situation is fluid and changing, European ballroom impacting on Kongo, Kongo distilling expressions from Russian Jewish dance.

As to the latter phenomenon, recent studies trace Russian and other Eastern European Jewish presences in the formation of tango music. It is an influence perhaps present as well in milonga, as symbolized by the frequency of a dazzling move, *la viborita* (the little snake), so called because

it winds and curves. Viborita is a move based on pivots, so another name for the move is "pivot run." There is a similar move in Eastern Europe called the "grapevine" so named because it curves and winds. It too is based on pivots. It is common in the group dancing of Eastern European Jews, for instance the hora: dancers lock hands and move in zigzagging, figure-eight patterns, constantly pivoting on the balls of their feet. Emergent in milonga, viborita becomes a

PLATE 35

danced incantation, luminously traced by the two partners across the floor. Just as African solo moves become partnered in milonga, the hora-like sequence may have been lifted out of group dancing and compacted to two dancers also.

In de Santana's sense of milonga as cultural fusion, shared moral values bind different black peoples together in the milongas of Bahia. But where were the equivalent theaters of creolization and fusion in Buenos Aires? The answer is black dance clubs. Here black dancers of candombe met black dancers of jazz, vals, and polka. But the main cultural engine was candombe.

Candombe dancing did not disappear with the closing of the salas, or for that matter with the death of the last of the societies' African-born members at the turn of the century. The intense candombe solo dancing, witnessed and drawn by Figari in the 1920s in the Barrio Sur of Montevideo, compacted the formal candombe of the late nineteenth century, with its four clear-cut sequences. By the 1940s, the four-sequence format had long since been replaced in Buenos Aires by freestyle expression, apart and improvised. But like all things creole, it both kept to continuities and took energy from change, becoming a new language. As Facundo Posadas recalls, "The candombe of today is not the candombe danced a long time ago. But the little that remained we put in milonga."

Where did blacks dance candombe and milonga in the twentieth century? In Montevideo they did so in certain *conventillos* (tenements) and in the 1920s at the Haraganes sin Producto club in the Barrio Sur, where Figari went to observe.

In Buenos Aires facets of candombe were absorbed into milonga at an Afro-Argentine dance club of the 1920s called the Reunión de Amigos, on Calle Montevideo, and later, between 1920 and 1930, at a place on Calle Azcuénaga.[29] Later still, in the 1950s, Carlos "El Negro" Anzuate danced milonga with a black colleague, Manuel García López, at the Mitre club, at 1332 Avenida Segurola in Monte Castro. In the same decade yet another black stylist, El Misto, danced a hot Africanizing milonga at the Club Buenos Aires.[30]

The unquestionable epicenter, though—the place where milonga most deeply took energy from candombe—was a space rented out by dance-loving blacks on the first floor and basement of the Casa Suiza at 254 Rodríguez Peña, between Perón and Sarmiento in Centro. They called it the Shimmy Club, in partial salute to black North American jazz culture. The Shimmy Club was active from the 1940s to the 1970s, essentially bridging the mid-twentieth century. The blend at all times was remarkable, because the rhythms of candombe and milonga are different. The drums of candombe overwhelm the ear in complex interlocks of three and four pulses, whereas milonga, the fast habanera, rolls out straight patterns of four.

In the 1940s key tango dance masters found ways of combining the three of candombe with the four of milonga: they inserted three steps over two. This was allegedly the origin of the *milonga del traspié,* and it was worked out by white artists like Petróleo and Arturito Intile, who were in touch with black circles, as well as by Afro-Argentine stars like Félix Luján, better known as El Negro Lavandina. So, at any rate, it is reported—but there are many stories about the origin of this step.

Meanwhile, candombe stepping wafted into the milonga at the Shimmy Club. The Shimmy, like the Harlem Savoy in the heyday of lindy, or the New York Palladium in the peak years of mambo, was a black cultural bastion. Both the Savoy and the Palladium had areas for ordinary dancers as well as "cats' corners" set aside for experts. So did the Shimmy, but for a deeper, spiritual reason: ordinary social dances—jazz, tango, vals—took place on the ground floor, but the basement, with paneled columns and a polished floor, was reserved for candombe and for the traditionalist black aristocracy. Consider a chapter in Alejandro Frigerio's book *Cultura negra en el cono sur* (Black Culture in Southern South America). A landmark study of the continuity of candombe in Argentina, it was the first work to signalize the importance of the Shimmy Club in the maintaining of that continuity, about which one of the participants recalled:

> In around 1973, 1974, I frequented the Suiza. There were tables where the prominent patriarchs were seated and where a powerful old black woman, La Negra San Martín, presided as well. [Prominent black families included] the Núñez, and the Lamadrid. And people danced.[31]

The tables, where the elders and others were seated, formed a circle around the dance floor. In this circle blacks danced "contrapuntally" (*haciendo contrapuntos*), in the same call-and-response manner that J. Van Wing witnessed in Kongo in the 1930s. A woman dancing solo was answered by a man dancing solo; a man alone was answered by a woman in front of him. Couple followed couple in an atmosphere of laughter and light conversation. This went on until midnight. Then suddenly:

> All the old blacks came out to dance candombe. They would not allow a single white person to remain. At the stroke of midnight [the candombe]

began. The elders would start shouting: *e e e, bariló!* which meant "bring on the drummers." If there were whites they would banish them, shouting "all whiteys out!" [*afuera los chongos*]. Then all the old blacks danced candombe in earnest, singing *e e e, bariló, e e e, bariló.* (Informant mimes, at this point, looking from one side to another, with one hand held over an eye, like a visor, and the other hand akimbo at the waist.)[32]

But *e e e bariló* did not mean "bring on the drummers"; nor was hand-on-brow a mere scouting gesture. In fact, it was normally executed as an alternating, mirroring gesture: right hand over eyes, then left hand, repeated and repeated, as demonstrated by a former Shimmy Club regular, Tete Salas, in 2003 (Plate 32). As we have seen, they were matters of ritual, kept from the *zongo* (gunshots), the *muzungu* (whiteys) Central African words fusing "danger" with "outsiders" that Argentine blacks had apparently creolized into *chongo.*

The phrase *e e e bariló* clearly derives from the Kongo lament *e, e, e, mbadi lo* (oh, alas), likely reinforced by a similar phrase, *e, mbadi ona* (oh, alas).[33] And in Kongo, dancers singing such phrases during a funeral may place their hand on their brow, making a sign of depression (*kyaadi*). Or they may make a sign of shielding the eye, "to blot out a picture of sadness."[34]

Starting at midnight was ritually significant. In Kongo this time was the "noon of the dead." It was time gone beyond—the sun was now shining on the world of the ancestors. Shimmy Club elders, by waiting until after midnight to perform the candombe, were dancing in the world of their forefathers. So Bakongo would have thought, and the more ritually wise black porteños are likely to have been dancing with the same conviction, to judge from the frequency with which a Kongo term for the other world, *kalunga,* turned up in their rituals. In the late nineteenth century River Plate blacks would shout out *Calunga güe!* a creole expression of the Ki-Kongo *Kalunga, Ngwe!* meaning "Hail the other world, our mother!"

After midnight, in this basement dancing area, the other world sometimes answered. Outwardly recreational, candombe became *makinu ma songa,* dancing to manifest ancestral presence. Buenos Aires blacks became momentarily possessed by the spirits of the dead.

Facundo Posadas remembers being admonished as a child in around 1945 not to bother people when they fell into this state. He was told that "a saint had grabbed her" (*la agarró el santo*) or that a spirit had taken him (*le tomó el santo*).[35] Posadas and other black children who frequented the Casa Suiza at that time—Puchi Zambrano, Pochi Luna, Osvaldo Marín (later famous as the boxer who beat the champion Monzón), and Tete Salas—were eavesdropping on a spiritual setting. Black saints came marching in, shaping and valorizing a universe of dance.

It is surely no coincidence that all of these children became fine tangueros and, in the case of Salas, one of the leading interpreters of candombe today.

Posadas remembers saints dancing barefoot, like the Kongo celebrants who danced before Rosas in 1838. A tall and imposing black man, Precinto, took off his shoes when dancing the tango. Posadas remembers him, dancing with hands held in front of his body, palms parallel to the floor (*lembika mooko*). From time to time he would push out both hands in front of his body (*empujando así con las manos para afuera*) or bring them both in to his heart, like the dance leader of n'kwanga in North Kongo. Sometimes in the 1950s he would push out both hands to one side while freezing one foot and inching the other forward, like *teeza maza* in Kongo.

The vitality of Precinto's dancing, improvised from various sources, taught Posadas and others that beauty of motion bursts through frontiers. That quality gave candombe momentum. It immersed it in pleasure and timelessness, a timelessness emerging in the return of the saints and the spirits. Respect for these values, like the undying respect for ritual obligations in Bahia, built social cohesion at the Shimmy Club. Facundo Posadas remembers:

> In the Casa Suiza I saw everything danced, everything black and rhythmic. I saw a lot of candombe dancing. It was different from the candombe of Uruguay. Black Uruguayans dance candombe in their shoulders. We dance it down in the hips.[36]

He demonstrates, taking two steps to the left, two steps to the right, rolling his shoulders in sympathy with his hips, weaving his hips in relation to his feet. Rolling the shoulders is *mayembo,* pluperfect expression of spiritual presence in Kongo. Posadas's undulation is total and snake-like. He remembers—and demonstrates—the "scouting" gesture, with alternate right and left hand held above eyes, rephrasing the Central African gesture of grief (*kyaadi*).

Other Kongo dance motions, alive in the body memory of black Buenos Aires, included leaning forward and leaning back (*yinama, yekuka*), circular pelvic motions (*tyenga*), and stylized modes of rhythmical walking (*tangalala*).

Candombe line- and circle-dancing had apparently vanished by the time Facundo Posadas came in contact with the tradition. But blacks put quintessences in the milonga. Eighth notes fostered short steps. With rhythmic erudition, star dancers at the Shimmy danced the milonga contratempo, "playing," says Posadas, "inside the time."
Black saints danced candombe in the basement. Talented persons danced the tango on the first floor. Milonga was the dance that reconciled floors, fusing two modes of pure action.

Candombe flared with crossover steps, plus backward-and-forward moves that dancers threaded along the lines of their motion like pearls. So did milonga. This stylized release of the energy of the body attracted onlookers. Milonga quick-stepping impressed two gifted songwriters, Dante Gilardoni and Raúl Capablanca, who revisited the style in the words to their milonga "Taquito militar" (Military Snap), which they wrote in 1953:

Al compás de esta milonga
vuelvo a ver igual que ayer
un bailar de meta y ponga
y un vivir para querer.

Aquel ritmo compadrito
marcábamos así
un paso atrás por aquí
otro avance más por allá
la sentada limpia y después
viene el taconeo final.

At the sound of this milonga
I see, as if yesterday,
the powerful moves, of women
with men, living for love.

In time with the hipsters
mark out the moves:
back one step, here
forward one step, there
she sits on your thigh,
then hit the strong heel-stamp.[37]

This nostalgic milonga brings back street fusions added to the Kongo influences in the Shimmy Club. Gaucho heel-stamping comes in from the country. Andalusian taconeo meets the improvised sentadas (a brief seating of the woman on her dancing partner's thigh) of the city. The seating of the woman on the man's thigh seems a playful rephrasing of the fleeting strong contacts of bumbakana. Riffs of small steps, backward and forward, recall similar insertions in the Carnival parades of candombe. Return to the Shimmy Club. There was more to the black action there than candombe and milonga. There was vals, there was tango, and there was jazz:

> At the Casa Suiza I learned candombe, milonga, and jazz. There were always two orchestras. The típica played tango, milonga, and vals. The jazz band played swing. Sometimes there was a característica, a band that played everything, jazz, mambo, paso doble, bolero, and boogie.[38]

Alternating with típica music, there were bands that played swing, Afro-Cuban, and blues. The three musics Troilo combined in "La Trampera"—habanera, jazz, and old samba—mirrored the cultural pandemonium that raged on both floors of the Shimmy Club. Not only that but, as the gifted Argentine scholar Ricardo Rodríguez Molas points out, further African influences flowed into tango and milonga from jazz.[39]

What is the point of living in a city if you can't take its poetic measure? Borges did. So did Blázquez and Piazzolla. But so did the black milongueros. The masters of milonga made sense of Buenos Aires with the taconeos of gauchos, the knee-bending crossovers of old black processions, and the pivoting runs—viboritas—that hinted of European hora. They were dancing an ode to both creoles and immigrants.

Milonga took energy from candombe in basement settings, on Rodríguez Peña in Buenos Aires, at Gaboto and Salvador in Montevideo. In the most famous of his "fictions," Borges wrote of a miraculous basement on Calle Garay in Buenos Aires, the street named after the founder of the city. It harbored an "aleph," a bright shining crystal that harbored a view of every place and every moment in history.

But the alephs of black basements were real. They sheltered the past that came in with black saints. They sheltered the present with tango and jazz. Their eye was also on waltz and on lindy.

This alephlike power, bringing country to city, north to south, Europe to America, gave dancers confidence. They could read Buenos Aires. They created a crystal to defy time itself.

TACKING AGAINST THE WIND: THE MILONGA
OF THE MASTERS

> I'm a true milonga dancer because I live every note.
>
> —LAMPAZO (November 1995)
>
> I dance milonga with hand, face, and body.
>
> —EL PIBE PALERMO (February 2002)

Begin with José María Baña, more famously known as El Pibe Palermo. He was born in the barrio of La Boca on November 30, 1921, in a house near the corner of Brandsen and Del Cancero. Handsome even in his eighties, Pibe and his wife, Norma del Carmen Soto Mayano, invest their milonga with playful assurance and aesthetic cunning (*picardía*). They staccato their steps. They transform them: walking transmutes into zigzagging, crossovers end with an air step. Sometimes Pibe's work takes on a Chaplinesque quality, as when he makes fun of the vanity of a dandy by smoothing down his eyebrows, or taps on his knee as if telling his leg what to do next. The truth of his milonga lies in the details.

Jealous of Pibe's stature, rivals claim "he can't even 'mark' [lead] a woman properly." But Pibe seeks intensity, not conventional leading. As his wife, Norma, remarks:

> Pibe breaks all the boundaries when he's dancing because he feels music so much he goes into another world. He comes out of time's tunnel to improvise wildly. . . . My whole life is dedicated to attempting to follow him. He becomes a velocity he's not even aware of, that carries me into the air.[40]

When Pibe bends down, sweeps out a hand, and shoots out a foot, sometimes he looks like Moraes, famed black master of the Brazilian martial art capoeira, dancing an Angola-inflected move called the *ginga*. His milonga *is* milonga, a cultural argument, with counterpoised elements—air steps and satire and Chaplin and down-dancing. Much of this is Afro. He takes pride in candombe.

In his youth Pibe hung out with black dancers. He studied them, idolized them, became one with their style. One afternoon in around 1937 a black friend, Miguel "El Negro" Ortiz, came up to him, saying "Poroto

[Pibe's adolescent nickname, meaning "bean"—he was lean], I'll come by tonight, for you and your cousin, if you like—we're going to the tango practice of Alfredo Núñez." Núñez was a black master who had inherited the style of El Negro Santillán. Pibe said yes and passed through the door of his fate.[41]

The practice took place at the Academia Hidalgo at 780 Calle Hidalgo in the Caballito barrio, between Almagro and Flores. There were two bandoneones. Hipsters were everywhere, trying out moves and challenging one another. El Negro Pavura (Black Dread), a famous Afro-Argentine dancer from Bajo Palermo, was there; he and Núñez traded dancing with a woman, La Peti, who had won their respect by mirroring whatever they threw at her. Pavura, Núñez, and another black, nicknamed "El Mocho," were also involved in hot Afro-Brazilian maxixe, which they danced with great flair.

Pibe met the two men and their partner. They liked him. He had a talent for riffing, which is essential for milonga. He had *pinta* (good looks). He had poise. Pibe eventually became a star pupil of Alfredo Núñez. (He also trained with his father.) Among the black cognoscenti of the Shimmy Club, Alfredo Núñez was famous for his elegant presentation. He opened up a whole world to young Pibe, a world tracing back to candombe.

Pibe kept practicing tango and milonga, dancing to old 78s on his parents' Victrola. He rehearsed in his mother's parlor, "working out things like taconeo, ta-ta." He soon had his following, including Vicente "El Flaco" Plá, who danced with a woman named Elvira and who partnered the great Cachafaz in the Cine Londres, where they danced as a male couple. As Pibe recalls:

One day when I was dancing milonga, strongly candombeized, the way it should be danced, in comes my father and he sees us. There I was, turning milonga into candombe like one extra black person, with El Negro Ortiz and El Flaco Plá. Dad said: "No! Stop! My kid's turning black right in front of me!" Flaco Plá stood up for me: "Aw, let him do it. The kid knows his stuff!"[42]

In 1960 Pibe took his black expertise into film, dancing milonga to a trio of flute, violin, and guitar in Leopoldo Torre Nilson's movie *Un guapo del '900* (A Tough Guy of 1900). His eagerness is palpable. He gives us a taste: a quick back-and-forth, a light skipping segment, a swaying of shoulders as in a step called rock-a-bye baby (*cunita*), and a single fine air step, traced with a foot off the ground. His partner is the beautiful mulatta dancer Rosario Blanco. She ganchos one leg around him, falls into a sentada on his thigh, and they spin. It is a sample from a larger horizon, steps drawn in air (*dibujando en el aire*), show-off motions (*firuletes*), break patterns (*quebradas*), and "violence," vividly flickering moves, like the "electric-shock" sequence *calambre*.

Video footage shows Pibe dancing roughly ten years later at the Club Akarense. His arsenal of moves was by then even richer; performing milonga, he endlessly improvises runs and cross-steps, viboritas with small pivots (*ochitos*); with a copious smile he inserts a Charlestonish, pivoting side step, borrowed from jazz via his father and Alfredo Núñez.

In one striking sequence he flexes his knees, sharp and staccato, while crossing his legs going forward (Plate 35). El Negro Pavura did this step and inspired him. Some call it "scissors" (*tijeras*); it comes from candombe. Blacks danced it in the streets of Buenos Aires in 1899 (Plate 34). One of the ultimate sources was Kongo, where, to this day, persons dance forward, bending the legs while at the same time sharply crossing them (*weti diata ye malu ma betama va komosi mabindama*) in a stylized curtsy. *Betama* (bending) while *mabindama malu* (crossing the legs) manifests honor to the ancestors.

Back to the Akarense. Pibe races toward the camera and drops *taconeos* (heel-stamps). He makes the notes visible, one step to a syllable, one step to a note, in a very black way: this is *milonga hablada, milonga conversada con los pies* (talking milonga, milonga spoken with feet). In one single flow he reconciles five different dances: Charleston, candombe, taconeo, jazz, and viborita. The transformation is amazing: person into polyglot.[43]

PEPITO AND SUZUKI AVELLANEDA

Equally exciting is the milonga of Pepito and Suzuki Avellaneda, who traveled in triumph to Paris in 1995 to perform in the revue *Paris, New York, and Buenos Aires*. Women loved to milonga with Pepito; bighearted, jovial, and heavyset, he made them look good. Often he'd pause in a tangoish way, inviting a woman to spin out in orbit, tracing orchidlike lines round his large frame.

María Nieves danced with Pepito in Toronto in 1990 and remembers *mucha picardía* (a lot of playfulness, a lot of novel moves) in his milonga. Implying black influence, Facundo Posadas suggests that *picardía* in milonga stems from candombe: "it means taking liberty with form, sudden improvisations, challenging your partner with new sequences."

Avellaneda's playfulness comes out in small jokes, like shining his shoe on the side of his leg, or taking a woman's hand only to rock fast cross the room. Like Pibe Palermo, he inserted Charlestonish side steps with a mock-modest air, as if this were all he could do. When he came to viborita, he would face his partner and they would sweep across the floor in their own bravura rendering of this pivot-run sequence. He died in 1998.

LAMPAZO

I met Lampazo (whose given name is José Vásquez) on November 26, 1995, his sixty-eighth birthday. We became friends. He invited my colleague Alejandro Frigerio to videotape his style of dance: "Milonga is my forte," he said. Indeed it was. Lampazo, then a star performer at Sin Rumbo in Villa Urquiza, had developed a milonga admired across town.

Lampazo worked inside time. He translated seconds into art and minutes into emotion. He lifted his feet stylishly. He brought them down stylishly. He crossed his feet while swaying his shoulders. Dancing to d'Arienzo's 1935 recording of the milonga "De pura cepa" (The Genuine Article), he started out athletically: crossover, crossover, crossover. Suddenly the bandoneón squealed a sharp, high-pitched note. Lampazo caught that immediately, twisting his chest, crossing his hands, and bending his knees going forward. Now he was swaying from side to side, inserting *cunita* ("rock-a-bye baby," also called *hamaquita,* "the little hammock") into milonga. This step resembles the "little boat" (*botecito*) move that swept black Havana with mambo around 1945. There were two or three bars of this phrasing. Then he moved to the left, sliding 1,2,3, 1,2,3, 1,2,3, translating triplets into footwork. It was a tour de force reading of rhythm.

CARLOS ANZUATE

Carlos Alberto Anzuate is a legend, linking milonga to deep black achievement. He was born in the Flores barrio on May 21, 1930; the first house he lived in was at Francisco Bilbao and Culpina. He started dancing at the age of twelve in Almagro, near Palermo. Later he attended practice sessions at the Luso Argentino club on Calle Calderón in Devoto; here blacks made up steps, and Anzuate trained with Afro-Argentine colleagues like El Negro Manuel (Manuel García López).

Anzuate was inspired by the great 1940s innovators—El Negro Lavandina, Petróleo, Finito, Vasquito, El Pescá—whom he saw in action at the famed Club Nelson, not far from the intersection of Avenida Jonte and Avenida Segurola in Monte Castro. In the process he developed his own laid-back manner.

That style is a cool milonga made up of small steps, not telegraphed but

PLATE 36

delicately revealed. Twisting his heels, Anzuate gingerly moves backward, then onward, with short traveling steps. He kicks out both feet very subtly. His hips move discreetly. He kicks, twists, and glides very quietly. When he does a crossover, sometimes he drags it.

In many of these maneuvers he is moving his feet a half-inch at a time, making his milonga unique. In crossovers, kicks, side slides, and shuffling, Anzuate plays the floor as a candombe moment, shading ideas with miniature expressions and play. *Epa!* (Phew!) cried out his Afro-Argentine colleague, Facundo Posadas, watching him dance with exasperated admiration. Posadas studied with Anzuate for nearly ten years.

Anzuate is not only one of the greats of milonga but a historically important teacher of tango. He plays the role generously. Back in the late 1940s, noticing a young Juan Carlos Copes at the Club Nelson, he offered to show him a spin to the left (*giro a la izquierda*) and other steps. In 1997 he married Eufemia Delsa Cerallo, whose father was a tanguero and a friend of Cachafaz (Plate 36). When Anzuate dances at Sunderland in 2005, knowing couples slow down and watch. They want to absorb what he's doing.

KELY AND FACUNDO POSADAS

Clara Raquel Lamdan and Carlos Facundo Posadas Beard, known professionally as Kely and Facundo, are famous top dancers of milonga. They are as fluent in jazz dance as they are in milonga and tango. This deepens their impact.

Honoring the crossovers in Afro-Argentine milonga, Kely and Facundo season them strongly with improvised departures: crossover with a stamp, crossover with a heel-tap, crossover with a slide, crossover with a heel-tap, crossover with the right foot drawing accents on the floor. Viborita appears. Facundo will set a course for three repetitions of this run to the side in small pivots (*marcará ochitos en tres corridas de costado*). Their milonga locks style into sequence: open-close-*forward*-move, open-close-*backward*-move. Spatial contrast is continuous: figures forward, figures sideways, figures straight ahead. Sometimes, when moving, they hit the fourth accent with a differing design: one-two-three-*pose*, one-two-three-*charge*, one-two-three-*twist*, one-two-three *break*. As Facundo explains, "It's a game—three changes of weight and then a stop on a four. We play on the four, then return to the sequence."[44]

Sometimes they weave in a jazz sequence—lindy swing-outs and swing-ins—that they fit to the beat of milonga. Or Facundo suddenly dances apart, gets behind Kely, looms over her body, and mirrors her movements—a step from candombe. These moments of play unite them to Pibe, Lampazo, and Anzuate.

Kely and Facundo essentially dance to a fast habanera, but it always turns into milonga as they leap across cultures. They enter the world to take joy in its differences.

CONCLUSION: TACKING AGAINST THE WINDS OF CHANGE

Buenos Aires and Montevideo honor the importance of tango's co-presence by calling the place where people dance tango a milonga and calling devoted dancers milongueros. Milonga shares with tango old moves, like ochos and sentadas and corridas, but it's faster and more festive, in recollection of candombe street dancing. Two motifs remain constant—pivot runs and twists of the torso. Crossovers and side-to-side swaying are also important. A milonga without them is like a rider without spurs.

Pibe Palermo twists, sweeps, and heel-stamps; he becomes a candombero when bending and crossing his legs. Kely and Facundo Posadas, freezing one foot while moving the other, cite candombe as danced at the Shimmy Club. Lampazo's milonga has black-oriented passages, twist, sway, and metrics. Pepito Avellaneda inserts tango through sudden quick pauses, breaking the ongoing flow of milonga. But he too loves pivots, short runs, and accents.

The New York art critic David Frankel compares milongueros to navigators in sailboats, tacking against the wind. Dancers translate strong winds from Africa and Europe into maneuvers that lead to a creole safe harbor.

Over the past one hundred years Argentina has undergone—and is undergoing—severe economic and political dislocation. In the teeth of all this, dancers keep going with milonga. They danced it in the Depression. They are dancing it now. Optimism in this form is healing.

Abel Bruno Versacci's woodcut *Milonguita,* dated 1977 (Plate 37) puts some of these truths into action. Three worlds are shown: an orchestra playing tango or milonga, a couple dancing in a red spotlight, and a dance-hall devotee—a *milonguita*—sitting alone with a

PLATE 37

glass of red wine. She crosses her arms demurely, awaiting her lover. Versacci breaks the picture into large vivid fragments. The orchestra plays on top of a line. The couple dances in a ray of red light. The milonguita sits alone in a white oval space. But soon she will rise in the arms of her partner, balance music with dance, and transcend these divisions with spirit.[45]

To provide some perspective on the narrative of this dance: We saw rural payada turn urban milonga. We saw jousting in strong raplike verses and b-boy-like battles of dance. We understand milonga through comparison with hip-hop because both share competitive poetry and competitive action. But milonga has a life of its own. Its blackness is legendary. Many milonga steps derive from candombe, translating its solo moves into partnering patterns but retaining the black body line.

Contrasting traditions were not seen as incommensurable; they were languages to love and to master. Talented dancers like Anzuate, Lampazo, the Posadases, and Pibe Palermo lived this felicity. They could *pandikisa,* a term from Angola, meaning "to connect words" and in the process to recover oneself.

6.

DANCING ON THE EDGE:
THE EARLY TANGO
CALLED CANYENGUE

Reflected in the water: the moon above
reflected in our hips: canyengue
reflected in wild longing: the way we love.

—ENRIQUE SANTOS DISCÉPOLO AND JUAN CARLOS
MARAMBIO CATÁN, "El choclo" (The Green Ear of Maize, 1947)

Canyengue is a rhythm where you don't take long steps
because, if you do, you're stepping outside the music.

—MARÍA CIERI (January 1999)

Teresa Pereyra, an Argentine artist, painted early tango in her *Tango canyengue* (1998). Two dancers perform at the edge of the city, dancing on a dock in La Boca (Plate 38). The Avellaneda bridge, in the distance, tells us where we are. Siting canyengue at the edge of the port, Pereyra reminds us that it emerged on the margins.[1]

PLATE 38

According to legend, early protagonists of this stylized tradition included black sailors. Pereyra shows two men of the sea, observing the action. One is black. The musicians, too, combine races—a blonde on guitar and a mulatto on bandoneón—and so do the dancers, an Afro-Argentine hipster (*compadrito negro*) tangoing suavely with a white woman. She wears a short skirt and a short blouse. (If the setting is around 1900, when canyengue emerged, her dress is an anachronism.) He bends her back dramatically. Beyond in the harbor, rope, chain, and crane echo the slant of her body: the machinery of the city rolls with the tango. The dance becomes part of the port—indeed, a boat in the harbor is named *Tango*.

Pressing his cheek against hers, the dancer is dressed as a man-about-town: shoes with special heels, light blue suit, rich white cravat made of silk. Black dancer, black musician, black sailor—Pereyra drops hints about origins.

There is no stronger allusion, however, than the word *canyengue* itself: it originated in Kongo and Angola discourse on dance, where it meant "melt to the music," "step it down," "start to party."[2] Argentina retains awareness of this history. The dancer Marta Antón, for instance, saying canyengue means "rhythmical walking" (*caminar cadencioso*), identifies it as a gift of the blacks to the culture of Argentina.[3]

Back to Pereyra. The man pulls the hand of the woman to his waist. This, plus the cheek-to-cheek, is canyengue.

So what *is* the dance called canyengue? How do we know it when we

PLATE 39   PLATE 40

see it? First, it's the dance that emerged in the period of "the old guard" (*la guardia vieja*), among the first tango dancers during the first two decades of the twentieth century. Marta Antón remarks, "Canyengue is the pure essence of the beginning of tango around 1900" (*la esencia pura del comienzo del tango alrededor de 1900*).[4]

What is the dance's structure? I posed this question to Lampazo, the late and legendary tanguero of Villa Urquiza, one night in the winter of 1995. He answered with a gesture: he pressed his fingertips together at an inward-leaning angle. The bottoms of his hands flared out like a bell. This was canyengue, bent forward and crouching; like Antón, he dated it to around 1900 (Plate 39). Then he held up his hands a second time, bringing them in close to each other, positioning them vertical and parallel (Plate 40). This was *tango liso* (smoothed-over tango), which emerged about 1905–10, according to Jorge Novati and Inés Cuello, historians of Argentine dance.[5] He was diagramming, at the same time, *tango de salón*, the tango as it was codified in a dance instruction book published by Nicanor Lima in 1916. In both *liso* and *salón*, dancers hold the back straight.

The same resolutely vertical torso defines *tango criollo* (native tango), the alternate form of the earliest tango that emerged, for one instance, among the Argentine-born compadritos and the creolized Italian immigrants of La Boca. Five tantalizing photographs of tango criollo appeared in *Caras y Caretas* on February 7, 1903. They show the noted payador and milonguero Arturo de Navas practicing tango with a man. Most of the steps are tango criollo, upright and piquant. Once, however, Navas's partner bends his knees deeply, flexing them dramatically, as he crosses one foot over the other. This is candombe, the step called the "scissors" (*tijeras*). We have here a quebrada, a down-flexing break.

De Navas appeared again in *Caras y Caretas* on August 15, 1903, this time dancing tango with a woman. At one point he presses his thigh against hers. It's a fragment of canyengue caught in the format of tango criollo.

Canyengue is a constant quebrada. The knees keep on bending; the bodies stay "down" as the couples revolve, each inclined against the other's chest. "The pose does not vary" (*la pose no varía*), María Cieri informs us, "except when we make a figure called *la hamaquita* ("the little hammock," a side-to-side rocking (*balanceo*) or a run to the side (*corrida de costado*).[6]

Dancing "down" is culturally black, going back to Pellegrini's painting and beyond. Emphatic leaning is Afro-inspired, too. Bending forward or back recurs in a number of Afro-Atlantic dances: Caribbean limbo, U.S. cakewalk, U.S. drum major strutting, Kongo n'kwanga.

Things changed in Argentina. Leaning, performed solo and apart by Afro-Argentines, met the two-person lean of the polka. The polka embrace brought a great deal of pleasure, intensifying the action with feeling and touch. Lampazo, pressing fingertips, was abstractly diagramming nothing less than the handing-over (*entrega*) of the body: cheek to cheek, chest to chest, and—remembering de Navas—thigh to thigh.

That intense body contact has inspired local poets. Witness Atilio Jorge Castelpoggi's 1991 "Buenos Aires mi amante" (Buenos Aires, My Lover):

> From the curve of my body I loved you.[7]

And Luis Luchi's 1964 "Tango Apology":

> Tango, no one lets you be ingenuous . . .
> the will to dance takes over,
> holding tight, closing eyes
> as in the culminating moment of desire.[8]

The canyengue embrace involves its own logic. She falls on his chest. He falls on *her* chest. The pressure is shared as both bend their knees. Should one partner step back, so dancers argue, both would fall down. María Cieri defines the *entrega* (the surrender to the pattern) as "melting

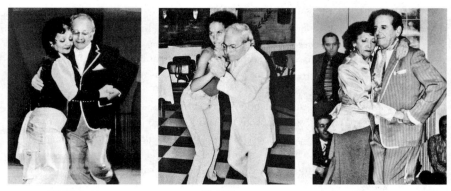

PLATE 41   PLATE 42   PLATE 43

into another half to make a whole" (*derritiendo, con otra mitad, por hacer un todo*). And what does it *feel* like? María sighs. "It's giving yourself over to love, it's understanding that nothing is more powerful."[9]

The blend is extraordinary: love in the Western world (cheek to cheek, chest to chest, thigh to thigh) combines with African close-to-earth motion ("performing from a crouch, knees flexed, body bent at the waist").[10] This is clearly so in the Cieri-school style of canyengue (Plate 41). Lampazo's style is even more African: he loved the crouch, knees bent, bottom out (*cola afuera*), torso inclined forward, and face frozen (*cara fea*, "ugly face") (Plate 42).

Styles vary.[11] Manolo "El Gallego" Salvador and Marta Antón generally move without the *cola afuera* thrust and also perform with a slight smile, bypassing the *cara fea* as well (Plate 43). Lampazo's partner's pose, though, is intriguingly close to the "original stomp" of West African dancing: loose, bent, and *down*.

Remarkably, two centers of gravity emerge in canyengue: the lean on the chest and the feet on the ground. "We lean," says María Cieri, "but we also bend down to the earth." In this close, compact form they dance with the small steps (*pasos cortos*) that flow as a consequence of the *ritmo cuadrado*—the tight choppy beat of tango pre-1925, which cayengueros prefer as their dance music. They like compositions like Manuel Gregorio Aróztegui's "El apache argentino" (1913), Francisco Pracanico's "Pampa" (1917–18), and Tuegols Rafael's "Zorro gris" (1920), plus early Francisco Canaro.

Afro-Argentine masters El Misto and El Negro Pavura were prominent among the early stars of canyengue. They emphasized stops and descents:

breaks (*quebradas*), cuts (*cortes*), and knee-bends (*flexiones*). Strong beats inspired them—they improvised when the rhythm was decisive.

Around 1916 in the Montmartre cabaret in Buenos Aires, one of the founders of canyengue as music, the remarkable Afro-Argentine bassist Leopoldo Thompson, while playing for Francisco Canaro, started striking the strings of his instrument "with his bow and his left hand in combination with the [beat of the] piano and the bandoneón, on and off the beat."[12]

Nor was this the only instance of a dominant percussive philosophy. The swing of the black guitarist Luciano Ríos, in Juan "Pacho" Maglio's band in 1912–13, is superbly audible (on Bandoneón EBCD 36). Between 1900 and 1910, a *tano* (Italo-Argentine) named Ernesto Ponzio is said to have intensified pizzicati in the playing of violin: instead of plucking his strings with one single finger, as in the classically trained manner, he strummed with all fingers but the thumb, attacking his violin as if it were a black banjo.[13] In fact, a banjolike violin is clearly audible, for a few fleeting seconds, in Argentina's first sound film, *Tango*, made in 1933. This challenged the dancer El Cachafaz, who immediately began to improvise. Canyengue on the bandstand sparked canyengue on the floor.

Meanwhile, blacks kept on improvising. The dancer-historian Petróleo documents one clear-cut contribution: "the blacks modified posture—they carried the hand down to the level of the hips."[14] White toughs, he added, picked up on this trait, and on the black manner of making stylish runs (*corridas*) across the floor. Carrying the right hand of the woman down at the man's waist remains part of canyengue to this day.

The short steps (*pasos cortos*) of canyengue follow the beat. "It's a rhythm," says María Cieri, "that does not permit taking long steps because, if you do, you're stepping outside of the music." "In tango de salon," adds Manolo Salvador, "one can bypass [*obviar*] the beat, but this is ordinarily not so in canyengue."

Taking small steps to choppy quarter and eighth notes recalls dancing in Congo-Brazzaville. Consider the Kuyu *kano*, a woman's circle dance celebrating the birth of twins, recorded in the 1940s. Two quarter notes sound on a gong, followed by a quarter rest, followed by two eighth notes, followed by a measure of rest and the repeat. The beat is brief but drives and compels. Women dance to it, taking short steps.

Canyengue is also distinguished—and this is critical—by an African-inspired sense of inner pulse. This gift, also known as "metronome sense," involves dancing to an inner rhythmic common denominator, regardless of what is sounding in the music. Masters of canyengue dance to a timeline held firmly in their minds. The late Rodolfo Cieri, when making a *corrida de frente* (run to the front), danced 1, 2, 1, 2, 3, 1, 2, 1, 2, 3. He moved against the beat of the tango. In Afro-Cuban terms, he was dancing "in clave," the strict two-bar artery of son and mambo. Moving to a beat in the mind is common in Afro-Atlantic dancing.

To maintain variety, Rodolfo and María sometimes dropped clave and followed the beat:

> In runs to the front there is counter-time, 1-2; 1-2-3. In runs to the side, forward or back, there is not, it's 1-2; 1-2. It's also 1-2 when we rock side-to-side, in the figure we call *hamaquita* [the little hammock].[15]

This sophisticated pulse consciousness almost certainly flowed into canyengue from candombe and milonga at the end of the nineteenth century.

The main pose of canyengue, down, tight, and trim, was strong at the start of the century. One way we know this is via foreign reflections. A Parisian tango postcard from 1910–13 confronts us with an unmistakable image: we see two women, cheek to cheek, chest to chest, knees deeply bent, hands held down low, and tails sharply out (Plate 44). The picture is posed, and the arms are European in their stiff presentation, yet canyengue experts find traces of authenticity here. María Cieri: "Hands are placed low, they move chest to chest, bending their knees very sharply." Marta Antón: "Definitely shows some traces of influence— knees bent, hands low, and they are pressing together their heads and their chests." Waves of mimesis must have also reached Warsaw: there is an undated photograph, from between the two wars, of a young Polish man and his tangoing partner. They pose cheek to cheek, with hands held down low—canyengue—but without the bent knees. It must have been difficult for a full expression to unfold in a city where in around 1923 high society "looked down upon with horror, and immediately wanted gone, African *quebradas* from the parquetted floors of Warsaw."[16]

Meanwhile the bold and the brave in Buenos Aires, including two of the most illustrious dancers of the time, El Pibe Palermo and José Méndez, kept doing canyengue straight through the 1930s. By the late 1930s and early 1940s, however, canyengue more or less went underground. Or perhaps it would be more accurate to say that an emerging revolution momentarily upstaged it: the elegance of Carlos di Sarli, the spark of Juan d'Arienzo, and the Stravinsky-like brilliance of Osvaldo Pugliese demanded their own codes of motion. But Pibe and Méndez, and the father of Miguel Ángel Zotto, and the father of Rodolfo Cieri and others kept on performing canyengue.

The eventual transformation of canyengue, from stigmatized dance style into recognized art form, was linked to the widening acceptance of tango: "With the extension of tango to all sectors of society, the salon synthesis being seen as synonymous with tango, and the compadrito progressively abandoning his native choreography, tango canyengue would no longer have the immoral connotations of earlier times."[17]

Final acceptance came with the tango renaissance of the 1980s. Suddenly it was clear that canyengue was special: leaning and turning, in short steps and flexions. Its control over pleasure, its ease and flexibility, turned the best dancers into icons of Africa.

PLATE 44

Contrary to every primitivist trope ("the tribal lacks restraint," say), the cool and the distancing powers of canyengue were unmistakably strong. Actually, as we have seen, continuous body contact in dance had been a Western phenomenon; Bakongo couples danced far "apart" (*tatuka*). So did candomberos, restricting their contact to a bump of the thighs.

Reason and control mastered the flow of sexual energy, shaping and diverting it with breaks, cuts, and flexions—equivalents to Kongo bumbakana. The intimacy was Continental. The control was sub-Saharan and exactly the opposite of what the elite of Buenos Aires assumed was going on. Mastering these challenges, canyengue dancers mastered the world they lived in.

In the process, they turned the word *canyengue* into a term of high praise, a salute to rhythmic authenticity and feeling, like the concept of "swing" in jazz or the notion of *duende* in flamenco. Rosita Quiroga, for instance, a powerful vocalist who found selfhood in tango, is esteemed for the "spontaneous and natural canyengue that always distinguishes her singing."[18]

But the original senses included matters of motion. In the Kimbundu language of northern Angola, for instance, *kiyengu* (also spelled *kiiengu*) means "dance."

Even deeper roots are found in Ki-Kongo, the main ancestral idiom of black Buenos Aires. *Kanienge* is the imperative form of the Ki-Kongo verb "to melt" (*mu nyenga*). It means "Melt into the music!" or "Let the party begin!" "Melt into the music," in turn, means leaning forward and leaning back, bending down and coming up—spatial assertions that defined canyengue in Argentina and that passed on into tango. Bakongo are famous for dance cries like *kanienge!* ("melt!") and *twisa ndungu!* ("pepper it!" "get hot!" or "step it down!"). This continued in the Americas, where nineteenth-century Afro-Cubans could be heard shouting, in creolized Ki-Kongo, *Kina, José, kina!* (Work out, Joe, work out!).

One can well imagine how the cry *kanienge!* constantly repeating the demand that one shape one's body to the beat, would ultimately name a whole dance. This happened in Cuba, where another Kongo dance cry, *rumba!* (work out!), became the name of the island's most famous dance. *Mambo* too descends from an imperative creole Kongo phrase—*abrecuto y güiri mambo* (open your ears and hear what we're saying).

Kanienge as an adjective, however, means something different in Kongo: "worn out" or "tired," that is, "melted" by the passage of time. This alternate usage went straight to black Cuba, where the word *cañengue* means "done," "tired," or "weary" (*demedrado y cansino*).[19] In the 1950s the great Afro-Cuban *sonero* Beny Moré sang a song about a *viejo cañengo,* an old, beat-up duffer, with *cañengo,* a creolized variant of the Ki-Kongo term. The use of the word *canyengue* in this sense also emerged in Buenos Aires, where (the famous tanguero Petróleo informs us) it can sometimes make reference to things "graceless" (*desgarbado*) or "tired" (*cansado*).[20]

Building on these usages, it is possible to suggest a composite translation for *canyengue:* the *oldest* form of tango dance, where one *melts* to the music, taking short steps, keeping knees bent, and leaning on the chest of one's partner. But the best way to savor its color and characterization is to see it in action.

BASIC CANYENGUE: MARTA ANTÓN AND
EL GALLEGO MANOLO

Canyengue is dancing, not waiting for a bus.

— EL GALLEGO MANOLO (February 2002)

Marta Antón and El Gallego Manolo, both Buenos Aires born, are leading
performers of canyengue. They study and share its rich history. According
to Manolo:

Milonga preceded canyengue. It gave canyengue the side-to-side swaying
we call *vaivén* [swing and sway]. Milonga was danced by *orilleros*. They
were the men who, after the border wars with Paraguay [of 1865–70] did
not integrate into society because of their [rough] style of life. They were
action people [*gente de acción*]. They preferrred open country to houses.
They had no interest in manual labor; they disdained work in the Italian
shoe factories. They remained—by choice—on the margins of society.
That's why we call them *orilleros* [men on the margins]. When these men
came together, what they loved to do was dance. Men started practicing
with men; it was in this way that *canyengue* was created, around 1890.
Later dancers picked up this turn-of-the-century style and kept it going.
One such person was the father of Rodolfo Cieri. He danced canyengue.
His sister and her husband did too. We are talking about around 1940. His
son Rodolfo and I grew up together. We lived within ten blocks of one
another. We trained with a canyenguero named Juan Carlos Jirafa who
taught me a step when I was fifteen [i.e., in 1947] which I teach to this
day.[21]

This shared adolescence explains the closeness between Manolo's
style of canyengue and the Cieris', and why they are friends who have
performed together. El Gallego Manolo sees canyengue as a style of tough
men: "We dance canyengue, walking and moving, in a very strong way. I
love to *compadrear* [dance in the style of tough guys] and say everything,
but say it in dance. In canyengue you bend down, and break to the beat,
play with the rhythm, and have fun."[22]
     Playing with the rhythm means dancing to timelines, not only in the
music but in the head, departing from two-four, then coming back, the

dancers controlling the beat. This fine inner pulse control links up El Gallego and Rodolfo Cieri. According to the former:

> Walking in rhythm is the challenge of canyengue. Such few figures as there are, those can be taught later. You first have to move to the beat, know what a full stop is, know what a comma is, and respect all the signs when they happen.[23]

When I asked Marta and Manolo whether canyengue had a basic move from which one departs and returns, like the *ginga* in capoeira or "breaking on two" in the mambo, Manolo answered yes. He said the "elemental step" was *enganche*, "the hooking-up action." "This step begins and ends all the others." The gist of enganche, as danced by the male, is: left to the side, right foot forward, left forward. Then left back, right back, double step, and cross-step. The woman reflects this in mirrorlike fashion. Marta adds: "You're dancing 1, 2-3-4, 1, 2-3-4, and on the 4 you end with a beautiful pose. Enganche unifies step after step."

In demonstrating enganche, Marta and Manolo emphasize a critical nuance—the male turns his chest (*gira su pecho*) slightly to the side, thus departing from the frontality of many Western forms of dance. In addition, Marta reveals the importance, for the woman, of remaining on the balls of her feet when she falls into her partner, giving her poise to pivot in response to the circling demands of canyengue. This distantly reflects Kongo style, for Afro-Cubans performing old Kongo dances are famed for dancing on the balls of their feet, in contrast to the shuffling steps of Yoruba/Fon styles. The painter Martín Boneo portrayed Kongo blacks in Buenos Aires dancing on the balls of their feet in the mid–nineteenth century (Plate 19).

Canyengue is composed of steps that would become the earliest foundations of tango—ochos, sentadas, corridas, cortes, and quebradas, plus drags of the feet called arrastres. The repetitions of these phrases are seasoned with zest and high spirits, in commitment to beauty and play. You sense this when the legs of the woman and the man stylishly unite as the two stride together. You sense it in the relaxed upper body when they swing and sway, with a lilt that betrays familiarity with candombe and black milonga. You see it in the cock-of-the-walk strut, and in the tracing of half-circles with foot fully extended, poised to show off and compete. The verve in all this vaporizes stereotypes of the tango as sadness or emblematic depression.

RODOLFO AND MARÍA CIERI

When Rodolfo Cieri died on June 4, 2000, in Buenos Aires, Argentina lost a master. Cieri and his wife, María, had brought canyengue to the attention of the world.

Italo-Argentine by birth and upbringing, Cieri honored his late father, José Cieri, with the faith and devotion of a Central African attending the memory and spirit of an ancestor. When problems occurred in his career, he went to Chacarita cemetery to tell José about them. "I have my father in my pocket," he told me once. He meant this literally: out of his wallet came two tiny photographs of Cieri senior, one of which he gave to me for luck.

The art of José Cieri—*canyengue acompadrado,* the pure compadrito style—became the grand allegiance of Rodolfo's life. But he danced it privately, before family and close friends, resisting his wife's pleas to put it onstage. Rodolfo thought performance would diminish (*desvirtuar*) José's heritage. But one night in the fall of 1992, José appeared to him in a dream, asking him why he was not dancing canyengue. The dream was a determining moment.

José Cieri was born in Buenos Aires on June 26, 1902. He was a bricklayer (*albañil*), tough, short (*petiso*), and wiry. Weekends he spent on canyengue. He came alive in the laughter and footwork. Dancers would stop to admire him.

José Cieri danced in the 1930s in two favorite places, La Paternal and the Anazco, neighborhood dance clubs in the Paternal barrio. Meanwhile he doted on Rodolfo, his only son, born on October 30, 1932. The family resided in Villa Devoto, at 4154 Calle Nazarre. Cieri taught Rodolfo tango de salón at home. It was 1940. Rodolfo was seven. Impressed by his talent, José also taught him canyengue. The boy mimed the pose, the circling, and the swaying as if he had been born to them. José took him to La Paternal to show him off. There little "Rodo" danced canyengue with an equally talented child, Carmen "Chocho" de Firpo, niece (*sobrina*) of Luis Ángel Firpo, the Argentine champion boxer who once fought Jack Dempsey in 1928. Applause sealed the moment—and Rodolfo's life.

José continued to canyengue. His partner was his wife's sister, Josefa "China" Testa. (In 2002 Josefa, in her eighties, was living north of Buenos Aires in Arrecife, near Pergamino, of payada fame.) José and China danced tango de salón and canyengue.

Who inspired them? At that time, in the 1940s, a tall light-skinned mulatto, El Negro Jirafa, and his Afro-Argentine partner, La Negra Maturana, frequented certain dance clubs that Cieri senior knew, like the club Estudiantes and the club Amanecer. El Negro Jirafa and La Negra Maturana kept canyengue visible in the time of Petróleo and El Negro Lavandina, the great tango stylists of the 1940s. They were links to black origins. José Cieri knew their work. But his son believes that his father's canyengue was influenced more by the dance styles of the barrio tough guys (*guapos de avería*). José Cieri knew and was respected by such men. No veil of self-consciousness fell between them. He learned from their proud and cocky moves.[24]

Some of the original compadritos were mulatto. But even the whites cultivated black cortes and quebradas. Others danced black without realizing it—as when they danced backward, or off to the side, or circling behind their partner. In later "whitened" versions, "the man only danced forward and his steps to the side were choreographic sophistry (*argucia*) meant to make the woman spin, just back to forward, forward to back. But never did the man spin or move out behind his companion [as in black styles]."[25] Yet when I first watched Rodolfo and María Cieri dance canyengue, at the milonga Almagro in 1999, the first thing that struck me was how he circled her, and how she circled him, and how at one point he fell in behind her. An originally black trait had passed intact from compadritos to Cieri senior to son.

Nor was that all. Consider Manuel Galvez's 1922 realist novel on life in the barrios, *Historia de arrabal* (Neighborhood Story). Based on the period 1900–20, it freezes in time further aspects of canyengue:

> The whole patio was dancing. The couples bent down, then lifted up their bodies, twisted them from one side to the other, and came to a full stop to rock themselves forward and back. Each man was stuck very tightly [*pegado*] to his partner . . . [and danced] with a surly look on his face, wearing a wide-brimmed homburg that fell over his eyes.[26]

With homburgs like visors, they were dancing a dream of Gardel. Note the cara fea, the surly expression. Stuck to their partners, they were clearly dancing

PLATE 45

canyengue. Not only that, but bending down, bending up, twisting the body, and rocking side to side were Afro-Argentine traits, performed in candombe-influenced forms of milonga. Illustrating this very passage of Galvez's in 1922, the Argentine artist Adolfo Bellocq showed further traits of the *canyengue coloquial:* dancers cheek to cheek, arms on high, and a woman falling on a man's chest as she danced (Plate 45).

PLATE 46

Such were the styles absorbed by Cieri senior. They took on new life when he taught them to Rodolfo in the 1940s.

When José started his instruction, the first thing he revealed was how the male dancer should hold the woman's hand. There were three special ways: *one,* he held her hand high, like Cachafaz and Lampazo and as drawn by Bellocq, his fingers curling over hers (Plate 46). *Two,* he took her right hand in his left and brought it down to his waist—this was the style José valued most and so did Rodolfo (Plate 41). And *three,* the most compadrito, he kept one finger in his left-hand side pocket while the woman took hold of his wrist.

If you struck the last pose, you were challenging the women on the floor. One might walk up, hands on her hips, saying "Okay, hotshot, let's see if you're man enough to handle me!"

MEETING MARÍA Rodolfo and María met in 1954 at a dance in Caseros, a small town in Buenos Aires province, to the west of the capital. María, who was born June 4, 1939, was fifteen. Rodo noted her entrance and was entranced with her beauty. In the style of the time, he sent coded nods (*cabeceos*), inviting her to dance. María thought not: "Even my mother had said 'look at that guy, how beautifully he tangos,' but my fear was that he was probably in love with himself [*engrupido*]. But when the dance was almost over, I thought it'd be criminal not to dance with the best dancer there. So I did." They were married three years later.

The Cieris lived in Caseros from 1957 to 1976, when they moved to Haedo, a little farther out from the city. To make his living, Rodolfo worked at various jobs, and so did María. But they always kept dancing—canyengue, salón, and sometimes some vals. When the great dance-hall boom came, in the wake of *Tango Argentino* in the 1980s, they were ready.

In 1990 their talents took them to Europe, where they performed a mixture of drama and tango. In a London boîte called Cafetín Porteño (Small Buenos Aires Café), for example, they danced a theatricalization of Cátulo Castillo's 1956 tango "La última curda" (The Last Drink of the Night).

Rodolfo was seated, glass and wine bottle on the table, playing the role of a lush. María sang the lyrics to "La última curda," specially accenting the most famous line, "Life is an absurd wound." She went on to the end:

I come from oblivion, a land always gray, filtered by alcohol.

María made a half-turn. She stood before Rodo. She had, in effect, subtitled his grief. Now she was challenging him to snap out of his depression. Rodolfo got up. He took her into his arms. They wheeled in a suave tango liso. The English were enchanted.

But this was only half of what María and Rodolfo were capable of: the secular half, as it were. Canyengue was sacred. That was the problem. María wanted to add the old style, to double their impact, but Rodolfo was hesitant. He needed a sign. Once when he was having trouble remodeling a part of their home, working with tools he had inherited from his father, Cieri senior appeared in a dream and told him what to do and how to do it. In effect, he tendered Rodolfo a blueprint from the beyond.

Then one night in early October 1992, in Buenos Aires, Rodolfo had another dream in which he spoke to his father. "Papa," he said, "we've made it. María and I are making money like we just can't believe." And his father answered, "Yes, I know. But I don't see you dancing the canyengue I taught you." Rodolfo woke up, immediately recounted the dream to María, and told her, "We're taking canyengue to London."

The Cieris performed canyengue in late October 1992, in the Cafetín Porteño. The audience was enchanted by the logic and romance of the form. The Dutch loved it more: Amsterdam had never seen such a dance, the mutual surrender, the lean, the walk, the sass. They were *shouting* when it finished. As Rodolfo would recall, "My legs were trembling . . . I couldn't believe it. It meant that canyengue could be appreciated any-where." Success followed success. They performed in period costumes: María in small boots with high heels, a hoopskirt (*mirinaque*), and a blouse that resembled a vest, Rodolfo as an elegant compadrito in white cravat, tailored navy jacket lined in white, and pin-striped trousers with a sewed-in ribbon on the side. Once, when dancing in Europe, María broke away from her partner and knelt to the floor. Her level was so low, Rodolfo had to stoop to keep dancing with her. Another vivid improvisation: Rodo opened his feet and then closed them; María answered with an elegant zigzag. The climax was Madrid, where Juan Carlos Copes saw them in action. He came up after the performance and said, ¡Rompiste la noche, Rodolfo! (You broke up the night, Rodolfo!).

Rodolfo and María helped trigger, in 1996, a renaissance in Argentine vernacular dancing, meaning the steps of the earliest tango, at the Akarense club on Calle Donado. They put together a program called "A Night of Canyengue," starring three well-versed couples: Aurora and Jorge Firpo, Marta and Luis Antón, and themselves.

REVELATION IN FLORES On a clear austral summer evening, January 7, 1999, Rodolfo and María Cieri danced canyengue in the house of Héctor and Graciela Menéndez, two friends in Flores. Rodolfo danced in shirtsleeves and pants, keys swinging from his backside pocket, María in a pink sweater and black pants.

Their dance signed itself, in time and in space, with strong circling gestures and relaxed body lines. Rodolfo's thrust-out left elbow added angularity. Whirls blurred his lead and her following together until both fused as one.

Down and locked in, the Cieris kept their steps short to the swift staccato of "Vieja calesita" (Old Carousel). They crouched while executing heel-and-toe diagonals, side-to-side rocking, and other steps. Rodo sometimes moved backward, indenting his knees.

Rodo executed a minute little ocho, then ended this sequence with a smartly bent knee. María answered with an ocho of her own, soft and delicate. The deft, gentle manner of her very small pivots was amazing: had the floor been an apple, she would have been taking small bites. Rodo extended his right leg and humorously twisted María halfway down over it, then brought her back up, twisting her body continuously. It was sexy, but prettiness ruled. Then they rocked back and forth to the side, 1-2, 1-2, swinging their bodies in an invisible hammock.

Rodolfo dragged his foot on the side of his shoe; he trimmed down and kicked up around the side of María's body, just like Cachafaz in the 1933 movie Tango. Their dance, at the end, was an endless seduction, a catlike prowl, a virtuoso display of pizzicato footwork.

Canyengue sees value in spins, turns, and circles, plus footwork in well-humored phrases. The patterns add up, creating meaning: art under pressure. When the Cieris raced forward (corridas de frente), they danced contratiempo 1-2, 1-2-3—that is, in clave. But in corridas de costado (runs to the side), the down pose and clave beat vanished; now they were stepping 1-2, 1-2, and a fraction of space between their bodies opened up. They also switched to 1-2 when they did hamaquita. Clave-led passages became marvelously segmented: step, step, *pose-pose-pose,* step, step, *pose-pose-pose.* "Vieja calesita" came to an end. Rodolfo and María left the track with deep smiles, at one with the grin of Gardel.

FELIPE DE LA FUENTE: PORTRAITS OF CANYENGUE

Felipe de la Fuente was born on January 12, 1912, in the village of Bella Vista, near San Miguel del Monte, in northeastern Buenos Aires province. He died in Buenos Aires in May 25, 2000. De la Fuente started painting around 1932, when he was twenty. He experimented with impressionism, cubism, and the design of stained glass, useful training when he found his métier: drawing denizens of the Argentine night.

Sketch paper in hand, for years he frequented the Bar San Bernardo (now closed) in Centro, a block from the obelisk on the Cortada de Carabelas. He met men there who reminded him of the compadritos whom Borges had distinguished by the strength of their arms and their incapacity for fear. They helped him find his own voice.

From 1950 on, de la Fuente started making small but furious sketches of compadritos and milongueros, meeting in doorways, hailing friends on the street, drinking in bars, improvising tangos before friends.[27] He was preparing his eye. By 1970 he had been sketching these men and their dances for twenty years. His gaze was intense enough to reveal them. His brush was as fast as their moves. In cinematic black and white, he got the darks right, the smokiness right, the emphasized curves of the motion right. He captured fluidity in dark, solid spaces.

These qualities are clear in a 1971 painting of two solidly realized compadritos who project the transcendent freedom inherent in tango (Plate 47). Standing in a bar, relaxed but dynamic, they dramatize the scene with their look. Other men drink grimly and passively, their hats tucked down, each at a table alone. A man walks in, carrying blank papers (*papeles en blanco*) for sketching. It is the artist, come to draw. De la Fuente, like Alfred Hitchcock, puts himself in his pictures.

The tough guys are unwinding. They are feeling their wine (*un poco pasado al trago*). They thrust out their thighs and hunch their broad shoulders. Every limb bends for action. They stand for the curved, the relaxed, the natural. They are preparing to dance. Together they will practice canyengue and forget where they are.[28]

De la Fuente's *Tango canyengue,* dated 1984, carries us again into tradition. In a dark basement setting dancers move in strong light, like boxers.

PLATE 47   PLATE 48

Someone peers down through a street-level window. A swaying bandoneón player makes them all move. De la Fuente saunters in, carrying his
signature papers (Plate 48).

Meanwhile, two couples canyengue in the style of Lampazo, hands at
shoulder level and bottoms thrust out. They streak like strange phantoms,
abrupt and uncanny. Flexibility and ease, established in their knees, have
turned them into icons. They are larger than the audience silhoutted at
their feet. They are giants of Argentine culture.[29]

CONCLUSION

When the youth of the world becomes aware of canyengue, it will sweep
many cities. Already some Germans prefer it to tango. Its overlaps with
black form—the twist, the swinging and swaying, the sweeps of the foot,
the dotting of the floor with clave-led structures—will accelerate the
spread of the form.

Literally a command to melt and get flexible, canyengue delivers its
truths through its initiates, Rodolfo and María, Marta Antón and El
Gallego Manolo, Aurora and Jorge Firpo. They make you feel the original
textures, compadrito and black creole, and the original decade, 1900 to
1910. Canyengue drives a dancer to think historically—to the point of
dressing up in period costumes, as María Cieri and Marta Antón do when
touring in Europe. Their audiences witness fast-paced amalgams of cos-
tuming, choreography, and nostalgia.

But forces beyond history pull in the partners: the self-extinguishing
elixir, the surrender of the body, the earth-honoring flexion, the audacious
runs, strolls, and footwork. With smart moves and short steps, canyengue
exalts us.

7.

TANGO AS MUSIC

From somewhere there came music. It was the tango.

—WILLIAM GADDIS, *The Recognitions* (1955)

The tangos of Pichuco and Piazzolla are rich in meaning.
If their sound weren't around, what a lonely town Buenos
Aires would be!

—ELADIA BLÁZQUEZ, IN RAÚL ALBERTO MARCH,
Eladia Blázquez: Síntesis de la canción porteña (1993)

N eedle poised in vinyl grooves, laser grazing silver disks, we stalk the history of the sound called tango. Begin in medias res with a painting, now in the Neuquén Museum, by a distinguished Argentine artist, Antonio Berni (1905–81), *Orquesta típica* (The Tango Orchestra) (Plate 49). Berni started this work in 1940 and completed it in 1975.[1] He depicts a classic big band of the 1940s. How do we know they are playing tango? Framed by a proscenium, three men play the bandoneón, tango's signature instrument. As Berni shows, the bandoneón is an accordionlike squeeze box with button keys on either side. Invented around 1835 in Krefeld, Germany, by Heinrich Band, a later-refined

PLATE 49

model, labeled "AA" (*doble A*), emerged in the 1860s.[2] The *doble A* is, as it were, the Stradivarius of tango.

In the evolution of bandonéon, two types emerged, the *chromatic,* giving the same note whether the bellows are opening or closing, and the *achromatic,* where opening and closing varies the expression, creating different sets of sounds.[3]

Each of the three bandoneonistas has placed a cloth on his thighs to protect his pants from the instrument's sharp edges. The shadowed notes of a bowed bass resound in our minds, if not in our hearing, through the presence of a bassist beside an accordion player. Behind them stand three men: two are violinists (one is black), and the third has apparently strayed from the upright piano at the right. All the faces are deadpan: this may be a reflection of original tango cool but more likely represents idealized working-class dignity.[4]

Note that all the instruments are European. None comes from Africa. There are no *güiros* or tambourines, as in Puerto Rican *plena;* no conga drum and bongó to heat up the son called *montuno;* no *cuica* and *recoreco* as found in the samba. Yet *how* the instruments are handled, their manner of play, can yield black swing or canyengue. Percussive conceits—drumrolls in melody called *arrastres*—and strong offbeat phrasings called *síncopas* keep a black pulse beneath transcience. In addition, whenever Berni's band played milonga, a creolized bass pattern, from Kongo via Cuba, enlivened the stage.

To the right of the orchestra, a woman belts out a tango on the microphone. She is making her name singing lyrics. She stands for a history of women's vocal accomplishment.

In the texts of the tango we savor a vernacular that was once exiled from the dictionaries. Similarly, certain manners of playing came to tango music not from the conservatories but from barrio improvisers. Striking the bass like a drum goes back to the black performer Leopoldo Thompson. String techniques like snapping muted strings sideways, or the *escoba* (broom) technique of moving the bow parallel rather than perpendicular to the strings, are special to tango. They start with founding virtuosi, like Julio de Caro, and extend on to Antonio Agri and Fernando Suárez Paz, who performed with different Piazzolla formations.[5]

Tango music is a kaleidoscope of heritages seething and shifting. It is a popular dance music, complex in transitions and mood shifts. From the humor of Ángel Villoldo in 1900, through the languor of "Mi noche triste" (My Sad Lonely Night) in 1917 and the hard drive of Juan d'Arienzo in the 1940s, to the classical daring of Piazzolla in the 1980s, we savor a narrative of ongoing change and excitement.

Tango starts with the neo-Kongo beat of the habanera. Scholars have known for some time that this bass was sub-Saharan. Writing in 1914, Henry Edward Krehbiel observed that the Cuban habanera "has an African rhythmical foundation" under a melodic superstructure elaborated by musicians of European descent.[6] Hélio Orovio refined this to Central African or "Bantu" origin;[7] Odilio Urfé refined it further: Kongo. Among several types of music appearing in Santiago de Cuba, Urfé showed in 1984, is the "congo tango," which shares its rhythmic bass pattern with the original habanera.[8] It remained for Fu-Kiau Bunseki to put the beat in its original context and reveal its true name, "the call to the dance" (*mbila a makinu*).[9]

Habanera first entered the written record in Buenos Aires on January 28, 1865, in a place called the San Nicolás Club.[10] Early tango would essentially take the form of a simple melody played over the habanera bass beat. Then came the beat called "the four" (*el cuatro*) and the rise, in the 1910s and 1920s, of the great bandleaders Roberto Firpo, Francisco Canaro, and Julio de Caro. These musicians expanded the rhythmic repertory, adding the percussive ornament called the arrastre; another percussive device that José di Giorgio (who played bandoneón for Aníbal Troilo and Osvaldo Pugliese) and others call the *carraspeo* (literally, "throat-clearing"); and the *síncopa*, offbeat phrasing, accenting the weak part of a measure. Some of these effects link to black artists, like

Thompson's drummed bass and the audible swing of Luciano Ríos, who played guitar for Juan "Pacho" Maglio. In the 1930s the distinguished composer Sebastián Piana revived the milonga. This renaissance was triggered by a woman, Rosita Quiroga, who commissioned Piana to compose for her the superb "Milonga sentimental," in which she passionately calls out to a lover, repeating key words and building a beat.[11] In sum, cultural borrowings were various. So were local inventions. They all stabilized and turned into the coherence called tango.

Pugliese traces the arrastre, or drag, back to the pampas, the world of the gauchos, many of whom, as we have seen, were black.[12] Significantly, the only writer to signal the importance of the arrastre in tango is the great black composer Horacio Salgán, who translates it as a drumroll-like ornament, "an effect of percussion where tonal clarity is not the goal but rhythm, in blurred sound."[13] For Salgán, it is arrastres that make tangos move, with a peremptory roll and offbeating sequence. The arrastre is a lower-register idiom. It is kept in the bass, where it rumbles and growls as it pushes things forward.

Salgán attributes the rise of the arrastre to Troilo's orchestra of 1943, which fits Troilo's well-known commitment to swing. In terms of broader history, however, the arrastre was more a reinforcement of an already extant element in the countrified dance music of the gauchos.

Not all jazz has blue notes, but subtract blue tonality, and whole chapters of jazz disappear. Similarly, not all tangueros play arrastres—"there are plenty of tangos that don't use arrastres and yet still are tangos"[14]—yet contemporary performers like Pablo Ziegler, Néstor Marconi, and Pablo Aslán see arrastres as quintessential to tango.[15] Aslán believes that arrastres relate to the walk of tangueros on the dance floor: their strong sliding push makes visible the sweep of the sound.[16]

Why is G. Matos Rodríguez's "La cumparsita" so extraordinarily popular? Because, in key interpretations, the arrastres are strong. Listen to Aníbal Troilo's 1943 "La cumparsita." Arrastres growl from the pianist's left hand, imperatives of action and energy.[17] They mix with staccato, a dialectic that drives.

Astor Piazzolla, tango modernist, pretended to despise "La cumparsita" as "the poorest piece of harmony you could ask for."[18] But it's not for its harmony that the world loves this tango; rather, as in the case we just heard, it's for the rousing immediacy of the arrastres and staccato. Piazzolla was jealous.

When the new beat called "the four" (el cuatro) came in with Firpo,

Canaro, and de Caro in the 1920s, it accompanied important changes in harmony and phrasing. Polyphony (parallel voices) and counterpoint (voices in alternation) emerged with de Caro.

Remembering that gauchos competed in dance battles bearing a pure Kongo name—*malambo*—it becomes relevant to recognize that Bakongo too slur notes to strike rhythm, when playing bass drums. Describing the effect, Central Africans use the same verb that Argentines do: "to drag" (*mu koka*); "to drag notes together is to affirm them [*mu koka n'ningu i mu singisa*]." It makes notes hit hard (*sika*) or hammer (*vo konkuta*).[19]

Return to Salgán's remark that dragging notes is percussion, the trading of pure tone for the dry, rhythmic spark of uninflected sonority.[20] "Drag" notes in Kongo, like bass piano arrastres in Argentina, flourish in low registers:

> Slurring notes together [*koka n'ningu*] on the bass drum awakens the spirit [*sikimisa mpeeve*] and sharpens understanding. We cannot achieve the understanding of heavy issues if sound cannot reach [*tuula*] the level where they're hidden [*ka tulendi sikimisa mambu vo n'ningu ka ulendi tuula ku nsia mampinda ko*].[21]

Bass notes have power. Bakongo believe they relate to the earth, the ancestral base that we stand on. In mambo, samba, candombe, and jazz, the importance of bass is primordial; "bass in your face" is equally strong in funk, soul, and hip-hop. So arrastres churning energy in lower registers, to say nothing of guitarists thumbing the bass to give the beat of milonga, suggest cognation between Afro-Atlantic traditions.

Pugliese, we have seen, reminds us that "tango has a characteristic that comes from the influence of the culture of the pampas, the *arrastre*."[22]

Slurred notes and syncopation punctuate old Argentine country dance forms like escondido and gato. In one recorded escondido you hear sliding, arrastrelike notes at the beginning of the piece. In another recording, "El gato del centenario," slurred notes herald offbeating. In other words, after the downbeat, syncopes come in over a basic three-four.[23]

"El gato del centenario" sparkles with meters, six-eight versus three-four. According to Michael S. O'Brien, a student of Argentine music, mastering the two time signatures simultaneously "is essential for anyone playing *música criolla* in the Americas and has received plenty of treatment in terms of its origin in the music of the Spanish Renaissance."[24]

More than has been recognized, the culture of the pampas conceals the excitement of creolized music from Iberia. This excitement helped spark the rise of the tango. *Taconeos* (Andalusian stamping patterns) and *pitos* (finger-popping patterns) were present at its foundation. At the start of the twentieth century, the famed early lyricist Villoldo even played castanets while singing tango.

TANGOS WITH HABANERA ACCOMPANIMENT, 1900–10

Begin, then, with Villoldo around 1900. His early recordings were tango-habaneras. People were dancing to the beat of the habanera bass. Despite the scratchiness of the old recordings, one hears very clearly the guitar player pick out the bass of the habanera with his thumb, just like Castor Pérez today in Calella de Palafrugell, on the Costa Brava. The propensity for riffs in low registers resumes.

The instrumental structure of the earliest tangos was simple and direct: the guitar furnished the rhythm (the habanera bass pattern) while the flute and violin played the melody in unison. Then, in the late nineteenth century, the concertina-like bandoneón came in, eventually replacing the flute and guitar. Its timbre and color would redefine powerfully the sound of the tango.

The Afro-Argentine composer Anselmo Rosendo Mendizábal wrote many tangos, including in 1908 one called "El Club Z" (The Z Club), where an instrumental call and response surmounts a habanera accompaniment. More important was an 1897 composition, "El entrerriano" (The Man from Between the Rivers), a classic in the history of the tango.

"El entrerriano" was the first tango structured in three sections, the first and third of sixteen measures, and the second of thirty-two measures.[25]

"El purrete" (The Kid), a tango performed by the Police Band of Buenos Aires around 1909, dramatized a habanera with clashes of cymbals. The tangos of the orchestras of Ferrer-Filipoto (1917–18) and Vicente Loduca (1917–18) were habaneras all the way.[26]

So were earlier recordings, of 1912–13, by the famous Juan "Pacho" Maglio,[27] but with a difference: the guitarist, Luciano Ríos, is black. Juan María Veniard signalizes Ríos's "rhythmic support."[28] A photograph of Pacho's quartet shows Ríos standing tall in the midst of his colleagues.[29] His guitar rings clearly in the recordings; it's not a beat that we hear, nor an accompaniment—it's *him*, a living embodiment of swing and dance motion. In all compositions he keeps his sound buoyant. One begins to understand why swing-and-sway (*cunita*) was a part of canyengue. (I once saw the tango bassist Pablo Aslán, who brought to my attention the importance of Ríos, listening to Ríos on 1912 recordings, rocking his body to the guitarist's beat in a side-to-side sway.)

Villoldo's "La bicicleta" (The Bicycle) of 1909 began, nobly, to mix cultures. From the famous black *payador* Gabino Ezeiza, Villoldo borrows jump-cuts from singing to speech. He hits certain words, like *damas* and *ramas,* with flamencolike trills, Arabized melismas that add savor to rhyme. And while he's singing, Villoldo plays castanets!

It is an acoustical equivalent of the "Moorish" tiled floors, with diamond patterns (*pisos dameros*), and the "Moorish" flat-roofed terraces (*azoteas*) favored in Buenos Aires and Montevideo at that time.

Turn-of-the-century Buenos Aires had an idiom for being stood up: *el esquinazo.* As the bandoneonista di Giorgio explains: "You tell a *mina,* I'll meet you at such-and-such a corner [*esquina*]. She doesn't show—you're 'hit by the corner' [*le dió un esquinazo*], you're stood up." Ángel Villoldo titled a tango with this colorful term.

"El esquinazo" (When I Got Stood Up) starts off with four knocks (*golpeteos*), struck on the side of an instrument. They are sharp and precise, like the heel-stamps of dance on the pampas, like Ríos's thumb in action. This tango premiered at Café Tarana (earlier known as Lo de Hansen) in Palermo around 1900:

> In the famous Café Tarana of Buenos Aires there appeared a tango-milonga, "*El esquinazo.*" At first the clientele accompanied [its passage of knocking] by drumming on tables. Then, progressively carried away, they used cups as gongs and chairs became drums.
>
> Men hit the beat with whatever was in reach, chairs, tables, glasses, bottles, [and plates.] Soon shattered glass and ruined chairs lay about. . . . The next day the owner, nicknamed "the Paganini of smashed plates," put up this notice: "henceforth it is strictly forbidden to play the tango, '*El esquinazo.*' We beg your cooperation in this matter. The management."[30]

The commotion recalls the Havana blacks who used to pound on doors, walls, and bar counters to make a beat for their rumbas.

THE EMERGENCE OF TRUE TANGO TIME: "THE FOUR"

Nothing swings like 4/4.

—JOHN COLTRANE, liner notes of *Africa Brass* (1961)

During the second decade of the twentieth century, in the work of the early masters Pacho, Eduardo Arolas, Agustín Bardi, Carlos Posadas, and

Firpo, tango music was starting to change. The music slowed down. Bass and piano came in. A critical shift took place in the rhythm. The distinguished tango guitarist Ubaldo de Lío tells us what happened next:

> The earliest form of tango was a type of habanera. The tango-milonga then followed. After that came "the four," four quarter-notes per measure. We still ask ourselves who invented "the four." Some say Canaro, others say Firpo, a few claim de Caro.

> To this Pablo Aslán adds: "One can detect several bars of four in the work of Arolas as early as 1913."[31]

Whoever was responsible, four equal quarter notes, streamlined to intensity, now formed the time of the tango. This straight-four design bears the name "the four" (*el cuatro*) or "the beat that's marked out" (*marcato*).[32] There is a parallel in the rhythmic evolution of jazz, from the two-step of New Orleans to the four-to-the-bar of swing.

Prudencio Aragón's 1910 tango "El pardo Cejas" (Black Cejas) is a striking sample of the rise of "the four."[33] Aragón dedicated this tango to Victorino Cejas, a young man of color who was one of the finest tango dancers of the era. (Canaro too had hung out with Victorino in his youth),[34] Cejas, who dressed as sharp as he danced, lives on in the shift to the four. Eduardo Arolas, who had hired a black bandoneonista for his band in Montevideo in 1915, also worked with "the four." He slowed the tempo down and developed fine themes.

"The four" arrived in force in the 1920s, with Firpo, Canaro, and de Caro. Important changes in harmony and phrasing came with it: polyphony and counterpoint emerged with de Caro. Tango was in a state of creative ferment. Black swing and black improvisation met innovations evolving within the Western-oriented tradition. The black composer Mendizábal, we recall, had designed the early structure of tango, involving a first and third part of sixteen bars each, with a bridge of thirty-two bars in between. Now de Caro and his peers swept this away: "After 1925 nobody writes [tangos] in three parts any more; sometimes introductions, bridge passages, and codas are added."[35] The trend was now to structure in two parts, doubled in execution: A B A B.

Tango was coming into focus, with two exact memories involved: a privileged world of formally trained men, many of them of Italian heritage, and a world of black improvisers. The music was creole and open. Italianate composers like de Caro were aware of and took counsel from street music themes; black virtuosi like Thompson and Ríos were corre-

spondingly interested in classical music, even while their concern with
swing and spontaneity kept tango intensity from dissolving in refinement.
The latter contribution is rarely talked about "because there were few
blacks in Buenos Aires." True, black numbers had been small in the
city—8,005 out of a total population of 433,375 in around 1887 for
instance[36]—and were getting smaller. But it only took one black to rhyth-
mize the use of the bass in the tango. This was of course Leopoldo Ruperto Thompson. He played bass for
no less than three major bands, Firpo, Canaro, and de Caro. Luciano
Ríos's guitar, identified as *moreno* (black) by Horacio Ferrer,[37] was as we
have seen the source of the swing in Pacho's historic ensemble. The earliest known players of bandoneón were black, too.

BLACKS AT THE BEGINNING OF TANGO MUSIC

During the last decade of the nineteenth century and the first quarter of
the twentieth, many black musicians were playing tango in Buenos Aires.
The profession of musician or dance instructor had been an acceptable
one for Afro-Argentines to enter for some time. Racially identifying nicknames—El Negro this, El Pardo that—help us to plot their contribution.
Carlos Posadas (1874–1918), an Afro-Argentine pianist and composer
who also played violin and guitar, was one of the most distinguished
tangueros of his time.[38] He was the author of "El tamango" (The Boot)
and "El taita" (The Tough Guy). His elder brother, Manuel Posadas
(1860–1916), was a director of one of the orchestras that played for
maskers in the Buenos Aires Carnivals of the early twentieth century.[39]
Carlos Posadas was the grand uncle of Facundo Posadas, today's master
of Argentine tango, milonga, and jazz dance.
Anselmo Rosendo Mendizábal (1868–1913) was "possibly the most celebrated of composers of tangos of the period predating 1900."[40]
Mendizábal wrote an all-time classic tango, "El entrerriano." His pianist
brother, Ceriaco Sergio "El Negro" Mendizábal, was active as well.
Among other early Afro-Argentine tango songwriters were Cayetano
Alberto Silva (1868–1920) and Plácido Simoni Alfaro, both of whom also
played piano.[41]
Harold Phillips (?–1915) was a North American black who played piano
in Buenos Aires. He came to the capital in 1900 and worked there for
fourteen years. Phillips arrived playing ragtime but soon learned the beat
of the city: by 1910 he was playing tango at Café La Marina in La Boca. At

least three other black pianists played tango about town: Luis Suárez Campos, who was born *circa* 1876 and who lived ninety years; Alejandro Vilela (1845?–?); and Juan Santa Cruz, who accompanied the bandoneón of his brother, Domingo Santa Cruz. In 1914 Juan and Domingo also opened an academy of dance together, at 1150 Calle Gascón.[42] At around the same time one El Negro Lorenzo was playing the traps in tango settings. This was years before Osvaldo Fresedo introduced jazz drums into tango.[43]

Early milongueros danced to the music of several black violinists: Domingo Castro Posadas (1880–?), El Negro Casimiro (1840?–1914), Eusebio Aspiazú (who was also a guitarist), El Pardo Alcorta, and El Pardo Cototo Almeida. Casimiro stands out. Some call this black man the inventor of tango because he was clearly composing long before de Caro. White-haired and "good-natured" (*bonachón*), he plied the dance joints of turn-of-the-century Buenos Aires.[44] "Viejo Tanguero," writing in 1912, affectionately remembers Casimiro "tickling" (*cosquilleando*) the strings of a well-worn violin.[45] The present-day writer René Briand attributes a famous early tango, "Cara sucia" (Dirty Face), to his hand and rescued the sheet music of his delightful tango melody "La yapa" (The Last Drink).[46] Playing gigs, Casimiro used "La yapa" to signal the last dance of the night.

Black clarinetists formed part of the scene: El Mulato Sinforoso and Gregorio "El Negro" Astudillo, a nice-looking mulatto who also played flute in 1912 for Arolas.

We come now to the most strategic of black musicians playing tango: guitarists. They were numerous. This is important, as Pablo Aslán points out, because the guitar was precisely the instrument that gave rhythm to the earliest of tangos.

Of all black guitarists, the most strategic was Ríos, and we will come to him later. Other Afro-Argentine guitarists included El Pardo Carnivari, El Pardo Emiliano, El Negro Lezcano, Lorenzo "El Negro" Martínez, El Negro Ortiz, and Justo "El Negro" Rodríguez.[47] The famed white bandoneonista Pedro Maffia made his debut in the trio of the violinist Justo "El Negro" Rodríguez. As usual, nicknames mark ancestry. Oscar Zucchi mentions another black guitarist, Enrique Maciel (1897–1962).[48]

The most famous mulatto guitarists were José Ricardo (1888–1937) and Guillermo Barbieri (1894–1935), both accompanists for Carlos Gardel. Gardel heard Ricardo play in 1915. He loved the way the man "talked" with his strings and wasted no time in hiring him. Later Gardel took on Barbieri.[49]

Gardel was a star. The world paid little notice to his accompanists. Even so, we catch glints of Ricardo's art when he backs up Gardel on "Mi noche triste" (My Sad Lonely Night) in 1917. His wine-colored chords are tastefully attendant. He strums at the end of each Gardel line, making a kind of muted call and response.

Ricardo worked for Gardel for fourteen years. Barbieri was with Gardel in the fatal plane crash of June 1935, in which both men perished. The parade of black guitarists is impressive, but there is more. Listening across the decade of 1910–20, one discovers the black guitarist Ríos. He played guitar for the pivotal ensemble of Pacho, with Pacho on bandoneón, José "Pepino" Bannano on violin, and Carlos "Hernani" Macchi on flute. Their recording in 1912 for Columbia was a revelation that sold briskly, and this was no accident: Ríos went beyond simple strumming; he gave early tango a groove.[50]

When the double bass, or contrabass, entered tango instrumentation, in the second decade of the twentieth century, the first noted player was black. He had earlier been a guitarist and knew Ríos and his work. We have mentioned this man several times: Leopoldo Ruperto Thompson.

The central tango instrument is of course the accordion-like bandoneón. Villoldo praised an Afro-Argentine of the late nineteenth century, Jorge "El Pardo" Machado, as "a true virtuoso of the accordion." Machado, who composed "Tango no. 1" in 1883, was a harbinger of the black musicians who picked up the bandoneón when it arrived in Buenos Aires from western Germany between 1870 and 1884.[51]

Juan María Veniard believes that a black virtuoso, Sebastián "El Pardo" Ramos Mejía, was the first master of bandoneón in Buenos Aires.[52] By day Ramos Mejía drove a horse-drawn tramway on the Buenos Aires–Belgrano line. At night he played tango. In 1903 he taught the distinguished tango composer Vicente Greco how to play bandoneón. Another black bandoneonista was El Negro Romero, who was working in Buenos Aires around 1890. He played in Palermo with Lorenzo "El Negro" Martínez, "the guitarist with a powerful thumb."[53]

The bandoneonista José "El Negro" Quevedo is remembered for composing "Boca juniors," to honor the popular Buenos Aires soccer team. Around 1915 he moved to Montevideo, where he worked for two tango stars, Arolas and Delfino.

The black musician Luis Adrián Almeida, "El Negro Cototo," taught none other than Pacho to play bandoneón around 1898.

Among early black bandoneonistas was Ernesto de la Cruz. Born in 1898, a boxer in his youth, he kept his trim into his seventies. He directed his own orchestra and in 1926 composed a hit tango, "El ciruja" (The Bum).[54]

A sixth Afro-Argentine came to the game somewhat later. Luis J. Martín, in a charming little pamphlet, *The Cafés of Patricios Park* (Los cafés de Parque de los Patricios), describes the Café Benigno, on Calle Rioja near the corner of Calle Brasil in the 1920s. This was the haunt of Floreano Benavento—"El Negro Eduardo"—an Afro-Argentine of Central African descent, via the Angolan port of Benguela. El Negro Eduardo played first guitar, then bandoneón. He was famous in his barrio for "a bellows that was backed by the spirit of Africa" (*un fueye pactado con Mandinga*).[55]

A distinguished Afro-Argentine musician and composer, Joaquín Mauricio Mora (1905–79) ends the list of early black players of the bandoneón. Born in Buenos Aires in 1905, he wrote several tangos, including "Divina" and "Frivolidad." He was a pianist until 1926, switched to bandoneón, then returned to the keyboard in 1934.

He was a keyboard player who threw his weight around (*pianista pesado*). He had a taste for strong bass arrastres. During his bandoneón days in the early 1930s, he befriended Troilo and attended the debut of that master's first orchestra in 1939. Mora left Argentina in 1943, toured Latin America, and settled in Medellín, Colombia. There he would work for the rest of his life.[56]

In sum, at least thirty-five black musicians played tango in Buenos Aires from 1890 to 1930: ten guitarists, eight pianists, two clarinetists, five violinists, one contrabassist, one accordionist, seven bandoneonistas, and one player of traps. There was no color bar for blacks, provided their instruments were European.

With the exception of Thompson and Ríos, we cannot link styles to performers. But we sense something that is Andalusian/North African, and also kin to the Kongo malambo, when a bandoneonista strikes his heel against the floor while he's playing. This gives "bite" to the notes (*muerde las notas*). The player stamps his heel. His knee rocks the instrument. The air rocks with the motion. The sound turns percussive.

In dance centers called *academias*, from El Bajo to Plaza Lorea, blacks learned to dance early tango.[57] Then as now, women and men occasionally resorted to brief but expressive heel-tapping sequences (*taconeos*), and these compare to the bandoneonistas who rhythmicize their phrasing by stamping their heels as they play. This creole procedure is taken for granted but likely was not the way bandoneón was first played in western Germany.

Marconi believes that other rhythmic strategies, like hitting the sides of the bandoneón as if it were a hand drum, came in "after Troilo" in the wake of the influence of jazz.[58] Troilo was a genius who constantly reinvented, guided by a love of flexibility and swing. Even so, Villoldo's castanets and Thompson's drumlike bass patterns are a matter of recorded history.

CANYENGUE TO LISO: FIRPO, CANARO, DE CARO

> The three of them played as one person,
> in a state of pure discovery
>
> — ANNE CARSON, *Tango* (1998)

"It is clear that the first tango ensembles [*conjuntos*]," writes Blas Matamoros, "copied the composition of small black orchestras."[59] In the process, early innovators, Firpo and Canaro, also incorporated black swing—canyengue—into their music.

When Firpo first played, in 1907, it was at a place where blacks played: La Marina, at the corner of Suárez and Necochea in La Boca, a kind of tango equivalent to Minton's, the famous site of early bop, at 118th and St. Nicholas in Harlem. Later, in 1916–18, Firpo pioneered piano in tango.[60] His signature way of playing the instrument is immortalized in Enrique Cadícamo's novel *Café de camareras*:

> The trio began to play "Una noche de garufa" [A Night on the Town], the first tango composed by Eduardo Arolas. Firpo continually embellished the right-hand melody with a left-hand accompaniment very special to him [*muy de él*], summoning, from the bass of his instrument to the treble, a moving, octave-tinctured chromatic scale that remorselessly mimicked the patterns of a guitar.[61]

There are black implications here: Afro-Argentine guitarists were numerous, and at least one of them switched from guitar to bandoneón. Firpo's tango compositions of 1916–18 include offbeat phrasing and pizzicato violins, struck not with one finger (the European way) but with several, making them sound almost like banjos, which itself was an African-derived instrument. Perhaps this kind of stroke, which enlivens Firpo's "De mi flor" (From the Flower of My Youth) and "Homero," reflects the influence of Thompson, the band's black bassist.

The *orquesta típica* had emerged in 1912–13, brought into being by Vicente Greco, the bandoneonista who had been trained by the black master Mejías. The ensemble was defined as follows: bandoneón, piano, violin, and contrabass.[62] Firpo thrived in this format. His rhythms on piano flaunted bass: he "introduced a rhythmized lower register—solid and flexible with deliberate accents."[63]

Firpo seasoned his tunes with offbeats, and they called the style *tango canyengue.*[64] Firpo's metric sophistication comes across clearly in an instrumental composition, "Didi," recorded with a quartet on January 21, 1948. Earlier versions go back to 1914 and 1916.[65] We hear pure percussion—somebody tapping the side of an instrument, mimicking a drum or guitar lick—*delátatátata.* Perhaps they were elaborating on the knocks in "Esquinazo." In any event, the piano simultaneously mirrors this fragment—*delátatátata*—pushing the tune in the direction of percussion. Then toward the end, the bandoneón reverts to pure melody.

"Didi" thus documents another source of tanguero swing, the so-called *carraspeo* (clearing of the throat). The term, as cited by a former bandoneonista to Troilo, José di Giorgio, refers to the transference of certain drum or guitar licks to the bandoneón or to other melodic instruments. In "Didi" the carraspeo is double—percussion and percussive melody all taking place at the same time.

The music displays another forte of the tango: inventive light textures. The lead voice and arrangement change every four bars. The strings are a marvel of technical variety—thrown bow, strong strumming, fast-moving triplet pizzicati—all in the service of building strong time.

In 1916 Canaro hired Thompson away from Firpo, his counterpart in canyengue. In so doing, he made rhythmic history. As Canaro himself would later write:

> The [black] contrabass-player, Leopoldo Thompson, was the creator of the beat called *canyengue,* which all bassists nowadays use. Canyengue consists of drumming the strings, with bow or hand, in time or against time, imparting great ecstasy and movement.[66]

Canaro, as we have seen, was friendly with the black tango dancer Victorino Cejas[67] and would remain so for the rest of his life.[68] In 1943 he even mixed candombe with tango.[69] No wonder canyengue dancers of the early twenty-first century, like María Cieri and Marta Antón, like to perform to recordings of Firpo and Canaro. They move to the swing of a black-inspired age.

Then something happened: a composer emerged, Julio de Caro, who transformed the musical order. He kept tango's rhythm but deepened its melody with an inimitable blend of symphonic and vernacular.

With a populist touch that honored buglers and organ-grinders and once even music boxes, he took pleasure both in European high culture and in Buenos Aires street textures. De Caro saw no contradiction in pleasing Italians who wanted bel canto and creoles who wanted a beat. He played the tango with well-trained performers who could read and write music. Many were Italo-Argentine, familiar with Rossini as well as milonga.

De Caro's accomplishment, blending concert and street, was extremely provocative. Pugliese, by drenching passages of his classic early composition "Recuerdo" (Fond Memory) in Rossini, clearly revealed that de Caro was his mentor—which inevitably attracted the master's attention. De Caro was the first to record this tango. Yet through all the changes the black beat remained, turning action into sound, and sound into action.

THE DRAG AND THE OFFBEAT (*ARRASTRE Y SÍNCOPA*)

One of the strongest manifestations of this enduring presence is the note-slurring weapon called arrastre. We have examined it before, but its richness sustains further inquiry. Indeed, the Afro-Argentine pianist/composer Horacio Salgán, a legend in his own time and the greatest tango musician alive, includes a chapter on arrastres in his recent book, *Curso de tango*.

Salgán defines *arrastre* as the intense rhythmic slurring of several notes together. Bass notes so blurred give push to the tango, like a roll on a bass drum. In an interview in New York in 2003, the tango pianist Pablo Ziegler demonstrated how he sweeps across bass notes with the base of his left palm to make his arrastres. Others use the forefinger or little finger. In so doing, no matter how briefly, they are "drumming" the left of the keyboard—a strong and significant rhythmic device in tango music.[70]

In tango, in the absence of congas or traps, piano and bass take the role of rhythm and percussion. On contrabass alone there are three different ways of making an arrastre. The contemporary tango bass player Ignacio Varchausky describes them:

1. *Arrastre with the left hand:* which slides along the string from one indefinite note to another. The bow is used normally.

2. *Arrastre with the bow:* the bass player puts more weight on the bow and, near the end of the arrastre, quickens the speed with which he passes it. (If the arrastre ends in a marcato or offbeat, it closes with a snap of the wrist.)

3. *Arrastre with bow and left hand:* the funkiest and most potent. The musician combines both kinds of arrastres above, being careful that it does not sound exaggerated. Note: when the arrastre comes to an end, the last note should resound, vibrating the string—otherwise swing is reduced and the effect sounds awkward.[71]

When vocally approximating the sound of an arrastre, tangueros often use the *s* as it sounds in the word *pleasure* or in extensions of *z,* because these voiced consonants all have a vibrating buzz: *zep, zoom, zum, zhoom.* Arrastres usher in downbeats. This form of anticipation, linked to strong syncopes (*la síncopa*), entered tango early. Arolas, who died in 1924, is believed to be the first to perform an arrastre on bandoneón.[72]

Finally, Ignacio Varchausky decodes the link between arrastres and swing:

> The arrastre is generally played with a slight delay [*retraso*] with respect to the tempo of the piece. This generates a feeling of expectation and desire, almost physical in quality, for the arrastre to reach the last note and return to correct time. This delay in execution, when realized, makes the work swing in tango terms.[73]

Such rhythms kept tango moving even while classically trained musicians of various descent—Italian, Spanish, Catalan, Russian Jewish—poured into it. In the 1920s, the time of the ascendancy of Julio de Caro, European harmony became increasingly important. Ever since the landmark tango-canción "Mi noche triste" of 1917, straight-ahead tangos intended for dancing had coexisted with lyrical tangos drenched with nostalgia. Alternative treatments of tempo were emerging, passages in rubato versus passages in strict time. Now one was savoring both arrastres and counterpoint, Weltschmerz and cool.

Julio de Caro exemplified all this and more. He dared to create a sound in which classical phrasing marched with street textures, even laughter and whistling, plus rhythmic motifs. He invented a text with a creolized matrix—European classicism + Argentine vernacular (a vernacular with black gifts intact). How did he achieve this? By living and loving both languages equally, barrio and concert hall.

JULIO DE CARO (1899–1980)

Juan Julio de Caro was born December 11, 1899, on Calle Bartolomé Mitre in Buenos Aires. Both of his parents were Italian. As a child, Julio was frail, so his mother dressed him in the habit of St. John for a spell, for spiritual protection. Meanwhile, his father set him to studying piano. One evening in 1917 Julio and some of his friends wandered into the Palais de Glace in Recoleta. Firpo was playing canyengue. Firpo opened a world to de Caro, who took in its poetics. He started playing tango violin. Seven years later, in 1924, he formed his first orchestra: his brother Emilio de Caro on violin; Luis Petrucelli and Maffia on bandoneón; another brother, Francisco de Caro, on piano; and himself on violin. They were young and had poise, yet like Gardel, they needed black swing—so as their bassist, they hired Thompson, who had recently left Firpo for the second time.[74] The star of canyengue now worked for de Caro. On August 25, 1925, Thompson tragically died from hepatitis, but his technical revolution, absorbed and alive, was unstoppable.

By 1928 de Caro was internationally famous. He performed that year at the Copacabana Palace Hotel in Rio, introducing the tangos "Tierra querida" (Beloved Land), "Copacabana," and "Olimpia." The first of these would become a standard. In 1934 de Caro played the Hotel Negresco in Nice, in the south of France—another posh spot. Here he became the toast of French society and met his compatriot Gardel.

De Caro attracted bright minds to his band: Troilo, Elvino Vardaro, and Pugliese. He kept the music flowing, with changes in mode and in texture.

These gifts are audible in "Mala junta" (Bad Crowd), a barrio tone poem recorded on September 12, 1927. "Mala junta" opens with laughter, two-part whistling of a tune, and classical piano. So far the music is not tango; there is no syncopation. The F-sharp major tune in fact sounds neapolitan, like a fugitive canzonetta. De Caro, open to street sound, an acoustical universe of whistling and laughter, is using it to build a provocative introduction. Then, bam—Pedro Laurenz comes in like an army on bandoneón, playing classical sixteenth-note counterpoint over syncopated accompaniment. He has switched to F-sharp minor. The swirling intensity of his bandoneón is amazing: he electrifies everything. Bandoneón has come of age in the discourse of tango.

Meanwhile pizzicati underscore the straight four. "Mala junta" is a transforming tango, major to minor, Neapolitan to porteño, informal to classical. There is a section of rhythm and a section of lyricism, each rounded off with two notes at the end. These punctuating notes are the chan-chan, the tango beat signaling an ending. De Caro plays with time. Led by the bandoneón, three eighth notes slow down, briefly suggesting a shift into waltz time—into six-eight—then immediately returning to the four. It's a metrical conceit that differs from, say, the music of Spain, where old genres like *canario* strictly alternate bars in three-four and six-eight; here the shift is mixed and spontaneous.[75]

At one point in "Mala junta" there is a solo in the high register of the piano that sounds like a music box. The composer is not afraid to mix vernacular with high purpose. That is his genius: to arouse countermusics.

All this and more is evident in the masterpiece "Tierra querida," recorded on September 12, 1927. Symphonic and street once again swing into consonance, over a single rhythm (with variants). "Tierra querida" opens with a polkalike A section. Suspensions of rhythm are announced by slurred notes on piano, leading into violin glissandi. Major and minor alternate superbly; piano introduces them with short, snappy solos. The violin takes on a buglelike quality, pulling the tango toward street mimes or marches. There is humor behind this, too, as in de Caro's "Derecho viejo" (Old Right), recorded August 4, 1926, where violinists sweep their bows down their strings, then playfully break into bird sounds.[76]

De Caro is more than the golden boy of the classicizing tango. True, he manipulated modes and rubato, but he also loved street songs. In wresting supremacy from opera and the concert hall, he was asking a question: who is really cultured in Buenos Aires?

His fame and his fortune arose from his power to make people feel elegant. He mastered the orchestra but kept things lighthearted. Julio de Caro died in Mar del Plata, Argentina, on March 11, 1980.

BANDONEÓN: MOOD INTO MELODY

The first documented player of the bandoneón in Argentina was a black man, José Santa Cruz. He played in 1865 as a soldier during the War of the Triple Alliance.[77] He was the father of Domingo Santa Cruz, who in 1905 became the first bandoneonista to direct a dance orchestra.[78]

Historians of tango take for granted the rapid acceptance of the bandoneón in Buenos Aires between 1870 and 1876. But there was an earlier, Italian-led, rural introduction of instruments—accordions and bandoneones—on the plains of Brazil and Argentina. In the bordering Brazilian state of Rio Grande do Sul, for example, country musicians played songs on the *sanfona,* a button accordion brought to Brazil by Italian settlers around 1836. It's the signature instrument of the gauchos of Brazil.[79] In northern Argentina, in the town of Corrientes, polkas on sanfona sparked a popular music called *chamamé.*

Rural migrants in Buenos Aires, then, were culturally prepared to greet the bandoneón when it came to the capital in the last quarter of the nineteenth century. Even so, for those who had never seen one, the experience must have been like staring at the instrument panel of a jet. The bandoneón is formidable—a seventy-one-button squeeze box, with thirty-eight buttons on the right side and thirty-three on the left. Unlike piano keys, these keys are outside the player's field of vision; they have to be felt with the fingertips. In the favored achromatic bandoneón, each button makes two notes, one when the bellows are opening, another when the bellows are closing. The wind from the bellows vibrates tiny reeds—*lengüetas* (little tongues)—inside the instrument. The tongues, not the box, make the sound.

Piazzolla contrasts the "velvet" sound of the bandoneón with the clear sunny accent of the accordion. To Piazzolla, the bandoneón was the true voice of sadness. That is the way he often played it. In fact, though, bandoneones were first made as portable organs, playing church tunes and polkas and waltzes in towns by the Rhine.[80] They were marked for belief and high spirits, not bereftness. In the hands of a master like Troilo or Marconi, the bandoneón can make a man cry, but melancholy gives way when dance drives the music. Troilo's 1962 milonga "La trampera" (Cheating Woman) is surely one of the happiest pieces of bandoneón music in recorded history, but Troilo turns nostalgic when playing "Mi noche triste."

Bandoneonistas "dance" their instrument when playing tango. African flutists and drummers also dance when they play, turning their action into acoustical terms. Five early players of bandoneón were Afro-Argentine. We intuit their influence when a bandoneonista stamps the floor with his right heel, making the thigh rock the instrument. Varchausky explains:

Bandoneonistas use the pressure of the thigh against the bellows (when the heel is going up and going down) to achieve the effect of staccato articulation. This happens when the air inside the instrument is caused to come out with much more pressure than if it were simply played with the fingertips.[81]

Bandoneonistas have their own idiom. They call their instrument the "bellows" (*fueye*), for clear reasons. Pedro Goñi, teaching José di Giorgio his instrument, used to tell him, "Don't lift the spider!" (¡*No levantes la araña!*), meaning: Keep your fingers on the buttons—don't lose your speed or your accuracy.[82]

EXPERIMENT IN INTENSITY: THE MUSIC OF
JUAN D'ARIENZO

> The music of d'Arienzo is a shot of raw whisky. It burns
> your throat, but your palate adores it.

— JOSÉ DI GIORGIO (2003)

The tango historian Luis Adolfo Sierra, wriing on May 5, 1949, took note of a revolution that had been led by Juan d'Arienzo: "He animates dance floors with a big pounding pulse, overwhelming and fast, in ceaseless collisions of staccato and silence."[83] What lay behind this artist's success? First of all, Carlos Posadas, the black master of early tango, taught him piano.[84] The tangos of Posadas were happy and strong; so were the tangos of d'Arienzo.

He came on the scene with a hit, a transformation of Pintín Castellano's "La puñalada" (The Stab of the Knife) into a swinging milonga, recorded April 27, 1937. His pianists—Rodolfo Biagi, Juan Polito, and Fulvio Salamanca—were to a man superb. They made his beat ring, as did staccato passages of instruments playing melody.[85] Finally, his songbook was cast in street idiom, in a revalorization of *lunfardo*.[86] Milonga-like pace and intensity, good-natured moods, hard-driving pianists, and lyrics in the vernacular—all this proved irresistible. The youth of Buenos Aires crowned d'Arienzo "king of the beat."

No one came on as strong as d'Arienzo. As the contemporary bass player Aslán points out, he got his punch more with staccato than with arrastre.[87] His momentum carried over into the 1940s and beyond—happy, fast, and pianistic, it was an ongoing experiment in intensity. It kept him the house band at the prestigious Chantecler nightclub from 1924 almost to the end of the 1950s.[88]

The star dancer Gabriel Angió evaluates d'Arienzo's achievement: "Tango was languishing until D'Arienzo came along. He revitalized things. He started them flowing again. All the top orchestras copied his beat, then branched off into personal expressions."[89]

D'Arienzo made music for dance. Excitement rules in "Milonga de mis amores" (Milonga of My Loves), while the offbeat bandoneón phrasings in "De pura cepa" (The Genuine Article) are amazing, briefly going into jazz—cakewalk and ragtime.

There was more to d'Arienzo's prowess than a strong sense of percussion: harmony and melody factor in, too. "Sábado inglés" (English Saturday) has a passage like laughter, where two violins play in falling chromatic parallel thirds. D'Arienzo was not formally daring, like Pugliese or Salgán, but this hardly mattered to his boisterous fans. They were in love with his rhythm and followed him around like a soccer star.

A MAN FOR ALL BARRIOS: CARLOS DI SARLI

> Hey, tango, tell us who you are . . .
> I'm bread, I'm a banner,
> I'm a shout, I'm a prayer.
> And the friends in your gang?
> Special-close, like a brother,
> is Carlos di Sarli—there's really no other.
>
> —ANTONIO CANTO, "Carlos de Sarli," La historia del tango (1998)

Carlos di Sarli, master bandleader of the 1940s, appears in an undated photograph wearing dark glasses (covering blindness in one eye) and a tuxedo (esmoquin), one hand in pocket. In the other he holds a cigarette, completing the pose.[90] He's relaxed, but you sense his command. Di Sarli faced tough competition in d'Arienzo, but he countered the pressure with suaveness and elegance. His mentor was Fresedo, with whom he had worked in his youth. Di Sarli's early-1940s tangos moved fast, caught in the turbulence of d'Arienzo; like all the 1940s masters, he knew how to swing. Then gradually he accomplished a beat of his own.

Juan Carlos Copes has proclaimed di Sarli's piano the most tanguero of all.[91] The Argentine critic Federico Monjeau finds in his work "a certain spareness" (una cierta parquedad) and means this as praise; his bass-register phrasings are unpretentious and cool.[92] Like Firpo before him, he creatively transposed guitar lines to piano. Confronted with strong rhythmists—Pugliese, Troilo, and especially d'Arienzo—he answered with elegance and more elegance.

Listen to his hit "Bahía Blanca" (The City of Bahia Blanca), recorded for RCA Victor on November 21, 1957. The strings make their entrance with Zen-like economy. Out of the blue comes a strong phrase, like a reverse falling star, moving from bass to high register. It recurs, this time softly. Di Sarli is recalling where he lived as a child. Breaking the canon of bereftness, "Bahía Blanca" proffers the past as a luminous cameo.

Many have danced to this song. The late José "Poroto" Oviedo, a talented Buenos Aires milonguero and night person, here shown dancing tango with Milena Plebs in January 2000 (Plate 50), told his friends: "When I die, play di Sarli at my wake [*velorio*]." When he passed away in April 2000, his comrades honored his request. Milena performed. Kely and Facundo Posadas tangoed to a recording of "Bahía Blanca" before his open coffin. Kely recalls, "You could swear that Poroto was smiling."[93]

When *vitroleros* (tango DJs) play di Sarli, the restraint of his style takes over the dance floor. In 1995 Néstor Fernández, late vitrolero of Sin Rumbo, in Villa Urquiza, ventured that:

> the rhythms of an orchestra tell dancers how to move. d'Arienzo inspires you to make flashy figures. [But] dancing to di Sarli, you'll walk and you'll stop, making elegant pauses, because the sound of di Sarli is "downtown."[94]

The dancer Angió responds: "It's true you make pauses when dancing to di Sarli, it's true you don't make numerous figures. You walk, you pause, and you walk again." Di Sarli, in other words, makes a world of his own. His fans mocked the followers of d'Arienzo:

FACUNDO POSADAS: People who danced to the music of di Sarli called d'Arienzo followers "cabbage-heads" [*repolleros*].
ALEJANDRO FRIGERIO: Because they piled one thing on another?
POSADAS: Exactly. One figure stuck to another. Pam-pam: a "run." Pam-pam: a "hook." Dancing the *melody,* forget it. But the dancers of di Sarli—

PLATE 50

FRIGERIO: —were more elegant?

POSADAS: You betcha. Instead of making ten figures in one single tango, they'd make maybe five. Plus, they left space for walking. You could see the beginning and the ending of a phrase. It was not a *repollo* [a cabbagelike mess].[95]

The man who led dancers into poise and economy was born Cayetano di Sarli in Bahía Blanca, three hundred–odd miles south of Buenos Aires, on January 7, 1903. At the age of thirteen he joined a touring *zarzuela* (Spanish light opera) troupe as the piano player. Applause and adventure changed his life. He spent two years performing tango in a remote town in the pampas, then moved to Buenos Aires around 1919.

When di Sarli got off the train, he entered a world in which Firpo and Canaro were kings. But it was the smooth, aristocratic Osvaldo Fresedo (May 5, 1897–November 18, 1984) who would affect him the most: in 1926, after José Pécora, an old-guard violinist, recommended him to Fresedo, he joined the older man's band and played in it for the next two years.

When he founded his own band in 1928, he was imbued with the Fresedo aesthetic. This meant, among many other things, a piano liberated from the role of keeping time, a piano that shaped melodies of tasteful simplicity.[96]

Di Sarli's magisterial restraint, which he inherited from Fresedo and passed on to Florindo Sassone, has been characterized as a rescue of old-guard nobility. But di Sarli in fact worked out a blend of periods.[97]

Thus armed, by 1939 he was the toast of the town. From Fresedo he had learned how to liberate, with supersuave sounds, the aristocrat in every woman and man. During the Carnival of 1941, at the large Atlanta Club in Villa Crespo, where Copes would later become the *cacique* (top leader) of the youths, di Sarli was paid fourteen thousand pesos to play seven dances.[98]

To understand di Sarli's style, listen to two pieces from the 1940s. One, "El jagüel" (The Country Cistern) is an instrumental, recorded for RCA Victor on November 4, 1943. He invites us to dance to his own special stimulus: "the sound seems to hang in the air [*algo colgado*] with notes that keep vibrating, languid notes [*notas lánguidas*], giving you time to work out your motion."[99]

The other is di Sarli's version of Lasala Álvarez's tango "El estagiario" (The Intern), recorded for RCA Victor on April 18, 1941. The beginning is graceful; then a loud, clanging pattern interrupts our attention. It heralds the coming of traces of ragtime, as if to recall the memory of Harold Phillips on piano. Riffs meant for marching cause elegant walks on the floor.

When a Sin Rumbo DJ characterized the sound of di Sarli as "downtown," Angió disagreed:

> "Downtown" refers to "the beautiful people," Barrio Norte, Recoleta. The sound of di Sarli *is* certainly elegant. That elegance can be associated with the Barrio Norte. Nevertheless, if one goes to Villa Urquiza, we find [the famous dancer] Gerardo Portalea who specialized all his life in dancing to di Sarli. Portalea is the pure spirit of Villa Urquiza. There are other tango masters of artistic walking, in Villa Urquiza and Devoto. They all danced to recordings of di Sarli.[100]

Black dancers of the early twenty-first century—Facundo Posadas, Margarita de Guillé, Carlos Anzuate—to a man and a woman all love di Sarli. Dreamily dancing to his tangos, eyes closed and lips pursed, they extend his restraint and economy.

When di Sarli died in Buenos Aires on January 12, 1960, his admirer Troilo remarked, "the blind man took his secret away to the tomb" (*el ciego se llevó el secreto a la tumba*).[101] On one level this was true, but on another it was not: in calling for elegance, di Sarli goes on forever, awakening the barrios to the possibility of freedom.

TROILO: FINDING THE TRUTH OF THE TANGO

> When it came time to play, he was alone with his soul and his instrument. But he always knew where the truth of the music could be found.

—EDMUNDO EICHELMANN, *Aníbal Troilo* (1980)

D'Arienzo designed tangos for hard, loud encounters. Di Sarli favored elegance. Aníbal Troilo (July 11, 1914–May 18, 1975) embraced both extremes and more. He played whole spectrums, action to meditation, nostalgia to celebration.

Troilo's remarks could be lapidary. Marconi remembers, "Troilo said that his bandoneón was a cage, filled with notes that were birds, which he liked to set free when he played." This is not sadness. This is mind being liberated. Unleashing sensibility and taste, Troilo made different people interactive. He could play two sides of an argument: he could grumble (*rezongaba*) with his left hand and rejoice with his right. These qualities are evident in "Quejas de bandoneón" (Lament of the Bandoneón), recorded in 1944 and considered his signature piece.

The mambo king, Dámaso Pérez Prado, when he wanted his men to "cook," used to give them a cold stare and a grunt. Troilo, similarly, used to shout, ¡*Dále grasa!* (Put grease on it!) when asking his men for their rhythmic most.[102] And when they gave it to him, he'd shout out approvingly: ¡*Subieron al tren!* (You got on the train!)[103] Swing was the issue—freeing up the beat so the music could go forward.

Adoring Troilo, Buenos Aires gave him an affectionate nickname linking him to an Argentine comic strip character of the 1940s, Pichuco, drawn with a grave face, both lips projecting (*con la trompita que ponía*). Call him Troilo or Pichuco, his contribution was nonpareil: "In his bandoneón sounded the canyengue of Maffia and Laurenz, the delicacy of Vardaro's violin, and the hard pounding piano of Don Osvaldo Pugliese. . . . He reconciled styles and generations."[104]

Connoisseurs cherish the period in the 1960s when he played in a quartet with the remarkable guitarist Roberto Grela. Somehow fewer instruments meant more. In "Ivette," recorded August 27, 1962, Grela flirts with the beat of the old habanera. Troilo counters with cuatro. They are playing with time.

Juan Carlos Copes loves dancing to Troilo. He renders his history in affectionate shorthand: "First there was his orchestral period, backed by great pianists, Orlando Goñi [who worked with Troilo from 1937 to 1942] and Osvaldo Berlingieri [the late 1950s]; then came the incredible quartet of the sixties."[105] Troilo's work of the 1960s gives back a refined essence of his style.

Troilo was born in Buenos Aires on July 11, 1914, at 3457 Calle Cabrera, between Laprida and Anchorena, in Buenos Aires's Almagro barrio. His childhood was active—he loved soccer, playing half center and forward—but a landscape of sound soon absorbed his attention. Passing bars and cafés, he would hear bandoneones. His brother, Marquitos, remembers him riveted whenever bandoneonistas played barrio picnics—"as if he were hypnotized."[106] His mother noticed: she bought him a bandoneón and arranged for lessons.

By the time Troilo was fourteen, life was tango. He put together a short-lived quintet that played with respectful adherence to the style of de Caro.[107] His ability to unify the work of the masters with his own rhythmic logic attracted the attention of Vardaro and Pugliese, who in

December 1930 invited him to play in their orchestra. Other masters also beckoned: Juan Maglio in 1931, de Caro and Laurenz in 1932. Troilo unveiled his own first orchestra on July 1, 1937, in the Marabú cabaret, on Maipú near Corrientes. He was twenty-three. On hand to wish him well was his colleague Mora, the black pianist and bandoneonista. Troilo's rhythmic sophistication was enhanced in the 1940s when he visited Rio and heard samba. Years later a dash of 1940s samba would deepen his 1962 masterpiece, "La trampera."

Troilo's classic "Milongueando en el 40" (Hanging Out in the 1940s), recorded on June 17, 1941,[108] starts with a dazzling cascade, notes tumbling down a staircase of sound. This sets the stage for a flourish-filled tango, sparkling with stops, zigzagging lines, and deft glides. Twenty-two years later its fervor would inspire the dancers of *Tango Argentino*.

In "Guapeando" (Hanging Tough), recorded on July 11, 1941, Troilo plays in short rhythmic bursts. "Cachirulo," an instrumental recorded on March 4, 1941, interrupts its own flow with stops, starts, and pauses. Musical cameos become arabesques. Troilo was now famous for acoustical richness—so much going on one can scarcely absorb it.

Troilo's interpretation of Alfredo Gobbi's "Orlando Goñi" (1950) reflects awareness of Pugliese—but the borrowing is muted. There is one small brief moment of Iberian phrasing. In his version of "Chiqué," contrasts emerge, dark, then lambent. He was seeking a synthesis.

Adding viola and violoncello to the texture of tango, Troilo experimented with new timbres. His orchestra of the late 1940s was a modernist proving ground—until Piazzolla, the main instigator, wore out his welcome and left. In the late 1950s, with big bands collapsing, Troilo switched to a format of four: himself on bandoneón, Grela on guitar, Edmundo Zaldívar (and then Héctor Ayala) on guitarrón, and Kicho Díaz on contrabass. The way they played was socially revealing: "Roles switched. Piano might keep time but solo as well. Bandoneón might attend to harmonics then take over rhythm. [Troilo's band] was more democratic."[109]

It was in this freewheeling way that Troilo and Grela with the quartet recorded the classic "Mi noche triste" on August 21, 1962. The music starts off with the expected air of regret, then suddenly veers into offbeats. A sad thought meets energy. At the end, as if to warn what will happen if we focus too intently on melancholy, the music dwindles down to darkness and rhythm, then only darkness.

Troilo was fond of his food and wine and ended his years with a serious weight problem. His last performance was May 17, 1975, in the Odeon

Theater. The event was titled *Simplemente Pichuco* (Simply Pichuco). He died the next day. The striking bronze likeness marking his grave in Chacarita cemetery, seated in the sunlight, captures the way he looked down when he played.

HORACIO SALGÁN: THE ONE-MAN CONSERVATORY

If you talk about so-and-so, the pianist, fine. But if you compare him to Salgán, better watch out. Salgán is a genius.

— ROBERTO GOYENECHE (N.D.)

The Stoics cautioned us to keep our philosophical precepts few and simple, as we might have to refer to them at a moment's notice.

— DAVID MAMET, "Hearing the Notes That Aren't Played," *The New York Times* (July 15, 2002).

Horacio Salgán was a star tango orchestra leader in the 1940s and 1950s and dominated the tango for the rest of the century. Pugliese and Canaro honored and incorporated black elements, but Salgán *was* black. From inside the culture he played with blue notes and syncopes, sambas and bombo drums, making sparkling contributions like nobody else. Instructed in Western harmonics, his tango was chordal as well as percussive. In his music—and this was the equation that inspired Piazzolla—popular was equal to erudite.

In 2003, at the age of eighty-seven, he was packing them into the Club de Vino, the famous café-concert venue in Palermo. Two years earlier he had published *Curso de tango,* a landmark text on the music—its execution, theory, and practice. Salgán, in short, opened up a whole cultural universe in Argentine music.

Listen, for instance, to his "Tango del eco" (Echoing Tango), written between 1960 and 1970 and recorded in 2000 with Salgán's Nuevo Quinteto Real (New Royal Quintet).[110] Chords become echoes, establishing a shimmering quietude. Marconi comes in on bandoneón, with his drive and propulsion. Suddenly there's an ambush in sound: a bass roll on piano ushers in eighth notes. These chimed exclamation points fall on the offbeat. *This* is the tango, Salgán seems to say, a percussive aggression that cuts through decorousness to drive you to dance. Conversation between instruments takes place, then back to the offbeating bass roll. Salgán prompts many musics. He can quote short motifs from show tunes or ragtime. His command of Western classicism is nonpareil. He has composed sambas as well, reminding us how cosmopolitan tangueros can be.

Salgán was born on June 15, 1916, in the Abasto, Buenos Aires, the barrio of Gardel. His black ancestors lie on the maternal side of his family: his mother Doña Emma Méndez, was a light-skinned black woman, and *her* mother—Salgán's grandmother—was *negra,* African in appearance, and married to a white. Salgán's father, Don Adolfo Cecilio Salgán, was white, the son of a Catalan immigrant.[111]

The family moved to Calle Olaya, in Caballito, between Flores and Almagro. There Salgán grew up in a musical environment. At the age of nine months, he crawled from a patio, seeking the sound of his father on piano. Don Emilio was playing a tango.[112] Emma read this as sign: her child would become a musician.[113]

He started his career as a pianist, playing background music for silent movies at the Cine Universal in Devoto. He was also the organist at the Iglesia de San Antonio in the same barrio. He was learning to play in large, dramatic spaces, figures flickering on the screen above his head, or with worshipers below, kneeling or seated in pews.

He grew into manhood, handsome and neat (*guapo y pulcro*). Women adored him.[114] He sought out the dance styles around him, U.S. jazz, Brazilian samba, Afro-Cuban habanera, Argentine vals and milonga—and his first composition (dated 1936, when he was twenty) was actually Brazilian in style. In 1943 this song, "Choro en Fa #," became his first recording. Salgán also worked out a six-eight piece based on the malambo, the Afro-Argentine rural black stamping dance; he was fond of milonga as well and spelled out its roots with a composition called "Milonga casi candombe" (Milonga That's Almost Candombe). But his primary passion was tango.

Salgán formed his first tango orchestra in 1944. He hired a young singer, Edmundo Rivero, who was rejected at first, then later became nationally popular. The band ran until 1947. With his second tango orchestra, in 1950–57, Salgán's stylistic power achieved major significance. As his singer he hired Roberto Goyeneche, who would become the Frank Sinatra of tango.

It was during this period that Salgán began to compose superlative countermelodies to be inserted in major works as "inspirations."

In 1951 he added one of these gems to de Caro's "Tierra querida": listening to his version, one waits impatiently for the part he composed, with its peremptory beat and notes that shine like chrome. He was also writing full tangos of his own, "La llamo silbando" (I Call Her by Whistling), recorded in 1952, and "A fuego lento" (To a Slow Fire), composed in 1950–51 and recorded in 1954.

In 1957 Salgán started a lifetime friendship with the brilliant guitarist Ubaldo de Lío, with whom he played in the nightclub Jamaica. Their first disk, recorded in 1958–59 on the Phillips label, spotlit four numbers: "Malena," "Un tropezón" (A Moment of Stumbling), "Taquito militar" (Military Snap), and "Risa loca" (Crazed Laughter). "Malena" and "Taquito militar" would join the two men's permanent repertoire.

In 1965 Ella Fitzgerald was performing in Buenos Aires and happened to hear the work of her black colleague. She persuaded the North American jazz entrepreneur Norman Granz to record a Salgán LP, *Buenos Aires at 3 a.m.* Then in 1970 the Aga Khan included Salgán's orchestra in an All-Stars LP recorded in Osaka, Japan. Salgán's reputation had become international.

In the 1950s three major bandleaders—Salgán, Pedro Laurenz, and Enrique Mario Francini—were forced to break up their bands because the manning of full orchestras had become unaffordable. Salgán and de Lío began to play as a duo, as did Laurenz and Francini. In 1960, the two duos fused and, adding the contrabassist Rafael Ferro, formed the Quinteto Real.[115] Their first LP was *El Quinteto Real* (1960), followed by *Su majestad, el tango* (His Majesty, the Tango) in 1961. They played together from 1960 to 1970. Later, in 1987, Salgán formed the Nuevo Quinteto Real, again with de Lío on guitar, Marconi on bandoneón, Antonio Agri (later Hermes Peressini) on violin, and Oscar Giunta on bass. In 1982 Salgán and de Lío performed at a café in Les Halles, Paris, called On the Sidewalks of Buenos Aires (Sur les troittoirs de Buenos Aires). Coming one year before *Tango Argentino,* their appearance helped set the stage for the Parisian success of that production. Many who heard them, baptized by their sound and their feeling, flocked to the later event. They reacquainted Paris with *tango porteño.* Critical reaction noted a distinct black dimension in the work of Salgán. Claude Fleouter, writing for *Le Monde* in 1982, observed:

> Salgán on piano moves with spectacular velocity. He deepens the rhythmic sense of the tango, adding a touch that is black. He creates a new tango, profound in its traditionalism, but open to Bartók, Ravel, jazz, and black popular music from Brazil.[116]

Salgán's style indeed involves two narratives, one classical, one black. He performs works by classical composers—Chopin, Ravel, Debussy—out of personal predilection; in 1950–51 he spun an aria from Rossini's *Barber of Seville* into the riff of his tango "A fuego lento."[117] This was five years before Piazzolla began blurring the boundaries between tango and classicism. In 1993 Salgán himself remarked:

> Training in Western symphonic music opened up a whole world of harmony, orchestration, and pianistic execution. But there's also a black dimension to my music. It's not casual, nor flagrant, but part of my origin . . . my style, and my truth.[118]

Tango is a partly African-derived dance that is nevertheless played without drums. A number of tango musicians have addressed this paradox: in the 1930s and 1940s Fresedo and Canaro added traps to the tango, not to change the beat but to reinforce it.[119] Villoldo once played castanets.

In 1961 Salgán added percussion to two numbers: "Con bombo legüero" (To the Beat of the Large Bombo Drum) and "Tango del balanceo" (Rocking Tango). The *bombo legüero,* literally "the bombo that can be heard across many leagues," is the larger of two drums in a rural Argentine drum choir.

Salgán took the bombo from the pampas and caused it to be played with a bright rolling pattern that sounds like merengue. Salgán also scored in a line of five coconuts, adding another sequence of rhythm. Each uttered but one note, like Central African and Haitian hocketed, one-note bamboo trumpets.

In "Con bombo legüero" Salgán also brought in a chorus, which sang with a fervor reminiscent of samba. (In fact, they sound like Quarteto em Cy, who were big in Brazil at the time.) The chorus chants drum syllables of Kongo-Argentine origin: *karankanfu.* To Kely and Facundo Posadas, *karakanfu* suggests "dancing without losing elegance." This is not so far from the sense of the original Kongo idiophone *kalakanfu,* meaning "drum slowly" or "step slowly." Compare also the Ki-Kongo *kala-kala,* "wait for a moment; catch your breath."[120]

By deepening percussion and chanting the word *karakanfu,* Salgán recalls the gifted black Cuban lyricist, Antar Daly, who galvanized the worldwide mambo hit "Babarabatiri" with the word *babarabatiri* in around 1950.[121] In sum, *con bombo* swings.[122]

Salgán rips off the mask of melancholy. To emphasize sadness, he argues, is to forget the exuberance of Mendizábal's "El entrerriano," to say nothing of the bright music of Villoldo's "El choclo."[123]

Salgán builds "Milonga casi candombe" (A Milonga That Is Almost Candombe) on black street drumming but transposes the beat from drums to the orchestra, in a move that presaged Piazzolla's "Marrón y azul." Notes grouped in patterns of Afro-Cuban habanera appear in parts of the bass.

Salgán became playful in "La llamo silbando" (I Call Her by Whistling), recorded April 9, 1952. In Howard Hawks's movie *To Have and Have Not* (1945), Lauren Bacall immortally purred to Humphrey Bogart, "If you need me, just whistle." Salgán transformed *his* love whistle into music, scoring for violin an ascending motif in two notes. Touching the string lightly, the violinist extracts a harmonic tone that mimicks a whistled phrase Salgán once used to call a former wife, Sarah, to his side. Then he segues into the main melodic theme of the Tin Pan Alley standard "Ain't She Sweet," deepening the amorous allusion. He whistles for his lover—he is calling her "sweet." And then he bears her, like roses, chromatic offerings that move down the scale by three half-steps.

The late Alan Lomax found playfulness in many key musics of tropical Africa.[124] But it's also a part of Jewish popular music, like klezmer. On the night of October 11, 1997, at the Club del Vino, I heard the late and great violinist Antonio Agri make his instrument twitter, as if a nightingale were caught in the upper range of his strings. Nearly five years later, on the night of August 24, 2002, Agri's successor, Hermes Peressini, playing for Salgán, made *his* violin chirp like a canary, and so did Ramiro Gallo, first violinist of El Arranque, on August 1, 2003. On yet another night, when Gabriel Angió danced the tango, unaware that his hair was standing on end, a violinist broke into the Woody Woodpecker theme. The New York tango bassist Aslán has heard Jewish violinists make bird calls with their strings. This may be a source. Jewish presence in tango is well documented.[125]

Classical erudition and other qualities meet in the style of Salgán: he works with orchestral call and response. He likes to toss themes around. In addition, he has a signature way of using rubato: "magically restoring the beat, or setting a subtly slower tempo for a lyrical section," according to the New York composer Herschel Garfein.[126]

Salgán's music is streamlined and sophisticated. Sometimes one note coincides with the silence of another in a technique known as *hocketing*.[127] And Monjeau has ventured: "Absence of heaviness sets his rhythms in flight."[128] He works with strong riffs, which he vaunts in the improvised double-time sections (*variaciones*) that he adds to tangos by other composers, like Arturo Bernstein's "Don Goyo" or de Caro's

"Boedo." In concert, though, his exposition may narrow to single-finger "plinks" in the upper range of his keyboard, underscoring de Lío on guitar. Listen to Salgán remaking "Tierra querida." De Caro recorded the landmark original on September 12, 1927.[129] Salgán recorded his version on May 30, 1951. Confirming his cosmopolitanism, the piano breaks into blue notes. Salgán's version is rhythmically more aggressive, with wild clusters of piano notes. He enlivens the bridge with classical counterpoint. He plays with rubato more than de Caro did, shifting the tempo. Like de Caro, he adds blue notes to the double-time chorus, confirming cultural richness and fervor.

Salgán turned tango into art music. Astonishing as it now seems, major companies once had no interest in recording him, but the support of musicians kept him going: "I played in the Tango Bar and the café was always crowded, much to the delight of the owner. But who formed the audience? Musicians. One of them was Astor Piazzolla."[130]

Salgán prevails. With his writing, his quintet, and his art, he is radiantly present in a time of great stress. He finds nobility in rhythm, healing in humor, transcendence in blue notes, and dignity in human communication.

THE CARNATION ON THE KEYBOARD: THE ART OF OSVALDO PUGLIESE

> One could speak, with total justice, of compositions before and after Pugliese's *Recuerdo* and of instrumentalists before and after *Recuerdo*.
>
> — HORACIO FERRER, *El tango: Su historia y evolución* (1960)

Osvaldo Pugliese was born December 2, 1905, on Calle Canning (now Scalabrini Ortiz) in the barrio of Villa Crespo. He gave the world the first modern tango, "Recuerdo." Later, with three classics—"La yumba," "Negracha," and "Malandraca"—he rethought the tango with blue notes, Stravinsky, and undreamed-of intensity. Rossini overtures, Verdi operas, and Beethoven were grist for his mill. Like his idol de Caro, he challenged his city's Eurocentrism. No one had to point out to Pugliese, as Juan Álvarez did to an earlier generation in 1908, that "even if blacks are now few in number, their presence still resonates—in habaneras, milongas, and tangos."[131] Pugliese honored the black music of his nation to an artistic degree rivaled only by Salgán and Piazzolla.

The writer Arturo Marcos Lozza once asked Pugliese what had triggered his percussive 1946 hit, "La yumba." Pugliese responded, "I kept my ears open. I remember, around 1930, a young black pianist who used to hang with us. He played by ear in tango dance halls. He was marvelous. We loved this black guy. Me and him used to play, four hands on a keyboard."[132] Pugliese was not saying this single black pianist inspired "La yumba." But he was hinting at a generalized influence. Note the black names of two of his masterpieces—*yumba*, meaning "dance!" in creole Ki-Kongo, and *negracha*, which translates broadly as "woman of color." Perhaps his most important work, "Malandraca," affectionately refers to his daughter. When Beba Pugliese was a little girl, racing up and down stairs and knocking on doors, her father lovingly called her "my little rascal" (*mi malandraca*). "Malandraca" is dazzling: its boilerhouse intensity melts into yearning, and a factorylike ardor, metallic and hard, turns into thought and nostalgia. Be vastly intelligent, the music seems to say, be tough and be hard, but keep the mind free with dreams.

Young toughs admired Pugliese, following him around like football fans.[133] They translated feistiness into motion. "How did you move when 'Yumba' came out?" I asked the legendary Pibe Palermo in 2002. Pibe stood up, took his wife in his arms, and started dancing a series of dazzling crossovers (*cruces*). He scatted the whole time that he did them, translating remembered notes into syllables. Pugliese's followers lived for his sound. They were also inspired by his courage—"he was slight but all steel"—and his social conscience.[134] Disillusioned by the progress of the Spanish Civil War, Pugliese joined the Argentine Communist Party in 1936. He remained a member to the day he died. Perón jailed him for six months in 1955; the military regime that ousted Perón jailed Pugliese, too. So did General Farrell, even before Juan Perón.[135] Whenever he was arrested, his men placed on his piano a red carnation or rose. It was a "symbol of absence" (*símbolo de ausencia*), alerting the dance hall that Pugliese was in jail.[136]

His fans had a war cry: "¡Al Colón!" (To the Teatro Colón!), the Colón being the opera house where the top musicians went. The management of the Michelangelo, a San Telmo nightclub that staged big tango shows, loved him, too: ignoring bomb threats, they kept him employed during the grim days of the Proceso, 1976–83. The junta did not dare "disappear" him; as Copes explains, "he was simply too popular."

When democracy returned in 1983, with the election of Raúl Alfonsín as the country's president, Pugliese received a long overdue honor: a concert on December 26, 1985, in the Teatro Colón.[137] The war cry had become a reality.

Pugliese had come a long way. By 1920, as a lean teenager, he was playing piano bar tango in Buenos Aires. In 1929 he and the brilliant tango violinist Elvino Vardaro formed the Vardaro-Pugliese sextet. A photograph shows them together: Vardaro looks pensive; Pugliese wears a pencil-thin smile. In 1924, before turning twenty, he wrote the first modern tango. The melody came to him in a streetcar; humming the tune to keep it alive, he raced home to write it, adding a variation later. He called it "Recuerdo" (Fond Memory) and dedicated it to the young numbers-runners (*quinieleros del café*) with whom he played pool and drank in cafés.[138] Two years later Pugliese was playing "Recuerdo" in the Café ABC, at Canning and Rivera, when the famed bandoneonista Pedro Laurenz happened to hear it. Impressed, he relayed his reaction to de Caro, who became the first to record "Recuerdo," on July 9, 1926. This piece made Pugliese's reputation.

The opening notes of "Recuerdo" are resonant and dark. They lead to a mixture of styles. The pizzicato first section ends like Rossini; then comes a strong Afro syncope. Pugliese was creolizing, submitting Rossini to Argentine stops and syncopes. These contrasts in culture establish its modernity and separate "Recuerdo" from what went before.

When the 1940s arrived, Pugliese was ready. Now he was playing for star dancing couples like Petróleo and La Negra Martita. Petróleo believed that those who lived best were those who danced best. In such a world Pugliese was perfect.

Fans dressed to match the excitement:

> In the 1940s each band had their followers. Their fine rented clothes [*pilchas*] were wonderful to look at. Each band had their fans [*hinchas*], each fan-group their "uniform." Ours dressed *a la divito* [in the style of a famous Buenos Aires comic strip]—wasp-waisted women and zoot-suited men. Our guys would arrive at the dance halls in trucks, [wearing] jackets with big lapels [*solapas*], padded shoulders [*hombreras levantadas*], pants with the seat [*fundillos*], and the legs [*perneras*] all cut tight.[139]

Pugliese's daughter adds that there was "a sashlike extension of the pants that went around the waist, studded with small buttons" (*una faja con botoncitos*).[140] Mimesis of 1940s black vogue—the Harlem zoot suit—had entered the milongas, cut, set, and modified to tanguero taste. The Buenos Aires cartoonist Guillermo Guerrero reminds us that one of the models of Divito was the elegant clothes worn by the blacks of Harlem.[141]

One group of followers shaved off their sideburns; they were *los sin patilla*.[142] Others sauntered in with a small cross made of Band-Aids (*curitas*) pasted on their right cheek.[143] The ultimate fans were Pugliese doubles, Beba Pugliese recalls—"guys who dressed like my father, wore his same glasses, and even barbered their hair in his manner."[144]

Women were no less provocative: they wore high heels, erotic anklets, skirts split on both sides (*tajos en la pollera, abierta en dos costados*), like women from Shanghai, plus Divito wasp waists.[145]

Pugliese's "La yumba," first recorded on August 21, 1946, rattled the landscape, like the Africanizing figures of Picasso's *Demoiselles d'Avignon.* Pugliese was mixing Stravinsky-like rhythms, an indirect "Africanism," with rich, yearning passages suggesting the blues.

The word *yumba* itself comes directly from candombe:

BASTONERO: *Calunga güe!*
CORO: *Oyeye yumba!*

STAFFHOLDER: Hail the infinity of the other world, our mother!
CHORUS: Sing it! Dance it![146]

Yumba is a holy word in Kongo: it means God's command, or a strong building force that makes things happen, like the concept of *ashe* in the Yoruba Atlantic.[147] It's the imperative form of a verb of strong action, like *lumba!* (march! go forward!), which compares to the Ki-Pende imperative *umba!* (dance!) not to mention *rumba* in black Cuba.[148] Pugliese christened his work with this word from candombe.

Pugliese formed his first orchestra on August 1, 1939. Swing was in the air. Orestes López was dreaming up mambo. Pugliese intensified arrastres and offbeats. Like Salgán and di Sarli, he worked with "robbed time," speeding up tempi and slowing them down.

"Yumba" starts off strong and peremptory. After a fusillade of accents comes a shift to the lyrical. The rhythmic revolution took place in the first and last sections. The middle section is more traditional—the young composer hedging all bets. He followed that composition with "Negracha" (Black Woman), recorded on June 24, 1948. Beba Pugliese says that in writing this number, her father was thinking of a woman of color who danced tango in the cafés of Buenos Aires in the 1940s. She remembers him talking about her, admiring the way she sketched patterns on the floor (¡*cómo dibujaba!*).[149] Perhaps he was alluding to La Negra Martita, the superb black partner of Petróleo, who certainly danced before Pugliese and his orchestra in the Atlanta dance palace, though whether before or after "Negracha" remains to be confirmed.

In "Negracha" violins pulse with minimal tone. Strings become drums.

It was partial homage to the strong rhythmic passages in Stravinsky's *Rite of Spring*. Like the Russian composer, Pugliese scored strings for eighth notes while the rest of the band merely punctuated. Erudition meets intensity—the blend is incredible.

Evenly accented eighth notes impart machine- or pistonlike qualities, severe and industrial. Then the music slows down like a train entering a station, a transition perhaps later copied by Horacio Malvicino, in a 1955 composition for Piazzolla.

Pugliese climaxed his revolution with an all-time instrumental masterpiece, "Malandraca," recorded on May 31, 1949. Uninflected eighth-notes return with a vengeance. Riffs pound like pistons while the piano goes down scale in a bright little fragment. An arrastre takes off—*vwooom!*— and the music does, too. Then comes a moment of yearning, a minor mode passage illumined with blue notes.

Copes and Nieves danced "Malandraca" with sharp lunges and angles.[150] Virulazo did, too.[151] They were dancing to music inspired by a black pianist, a black woman, the blues, and Stravinsky.

"Malandraca" achieved musical cubism, turning tango into vivid abstractions. The opening was pared down to riffs and intensity. Its influence on Piazzolla would be strong.

Pugliese died July 25, 1995, at 8:40 in the evening. Tangueros today, inspired by the memory of his famed generosity, consider him a saint. He ran his band as a cooperative: equal cuts for all players. His sidemen were able to buy houses and cars. Musicians make pilgrimages to his statue, at the corner of Corrientes and Scalabrini Ortiz in Buenos Aires. Touching his image is said to bring protection from envy. Many visit his tomb in Chacarita, where he is seen playing a bronze keyboard—laden, of course, with red carnations.

Buenos Aires musicians today, even rockers and players of *cumbia villera,* will often mention his name before going onstage to counteract the forces of envy and bad luck (*mufa*).[152] There is a prayer card printed in his name and bearing his lean image, the red rose of absence, and the legend *San* [*Saint*] *Pugliese*. On the obverse we read: "Carry us, with your mystery, towards a passion beyond death."[153]

In the context of these beliefs, "Malandraca" becomes an altar of sound, composed by a generous, uncompromising man. In the intensity of the last chorus he stands right beside us. As the pressure builds up, I find myself shouting: *Say it! Say it! Say it, brother! Teach us the power of refusing to suffer!* "It's a melody for shouting," says his own daughter.

Beba Pugliese became a prominent woman orchestra leader in tango, with a distinguished career of her own. Her father has his statue; she has her corner, designated by a plaque, where Rodríguez Peña crosses Corrientes in the capital. Pugliese also inspired his granddaughter, María Carla Novelli, who performed tango piano in Japan with her mother, Beba, in June 2003.[154] At the end, Pugliese turned talisman. His aura enhances Argentina.

ASTOR PIAZZOLLA'S NEW TANGO

> Uri Caine's talent [involves] seeing connections where others see distance.
>
> —JEREMY EICHLER, "Bach Meets Klezmer and Bossa Nova,"
> *The New York Times,* April 20, 2003.

Start with a still from the 1965 Argentine film *Fueye querido* (Beloved Bandoneón). Astor Piazzolla is playing. He stands with his left foot on the ground, his right propped up on a stool. The bellows of his bandoneón spread open, like a fan, across his right thigh. He reads from a text of nostalgia, open to a secret page.

This was Piazzolla's signature playing position. It's not unlike the stance of a payador, guitar propped on knee, as in Juan Carlos Morel's *Payada en una pulpería* (Battle of Rhyme in a Country Bar) from about 1840. Both payador and tanguero are in control of their iconography, Piazzolla more so, because from that position he can see what his sidemen are doing.[155]

With an epic surge of compositions and concerts between 1955 and 1990, Astor Piazzolla took modern tango to the world. Inspired by the music of the 1940s, by Salgán and Pugliese transforming tango into art music, he elaborated on their gifts, adding Bartók and Bach, cool jazz and free jazz. Piazzolla put a new face on the tango. When he died on July 4, 1992, he was the most famous Argentine musician in the world. Today his CDs sell in classical, jazz, tango, and world music bins, impervious to one single rubric.[156]

Tango met jazz a long time ago, but the encounter took on momentum and depth with Piazzolla. Recall the ragtime of Harold Phillips, the black North American pianist who played tango in La Boca in early twentieth-century Buenos Aires. In the 1940s the major dance halls of the capital routinely featured a tango band, a jazz band, and a band that played rumba: "Musics were in the air, ears were open, sounds were mixing."[157]

Dizzy Gillespie's 1956 appearance with Osvaldo Fresedo's tango band at Fresedo's Rendez-Vous nightclub constituted a legendary moment in Argentine music. Listen to the CD *Fresedo: Rendez-Vous Porteño,* particularly to the cut "Vida mía" (My Darling): Gillespie plays tango, then breaks into bop, scatting his way to the stars. The blend is quite tight in "Preludio no. 3" as Fresedo and Gillespie rediscover together the beat of the habanera. The experiment stands as an influential precedent.[158]

Dominic Frasca's important unpublished study "The Influence of Jazz in Astor Piazzolla's Music" helps us examine a north-south encounter. Bartók and Bach, milonga and candombe, factor in, too. The titles of Piazzolla's recordings, whether written by himself or by others, document an openness to musical experience. He was obviously aware of Afro-Argentine culture ("More Candombe") and of Pugliese's take on it ("Negracha," "La yumba"). He honored key works by black composers (Salgán's "Fuego lento," Mendizábal's "El entrerriano"). He was memorably inspired by de Caro ("Boedo"). In New York in 1959 he arranged music for a Puerto Rican (*boricua*), possibly Tito Puente, the Manhattan mambo king for whom he allegedly wrote a few scores. He learned words from Jewish friends (hence the composition "El goy"). He had classical ambitions (*serie de tangos sinfónicos*). There were three women in his life ("Dede," "Amelitango," "Sueño de Laura"). He knew all about protection from bad luck (*la mufa*). He worked with Jorge Luis Borges (*Alguien le dice al tango*). He was turned on to tango by Vardaro ("Vardarito"). He esteemed the milonga as a form in its own right ("Milonga en ay menor," "Milonga del ángel," "Milonga del diablo," "Milonga loca," "Milonga del trovador").

Whatever Piazzolla did, his true love was tango. He loved her in word-play (*libertango, meditango, tristango, tanguedia*), he loved her in ecstasy, he loved her in sadness. At the end of his career he was as renowned as a rock star. Thus Frasca:

> One year after the birth of Charlie "Bird" Parker in Kansas City, there was born in Argentina a child who was to change the face of his homeland's music as dramatically and forcefully as Bird was to change his country's original music. His name is Astor Piazzolla, and his instrument is the bandoneón [which is] to tango what the saxophone is to jazz.[159]

Astor was born on March 11, 1921, in Mar del Plata, on the Atlantic, southeast of Buenos Aires. That same year his family moved to New York, where he lived for the next sixteen years, until 1937. There he heard jazz,

Cab Calloway in Harlem, and Bach, as played on the piano by a Hungarian neighbor, Béla Wilda.

Young Astor was tough. He defended himself on the streets of New York. Once he tried to steal a harmonica—a policewoman gave chase, but Astor escaped by jumping onto a passing truck. To deal with the boy's wildness, to give him focus, and to remind him he was Argentine, his father gave him a bandoneón. Soon he was playing bandoneón in New York. His first recording took place in Manhattan on November 30, 1931, a solo interpretation of a piece called "Marionette espagnol."[160] By December he was known in Latino New York as "the boy wonder of the bandoneón." The following spring he performed at Rockefeller Center. The Mexican muralist Diego Rivera was there, too. Impressed, he sketched Astor's face and gave him the drawing—recognition of one artist by another. Rivera captured Astor as Picasso might have, with delicate lines and strong darks. In the musician's luminous forehead and intent flashing eyes, Rivera clearly divined a passionate future.[161]

The great tango singer Carlos Gardel, working in New York in 1935, must have felt similarly: he had Piazzolla hired to play a newspaper boy in John Reinhardt's film *El día que me quieras* (The Day You Love Me). A still from that movie shows Piazzolla with the shining round face that Rivera captured, pointing into the distance beside a policeman and three men. One of the men is Gardel.

In 1937, when Astor was seventeen, the family moved back to Argentina. There decisive things happened. First, in 1938 he discovered the tango orchestra of Elvino Vardaro, working in Mar del Plata, and was enchanted. Then and there he resolved to be a tanguero and to play the music as well as Vardaro did.

Second, after moving to Buenos Aires, Astor fell in love with the music of Troilo and also with Dede Wolff, who would become his first wife. He memorized Troilo's book and dreamed of playing in his band. In December 1939, when one of Troilo's bandoneonistas fell ill, Piazzolla stepped up. Troilo said: "So you're the *pibe* who knows my whole repertoire. Okay, get up on stage and play." When the audition was over, Troilo simply said, "Wear a blue suit, tomorrow [night] at seven" (*Pilcha azul, mañana a las siete*).[162] Piazzolla had played his way into one of the most exciting bands in tango history.

But it wasn't enough. During intervals he slipped out to the Moulin Rouge to listen to Pugliese—the rhythm of his orchestra drove him wild with enthusiasm. He listened as well to Salgán; "Negracha" and "A fuego lento" would eventually appear in his repertoire. Meanwhile he was studying classical music and trying to compose in that idiom.

Piazzolla's life was a quest: don't just let things happen, *make* them happen. There is no better example of this than the time Arthur Rubinstein came to town in 1941: Piazzolla talked himself into the maestro's apartment and got the great pianist to play a piece he'd composed.[163] "You need study," said the master; he picked up the phone and generously recommended Piazzolla to Alberto Ginastera, a promising young Argentine composer.[164]

Piazzolla started to study with Ginastera that same year. He learned many things, especially orchestration. To deepen his understanding, Ginastera urged him to keep up with literature and art.[165]

Unfortunately for Troilo, Piazzolla was eager to try out what he was learning from Ginastera. Billy Eckstine once admonished the young Dizzy Gillespie, when the latter played bop in his band, "Get that Chinese music out of here!" Piazzolla, similarly, upset the traditionalists. They didn't want fugues, they wanted tango.

Like the young Debussy (an infamous prankster),[166] Piazzolla worked out his resentment with practical jokes. He once lit a long-fused string of firecrackers beside Troilo's bandstand. It exploded while everyone was playing; Troilo knew. He loved the younger man and called him *gato* (cat), but he was not about to let the budding genius turn his sound into chamber music. In 1946, inevitably, Piazzolla gave notice.

Next Piazzolla briefly directed the orchestra of the singer Francisco Fiorentino at the Marabú nightclub. One night Piazzolla introduced an arrangement of the tango "Copas, amigas, y besos" (Drink, Girlfriends, and Kisses) that opened with a long cello solo—whereupon women who worked in the Marabú raced out onto the dance floor and started dancing on the tips of their toes in a grotesque imitation of ballet.[167] They felt Piazzolla was pretentious. They were putting him down. Crushproof as always, Astor just formed his own orchestra and played with close colleagues who shared his ambitions.

Piazzolla's first orchestra lasted three years, from 1946 to 1949. He was absorbing fine tango (Pichuco, Salgán, Pugliese) and compositions like "Taconeando," then intertwining it all with classicizing touches. He played, mostly for listeners, at the Tango Bar and the Café Marzotto on Avenida Corrientes. The format was influenced by Troilo. At this point Piazzolla was playing other musicians' music, plus some of his own compositions. He would recall that he wasn't certain what he wanted until he discovered his own way of phrasing. The titles of pieces written between 1950 and 1952 reflect a gathering cockiness: "Prepárense" (Get Ready for It), "Lo que vendrá" (What's Coming Next), and "Triunfal" (Triumphal Entry). What triumphed in "Triunfal" was the composer, taking tango away from charted coasts, dance halls, and love songs, and into a realm that was dense, strange, and new. Still to be worked out was a truce between hardness and sentiment. Piazzolla was honing his powers to create in several languages. All he needed was one major break. It came in 1954: one of his symphonies won him a French embassy scholarship to study with Nadia Boulanger, who had worked with Ravel and taught Aaron Copland.[168] In Paris she taught the young Argentine counterpoint and other techniques he would weave into tango. But her critical gift was to retrigger his self-confidence:

> I brought [Nadia] almost everything [classical] I had written. She looked it over for quite a while. Then she asked me how I made my living. I embarrassedly told her I wrote and played tangos. She said she loved tango and asked me to play some for her. I began to play ["Triunfal"] on the piano. After about a minute she grabbed my hands and said, "Now that's the *real* Astor Piazzolla." She told me not to give up the tango. I went back to Argentina and started my first [modern] tango ensemble.[169]

It was not quite as simple as that. Boulanger liberated Piazzolla, but so did the octet of Gerry Mulligan, the cool jazz performer whom he heard during his stay in Paris. Piazzolla would recall:

> It was really marvelous to see the enthusiasm of the musicians, each for the other, while they were playing [as well as] the euphoria of the ensemble when they came together harmonically.[170]

The key idea was enthusiasm—to build his new music, he wanted animated colleagues, not the frozen-faced players as documented by Berni. Returning to Buenos Aires in 1955, Piazzolla formed the Octeto Buenos Aires. He brought aboard the finest tango musicians he could find: Enrique Mario Francini on violin, Atilio Stampone piano, Leopoldo Federico second bandoneón, Hugo Baralis violin, Horacio Malvicino electric guitar, José Bragato violoncello, and Juan Vasallo bass. He rehearsed them at the Rendez-Vous, where Dizzy Gillespie would play jazz with Fresedo the next year.

Ideas flowed in from everywhere: Boulanger-inspired counterpoint between the strings in "Arrabal"; a waltz *à la* Ravel in "Haydee"; Afrotinged percussion in "Marrón y azul" (Maroon and Blue). Malvicino's electric guitar automatically added color, like putting a Matisse in a room full of old masters. His tune "Tangology," with its Parker-like title, made clear the intention to hook up with jazz. Malvicino begins with a "slow, misty theme on guitar."[171] Then rhythm takes over, carrying us into zones of excitement.

The Octeto was an artistic triumph. Two years went by; then in 1957 Piazzolla struck gold with a vivid composition entitled "Tres minutos con la realidad" (*Three Minutes with Reality*). He composed it after listening to Béla Bartók's second violin concerto. As Piazzolla told an interviewer, "Above my bed I have a picture of Bartók. He is my idol."[172]

Bartók (1881–1945), who mixed Hungarian folk and European art music, was a perfect inspiration for a man blending tango with other world musics. As Paul Griffiths has written:

> In one of the lectures he gave at Harvard in 1942, Bartók distinguished two ways in which composers could respond to folk music: they could quote tunes, or they could examine the elements of those tunes—modes, melodic patterns, meters, manners of ornamentation—and create anew in similar style.[173]

Piazzolla, like his mentor, chose the second, more challenging way. In the process he wound up enhancing not only tango but the work of the Hungarian master. Bartók worked with Hungarian folk scales. Piazzolla, in "Tres minutos," adapted a Bartók scale of eight notes, alternating half steps with whole steps.[174] In the process he did more than introduce a distant intelligence to the music of Buenos Aires—he made Bartók exciting in popular terms. In 1959 he would blend a lament with a Bach passacaglia.

Jazz improvisation also lit up his work. Piazzolla experimented with three different idioms of jazz spontaneity.[175] First was embellishing. He would parcel out a spare line to a musician, then ask him to build on it, to make it new. Embellishing enlivens Piazzolla's "Verano porteño" of August 1965. Two black traits meet, jazz improvisation and the milonga beat. The composer himself shows the way: he plays a theme on his instrument, then alters its shape and its color.

Piazzolla's second mode of improvisation simply built on strong riffs, riffs to excite instrumentalists to improvise, as in mambo or jazz.

Pablo Ziegler, one of Piazzolla's most gifted pianists, remembers that Astor would write out a groove, then ask whomever to improvise over it. One clear example: "Concierto para quinteto" (1984).[176]

The third way of improvising occasioned a masterpiece:

> The . . . most interesting style of [Piazzolla's] improvisation is [a restrained form] of free jazz—one instrument playing a scored tonal melody over a

bass line that also is scored. Then Piazzolla has the rest of his ensemble improvise freely between these two lines. The result is polymusical. *Tristezas de un doble A* [Tristesse on a Vintage Bandoneón, 1972] is an excellent example. In this one piece Piazzolla incorporates all his musical techniques. *Tristeza* begins with a bandoneón solo followed by the entrance of the ensemble, playing direct from scores. Then slowly it slips into free jazz and then back to scored music.[177]

The free jazz of the 1960s had abandoned tonality as well as predetermined chord sequences.[178] But Piazzolla used standard chord progressions in a classical way, returning harmony to jazz-inspired playing while simultaneously augmenting the vitality of tango. Vivaldi-like melodies met rich jazz progressions while the bandonéon maintained tango tonality. "Tres minutos" intensified tango *and* Bartók. "Tristezas" vitalized tango *and* free jazz. As if that were not enough, it also incorporates passacaglia—the improvisations go over that ground bass enactment.[179]

Thus did Piazzolla attune tango to jazz and to concert music. Of course, mixing these forms bent traditionalists out of shape; he was playing with the national emblem. But the ghosts of Afro-Argentines were smiling. Piazzolla was renewing a process that had begun when jazz bands alternated with tango and that was continued by Gillespie with Fresedo. Piazzolla himself played tango with jazzmen—Gerry Mulligan in 1974, Gary Burton in 1985.

In sum, there are elements of classicism in the work of Piazzolla—Bartók-like scales, Bach passacaglis, and rich counterpoint. But indirect black influences, especially jazz phrasings, offbeats, blue notes, and improvisation, filter in, too.

Piazzolla's music is often called a break with the past. With tango as ballad, yes; with tango as dance music, partially. But with tango as a tissue of national rhythms, no. The composer himself puts us on warning: "I wanted swing in terms of tango, not jazz or classical."[180] How would he find it? By bringing back milonga and other local black beats. Critics have been so dazzled (or dismayed) by Piazzolla's experiments with jazz and classical counterpoint that they have overlooked his respect for Afro-Argentine rhythms, not to mention his affinity for decades of sadness in the texts of the tango. Porteños have a saying: *el tango siempre te espera* (the tango is always out there, waiting for you). You can lead a full life, but sooner or later someone you love dies without warning, or your lover walks out, or you're laid off your job. Then tango will get you, just like the blues. But tango is also the antidote—its solace awaits you, again like the blues.[181] As Piazzolla's daughter Diana points out, "Adiós Nonino" (Farewell, Dear Father) from 1959 is the ultimate phrasing of tango tristesse.[182]

Diana Piazzolla remembers her father playing her an LP of African drumming, brought back from a voyage to Europe.[183] He was sharing an enthusiasm. To reach swing in black terms, though, he had no farther to go than the beat of milonga and candombe. He hinted at this in the titles of compositions, such as "Milonga del mayoral" (Milonga of the Foreman, 1953), "Milonga del ángel" (Angel's Milonga, 1965), "Milonga del diablo" (Milonga of the Devil, 1965), "Milonga de la noche" (Nighttime Milonga, 1972), and "Milonga del trovador" (Troubador Milonga, 1981).

Listen also to "Verano porteño" (1965), "Libertango" (1973), "Tanguedia II" (Milonga loca, 1986), and "Tanguedia III" (1986). With these works Piazzolla was reinventing the tango but seasoning his advances with the swing of canyengue. "Libertango" builds on a 3-3-2 rhythmic pattern. The bass box is struck smartly amid sparkling lines of melodic percussion. All this goes farther in "Tanguedia III," Piazzolla's ultimate triumph of rhythmic decisiveness. The piece, as we will see, virtually conjures the image of a swaggering male, leading with chest and two fists.

By the 1980s Piazzolla had turned his experiments into a world-class tradition. In four of his landmarks—"Adiós Nonino" (1959), "Tristezas de un doble A" (1972), "Chin-Chin" (1979), and "Tanguedia III" (1986)—imagination turns into action. "Adiós Nonino" is Piazzolla's most famous tango.

In 1959, while working in Puerto Rico with Copes and Nieves, Astor was stunned when they told him that his father had just died. He burst into tears. In New York a short time later he transformed an earlier musical tribute to his father into "Adiós Nonino."

The progression is classical, a repeating harmonic pattern over a chromatic bass pattern (passacaglia). The nobility of this repeated slow pattern assists shock and grief. Lament turns to lullaby. Piazzolla sings his father to sleep. Child becomes parent. Father becomes son. Linear time blurs in a prism of tears.

Piazzolla thereafter dedicated much of his life to turning grief into melody, making abstractions of vicissitude, exalting us all in the process. This too was tango, no matter how modern. Listen again to his 1984 Montreal Jazz Festival version of the 1974 classic "Tristezas de un doble A." Pablo Ziegler considers "Tristezas" the most exciting improvisation in all modern tango: "The tune is five minutes but we played twenty-seven."[184]

What is jazz about "Tristezas"? asks the New York composer Herschel Garfein. He answers his own question: "textures, basic structure, soloing and trading of solos, Piazzolla's opening long solo, occasional left-hand chords, coloring long right-hand melodic flights, and of course the passage of free jazz." And what is tango in the piece?

"Minor-mode chord progressions, basic melodic construction, and improvisation. 'Tristezas' isn't bop, which has colored jazz improvisation since the 1940s. The instruments used and instrumental techniques showcase the fluency of abstracted tango rhythms."

And what is classical?

"The ground bass (passacaglia); free jazz insertions resembling aleatoric music. The way Piazzolla and his players bring motives in, like found objects, compares with John Cage."

To mix tango with jazz, modern and free, plus Bach passacaglia and perhaps a dash of Cage, betrays an amazing degree of cultural coherence. Piazzolla and his men had become linguists of possibility. They were tilting the tango toward freedom.

The liberation continued—witness "Chin-Chin," as performed at the Montreal Jazz Festival on July 4, 1984. *Cin-cin* (Cheers!) is an Italian expression for the clinking of glasses and the making of toasts. This is how the piece begins, percussive and festive, madly half-klezmerlike, half-tambourine. Pablo Ziegler, the pianist, blends McCoy Tyner–like runs with shooting-star accents. He makes his piano chase its own tail. He's playing deep games beneath the canyengue.

With "Tanguedia III," recorded in 1986, Piazzolla achieved his epiphany. The title is wordplay, a fusion equally arguably of *tango + tragedia* and *tango + comedia* and therefore surely of both. Out of the maelstrom emerge precedents to make our lives possible. How so? Listen.

From the very first bar, the sound is valor. Astor shoulders his way into consciousness with two hard-hitting measures in A minor. Superimposed chords build a rich polytonality. This section ends with a tiny release.

Then, as if we were Jericho and Piazzolla Joshua, he hits us again, with an identically accented two-bar motif, this time in F-sharp minor. Violent glissandi follow on violins, an effect called "the whip" (*el látigo*). They're action equivalents to the step called *boleo,* where the dancer's foot lashes back without warning. (In fact, as Aslán reports, dancers love to *boleo* when *látigos* sound.) Then comes a B section, piano hammering away. Piazzolla on bandonéon shapes notes like brushstrokes, blurred, loose, and luminous. Big stop.

The composer uses silence to separate sections. In come the A and B parts again. In the B section there is more polytonality and sustained violin notes with exaggerated vibrato. There is subtle acceleration in each section followed by return to slower tempo after each halt. Stop. For the third and last time, we savor strong accents, here with a backbeat, struck on the side of an instrument. The coda cites Bartók. The end. Piazzolla abstracted qualities—polytonality, key changes, offbeats, gradual accelerations, the scales of Bartók. He put together a hard-hitting music that is amazingly new. Even the rhythm, 3 + 3 + 2, synthesized Middle European metrics à la Bartók with that old rhythmic warhorse habanera. "Tanguedia III" is an orchestral tone poem about grace under pressure, turning shock into work, so we all can get on with it.

Piazzolla died in Buenos Aires on July 4, 1992. His art celebrates nearness where others saw distance. He joins the immortals, especially Borges. The connection to Borges is tantalizing: both developed a vernacular kind of classicism, both loved milonga, and both brought Argentine art to the world.

TWENTY-FIRST-CENTURY UPDATE: ZIEGLER, ASLÁN, AND EL ARRANQUE

The music continues. Argentine virtuosi now routinely play North America, Europe, and Japan, as well as Argentina. They have doubled the range of their music. They inspire musicians in many world capitals.

PABLO ZIEGLER Pablo Ziegler, the pianist in Piazzolla's last quintet, is a primary example.

Ziegler, who lives in Brooklyn, Berlin, and Buenos Aires, was born in the Argentine capital on September 12, 1944. It soon became clear that he was a prodigy: he started serious study of piano, at the Conservatorio de Música de Buenos Aires, at age four. Ten years later, in 1958, he was awarded a degree. At fourteen he was a fully accredited teacher of piano.[185]

Ziegler entered the Buenos Aires jazz scene in 1962. He met Piazzolla in 1978, when the composer was "looking for a man who could play tango differently."[186] Ziegler was his pianist from 1978 to 1988.

Ziegler leads to the future. In early CDs like *Conexión porteña* (Buenos Aires Connection, 1991), *Los tangueros* (1995), and *Asfalto* (Street Tango, 1997), the debt to Piazzolla is obvious. But *Pablo Ziegler: Quintet for New Tango*, recorded in New York and Buenos Aires in February 1999, broke

away. There is a cut on this album, "Alrededor del choclo" (A Ride
Around the Corn) that brilliantly rethinks Villoldo's classic. It is shocking,
at first, to hear jazz with "El choclo," but the ear soon forgives, because a
number of instruments are still playing tango. Ziegler also excels in
"Imágenes 676," a Piazzolla composition named after a famous Buenos
Aires jazz boîte at 676 Calle Tucumán. He sets up a groove, then saunters
into bass meditations. Enrique Sinesi, his electric guitarist, hammers the
strings. This abstract arrastre leads to an impressionist turn.

In a festival in Buenos Aires in March 2003, Ziegler "deconstructed *La
Cumparsita,* perhaps the best known tango, in much the way that John
Coltrane [reshaped] *My Favorite Things.*"[187]

Ziegler's *Bajo cero* CD, released in June 2003, engages the future with
a vengeance. A composition called "La Rayuela" (Hopscotch) jumps
across sections, like chalked squares on the sidewalk.[188] The opening riff,
strong and ringing, is milonga-candombe. The riff is conceived in the
Lydian mode, which is impulsive, less still as major or minor. It builds a
dance-seeking happiness, rivaling the staccato incandescence of mambo.

PABLO ASLÁN   One of the bassists in Ziegler's Quintet for New Tango
was a young Argentine man named Pablo Aslán. He too plays traditional
and modern. He too has lived a transnational life. Born in Buenos Aires
on May 5, 1962, and educated at the University of California at Los
Angeles, he plays tango in New York but remains in close touch with
Buenos Aires, where his father is a practicing architect and his mother an
artist. A scholar of tango as well as a performer of it, Aslán has published
excerpts from his M.A. on his own tango website.

Aslán's *Avantango* CD was recorded live at the Knitting Factory in New
York on May 8, 1996: Aslán on bass, the late Thomas Chapin on alto saxo-
phone, and Ethan Iverson on piano. Admiring Salgán's sense of rhythmic
subdivisions, Aslán interprets the black master's "Don Agustín Bardi" at a
tempo faster than the original.

Iverson improvises in the terms of Andalusian tonality; he takes tango
back to one of its roots. In "Petit fleur," conversely, Aslán turns a Sidney
Bechet jazz piece into tango.

At a concert at Yale University, May 13, 2003, Gustavo Casenave,
Aslán's Uruguayan pianist, slurred notes with the palm of his hand. He
was drumming arrastres. Aslán played his bass with a hard-bitten swing.
Moving his instrument into the center of the dance ring, he struck his
strings sharply while Kely and Facundo Posadas twirled in a milonga on
each of his downbeats.

EL ARRANQUE While Ziegler and Aslán hold the fort in Berlin and New York, a brilliant young group has emerged in the Argentine capital. The musicians in El Arranque (The Beginning) are led by the bass player, Ignacio Varchausky. They challenge the limits, as set by the old guard, the new guard, the 1940s, or Piazzolla. They cross borders of consciousness. They are also teachers. As Varchausky says:

> I organized the project, Orquesta Escuela de Tango [School of Tango Orchestra] of which, since its founding in 2000, I am the coordinator and artistic director. Ramiro Gallo is first violin and assistant to the permanent musician-in-charge, Emilio Balcarce.[189]

I visited their school in the Casa del Tango in Almagro on August 3, 2003. The students were impressive. They rocked to the beat of arrastres. There were seven women and five men.

The work of El Arranque appears on four disks. The first cut of their May 1998 CD, *Orquesta El Arranque: Tango,* pits the elegance of de Caro against the beat of Pugliese, with a dash of Alfredo Gobbi.

In their third record, *Clásicos,* of October 2001, El Arranque operates essentially as a repertory orchestra, sharing past genius but gunning for the future. They work in the manner that Piazzolla admired in Gerry Mulligan's octet, smiling at one another, shifting the center of musical gravity, first to Ariel Rodríguez's piano, then to the vocalist, Ariel Ardit, then to Varchausky, and finally to the first violinist, Gallo, and the first bandoneonista, Camilo Ferrero, and on through all the musicians.

I have seen El Arranque in action at the Club del Vino in Palermo, dancing in place, like a salsa ensemble, flaunting their youth and their energy. Ziegler, Aslán, El Arranque, and other important colleagues—Marconi, Raúl Jaurena, and others—dispense tango medicine for a dangerous age. While their disks spin, they outweigh our problems.

CONCLUSION

In the beginning, tango texts were humorous and bluesy—and charged with innuendo. Tango "Sacúdeme la persiana" (Shake My Blinds) recalled the blues "Tight Like That." When Villoldo wrote "Soy tremendo" (I Am the Greatest) in Paris, he had penned an assertion that would parallel blues, Muhammad Ali, and first-generation hip-hop. But by the 1930s only one major lyricist, Celedonio Flores, was black.

Most lyrics back then resonated with stylized sadness, stemming from traditions ultimately Spanish and Italian. Since the study of tango is biased toward literature, here was another reason for the belief that black influence, if present at the beginning, had long since disappeared. But the situation changes when one switches to music. Black presence is continuous, from Mendizábal and Posadas in the late 1890s to Salgán and his son in 2005. Not only do Afro-Argentines continue to make music, they influence major composers like Piana, Pugliese, Troilo, and Ziegler, all of whom have worked with black themes.

Pugliese, of course, wrote three black-inspired gems of the 1940s—"La yumba," "Negracha," and "Malandraca"—affirming the drive of Afro-Argentine culture. So did Troilo, with his milonga "La trampera," and Ziegler as well, with his matching masterpiece, "Rayuela."

The canyengue—the Afro-danceability—of three important early orchestras (Firpo's, Canaro's, and de Caro's) stemmed from the hand of one powerful black bassist, Ruperto Leopoldo Thompson. Striking strings, drumming wood, like his spiritual brother, the great Afro-Cuban bassist "Cachao" (Israel López), Thompson turned his instrument into a virtual drum. We do not have to imagine him doing this: there is a sound document, a 1916 recording of Canaro's orchestra playing "Didi."[190] You hear Thompson knocking a phrase like a drumroll—what di Giorgio and others calls a *carraspeo* (a throat-clearing passage)—on the side of the instrument. The rhythm is simultaneously picked up in the melody as well.

Canaro gives the impression that Thompson invented such effects only in his orchestra. But Horacio Ferrer, in his *Libro de Tango III,* reveals that Thompson was, earlier, a guitarist with Arolas, where he may well have come in contact with the key black guitarist Luciano Ríos, who was churning out rhythm for Arolas in 1912.[191]

Canyengue is a stratagem flowing into tango from Afro-Argentine sources, like Ríos and Thompson. But Africa in another sense, Moorish-tinged sound from Andalusia, is a variable, too. North African and Andalusian heel-stamping (*taconeo*) forms another body of danced sound, reflecting seven centuries of Moorish presence in Spain. The tradition reemerged in Argentine creole dances like gato and escondido.[192]

Stamping the heel and lifting the knee, while playing the bandoneón in one's lap, forces the air in a West German instrument into patterns reflecting creole interests and diction. Andalusians, when they strum as they sing, may slur notes together; flamenco guitar comes to mind. The technique was picked up by gauchos, as in the gato. It becomes the arras-tre. Zapateados and taconeos from southernmost Spain flow into tango just as Moorish azoteas (flat-roofed houses), checkerboard tile floors, serrated horse's manes, star pattern spurs, and alfajor sweets flowed into Argentine architecture, horsemanship, and cuisine.

Black impact on tango music is complex and rich. More is involved than candombe: it includes the milonga, Kongo and Moorish body percussion, and jazz. There are no African instruments in tango, but bandoneón, piano, contrabass, and violin, when struck on their sides, reverb as if they were. There is no "African" beat, either, but the neo-Kongo bass of the old habanera, nurtured by musicians of color in Cuba and brought to the River Plate by sailors, sheet music, and Spanish light opera, became the pulse of the earliest tangos. Blue notes enter, too, and fragments of ragtime. Piazzolla experiments with free jazz.

The music of Italian and Spanish immigrants merged with all this. Early blends with their world were inevitable. The tango "Hotel Victoria," for instance, was no more than a Neapolitan song in habanera time.[193]

The children of Mediterraneans played with the rhythms of tango, intriguingly shifting them by adding changes of tempo. In single compositions one might pass from percussive to decorous, fixed beat to rubato, accent to sentiment. In the process, transitions in feeling came to distinguish the tango from mambo or samba, where pulse and bright feeling run straight on through. It was an intricacy that would inspire two of the richest minds in all of the Americas, Piazzolla and Borges.

ENVOI: ALICE TULLY HALL, LINCOLN CENTER, MAY 3, 2001

Wynton Marsalis, artistic director of Jazz at Lincoln Center, performs with his own band and with El Arranque. The two orchestras are exploring together the links between tango and jazz. The *New York Times* jazz critic Ben Ratliff cuts to the problem: "since drums do not normally appear in the tango this, on the face of it, would make difficult finding common ground with jazz swing."[194]

But canyengue, as we know, bends classical instruments to sub-Saharan rhythm-making. When El Arranque came onstage and played Gillespie's "Night in Tunisia," the tango violinists scratched their strings and the bandoneonistas hit the sides of their instruments, bringing into being what Ratliff called "a unique rhythmic density." On the classical side of the equation, that night El Arranque premiered Gallo's *Suite borgeana,* a composition in seven movements.

Then came a magical moment. The groups played, as one, Marsalis's
Concerto Grosso:

Using both orchestras, it perfectly represented Mr. Marsalis's composing
style within the frame of tango, much lighter in humor [than in a brooding
work by Gallo] with quickly shifting strains, incorporating the jazz conven-
tions of the blues form, mambo-like piano figures, and four-bar trade-offs
among soloists.[195]

Writing for *La Nación,* the Argentine critic Gabriel Plaza savored the
blend, too, and also heard mambo:

In the second movement of [*Concerto Grosso,*] they played with the most
afro of all tango formulas, the *habanera,* and even with a certain rumba
rhythm that at certain moments recalled the glorious [mambo] orchestra of
Pérez Prado.[196]

Ratliff and Plaza divined together a new stratagem for blending traditions—bring in a third music. Mambo, shared cultural polyphony,
brought deeper perceptions to tango and jazz.

8.

TANGO AS DANCE

You'll see: life becomes a narrative when you dance
"La cumparsita."

— MIGUEL RAMÓN FRANCO, *Lunfardia en Villa Gesell* (n.d.)

The shape of the tango is made up of moments: a swift
sudden entrance, a sweep of the feet, an advance, a
retreat, a halt and a start, a displacement of hips, and a
freeze, as if hanging in air.

— PABLO ZIEGLER (1997)

Juan Carlos Copes stamping out four beats on the floor in 1988, in
Tango-Tango, echoes the percussive knocks in "El esquinazo" (Being
Stood Up), the notorious tango-milonga of 1900. María Nieves Rego
pivots and poses; the twist of her hips brings back Kongo. In short, the
steps of tango open vistas.

Another instance: Catherine Deneuve and Linh Dan Pham moving
forward, faces profiled, arms straight ahead, in the film *Indochine* (1992)
reenact the "hard" (*duro*) style of tango seen in Paris before World War I.
The Argentine tanguero Bernabé Simarra, in a photograph published on
March 28, 1913, appears in Paris brandishing the same stiff-arm position

PLATE 51

(Plate 51). Argentine dancers brought it to France; including Simarra, who streamlined it.[1]

When the step came back to the barrios of Buenos Aires, milongueros reacted variously. Ester Pugliese overtly makes fun of it: moving forward, then back, nose in air, she takes sharp, sudden looks to right and left. An occasion for satire among Buenos Aires experts, the arms-straight-ahead gesture dazzles innocents who think they are tangoing. Consider, for instance, a 1970 revival of the 1931 ballet *Façade* (Plate 52), or Jack Lemmon and Joe E. Brown in Billy Wilder's film *Some Like It Hot* (1959), or the mannikinlike sequences in *Last Tango in Paris* (1972), or the Nazi soldier dancing with a Dutch resistance hero in *Soldier of Orange* (1978). In each of these cases the step makes an appearance only to verge on parody.

But porteños devised it, and they can restore it to authenticity and sub-

PLATE 52

stance. El Pibe Palermo, his hand held out high, charges forward three steps, charges back three more steps, in this pose.[2] I saw Copes's troupe similarly stiff-arm and profile, moving quite fast, at the Nuevo Salón la Argentina in Buenos Aires on June 27, 2003. They had brought back a step of the tango of Paris.

According to Copes, the step has no name. "Personally," he adds, "I really don't like it, the woman gazing forward, the man gazing forward, as if both were looking for someone better to dance with." Likely it was invented by porteño men, practicing with other men: with this step they could strut as a team, facing forward, avoiding eye contact.[3] An early photograph in fact shows this happening. In 1909, in the Congreso barrio in Buenos Aires, a photographer caught men celebrating the closing of a day's work at Lorea Market, practicing tango. Tradesmen in white aprons with fine polished shoes, and a dapper businessman in dark suit and fedora horsed around for the camera.[4] Despite the joking, some of the poses are real: differing hand levels, for instance, reflect the independence of expression in porteño dance halls. The hatless man in apron at right grasps the hand of his partner and pulls it down to his waist, a black-originated trait that came in with canyengue.[5] Two men at center thrust out their elbows; they are razzing the photographer, not dancing. Farther left, though, two macho males in contrasting clothes pose good-naturedly, arms and faces forward. They hold their hands high, like the prow of a ship.

That prowlike device acquired a life of its own. It turns up on the streets of Buenos Aires a few years later: again all the dancers are male. Leaders guide followers, right arm round their waists. They are wearing bowties (*moños*), not cravats (*lengues*). They are not compadritos.

THE IRONY AND THE INTRICACY Tango, no matter how aesthetic, often is reduced to a context of dives and bordellos, in a process resembling the Storyville stereotype in jazz. True, men and women descended from Kongo, Andalusia, and Italy met and created a new dance in rough neighborhoods. Some danced for sex; some danced for art; some danced to show off their bodies. New steps could hardly have emerged, however, had the best not been dancing for dance. In a city in motion, bravura moves were the crest of all change.

The inventions proved lasting. Porteño virtuosos distilled lifetimes of dancing. Bars and bordellos were democratic venues, where blacks performed freely before admiring sets of people, like sailors and *tanos* (Italian immigrants). Passion for dance transcended condition. Making up moves was the aim. Meanwhile, the white oligarchy kept in thrall to Europe.[6]

When immigrants from Italy and Spain came in contact with the southern black barrios of old Buenos Aires—Montserrat, Concepción, and San Telmo—the strong creole dancers moved them. They inspired them to turn into Argentines.

WRITING TANGO DANCE HISTORY Early moments live in verbal and printed descriptions. It has been asserted that two or three minutes of El Cachafaz dancing represent virtually the sum total of early tango on film. Fortunately, that isn't so: there are films and videos of El Pibe Palermo, José Méndez, Antonio Todaro, Petróleo, and other masters, and of the poised, brilliant women who danced with them.

Paintings and photographs also capture gesture. One emblem of fine dance in West Africa is knowing how to match the end of a drum phrase to a strong final pose. The criterion reemerged in black Buenos Aires as the corte, freezing all motion for one telling second. That second could be photographed or drawn.

Written sources capture other traits. There is mention of the cold facial stare (*cara fea*) of tangueros—in contrast to Westerners, who often smile when they dance. In the telling of such patterns a narrative emerges, the process that led to the tango.

THE RISE OF THE TANGO, 1865–95

A description of habanera in nineteenth-century Buenos Aires mentions a quality that derives from West Africa: silence. In Kongo and in the kingdoms of the Yoruba, silence is prized in the dance.

A young man in the Nigerian Yoruba village of Ajilete once praised the dancing of the local master, Agbeke Asoko, in these words: "She did not speak until she stopped her dance."[7] Her face was a seal of composure, a calm that transcended all speech or distraction. The rule of not dissipating the energy of the body by talking or smiling while dancing is strong too in Kongo. Here silence and concentration grant dancers leeway to spiritual ecstasy: "The dancer does not speak when on the dancing court (*mbasi a makinu*) because his body is focussed to receive ecstatic waves of the spirit."[8] Fu-Kiau concludes, "The dance court in Kongo was not where you talked."

Compare porteños dancing to a black pianist in the Club de San

Nicolás as described in *El Pueblo* on January 28, 1865: "A mulatto returns to the piano and a dancer named Troya gets hot, turning this way and that, without talking. You want conversation? Get *this:* here we all gather to dance!"[9] Francisco Ebelot's book *La pampa,* published in Paris in 1899, mentions hip motions entering habanera, as they would later invade tango. These motions are marked with Central African implications. Ebelot saw them at a wake on the pampas, in a dance for a dead child: "As they danced by the bier, women moved their hips, with the provocative undulation characteristic of the habanera. At the same time, one by one, they crossed themselves."

Meanwhile Buenos Aires was absorbing choreography from myriad European sources. In 1880 the newspaper *El Siglo* announced a ballroom affair featuring polka, habanera, quadrille, waltz, mazurka, and schottische.[10] Like traditions continue: it is not at all unusual to find tango, milonga, waltz, and jazz dance alternating on ballroom floors. Other milongas routinely alternate tango with cumbia, rock, and salsa.[11]

Vernacular black dancers deepened habanera with their own cultural imprint: "Candombe was danced apart whereas polka and habanera were danced in embrace position. In translating the break patterns of African apart dancing into embrace dancing, the compadrito (as well as other vernacular stylists) were gradually creating their own empirical choreography."[12] In the process, Kongo quebrada took root in habanera. It was consistently described as "undulating," "rocking" (forward and back), and "swaying" (side to side). These traits plus frozen faces coalesced in canyengue.

MULATO ARROYO THROWS A PARTY FOR GAUCHOS, JANUARY 21, 1899
We run again into cortes (sudden sharp stops) at a black-hosted fete on the outskirts of Buenos Aires at the end of the nineteenth century. Back then, according to the writer Domingo F. Casadevall, the outskirts of Buenos Aires formed a link between pampas and city. Here rural migrants set up residence among cattle paths, ombú trees, and ranches as if they were still on the plains.[13] That permeability proved crucial.

On January 21, 1899, *Caras y caretas* published a drawing by Francisco Fortunay (Plate 53) of a dance organized by a man of color for his friends, men from the pampas, on the outskirts of Buenos Aires. The host was El Mulato Arroyo, a former regimental sergeant in the Argentine army. Military neatness still governed his life: his ranch house was said to be the most whitewashed on the outskirts of Buenos Aires (*su rancho el más blanqueadito de las orillas*). In pure pampas style, gauchos danced at his party, knives tucked in the back of their belts.[14] Dancing, the cowboys leaned forward and back, their strength and agility reflecting lives herding cattle.[15]

Men carry their right hands at waist level. Women rest their heads on the men's shoulders. They dance tight, in waltzlike embrace, his legs touching hers. The leaning, close embracing, and hands at the waist compare with canyengue as danced in the capital ten years later. "Mataco," the writer for *Caras y caretas* who reported on El Mulato's dance, tells us that a habanera was expected "as prelude" and that the guitarists later strummed a "mournful mazurka." But nothing sad, nothing languorous appears in this drawing. On the contrary, the swing and the joy suggest another kind of dance altogether.

Three modern milongueros suggest what it is. Carlos Anzuate sees polka, Gabriel Angió, too. Copes concurs and gives reasons: "This is not tango. This is not habanera. This is polka, the root of our own chamamé. Look at the movement, that strong swing and sway, leaning in, leaning back. It's a pendulum. It's polka!" The American dance critic Sally Sommer agrees: "This is polka, where you hold them in tight, you lean, and you twirl."[16] Leaning is clear in Fontanay's drawing. The accompanying article also mentions twirling, to the right, then the left.

According to tradition, a Czech servant girl invented the polka in the 1830s.[17] By the spring of 1844 the dance was the toast of Paris.[18] Some say it entered Buenos Aires one year later, others slightly earlier, in 1843, when it was spotted at Tandil.[19]

Argentina and Brazil mixed black sources with polka. This created hot hybrids: maxixe-polka in Brazil and polka-habanera in Buenos Aires, the

PLATE 53

latter dated to 1878. According to the tango pianist Pablo Ziegler, the arrival of polka changed languorous habanera into the quick-paced milonga.[20] It was in the barrios of the city of Corrientes, in Argentina's north, that the local variant of polka—*polkita correntina*—turned into chamamé, around 1930.[21]

Besides turns and strong leans, Argentine polka included rich waltzlike whirls and "fast-moving heel-and-toe action" (*taco y punta*).[22] A gaucho in Fortunay's drawing addresses the ground in just this sharp way.

Something else happened as well, the emergence of a style that the black host undoubtedly approved of: sudden stops, sudden freezes—the corte. Mataco describes it: men took advantage of "brazen pauses" in the music to stop for a second and press their hard chests against their partners' soft bosoms. That furtive quick pleasure had already caused cortes and quebradas to be banned from many a dance floor. Forty years earlier, on September 9, 1862, four men and two women had been arrested at 58 Calle Paraguay in Buenos Aires "for dancing and exhibiting forbidden cortes."[23]

When polka came in, imagine the reaction of black dancers: "We know those steps! Let's do them better!" In fact, El Mulato Arroyo and his colleagues were brazenly revitalizing black styles via the verve of the polka.

Something analogous was happening in Brazil with the maxixe. Early maxixe referred to the black way of dancing the polka and the habanera—with a "slurring of feet" and a quebradalike "rippling of hips."[24] So similar were the two dances, it is likely their dancers were in touch with one another.

BLACK AND WHITE WOMEN IN THE RISE OF TANGO, 1880–1911

> As a child I danced the fandango
> And joyful waltz, back to back,
> But tango gave me class
> because I learned it from a black.
>
> —LÁZARO LIACHO, *Cantos de tango y vida*
> (Songs of Tango and Life, 1970)

Tango Argentino, a silent short shot in Buenos Aires around 1900–06, starred a black virtuoso, El Negro Agapito. The print has been lost; one can only surmise about its contents. Did Agapito cut, break, and walk? Whatever he did, his was the first tango filmed.[25]

It was hardly an accident that an Afro-Argentine starred in the first film on the tango. It was recognized at the time that blacks were its major dance experts. More than twenty-five years later, in 1933, when the first Argentine sound film, *Tango,* was released, the figure of a black woman, tall, dark, and dashing, would swirl briefly into view, tangoing in the arms of a white man. It was like a salute to the contribution of black women to tango.

Women in general, Afro-Argentine in particular, sparked early tango. The docksides, haunt of the sailors who brought habanera from Cuba, were armed with strong women, unafraid to try moves from afar, unafraid to blend or to bend them. Sharp styles developed. An illustration in the Buenos Aires journal *PBT* (Plate 54) from January 1911 shows a man and a woman dancing.[26] The woman is bold. "Breaking" her body, defying the West, she pushes out her bottom, bends forward her torso, and rests part of her weight on her partner's chest. Her crouch counterpoints his tall stance. She dances intent on distant tradition, deriving from Kongo and elsewhere in Africa. The profile of her body mirrors a young woman dancing at Zoan Hounia, Ivory Coast, in the 1950s (Plate 55)[27] and recalls women dancing in Kongo. She is dancing canyengue, emblem of Africa in early-twentieth-century Buenos Aires. The independence of her motion relates to the pivoting ocho, expressed in full counterpoint to the male who stands by as she turns.

During the rise of the tango in 1880–1900, Nicole Nau-Klapwijk points out, women who danced well were definitely in demand. This gave them an edge: "Women indirectly shaped the course of the dance."[28] Women enabled men, including early stars like Ricardo Scalisi Saúl (known as El

PLATE 54   PLATE 55

Flaco, the thin man) and Mariano Cao[29] to make the most of black-derived cortes: "The corte, an abrupt stop, presupposed experience and talent on the part of the women. Without prior knowledge and cool, [their cortes] might have turned out inept or quite awkward."[30] Like the 1911 woman dancing canyengue, the working-class women of late-nineteenth-century Buenos Aires cultivated moves beyond those proposed by convention. Some were women of the night; others worked in bars frequented by sailors and men from the pampas, many of whom were good dancers. These marginalized groups built the central tradition of Argentine dance.

Writing in 1880, a contemporary observer mentions five women dancers.[31] Their nicknames give hints of assertion and ethnicity. Two were certainly black: La Parda Loreto, "feisty and gossipy" (peleadora y bochinchera), and La Parda Refucilo, "homegirl and hipster" (comadre y compadrita). Ramón Romero's 1880 novel Los amores de Giacumina (Loves of Giacumina) describes a dance at the Politeama, a contemporary dance place; he mentions nine women by name. René Briand, in his Crónicas del tango alegre (Chronicles of Tango When It Was Happy), describes two young men excitedly awaiting their talented dance dates, Matilde La Mondongo and Sofía La Nueva, at the Café de Cassoulet. Matilde was possibly black, to judge from her name—mondongo is a term associated with Central Africa. Both women had been invited to the Politeama Carnival of 1879. They were excellent dancers—that's why we have both their names.

Ricardo García Blaya has recently argued that the brothel theory of the birth of tango exaggerates to the point of absurdity.[32] Point taken. Brothels were certainly not the only places available for dancing; there were tenement parties, dives, cabarets, and, later, cafés, dance halls, and theaters. There were street-corner sessions, where men practiced with men to the sound of organ-grinders or their own whistled tunes.

Working-class women went to cafés and dance halls to dance. Nicknames like compadrona (tough gal) suggest girls who knew how to take care of themselves. One scared off wolves by flashing a knife. They certainly were not tragic, unlike Margarita Verdie (La Rubia Mireya, "blond Mireya"), who, in the late nineteenth century, "passed from dancer to dancer until she broke down and died of tuberculosis."[33] All took part in the rise of the tango. Even women of the night like María la Tero, famed for the beauty of her remarkably long legs, contributed to tango centrality.

Famed for their dancing, women like Clara La Degollada (Clara Who'll

Swindle You), Isabel La Turca (Isabel the Turk), Petra La Pinchadora (Petra The Penetrator), Rosa La Compadrona (Rosa the Homegirl), Juli La Ñata (Pug-Nosed Juli), Violeta La Panzuda (Violeta with a Weight Problem), Manuela La Chijete (Spitting Manuela), María La Vieja (Old María), and Juana La Pilladora (Juana the Woman with Attitude) live on in Argentine cultural history. Their nicknames attest their strength and their toughness. Finally we have the name of La Negra Laura, a woman of color who was an extraordinary dancer. She used to play records for dancers at a place on the corner of Bartolomé Mitre and Talcahuano. Black Laura and her colleagues live forever in the art history of tango, while most of the upper-class women of the era slumber forgotten in the tombs of Recoleta. Such is the revenge of the first milonguitas.

STYLISTIC HAPPENING AROUND 1900

Tango styles coexist in the history of the dance. As Africanized polka turned into samba in Brazil, so Argentine polka, with close-in embrace, hand placement on waist, and heel-and-toe work fused with black hip twists, knee dips, and offbeats in Buenos Aires around 1900.[34] They called it canyengue.

The situation that year was fluid. It was the time of "El esquinazo," the climactic milonga. Twenty years of competitive choreography—of *pasos de desafío* (challenge steps)—among blacks and their working-class colleagues, especially sailors, had sharpened milonga with an arsenal of stops, walks, and poses. Among the sailors, milonga and early tango were beautifully danced by talented men called *zarzuelinos,* the crews of Spanish ships that began their ports of call in Cádiz, voyaged on through the Canary Islands, Havana, Pernambuco, Bahia, Rio de Janeiro, and Montevideo, to arrive finally in Buenos Aires. Hanging out in these ports, each famed for its dancing, one can well imagine the expertise of the sailors, genially shared, amid drinking and laughter, with Buenos Aires women in street parties (*romerías*) in Palermo and open-air celebrations (*verbenas*) in Recoleta. They helped bring habanera and maxixe to Argentina.[35]

Meanwhile, superb Argentine dancers triumphed through hard work and practice. Juan Filiberto, a male tango star of the late nineteenth century, "spent hours and hours tracing curves with the point of his shoe . . . hours and hours 'profiling,' working up moves he would later present to the world."[36] With his shoe as a pencil, Filiberto elaborated versions of one of the earliest tango steps, the *media luna* (*Moon*) "Profiling" recalls men horsing around in Plaza Dorreo in 1909.[37]

To recap: as the twentieth century started, the lexicon of tango included these steps:

Arrastrada or **arrastre:** a dragging or "slurring" of the feet[38]
Balanceo: swinging and swaying, as in polka and Kongo
Corte: a sudden swift stop or quick pose; also called *parada*
Corrida: a run across the floor
Lustrada: a move in which the woman briefly bends down and simulates the polishing of her partner's jacket buttons or shoes[39]
Media luna: a half-circle traced with the toe on the floor, pioneered by Juan Filiberto in the late nineteenth century. (Later, in 1930, El Profesor Silva would assert that the media luna entered the tango via rumba, suggesting sources both local and outside in the rise of this step.)[40]
Ocho: a woman's figure-eight walk with pivots and a twist of the hip, "perhaps the most feminine figure of tango."[41]
Quebrada: a twist of the hips
Sentada: a brief seating of a dancer on her partner's thigh.
Taconeo: Andalusian- and Kongo-derived heel-stamping
Tijera: literally, scissors; bending and crossing the legs

This does not exhaust the list of early moves. Mingo Pugliese brings to our attention other old steps like the *arroje* (slingshot) and the *molinete* (simplified turn).[42] There was a zigzagging run, pivoting continuously and superbly, called *viborita* (little snake). Associated with milonga, it resembles "the grapevine," which appears in the hora and other Eastern European dances. It may have entered tango via "*ruso*" (Jewish) immigrants coming in from Odessa and other Eastern European locations.

Some steps from this period brought social realism to the image of tango. There was the *rueca* (distaff), in which the woman placed her foot on the man's foot and mimed the pedal of a spinning wheel. The *corrida del bolsero* turned the swaying walk of a longshoreman unloading heavy bags from ship to shore into a dance step. Finally there was a step called *alfajor,* named after the Moorish-derived sweet biscuit with filling that is found, in different versions, all over Argentina.

Naming dances after sweets is black. As we have seen, the national dances of both Haiti and the Dominican Republic are named after meringue. "Sugar" in salsa is synonymous with swing.[43] When the great Cachafaz famously danced against El Negro Santillán, a friend yelled out to him, "Show him the sugar!" Mingo Pugliese's suggestion, then, that it was Afro-Argentine dancers who named and developed the alfajor seems reasonable.[44]

African knee flexion enlivens many early steps: you can't seat a woman on your thigh, or mime shining shoes, without bending down. The polishing of buttons also reflects concern about style, a world where everyone ideally was *pulcro*—neat, clean, and brilliant. But it also is sexy—one can imagine someone saying "I'll polish *your* buttons, I'll shine up *your* shoes!"—in the risqué tone of such hits of early tango as "Sacúdeme la persiana" (Shake My Blinds).

The transformation of milonga into tango involved clear basic changes. The ocho of milonga, done in short steps (*pasos cortaditos*), becomes more expansive, sliding (*deslizando*), floating (*flotando*), and later, in salón styles, elegantly walked through (*caminado*).[45] At the turn of the century, then, artists knew where they stood. They got their inspiration, their everything, from tango.

THE TANGO OF ARTURO DE NAVAS, FEBRUARY 7, 1903

Arturo de Navas (May 1, 1876–October 22, 1932) was a "fine tango dancer and a friend of Gardel."[46] He was born in Montevideo, and his father, Juan de Navas, was a famous payador.

De Navas mastered the idiom of gauchos, and like Will Rogers, he brought the argot of the range to the stage. He also participated in payadas, the black-dominated battles of verse. Onstage performance in Buenos Aires gave him the power to carry cultural messages. Gardel was a friend and admirer; he borrowed de Navas's hit "La vida del carretero" (The Life of the Carter) to open his own performances in Paris.[47]

De Navas was dapper: "Tall, lean, and polished, he dressed very elegantly in a black dinner jacket, pin-striped trousers [*pantalones de fantasía*] of suave English cut, ankle boots of patent leather, and a gray hat cut in the style of a diplomat."[48] He danced as he dressed: superbly. He was much in demand at the turn of the century, dancing tango onstage. He lived to its rhythms. Early in 1903, in a windfall for tango art history, the Buenos Aires journal *Caras y caretas* called on de Navas and a talented friend to illustrate male practice in their pages.[49] The stylized poses of the two dancers attest to tango's richness at the start of the century. The photographs are accompanied by captions, written in the idiom of gauchos. Humorous and laconic, these inscriptions form part of the authority of the experience.

De Navas appears in his customary hat, black jacket, and ankle boots (Plate 56). He stands on his right foot while striking the ground with the heel of his left, a heel-and-toe action recalling polka and canyengue. (We saw a pampas man heel-tapping at El Mulato Arroyo's party four years earlier.) The men dance side by side, facing in different directions. De Navas holds his partner and extends his right arm. The caption reads "*Cópiame ésta paradita*" (Copy me doing this little pause), "*Y te hacés gente de golpe*" (And make yourself hip as all hell). De Navas is mischievous: his move leaves his partner hanging in air.[50]

Suddenly the partner makes a move (Plate 57): while de Navas shoots out a leg, the other man "breaks" (*hace una quebrada*) with deeply bent knees and crosses his feet, right over left. De Navas does one thing, his partner another. This cross-step with flexion, as we learn from the caption, has a name: "*Es al ñudo, hacha vieja*" (literally "It's useless, old blade," or as might be said today, "Don't fight it, dude"). "*Pal corte: aquí está tijera!*" (On to the next step: here come the scissors!). The partner's scissoring move comes from candombe. Its gist: crossing the legs while bending the knees forward. The limbs open and close like a scissors; hence the name.[51] The step came from Kongo, from a dance called *muluketo,* in which "to bend down and to cross legs" (*mu betama ye mu bindakana*)[52] was a characteristic sequence. Lowering the body showed respect to the ancestors, while crossing the legs built self-protection: "You are weaving a belt, preventing bad entrance, tying a barrier between yourself and all evil."[53] This Kongo-derived pattern surfaced in Buenos Aires in candombe street dancing toward the end of the nineteenth century. It continues in milonga-candombe.

El Pibe Palermo, tutored in his youth by the black master Alfredo Núñez, danced it superbly in the 1970s. It forms part of a current of proto-break dancing—from a black person "getting down" before the church of

PLATE 56   PLATE 57   PLATE 58

Santo Domingo in 1830 (Plate 18) to dancers of today, Natalia Games and Gabriel Angió, showing off their mastery of quebrada (Plate 77).

The partner again breaks away (Plate 58). De Navas draws a line with his boot, and the partner moves laterally, crossing right foot over left. De Navas, through the curve of his arm, is signaling (*haciendo marcación*) his partner: "Begin doing ocho." Making the move, the partner will cross his feet and pivot, once forward, once back. In the photograph he has already crossed right foot over left, going forward.[54] The caption takes note of the pivot: "*Pucha con la vueltita . . . que'es cantora . . . Enséñasela a tu hermana que tiene tan linda voz*" (Try your damn luck with this little turn. It's a song. Teach it to your sister who has such a beautiful voice). Ocho had become essential to tango.

Suddenly we enter a world of intrusions (Plates 59 and 60). De Navas shoots his leg between the limbs of his partner, who rides the leg, left thigh supported by de Navas's right knee. This small fleeting uplift is an early sentada, a step in which the dancer bends down, brings in his partner, and seats her or him on his thigh. Ten years later, in 1913, the Argentine painter Santiago Stagnaro would insert a sentada in the far-right section of a painting titled *Pierrot tango*.

Inserting a foot between your partner's two legs, then having him sit on your thigh, is provocative. The subtext is dominance. The caption reacts, in a strong, bluesy way: "*Pa que querés que haiga luz si tu mamá ve en l'oscuro*" (Why look for light [space between dancers] if your mama can see in the dark). The sentada ends. Another caption follows: "*Aura, avísale al inglés que l'están pelando el perro*" (Now tell the Englishman they're shaving the dog).

So tango in 1903 was full blown, strategically shaped by black style.

PLATE 59   PLATE 60

North African influence is apparent in Moorish taconeos, the heel-tapping sequence in the first photograph, tinctured with possible traces of polka. Later in tango, taconeo would take on a new form—striking the ground with the heel between steps. Carmencita Calderón taconeoed this way throughout her career.[55] Further black implications: the call and response in the making of ochos. The presence of ochos in 1903 meant that the tango tradition of calling for moves (marcando) with hand and arm pressure was in force at that time. You cannot make ocho without it. The dancer marks; the partner responds. It's an elegant rephrasing of call and response, or questioning and answering, as danced by apart couples in Kongo. It continues in tango, masked by embracing.

Milena Plebs, star tango dancer, cites a legend: ocho emerged among blacks making figure-eight patterns in the streets of Buenos Aires during Carnival.[56]

Shooting a leg between a partner's thighs is close to maxixe, the strong, sexy Brazilian dance that was spotted in its native Rio by the Gazeta da tarde on January 25, 1884, and was popular throughout the city by 1900.[57] As ragtime led to jazz, maxixe led to samba. Maxixe (pronounced "mah-shee-sheh") attained world popularity around 1910–15 but had already diffused southward into neighboring Argentina. Panchito de los Corrales and Lito Cerruti, early-twentieth-century performers of tango, danced the maxixe in Buenos Aires dance halls.[58]

Maxixe was a blending of blends, combining elements from afar with local ingenuity: "The polka gave it its movement, the Cuban habanera its rhythm, Afro-Brazilian popular culture its characteristic off-beating, and Brazilian creativity in general perfected its essence."[59] And the dance? Zeca Ligiero, Brazilian theater director and student of Afro-Brazilian culture, informs us that it has these characteristics:

1. Couples glued together but in choreographic dialogue.
2. Zigzagging motion, like a leaf floating down (male molente).
3. Bodies lean forward and lean back.
4. Lots of "leg play"—the male thrusts his leg between hers, and vice-versa.[60]

Maxixe resembles early tango through its cheek-to-cheek dancing, as in canyengue, and its leaning forward and back, as in candombe, canyengue, polka, and the dances of Kongo, and the zigzagging motion recalling viborita. In a 1907 drawing of a couple performing maxixe (Plate 61) the man's knee presses in between her two thighs, making a line of clear sexual assertion. It's hotter than de Navas sticking his foot between his partner's legs, or other tango entering steps. In maxixe, hands held high telegraph upper celebration of lower invasion. The dance is a test of sexual cool: can the partner dance on through all this allurement, her thigh between his, or his between hers, without losing poise or control? Were de Navas's penetrations maxixe-inspired or vice versa? Or were both dances creole rephrasings of Kongo bumbakana, the playful invasion, striking stomach against stomach, thigh against thigh, that took root in Argentine candombe and Brazilian *samba de roda?* All three cases may apply.

DE NAVAS AGAIN, AUGUST 15, 1903 De Navas loved tango, and he kept close to its motions. The issue of *Caras y Caretas* for August 15, 1903, reveals him in action again. This time he danced with a woman.

In one of his cortes he makes her feel the hardness of his leg. He presses up close, his flank on hers, while nonchalantly crossing his feet. The caption reads, "This is called being stuck together, even if we have no glue." After more steps he stops once again, pressing in hard from hip to knee. Caption: "This corte will leave Uncle cross-eyed!"

De Navas saunters cockily. What was she thinking, the woman who felt his strong leg? Something like novelist Anne Bernays's first conscious experience of sexual attraction when she was a teenager?: "[When] the edges of our shoe soles touched, I felt a rush of desire so violent it nearly knocked me off my perch."[61] Or was she simply concentrating on the dance? We cannot tell—possibly because the two partners had mastered a pact between desire and control.

De Navas also shows us that stops defined tango from its earliest formulations. Writing in 1959, Estela Canto observed, "In tango you advance, then stop for no reason, briefly immobile, as if you were concentrating. Then back to the march, the forward-thrust action, inevitably to be interrupted again."[62] Actually, the stops *can* be reasoned: they continue the African criterion of making hair-trigger stops to make a fine pose, cutting excitement with cool. They are made to show off the control of high pleasure.

PLATE 61

But also, it's love in the Western world coming in, dramatizing an ending, making it romantic, with frissons of touch. Meanwhile, Afro freeze and Afro break were so powerfully attractive that they developed into a dance of their own: canyengue. That dance went to Paris.

FUROR IN THE CITY OF LIGHT: TANGO TAKES PARIS

Tango took Paris in 1914, shortly before World War I. Because this world-class cultural center was aflame with it, Europe-worshiping upper-class Buenos Aires citizens were embarrassed into taking their national dance seriously. "Ossal" (Lasso de la Vega), a writer for the Buenos Aires journal *PBT*, pretended to be insulted: "In France they have transformed it and they've dubbed it 'le tango.' Let them dance this tango back where it came from, the Congo!" For all the wrong reasons, Lasso de la Vega had pinpointed one zone of influence, Kongo, the ancient urban kingdom where *nzéngolo* (freezing) and *tienga* (a break in the hips with deeply bent knees) had formed part of dancing since time immemorial.

Tango argentino hit Paris hard, like the *Demoiselles* of Picasso. How so? First, none other than Ángel Villoldo, the remarkable dancer-singer-composer, had come to Paris with the Uruguayan Alfredo Gobbi and his Chilean wife, Flora Rodríguez, before World War I.[63] Villoldo wasted no time in composing tangos for Paris like "Le petit salon" and "Soy tremendo." He must surely have danced tango too, startling Parisians with barrio moves. Second, Manuel Pizarro, Eduardo Bianco, and other Argentine musicians played tango music in a Montmartre boîte called El Garrón. Third and most important, El Vasco Aín, a famous Buenos Aires dance stylist, came to Paris, performed, and gave lessons. Another Argentine dancer, Bernabé Simarra, did the same.

That there were actual Argentines in town teaching real tango steps with real tango names comes across in a passage of *Les possédées* (The Possessed), a report on the tango's conquest of Paris, dated April 1912, by "Sem," a noted French caricaturist: "Oh, Fernando, what a lovely media luna!"[64] Xavier Sager's illustrations, published in 1913 and inspired by the French comedy *Le tango*, picture a mass liberation. Parisians loved leaning forward and back. (They had done this with polka.) They cherished brandishing arms to the side and in the air, banners of ecstasy. They loved de Navas–like lines in the legs, especially when his legs touched hers.

The American writer Marjorie Howard saw Argentines dancing in Paris in 1914, demonstrating to a select crowd how tango was done: "They stand absolutely erect, no motion of their bodies above the waist. Their feet move with exquisite precision and hardly seem to leave the floor. This is the real Tango Argentino."[65] It was indeed. Salón tango posture had invaded the French capital together with the black penchant for feet flat on the floor. There were even parallels with the racial democracy of the working-class bars of Buenos Aires: much to Howard's surprise, blacks openly tangoed with white women in the Bullier dance hall she visited. At the top of her article, there is an illustration of a couple dancing with a quebradalike knee bend, alternate legs extended.

Tango in France marked the start of a diaspora, of Argentine musicians and dancers abroad to make money and names. Paris, the world cultural capital, soon had London, Budapest, and St. Petersburg tangoing in mimesis of vogue. A young Japanese nobleman named Baron Megata, in Paris at the time, heard Pizarro's music and saw Aín dance. Enthralled, he took tango back to Japan. Teaching the dance to the Tokyo aristocracy without charge, he became a founder of a tradition. In 1956, at the age of sixty, he was photographed tangoing with the Duchess of Okuma.[66]

Tango left strong visual traces in Paris—postcards, billboards, drawings, photographs. Allowing for exaggeration (and there is plenty of it), these documents help us to assess tango expressivity around 1913. A series of postcards published that year show two attractive young women doing impressions of the dance. It is hard to get past their beauty, but once we do, we witness strong tango elements: leaning with extravagant gestures, one hand pointing out, the other on hip, with decorously flared fingers; opposition of levels, one partner up, the other bent down, a contrast we saw in Buenos Aires in 1911; and finally, unmistakable traces of canyengue—cheek to cheek, deep-bent knees. There is another wild step, in which one leads the other with arms flaring out like two wings. This move is close to maxixe, as danced in Buenos Aires in 1927. It provides one more instance of how much the two dances share.[67]

Paris was instructed. Argentine dancers like Villoldo, Aín, and Simarra brought actual steps from La Boca to Montmartre. A writer who knew both neighborhoods observed, "I see no difference between the way the tango is danced in the elegant salons of Paris and in the lowest night spots in Buenos Aires."[68] A critic, Sergio Pujol, dryly observes, "The classes Simarra taught had evidently borne fruit."[69] So had the media lunas of the Argentine known as Fernando.

THROUGH THE PRISM OF AMBITION: CACHAFAZ AND CARMENCITA CALDERÓN

EL CACHAFAZ

I did my best,
Among all the tough guys,
To prove I could move in the style of Cachafaz,
The ultimate dancing hipster.

— CARLOS PESCE AND ANTONIO TIMARNI,
"*El porteñito*" (1940s)

Carmencita Calderón,
You are the babe eternal,
Pure flawless motion,
Like the tango that carries you, deep in its beat.

— JOSÉ GOBELLO, "*La piba sin tiempo*"
(The Babe Eternal, 1984)

Benito Bianquet (1885–1942) and his brilliant best partner, Carmencita Calderón, still living in Buenos Aires in 2003 at the age of ninety-eight, indelibly shaped the dancing of tango. Bianquet is known by his nickname, El Cachafaz, "a guy who doesn't give a damn about making a good impression."[70]

Born on February 14, 1885, in the barrio of Boedo, El Cachafaz was a feisty young street dancer by the turn of the century, when he was fifteen. He started at the corner of Rioja and México, not far from where drums of candombe had once sounded. Hungry for training, he haunted a milonga at 1465 Calle Alsina, where he befriended a tanguera of color, María Celia Romero, known to the habitués as María Celeste. María taught him moves. Cachafaz explicitly said that he learned to dance with Maria Celeste in 1913–14. He did not elaborate. Nevertheless, armed with her training, he was able to assert himself.[71]

Cachafaz danced with various women, including Emma Bóveda (also known as La Francesita), Olga San Juan, and Isabel San Miguel, with whom he partnered from 1929 to 1933.[72] In 1937 he encountered Carmencita Calderón, the partner of his life. They met in the famous milonga Sin Rumbo, in Villa Urquiza. They danced together until the day he died: February 7, 1942. They didn't just tango; they *were* the tango.

When anyone challenged Cachafaz to battle in style, he was always game. Entering these challenge dances (*danzas de desafío*), he was participating in one of the hardiest of African- and Andalusian-influenced aesthetic traditions. One of his earliest victories was in 1911, in a movie house in Palermo on what is now Calle Puerreydón, between Gómez and Sarmiento. The dancer he vanquished was Juan Carlos Herrero, who, being noted for "sweeps" (arrastres, draggings of the feet), was nicknamed El Escobero (The Broom Man). In 1915 Cachafaz went up against a dancer who called himself Rengo Cotongo. He beat him, too. Then in the same year, he won a historic *tapada* (literally, "head-butting battle")[73] at a club called Parisien. Here he vanquished none other than El Vasco Aín, the famed milonguero who had taken tango to Paris and and danced for the pope.

Cachafaz went to Paris in 1919 and set his teaching fees at astronomic levels. When he got back to Buenos Aires in 1930, he taught a polished salon form of tango, remote from the street styles, to the city's upper class. The Argentine rich of the period, making their grand tours of Europe, had been astonished to discover that in Paris one of their countrymen was judged more by his tango than by his name, wealth, or property. Ever so slightly, the furor in Paris had democratized matters.

Back in Buenos Aires, Cachafaz resumed battling at a place called the Lido. There he had the audacity to challenge José Méndez, the 1930s king of canyengue. Cachafaz seemed unbeatable. Effort and attainment became one.

But Méndez would have his revenge. Dancers didn't fight once. They battled again and again, as equals in skill, in ongoing engagements rather than in win-or-lose-all competitions.

Petróleo, the famous dancer of the 1940s, witnessed Cachafaz dancing and wrote down impressions: he saw him dance a "well-measured" milonga figure in which the couple moved zigzag, left-right, right-left, left-right, right-left. Petróleo seems to have been describing the viborita, the flash pivot run. He praised the dancer's medias lunas, drawn with "exactness." He admired the way Cachafaz could slip a leg between a woman's thighs in the manner of a barrio tough guy (*ese repiquetear compadrón*). He remembers him "sliding one foot, dragging the other" (*ese deslizamiento con un pie, arrastrando el otro*). One thing was clear: Cachafaz had a dead-on command of canyengue. But he was equally fluent in tango de salón. He role-switched in dress, dance, and attitude: white cravat for canyengue, black tie for salón.[74] Calderón, comparing his cortes with those of a famous dancer of the 1940s, El Tarila (José

Giambuzzi), said that "the difference was that Don Benito danced his steps with impeccable timing, leaving no line without finish." She found him liberating, rescuing tango from notions of baseness.[75]

Black competition kept Cachafaz sharp. He was aware of the excellence of an Afro-Argentine tangoist nicknamed "Black Dread" (El Negro Pavura), whose given name was Luis María Cantero. El Negro Pavura danced with El Negro Santillán, the most famous of Cachafaz's adversaries, in the Parque Romano in Palermo.[76]

By the early 1930s Cachafaz was the king. He held court in a café at the corner of Corrientes and Talcahuano. The first table by the door was his *secretaría* (office), where he sat with fellow luminaries: Tito Lusiardo, star of the film *Yo quiero ser bataclana;* Elías Alippi, another famous dancer; and Gardel.

Cachafaz shaped the "look" of pre-1940s tango. When Cachafaz was starting out, some canyenguistas held their partner's hand low at the waist. According to Mingo Pugliese, this style was black. De Navas danced that way. Others, like a group of white men photographed around 1900 dancing on the outskirts of Buenos Aires, held the hand high, at the level of the shoulders.[77] Even canyenguistas, in their ecstasy of extremes, might dance with hands high while bending down low. But Cachafaz and Calderón rethought tango down to its smallest expressions: when Don Benito took Carmencita's right hand in his left, he lifted it up to the level of his eyes (Plate 62).[78] Cachafaz teaches us even in the way that he took Carmencita's hand: four fingers curled over the ends of her fingertips. This subtlety of grasp was a way of honoring her, unlike the tight fist of a brute. He was priming their flow with respect.[79] Parallel to this, Cachafaz addressed Carmencita, to his last dancing day, with the formal *usted* instead of the familiar *tú.*

Calderón would turn slightly

PLATE 62

forward, her face beautiful, resting her cheek on his chest. The relaxed line of her arm would echo the ease of Cachafaz's leg crossing over. Then he would sometimes go into a spin while she improvised tiny flourishes.[80] The pair kept a strict vertical torso, a trait tracing back to flamenco and the Renaissance courts of western Europe,[81] but from the waist down things were different: right leg crossing left, left leg kicking up, spurts of milonga and polka. They were working out an equation, of classical silhouette over intense creole footwork. Cachafaz and Aín smoothed things over when dancing salon, but they never forgot the orillero alternative: freeze, break, and whiplash (latiguillos). Copes adds, "Cachafaz had a way of stopping short [parando], then flowing right back into motion."[82] Everyone makes stops (cortes) and everyone walks (hace caminadas), but Cachafaz strung these moves together in bursts of high contrast.

Cachafaz danced in at least fourteen movies, starting with Resaca (Undertow), a silent film of 1916, and ending with Carnaval de antaño (Carnival of Yesteryear) of 1940, two years before his death. Tango (1933), the first Argentine sound film, features him briefly in action. We see couples revolving canonically counterclockwise to the music of Miguel Caló. Suddenly a man and a woman move in from the right, flashing corte after corte. It's Cachafaz.

He kicks out sharply: milonga. He sways side to side: canyengue. He hops to the right. He rejoins the circle with a slow drag: arrastre. With a deadpan expression, he packs in four figures—milonga, canyengue, a hop, and a drag. "He saw his moment," says Copes, "like a fast-moving soccer player, making a feint [rabona], then shooting the ball between his opponent's legs [caño]."[83] Mingo Pugliese notes additional style elements: "Orillero dancing appears in the film Tango, performed by Cachafaz. With a lifted left leg he touches a woman on her back. He [also] touches his foot with his hand."[84] Challenging a woman with a playfully placed kick recalls vacunao, the Kongo-Cuban dance game of sexual pursuit; touching foot with hand is pure Charleston. This jazz dance conceit would reappear in the 1930s improvisations of Méndez.

In Carnaval de antaño Cachafaz dances tango/milonga with Sofía Bozán. He enters moving backward, taking the woman's role for a second. He crosses left over right with obsessive intensity. His sobrepasos (crosssteps) become incantations, charms to keep things in motion.

The Cachafaz profile lives on in art history. Adolfo Bellocq, in a woodcut of 1922 (Plate 45), shows couples tangoing in a tenement patio to guitar and bandoneón. They dance in the style of Cachafaz: vertical torsos, legs swaying strongly, hands held on high. That Cachafaz "look" reappears

in a famous bas-relief on the
wall of the Caminito walkway
in La Boca, dated 1932 (Plate
63). We see two dancers. The
uplifted hands, on axis with the
eyes, are telling. The fingers of
the man enfold the extended
right fingers of the woman.
Pure Cachafaz. The woman
bends her torso slightly back.
They dance cheek to cheek,
thigh to thigh, in a poem of
attraction that brings back
Arturo de Navas.

PLATE 63

We end with Cachafaz's oft-
told battle with his famous
black rival, El Negro Santillán, in a version related by the former suitor of
the grandmother of the Argentine anthropologist Alejandro Frigerio:

> Once El Negro Santillán was dancing in Hansen's when Cachafaz walked
> in, without his gang and without his dance partner but with a tough side-
> kick named Paisanito. A dance battle started. El Negro Santillán began
> with a corrida. Cachafaz answered with two cortes. El Paisanito took out
> his knife [*finginga*] and hurled it into the hardwood floor, saying, "OK,
> Cachafaz, show them the sugar!" And Cachafaz danced round the knife
> and defeated Santillán. He let the blade graze the cuff of his pants without
> tearing the cloth or him getting scratched.[85]

It was a moment of bravado reminiscent of the rumba of the knives, in
black Cuba, and of the death-defying dancers, with knives in their hands,
in Kongo and Ivory Coast.

EL VASCO AÍN: DANCING THE TANGO FOR POPE PIUS XI

Cachafaz had another rival: El Vasco Aín (1874–1940). Born Casimiro Aín
in Buenos Aires in 1874, he was the son of a milkman, a Basque, and so
was nicknamed "El Vasco." He grew up in La Piedad barrio. Like most of
his peers, he learned tango on the streets, watching young toughs whistle
and practice. Aín learned to break with the best of them. He became

famous for media lunas and quebradas, the steps that Villoldo had mentioned in verse.

Aín turned professional in 1913, at the age of thirty-nine. That year he traveled to Paris, bringing to France both the street tango and what would soon be called tango de salón. Eleven years later he famously danced tango for Pope Pius XI. He was fifty. The session took place in the late afternoon of February 1, 1924, in the Vatican Library. The Argentine ambassador to the Vatican, García Mansilla, had arranged the encounter. Aín kissed the pope's ring. "Come forward, my son, proceed" (*Avanti figliolo, procedi*), said the pope, so Aín started tangoing, he dressed in tails (*frac*), his partner in a long dark-blue skirt. The choice of music, Francisco Canaro's tango "Ave María," was diplomatic, and Aín sheared off all hint of the sensual. An undated drawing of him suggests the vocabulary he used on that day: faces apart, moderate embrace, torsos straight, hand held high in the Cachafaz manner. Yet at the end, Aín dared to unleash two real moves: "As I came face to face with His Holiness, I made a small run, then froze with my partner to the left."[86] The pope was pleased.

Aín appeared in silent films of the 1920s, notably a Universal picture called *Destinos*. He returned to Buenos Aires in 1930 and died there ten years later, at the age of sixty-six. Teaching in Paris, beguiling the pope, Aín helped open tango to the world.

INTERMEZZO: THE PERILS AND PLEASURES OF
EUROPEANIZATION

The publication in Buenos Aires of *The Argentine Salon Tango: Method, Technique, and Practice of the Dance* in 1916 marked a cultural watershed.[87] The concept of *tango de salón* dates from this book, which codified tango, transforming an improvised, spontaneous club and street dance into set patterns and measured expressions.

Tango de salón was an intensification of tango liso, the "smoothed-out" tango that had gained ground around 1905–10. Supposedly it was dancers of Italian origin who were primarily responsible for the development of this style. Tango liso sheared off the street traits, the cuts and breaks, and concentrated on walks and "fine posture," that is, a vertical torso. The process of "Europeanization" also included the dropping of taconeo, or Andalusian heel-stamping.

But Cachafaz, Aín, and black dancers like El Negro Santillán kept alive all the styles of barrio animation. Tango liso and tango de salón did not replace orillero or canyengue among star tangueros. They simply widened the vocabulary: Euro verticality met Afro bent knees and legs intermingled (*entrevero de piernas*). In addition, two particular dancers, El Negro Santillán and José Méndez, would revitalize canyengue around 1930, continuing the steps of an earlier era—corridas, cortes, quebradas, ochos, sentadas, taconeos, and vueltas—plus the old cheek-to-cheek. Bypassing liso, they kept to a strong creole beauty.

THE MÉNDEZ CANYENGUE RENAISSANCE, 1930S

José Méndez, nicknamed El Gallego (The Man from Galicia), was a committed intelligence. A strong and brilliant dancer, he paralleled, in dance, the black-influenced movement championed in Sebastián Piana's revival of milonga in the 1930s. Méndez and Piana, working in the same decade, revitalized Afro-Argentine dance.

Méndez brought in canyengue, the steps that blacks danced at the start of the century. The authenticity of his vision would resound past the 1930s. His style of dancing made an impression on the father of Rodolfo Cieri. Father taught son; Rodolfo, dancing with his wife, María, in the mid-1990s, would become king of canyengue in Buenos Aires. The manner of Méndez also shaped the style, walk, and motion of the father of Miguel Ángel Zotto, great star of the early twenty-first century, who can perform in this style upon the slightest invitation.[88]

Méndez excited the city with canny, swift moves. In renewing canyengue, its postures and timing, he was renewing himself and his friends. He lived for motion; in a posed photograph from the 1930s, standing with his partner, La Cachito, his body breaks subtly into various angles (Plate 64).[89] Note the slant of his shoulders, the conversation of his hands (one thrust in pocket, the other poised with cigarette, just like di Sarli), the cut of his hat. (Thinking himself short, Méndez famously danced with his hat on to add to his stature.) His right leg is straight but the left gently bends, taking a phantom step forward. La Cachito moves into her man with the side of her body. She's dancing, too.

Petróleo extolled Méndez: "Without any doubt the best interpreter of canyengue in the history of our dance." He mastered the idiom by jousting with blacks, "in eternal duels in search of the best."[90] The action took place at a practice club called La Colonia Italiana, at 555 Paraná. Here, as we shall see, he was frequently challenged by El Negro Santillán.

PLATE 64

Méndez moved cheek to cheek, but kept his body apart from his partner (*cara junta, cuerpo separado*). Mingo Pugliese talks about his canyengue style: "Not like today, where one leans on the other, and the man takes the weight of the woman on his chest."[91] Mingo again: "Méndez brought speed to canyengue. Where ordinary dancers might make two steps Méndez took five. He showed off flash moves, where his hands touched his feet. Sometimes, when he kicked to the back, he slapped his hand on the ground."[92] He was vaunting his authority over foot, hand, and motion. Touching his feet, and slapping the ground while kicking to the back, echoes the jazz dance the Charleston.[93] The back-kicks predicted boleos—strong kicks to the rear, which would become popular in the tango of the 1940s—while at the same time relating to back-kicks in Kongo and candombe.

Petróleo admired Méndez's fluent, light legs (*piernas ligeras*), his break-neck speed (*tango a toda velocidad*), and the flash of his body (*una luz*).[94] His allusion to swiftness reinforces Mingo's. It distinguishes Méndez's canyengue from the canyengue of today, danced with a gentle swing and sway.[95] Petróleo claimed that Méndez changed the rhythm of tango, using steps that were short and staccato.[96] He was certainly the best dancer of the 1930s.

Méndez challenged and beat Cachafaz in a duel at the Confitería Niño in Costanera Norte in around the late 1930s. He had other rivals. One was Bernardo Undarz, known for his dreamy, slow tangos.[97] Another was El Negro Santillán, with whom he sparred constantly. Santillán developed his style with two famous black partners, La Parda Hayde (later his wife) and La Parda Ester. He frequented the club where Méndez performed, La Colonia Italiana, with its Wednesday-night duels. Santillán represented black style to Méndez. To ignore, or pass over, their mutual influence would be like subtracting Braque from Picasso.

One night in the 1940s friends gathered to honor José Méndez on the occasion of his retirement from dancing. Juan César Mendieta, nicknamed "Congreve," apparently after the nineteenth-century military rocket, organized the event. It was held at the Maipú Pigalle club, in front of the Marabú. Petróleo was present and wrote down an account. The royalty of 1940s tango danced for their man. Mendieta opened, moving to the beat of "El africano" (The African, 1919–20), an old tango by Eduardo Pereyra. Mendieta improvised steps "in the manner of Divito." This apparently meant that he moved with a suave body line. Then Petróleo made his entrance, parading to the beat of the tango "Comme il faut" by Eduardo Arolas. He danced 1940s style, with giros (strong spins), piques (hammering the floor several times with the tip of the shoe), boleos (kicks to the rear), and arrastres (drags of the feet), in a ceaseless parade of moves new and old. The next tango luminary, José Orradre, "El Vasquito," danced to the tango of the black composer Anselmo Rosendo Mendizábal, "El entrerriano" (The Man from Between the Rivers), mixing orillero and canyengue together. Méndez usually danced to Mendizábal, so he now wondered what he might dance to instead. Petróleo solved the problem by asking the bandleader, Sassano, to play a milonga in Méndez's honor. So Sassano broke out with "Viejos corrales" (Old-Time Corrals), which Méndez, drawing on the style of the blacks and the sailors, transformed into a dockside milonga.

When Méndez finished, men carried him in triumph on their shoulders, circling the dance floor several times over. In a sense it was roots night at the Maipú Pigalle. The roots—Mendizábal, canyengue, "El africano"—were allusively black. Whether or not they intended to, the participants were honoring black cultural intelligence as well the master who built on that strength.

Méndez did *not* retire. He set up a studio in the 200 block of Libertad, where Mingo Pugliese worked with him in 1950–51. He kept right on working till he died. Two films include fragments of his fast-moving style: a patio scene in *Derecho viejo: La vida de Eduardo Arolas* (Old-Time Custom: The Life of Eduardo Arolas, 1950), where he dances milonga in a conventillo, and *Los muchachos de antes no usaban gomina* (Guys in the Old Days Didn't Gum Up Their Hair).[98] Until the end, Méndez challenged his followers to rethink their motion and achieve richer goals.

THE *SOBREPASO*

In the late 1930s came the invention of the *sobrepaso,* the cross-step (also called *cruce,* or "cross"). Many things changed in its wake.

In the sobrepaso, the woman starts off moving backward, making a cross-step of left foot over right. Beginning this way aligns the couple and swings them into a symmetry of action. Two stories are told of the rise of the sobrepaso, one version stemming from Mingo Pugliese, the second from Eduardo Arquimbaud. Staunch adherents attach to both versions, and understanding both is critical: modern tango begins with the sobrepaso.

According to Mingo Pugliese, the revolution started with José Orradre, El Vasquito de Villa Crespo (1902–62). He danced in the 1930s with a partner named Lucy, and later he danced with his wife, Olga. He was honored *bailarín* with the orchestras of Juan d'Arienzo and Osvaldo Pugliese.[99]

In 1938–39 Orradre was practicing with a partner, a man named Recalde. As Orradre was bringing this man forward to start off the dance, Recalde reached the point where he had no room to advance. So instead he stepped back with a cross-step, left over right. A new possibility opened up.[100] Orradre recognized it.

Before the sobrepaso, at the start of the action both partners had sallied forth toward the front, side by side, in a joint forward step.[101] This starting step—performed in profile, side by side, two arms held ahead like a prow—transmuted into stereotype: Joe E. Brown and Jack Lemmon danced this way in *Some Like It Hot* in 1959, as did Catherine Deneuve and Linh Dan Pham in *Indochine* in 1992. With the emergence of the sobrepaso, all that disappeared. The man and the woman now started out opposite and facing one another, interwoven and balanced. Petróleo and El Negro Lavandina would seize that power as a basis for new moves.

This change is so important that there is another credited version of it, by Arquimbaud, one of the star dancers of the *Tango Argentino* show of 1985. He too underscores the crucial nature of the woman's cross-step, moving backward at the start of the dance, the *salida.* This is his commentary:

> Giros, boleos, piques—in the 1940s—were not what was most important. Back in the 1940s what did carry significance was the [backward] cross-over step [*cruce:* left over right] of the woman at the salida, the start of the

dance. Because from that flowed all the rest. Once cruce appeared, other figures came in. In the salida of early tango, the woman didn't cross-step. Man and woman started side by side. Now the woman moved backward [de espaldas] and did a cross-step.[102]

The couple was now poised to begin improvising steps, directly facing each other. The women could also show off her legs, revealed by the short skirts of the 1940s.

One little backward-moving cross-step changed a tradition that had been abused from Paris to Hollywood. In the new starting format, mirrored kicks, whirls, and probes would soon refacet tango. Tango would sometimes now look like a danced form of cubism.[103]

PETRÓLEO — PROTAGONIST/HISTORIAN OF MODERN TANGO
DANCE, 1940

In the 1940s a remarkable young bank clerk named Carlos Alberto Estévez, working with leading dancers and building on the seminal innovation of Orradre, enriched Argentine dance history. As Lili Palmer has observed, "He never set foot on the stage but in one decade he modernized tango de salón."[104]

There was nothing fortuitous about this. One reason the new steps took hold was that although the protagonists now practiced not on the street but indoors, in the barrio clubs, they still honored the tradition of informal all-male practice that had launched early tango. Mingo Pugliese points out that when the man learned the woman's way of moving, "it allowed him to sense with his own body what it meant to be led." It is probably no accident that the sobrepaso, the single most important element of change, grew out, as we saw, of a practice session, between Orradre and a man named Recalde.

A lot was changing, including social origins. Early dance stars were working class. Now tango's genius was a bank teller. He wrote tango history for the in-house journal of his bank, Banco Europeo para América Latina (BEAL). Caught up in the event, he could still look back, describe, and comprehend it. In Petróleo's best writing, it is as if Nijinsky were turning his talent to the writing of dance history.

Estévez—that is, Petróleo—and his partner, Esperanza Días, and his charming black colleague Félix Luján—that is, El Negro Lavandina—and his partner, a woman of color named Ester, challenged young tangoists to enter a new world. Afro-Argentines thus moved at the very heart of this action.

Petróleo ruled the 1940s as Méndez had the 1930s. How did he acquire his colorful nickname? One tanguero says they called him "gasoline" (*petróleo*) because the whirling pinwheel in the glass dome of 1940s gas pumps recalled his famed spins. This is one version. But most people say: Petróleo drank heavily. His beverage of choice was cheap red wine, called *petróleo* in lunfardo because of its dark color.

Petróleo was born in 1912, in Almagro. He grew up in Villa Devoto, farther out in the city. Petróleo was white, but he trained (*hizo su formación*) with a black virtuoso: in 1928, at the age of sixteen, he would hang out at a cabaret on Corrientes, riveted by the style of an Afro-Argentine dancer called El Negro Navarro, who had recently returned from a dance tour in Paris. Sensing a boy hungry to learn and probably enjoying his admiration, Navarro took Petróleo on as an apprentice. He told him, "Come to the cabaret tomorrow, but make sure it's all right with your parents—I'll teach you."[105] He was opening a door to a culture of moves.

Navarro introduced Petróleo to old-guard traditions—the rhythm of canyengue, hands held on high in the Cachafaz manner. "Oh, how I loved it!" Petróleo would remember. Like the famed salsa innovator Willie Colón, who smoked cigars in 1966 at the age of sixteen to make himself look older, Petróleo masked his extreme youth by donning compadrito attire. Meanwhile, Navarro taught him black style, opening his heart to canyengue. The style would remain in his bloodstream. Zotto's 2000 video *Perfumes de tango* has a precious filmed fragment of Petróleo tangoing, now as an elder in the 1970s. He dances canyengue, knees deeply bent, torso thrust forward.

Petróleo trained with Navarro from 1928 to 1930. His virtuosity and confidence attracted the attention of Esperanza Días, whom he met at a dance in 1930. Soon they were living together. They danced as a team for two decades; then suddenly, around 1950, Esperanza split, fed up with her partner's drinking. Petróleo handled the hurt philosophically: "So that was that for romance and the dance. I would never again mix business with pleasure. I would tango with professional partners." Translation: he refused to give up his red wine.

Petróleo next focused his attention on an Afro-Argentine woman, La Negra Martita (Black Martha). The two danced exhibitions at the Augusteo Club, on Sarmiento and Uruguay, and at the fabled Atlanta dance palace, where Osvaldo Pugliese played and Copes and María

Nieves would soon make history. A black had trained Petróleo. Now he was dancing with a woman of color.

La Negra Martita had style. Milena Plebs saw her dance with Petróleo in 1987. She deeply impressed Plebs with her smart, rhythmized footwork: "very percussive." Carlos Anzuate remembers her way of rendering a boleo back-kick: "close to the floor, not high like today." She was not good-looking, but men seldom cared because, adds Anzuate, "she danced like the gods." At Atlanta she performed in full view of Osvaldo Pugliese. If she danced there in the late 1940s (that is, before teaming up with Petróleo in 1950), she was feasibly the woman who inspired Pugliese to write "La negracha."

Petróleo and Lavandina kept things in motion. Their group included Monte Castro dancers like Ricardo Scalisi, nicknamed "El Flaco" (The Thin Man), plus dancers from elsewhere, like Cachirla and Antonio Todaro, who were dance stars as well. El Flaco was famous for walks laced with flourishes. Todaro's style was hard to pin down but immediately recognizable and powerful.

Petróleo, Roberto Marcos (who knew so many moves, they called him "La Biblia," the Bible), and El Negro Lavandina coached the modern master, Mingo Pugliese. Todaro had a similar impact on a young man named Jorge Martín Orcaizaguirre, nicknamed "Virulazo" (a hit in the game of bocce). The exceptional daring of all these men's dancing was creating disciples who would carry their excitement into the twenty-first century.

MINGO PUGLIESE, CENTURION OF THE 1940S

> If tango hadn't developed, it would have simply
> disappeared.
>
> — MINGO PUGLIESE (March 4, 1997)

Mingo Pugliese and his wife, Ester, keep 1940s dancing alive in the twenty-first century (Plate 65). He was at the heart of the revolution in tango that began at the start of that decade. Petróleo was the leader; he took on Pugliese as a valued private student. Petróleo wrote articles on new tango, its prowess and defiance. These works are important, but Mingo's published interviews add balance.

At the time of the revolution, Mingo points out, few milongueros were

PLATE 65

professional. Cachafaz and Aín had given lessons in the 1920s, Méndez and El Negro Pavura ran studios, and in the early 1950s Lalo and Julia Bello danced on stage with Copes and Nieves. But most milongueros danced for pleasure. The few times they charged was when trying to raise money to help a friend, someone sick or out of work or in some kind of trouble. In that case a few star dancers might put on an exhibition in a barrio club, charge admission, and give their friend the money.[106] It was a tango equivalent to the Harlem rent party.

Petróleo and his followers, then, were autonomous and unsponsored when they started inventing new moves in 1939–40. We cut into the story in 1948, some eight years after the revolution started. That was the year Mingo entered the game, in Monte Castro. But he had to pass tests.

Mingo was born on July 1, 1936. He learned his first tango steps from a girl; his brothers helped him learn more. They sent him to a friend, Arturo, at Club Miranda in Villa Parque in Buenos Aires. Arturo passed him on to a milonguero called El Rana (The Frog), because he danced with a very long stride. The Frog and another dancer, Salvador Maitía, taught Mingo steps and how to combine them.

The more he learned, the better he looked. He caught the eye of a handsome, heavyset mulatto, who came up to Pugliese in the Club Miranda one night and said, "Kid, if you want, I can take you to a place where you'll *really* learn tango." He took him to the epicenter, El Club Social y Deportivo Nelson (The Nelson Social and Sport Club), at 1650 Calle Bernáldez in Monte Castro. Here met the aristocracy of new 1940s tango to practice, on Mondays, Wednesdays, and Fridays

Mingo, on entering the Nelson, noted at once how everyone treated his host with deference and admiration. This man was none other than Félix Luján, better known as El Negro Lavandina, famed tango innovator (Plate 66). Félix Luján was born in Buenos Aires around December 1925. He was in his early twenties when Mingo met him. A family photograph dated *circa* 1974, showing Luján together with his mother, María Luisa

Ospeche de Luján, and her brother, documents the African-descended side to his family (Plate 67).[107]

Luján took young Pugliese to the bar, where he introduced him to a short man (*petiso*) named Roberto Marcos.[108] "Are you aware," Marcos said, "that henceforth your life will take place in the night?" Mingo nodded. Marcos summoned a waiter to bring two glasses of *formidable,* an orange-flavored firewater that was 59 percent alcohol. (An 80 proof whiskey is 40 percent alcohol.) Marcos drank. Pugliese followed suit. The liquor burned, but he was in.

Roberto Marcos promptly summoned a dancer named Miguelito Roscella. Together he and Miguelito taught the young Mingo complex combinations. It was 1948 and Mingo was just a kid—twelve years old— but definitely a prodigy. He intrigued Estévez, who mentored the boy. So did Luján, even as El Negro Navarro had once taken Petróleo under his wing.

FÉLIX LUJÁN, THE PRINCE OF MONTE CASTRO

> *Dancing down, stylish, tight*
> *in comes Black Lavandina,*
> *with an ocho and mina*
> *both out of sight.*

—ENRIQUE CADÍCAMO, "Villa Urquiza"

Monte Castro is a compact Buenos Aires barrio of 219 blocks and approximately 35,000 inhabitants. Two powerful thoroughfares, Avenida Segurola and Avenida Jonte, intersect near its heart. That crossroads, Jonte and Segurola, has come to symbolize the dance revolution of the

PLATE 66   PLATE 67

1940s. What it really refers to is the nearby Club Nelson, which in the 1940s was located at 1650 Calle Bernáldez. The Café Febo at 4475 Jonte (today a Día supermarket) was where the local tangueros gathered to drink after practice. Cine Febo, at 4465 Jonte, featured live comparsas and *murgas* (roaming street bands) at Carnival time. Félix Luján used to hold court during summers in the 1940s, seated in front of this cinema.

Thus far no history has identified Lavandina's given name, Félix Luján, but Afro-Argentines Carlos Anzuate and Margarita de Guillé, and Lavandina's half-brother, Ernesto Lopardo, give his name as Félix Luján. Another source gives his name as Salvador Sciana. I go with the Afro-Argentine version.

Lavandina danced by night and worked by day as a house painter. Preparing house walls with bleach (*lavandina*) gave rise to his nickname.

Luján was a fabulous dancer, blending milonga and canyengue with all that he saw going round him. Margarita de Guillé, one of the more famous black women tangoists, cherishes the memory of Luján teaching her viborita at a restaurant in Vicente López in around 1950. She remembers as well his subtle sentada, placing her gently on the top of his knee

Luján deeply enriched the consciousness of tango. His spins to the right were exceptionally brilliant. So were his air steps. He evolved skit-like little dances of derision, like making fun of a lush weaving wildly down the street.

THE CLUB NELSON MEN

Petróleo and El Negro Lavandina attracted an entourage of some twenty-one dancers who met regularly with the two masters to practice at the Club Nelson. New moves were their goal. All but two—Orcaizaguirre and Ramón Ribera—came from the barrio of Monte Castro. Mingo Pugliese has recorded their names and their *noms de combat*.

1. Julio Leme: El Gurí (The Kid)
2. Arturo Gardet: Perita el Experto (Perita the Expert)
3. Juan Neme: El Turco (The Turk)
4. Jorge Curí: El Turquito (Little Turk)
5. Rafael Cirulo: Rafael
6. Mario Zambán: El Rusito (The Little Russian)
7. Roberto Marcos: La Biblia (The Bible)
8. Francisco Hernández: Firpito (Little Firpo)

9. José Bernardo: Josecito el Lecherito (Little Joe the Milkman)
10. Miguel Roscella: Miguelito (Little Mike)
11. José Arena: Pepe Arena
12. Salvador Lorenzo Piazza: Piazza
13. Pedro Bernal: El Pescá (The Fishmonger)
14. Ricardo Scalisi Saúl: Ricardo: El Flaco (The Thin Man)
15. Roberto Estanislao Rolón: El Negro Rolón (Black Rolón)
16. Salvador Sciana: Cacho Lavandina (Cacho the Bleach Painter); also El Negro Lavandina (The Black Bleach Painter); also Monte Castro
17. Arturo Intile: Arturito (Little Arthur)
18. Carlos Alberto Estévez: Petróleo (Drinker of Red Wine); also El Bailarín Imposible (The Impossible Dancer)
19. Domingo José Pugliese: Mingo
20. José Maturana: El Negro Pepe (Black Pepe)
21. Raúl Leira: El Negro Raúl (Black Raúl)
22. Ramón Ribera: Finito (Slim)
23. Jorge Martín Orcaizaguirre: Virulazo (a hit in bocce)

Petróleo and Lavandina, twin leaders of the revolution, are the only dancers awarded more than two names. Finito and Virulazo, from outside the neighborhood, were welcomed for their talent.[109]

Blacks were supposedly "invisible" in Buenos Aires, but at least three—Luján, Maturana, and Leira—were members of the elite Nelson gang. Others also visited, notably Carlos "El Negro" Anzuate, who would teach Copes there his first giro.

Afro-Argentines formed an overwhelming majority in the Shimmy Club in the Casa Suiza in Centro and were artistically significant at Sin Rumbo, the famous milonga of Villa Urquiza. To Sin Rumbo came at least five milongueros of color: Margarita de Guillé,[110] Betti Pizarro,[111] Facundo Posadas, Luis "El Negrito" Russo, and Lydia "La Negrita" Rivero.[112] They established a context that was rich, full, and vivid, famously based on suave pauses.

Between 1940 and 1950, the postpractice hangout of Nelson Club regulars continued to be the Café Febo on Avenida Jonte. Anzuate, who lived only three blocks away, remembers that in 1950 a blond vitrolera (DJ) played tango records there.[113]

Back at the Nelson, Perita el Experto strutted special cortes (freezes) and firuletes (special figures). Neme, by contrast, was "boss of the elegant tango salón." (Mention of these dancers and the ones that follow stem from Pugliese's conversatons with Anne Hess.) They anchored the adventurous in the lyric power of the past. Piazza's acrobatic dances convey the feel of a period of experiment: as Mingo Pugliese tells us, "He held tightly on to his partner and had her do a headfirst somersault." One senses the influence of lindy athleticism, one more cosmopolitan source in the mix, and the rise of a tendency that would become *fantasía*.

Curí became "the king of the walk in the tango." Like Neme, he worked in the medium of tango de salón. Cirulo made his name working out a geometric step called *raspada* (compass). Meanwhile Zambán, like Curí, added his own special savor to salón.

Zambán and Curí posted another reminder to aggressive young colleagues that modern tango was inseparable from the past. In fact, it was an extract of all tangos danced. Thus, as we shall see, vuelta became giro. Maxixe informed gancho. Arrastres became magnetized, his foot to hers, slurring and dragging together.

Most of the changes stemmed from Lavandina and Petróleo, who rethought the tango. At some point Lavandina awarded himself a fourth name, "Monte Castro," citing the barrio in which he and Petróleo danced, lived, and flourished. Petróleo's admirers gave him a third sobriquet, "The Impossible Dancer"—that is, impossible to challenge, impossible to mimic. Petróleo, bold and autonomous, had his own test of excellence: how many people are copying you? Casting modesty to the winds, he noted in his writings that "The Impossible Dancer" (himself) left formative traces on several key dancers, inspiring, for example, the superb "arabesques" of Francisco Hernández, "Firpito." According to Roberto Tonet, Petróleo's arabesques were "danced pictures," "extraordinary poses."[114] They predicted the tableaux that would bring down the house at the finale of *Tango Argentino*. They echo the "living statues" who famously pose in the streets of Recoleta and San Telmo.

Dressed entirely in white and wearing white makeup, the "living statues" of Buenos Aires complement the city's commitment to culture. Standing absolutely still, they mime famous statuary—*Pietà, Venus de Milo*, or protagonists in history like Roman centurions. They come alive, gesturing thanks, only when money is deposited on the ground right before them. Their poses are like cortes that go on forever.

In any event, out of the pose-rich Nelson emerged tough-guy dance duos. The influence of Petróleo was again evident: José Arena paired up with him, as did José Bernardo, better known as Josecito el Lecherito. Josecito then danced with Piazza and with Leme, El Gurí. They danced orillero in exact, bold formations. Josecito and El Gurí were pulled into the orbit of yet another strong dancer, Pedro Bernal or El Pescá, a virtuoso of the night who sold fish by day. In all of these duos the concern was aesthetic excellence.

Arturo Intile, better known as Arturito, came late to the Nelson but advanced to the level of master. Arturito, it is said, pioneered the *milonga con traspié* (where one syncopates three steps over two beats). Lampazo insists that he invented the *sangüichito* (little sandwich), where the man encloses the woman's foot with both of his feet.[115] Scalisi enlightened his colleagues with elegance and transition, and finally El Negro Rolón astonished the club with new ways of attacking milonga. Here was a passionate improviser. Intile, Scalisi, and Rolón were all members of Petróleo's inner circle, upon which depended so much of the vitality of the 1940s.

Ambitious tangueros, however, were now entering from elsewhere—Devoto, Mataderos, Parque, Villa Urquiza, Pompeya, and Saavedra. They played back the steps in their own local clubs. The Nelson was not the sole site of happening. Beyond Monte Castro danced talented blacks like Alfonso El Negro, who performed in the Confitería Continental at Belgrano and Entre Ríos, as did La Negra Leonor, who was married to a dancer nicknamed Chichi. A passionate black dancer named El Mixto "danced very down [with deeply bent knees] in an original way."[116] He partnered with Carmencita Calderón after the death of Cachafaz in 1942. Two further protagonists were El Negro Capdevilla and El Negro Correa.

Afro-Argentine women like La Negra Martita were famed for their ability to complement any man's style, such was their richness of cultural adaptability. Hence in the 1940s we find Alfredo Carozzi paired up with La Negra María in the San Nicolás barrio, Luis Lobardo performing with La Parda Corina,[117] plus other instances remembered in the oral tradition.

Among the most elegant of Argentine dancers was Geraldo Portalea, who led Villa Urquiza in the translation of di Sarli into gems of salón. There was no canyengue in his mature final style; Portalea was a man of elegant stops, promenades, and ochos. Serious and intent, his guiding hand sometimes floated off the back of his partner. He gives the actor and director Robert Duvall a lesson in Duvall's 2003 film *Assassination Tango*.

About the Club Nelson, Petróleo remains a strong source. In the monthly house bulletin of the BEAL, the bank where he worked, he recorded his impressions and chronicled the taste of the men who changed tango.

Early tango had turns (*vueltas*). Lavandina and Petróleo transformed them into fast-moving spins (*giros*). They created a new language of rotation: single spins, double spins, triple spins, to the left, to the right.[118]

The distinguished Argentine artist Hermenegildo Sábat immortalized the giro in *Endless Tango,* 1987 (Plate 68), which shows a man whose dance-signal hand is enormous. His partner has ripped off her clothes in excitement. They are passionately in love. They whirl in a giro forever, leaving red-hot strong circles in the air.

Expounding on this freewheeling idiom, Petróleo and Lavandina introduced the pivot with *enrosque* (turned screw) around 1940. In enrosque, the dancer spins on one foot while the other foot rests on the ankle of the leg that is spinning. This trope was borrowed from ballet, where it is performed with the foot placed on the calf of the leg that revolves. Petróleo and Lavandina lowered the accent to the region of the ankle, keeping it close to the ground.

They were signaling: high culture is fair game. They would take what they liked from wherever they liked—concert halls, soccer matches, films, street games, club action.

Petróleo and colleagues elaborated *pique,* in which the dancer taps the floor with the tip of his shoe—a stylish rethinking of Andalusian zapateo, animating motion with pinpoints of percussion. "For me, doing piques," says the young tango dancer Gabriel Angió, "the accent is up, pulling the tip of the shoe quickly up."[119]

Further new sequences surged out of the clubs: raspadas, traspiés, and boleos. *Raspada* meaning "compass," and that's how it's danced: left foot, in place, revolves on its axis; right foot, extended, draws a pure circle. They also called this step *el lápiz* (the pencil). Doing lápiz-raspada, tangueros trace two or three circles, exchange right foot for left, then resume the same action and draw several more. It's dancing in geometric terms.

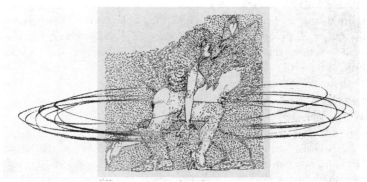

PLATE 68

Traspié, a counterstep, similarly keeps one foot still while the other moves. It echoes a step from candombe (discussed in the chapter on milonga) that in turn seems derived from the Kongo dance motion *teeza maza* (testing the waters), where one foot stays put (on the land) while the other rhythmically inches ahead (in the river).

We come now to aggression in dance, the *boleo.* In the boleo the foot moves backward while kicking up fluently. In fact, the leg flicks back and comes down like a whip. María Nieves adds grace to this step; she curls up her heel with classical elegance, as if tracing the volute of an upside-down column. Essentially she is hooking the air as she comes out of an ocho.[120] Petróleo developed this step and gave it its name: developed, not invented, for Méndez kicked back in the 1930s and so did black dancers in candombe and Kongo.

Jorge Márquez, a dancer of Pompeya, is said to have invented the gancho.[121] When air hooks collided with memories of the leg play of maxixe, the rise of the gancho was inevitable. In a gancho the woman wraps her leg around the leg of the man, then, just as suddenly, removes it. The man does the same. It's flamelike, limbs licking limbs, as if embracing with arms offered not enough heat. It's a high-octane blend of art and seduction.

Meanwhile tango women of the 1940s rebelled against men who bossed them around with peremptory hand motions. Some took the battle to the level of Lysistrata: guide me more tactfully, or start sleeping alone.[122] Not coincidentally, sharing of action, 50 percent male, 50 percent female, emerged in this decade. Nieves and Copes took that trend to the max.

The Argentine surrealist Juan Carlos Liberti portrayed a woman being ganchoed by a man in a pen-and-ink drawing of 1997, "La morocha," The Woman with Dark Hair (Plate 69). A dapper milonguero tangos with a woman whose head has turned into a scroll of sheet music. The meaning: "She carries tango in her mind." The painter adds that the milonguero's gancho, hooking his right leg around the woman's right, indicates the couple's unity and the extent of their concentration into one working force.[123] The man holds a guitar "to symbolize the sound that they follow." With deft surreal touches—guitar as third partner, sheet music as face—a man and a woman fall into synchronized motion.

In sum, Petróleo and his colleagues challenged the dance status quo. With hooks, whips, and spins, they dramatized tango. A new, secret ardor had entered the action. Dancers whirled like ballet stars or jousted like athletes in duels of the feet such as *la metida.* Legs flickering around legs

PLATE 69

abstracted the melody into action. It was air guitar scored for the feet.

Tango now reached the complexity of ballet, but it stemmed from a different aesthetic. Ballet ascends; tango gets down. Legs turn to sword-play, made more amazing by the still-ness of the torso. All this fired up the strong and the brilliant. Building on a tendency—of steps done for show or for flash—that goes back to canyengue, tangueros such as Todaro, Intile, and Piazza superdramatized tango. When the smoke cleared, peo-ple called the trend *fantasía*. Zotto's video of Todaro shows him breaking embrace and twirling out his daugh-ter in sizzling pirouettes. Extravagant leaps and acrobatic expressions came in with Piazza. Intile, too, took tango to the level of show.[124]

Tango fantasía combines showy figures (*figuras vistosas*) with momen-tary suspensions of the *abrazo,* the tango embrace. This frees the hands for strong gestures, especially for the very last pose. In short, fantasía begs for the stage. And two dancers noticed.

THE CONQUEST OF SILENCE: COPES AND NIEVES

> More important than applause, laughter, or tears is making an audience become silent.
>
> —JUAN CARLOS COPES (January 7, 2001)

> What exile ever fled his own mind?
>
> —HORACE

Horacio Salgán, Osvaldo Pugliese, and Astor Piazzolla turned tango into art music. Two brilliant tangoists, Juan Carlos Copes and his partner, María Nieves Rego, took barrio dance to the stage.

Copes was born on May 31, 1931, in Mataderos, a working-class neigh-

borhood of Buenos Aires. He passed time fleetingly in several other barrios—Floresta, Villa Urquiza, Devoto.[125] His father, an intense-looking
man with a moustache, was a bus driver (*colectivero*) whose real forte was
cooking. His barbecues (*asados*) were renowned, and in the 1920s he
became head barbecue chef (*asador oficial*) of President Hipólito
Irigoyen.[126]

As a young man, Copes studied electrical engineering for two years at
the University of Buenos Aires before deciding to become a professional
dancer. He knew that tango was the signature of the city: "Every self-
respecting neighborhood had its plaza, its cathedral, its club, and its
tango gang."[127] But somehow that world did not reach him—that is, until
one night in 1947:

> I discovered the milongueros, their women, their dress, and the incredible
> way they moved on the floor. I had showed up one night at the Parque
> Norte dance hall, in Palermo on Las Heras, where the *zoológico* ends and
> in front of [the jardín] *botánico*. I could not believe what I was seeing. I
> leaned on a column by the side of the bandstand, lit up a cigarette, and just
> kept on marveling.

The best dancers, he noted, had staked out their corners. He stared at
their cortes, quebradas, and sentadas, emblems of work and devotion.[128]
Women sported outfits that made them look "tall, racked, and big-assed."
Men all dressed "in the style of Divito"—of Guillermo Divito (1914–69),
that is, a noted cartoonist whose drawings of the 1940s and 1950s for his
Buenos Aires magazine *Rico tipo* (Good-Time Charlie) made him famous
for zoot-suited men and wasp-waisted women. Divito influenced the look
of 1940s tango.

Copes resolved to learn every bit of it. "Before I met the milongueros of
the Parque Norte, I only knew tango as a sound on the radio, an image on
the screen." Now it was life's major reason. In that same year of 1947
Copes discovered the Nelson. He went with a barrio chum, Néstor Ayala,
and upon entering that world of creative turbulence, the two men were
stunned.

Black dancers were present—Carlos Anzuate, Félix Luján, José
Matoral, and Raúl Leira.[129] Anzuate, sensing how out of it Copes and
Ayala felt, generously taught them their first 1940s giro—a fast turn to the
left, four steps for the woman, three for the man.[130] Copes would remember Anzuate's generosity: touring the United States in the early 1960s, he
would include in his troupe a black Argentine expressly to illustrate that

side of the dance. A racist promoter in Pittsburgh told him, "Don't come back with that nigger—that isn't tango." Copes ignored him.

In 1947 Copes started traveling the city: "All the barrios of Buenos Aires had their clubs. I went to all of them, good, bad, indifferent, looking for moves to make me complete." In 1949, strong with experience, he chose as his dance base the Atlanta, a legendary dance palace in Villa Crespo near the corner of Corrientes and Humboldt. Here two regulars were black: El Negro Manuel, who loved Afro-Cuban dancing as well as the tango, and El Negro Juan.[131] The Atlanta was enormous, on the scale of a skating rink. Nieves loved it: "It was huge. We could break out new moves with impunity."[132] Copes felt the same way: "Atlanta was beautiful and big. There were places to work out new steps."[133]

Pleasure brought danger. Young toughs from Mataderos, looking for trouble, invaded the Atlanta. They challenged the men. They flirted with their women. Fistfights broke out. Copes proved tough, not to be messed with. Battling confirmed credibility. He was soon tacit boss (cacique) of the young men of Atlanta.

He gave them advice: "First hang out stag [planchar] and just watch. Then, for about six weeks, practice with guys, until you get your form down. Then, only then, will the best women let you cut in." In other words, tango with a woman was a privilege, not a right. She would complete you, make you look grand, but you had to deserve her, with cool, style, and courage.

Copes himself had plenty of women. An early partner, one Marta, danced once to Osvaldo Pugliese with such depth of feeling that Copes burst into tears. But he still lacked the perfect companion. Then one night around 1948, once again crossing the city to Palermo, this time to hear the superb orchestra of Francini-Pontier, he walked into the Estrella Maldonado dance hall. There he met a good-looking young woman named Ñata Nieves. She had pinta (good looks) and agility. Men fought to dance with her. Copes and Ñata talked, laughed, tangoed, and became friends. Then Ñata got married—but not before she introduced Copes to her smashing young sister, María.

María Nieves was fourteen at the time. She had worked as a domestic since she was twelve, helping to support her widowed mother in Saavedra. She was thrilled by the tango, having watched it at neighborhood clubs on weekends since she was a little girl, chaperoned by her sisters and mother. As an adolescent, "she would come home from such evenings and stay up alone for hours, leading her broom in mad tangos across the kitchen floor."[134]

María's looks and dancing enchanted Juan Carlos. They fell in love. Their tangos reflected that. Other men stood while their partners revolved; Copes and Nieves turned together. They "scissored" together, did acrobatics and grace notes together. Sometimes they chose certain steps from the past, like the lustrada, in which Nieves would bend down and mime shining the shoes of her man. Whatever they did, they made it flow in one stream of motion. Friends made circles around them, on the floor of the Atlanta, each person rapt.

The Atlanta was not the only place where exploratory dancing was going on, however. Petróleo's revolution had spread far and wide. Copes picked up steps at the Palermo Palace, in Palermo on Calle Godoy Cruz, and at La Enramada, "where at the time there were a lot of blacks dancing."[135]

Copes and Nieves deepened their response and command. They were now *compenetrados,* María's word—interpenetrators, each understanding the other. They were ready.

TRIUMPH IN LUNA PARK, NOVEMBER 1951 In late 1951 Copes and Nieves entered a tango contest at Luna Park in downtown Buenos Aires. During the semifinals, Copes had to hide María from the police because she was under age. As she would recall, though, "when we won, over a hundred other couples, nobody thought about my age anymore."[136]

Victory in Luna Park gave Copes and Nieves the self-assurance to become fully professional. Around 1952, the following year, they lost their base when the management at the Atlanta changed, but that just made them rethink their options. Intergroup rivalries now seemed pointless; they would work together with their rivals.

Late in 1951, moral support blazed up on the screen: Gene Kelly in *An American in Paris.* Here was a guy with a smile like Gardel's, a dark, smoky voice, and an athlete's compactness who proved that vernacular was class. A tough guy who jazz-danced with a ballerina on his arm. Copes was enthralled: "What Kelly did with jazz, we'd do with tango—make history with dancers. Dancing not for ourselves but to illustrate lives lived for tango."[137] Copes and Nieves studied other North American film musicals "and tried to copy the smooth seamless dancing we saw in them."[138] Copes worked Kelly's hat, smile, and catlike (*gatuno*) appearance into the structure of his tango. In a photograph from the 1950s he even looks like Gene Kelly.[139]

Meanwhile, Copes and Nieves were touring the barrios in search of new talent. They persuaded thirty strong couples to join them in a presentation that they called First Recital of Porteño Típico Dances. This two-hour spectacle was held in the Salón Federal, at 955 Calle Chacabuco in San Telmo, on November 4, 1955. In front of a backdrop representing old Buenos Aires flat-roofed colonial houses (*azoteas*) with Iberian iron grillwork (*rejas*) guarding enormous street windows, paired dancers preened the new tango. Copes chose couples from differing barrios, knowing that dance wars were sure to break out. The stage came alive with competition and artistry.

PROFESSIONAL DEBUT, DECEMBER 30, 1955 Late that November, Copes set up an interview with an Argentine producer, Carlos A. Petit. Copes brought him a photograph: three swains and a woman. "What the hell is this?" groused Petit. "An argument," Copes answered. "Three guys and a woman. They fight for her favors, one guy finally wins, and they tango away at the end." Petit was intrigued and said yes. The show opened at the Teatro Nacional on December 30, 1955. The audience loved it. This was Copes's first formal contract.

Encouraged, Copes and Nieves started to experiment: the age of Cachafaz, the age of Méndez, and the age of Petróleo, if brought into consonance, they reasoned, would dramatically deepen tango's line and appeal. So they developed a style that mixed canyengue—short, small, fast steps—with the straight, frozen torso of tango de salón. They were turning into centaurs: half Cachafaz/half Méndez, half Carmencita/half La Cachito. The result would be legendary: "We discovered that we could be elegant and use our legs to do fast, intricate steps."[140] They would further perfect this on an epochal journey.

TANGODYSSEY, 1958-60 Copes and Nieves trekked north across the spine of the continent, first to Chile, then to Brazil and Venezuela in September 1958, and on up to El Salvador in October. They arrived in Mexico City in early 1959. Astor Piazzolla joined them there and became their musical director. Mexican unions and bureaucrats, however, made their lives miserable. Copes, eyeing their proximity to the United States, wanted out. In October 1959 he accepted a gig at the Club Flamboyán in San Juan, Puerto Rico.

That led to New York. On November 6, 1959, Copes and Nieves opened at the Starlight Ballroom of the Waldorf-Astoria. Many New York Latinos (and Anglos as well), including young lovers who needed to feel sad in order to feel more alive, were fond of the tango, but Copes countered that fadolike assumption with speed and intensity: "Back in Buenos

Aires, before setting off, we toughened ourselves by seeking out rivals and deliberately challenging them to battles of speed. Dancing the fastest, while keeping the beat, was the goal."[141] It was precisely this rocketing drive that electrified a capacity crowd at the Starlight Ballroom, winning the dancers a three-month engagement at the Chateau-Madrid nightclub, near the Plaza Hotel.

This led to other appearances. In 1960 Copes and Nieves showed up on the cover of an LP of milonga cut in New York.[142] They also made it to television: on *The Ed Sullivan Show* in late 1959 they danced a fast milonga, the first perhaps seen by a mass audience in North America.

Next, on *The Arthur Murray Show* in early 1960, they translated film noir into tango. Copes and Piazzolla are seen talking. Nieves strolls by. We hear a few bars of Piazzolla's dark tango. Nieves flirts for a second with the musician, then falls into dancing with Copes. His foot slides by hers, hers slides by his. He bends her to the floor, then brings her back up, a step for the stage called "the drop." Copes moves like Gene Kelly, hat over eye, jazzy lithe build. There are Andalusian moments as well, heels stamping down, staccato and trained. Copes wears bright shining boots to accent his velocity.

He and María left Mrs. Murray, the hostess of the program who pronounced Copes's name as if it rhymed with *topaz,* pleased, charmed, and taken.[143]

TANGO FILM NOIR In 1960 Copes, Nieves, and Piazzolla posed for a photographer in a studio in Carnegie Hall (Plate 70). It was a promotional shot, but it caught their charisma.

The lighting was atmospheric—film noir again—accentuating Copes as a street tough, jacket off and draped like a bullfighter's cape, ready for action. Piazzolla was his musician-accomplice, wielding his bandoneón in slouch hat and compadrito cravat (which he hated to wear). Nieves stands behind them, right hand on hip, left hand extended. She lights up the set with her beauty.

LA MILONGA DE LA MESA (THE TABLETOP MILONGA), 1962 Copes and Nieves returned to the United States in October 1961. There they met two famous Argentine jugglers (*malabaristas*), the Martin Brothers. These compatriots challenged them: do something strong, give the Americans an impossible number. So early in 1962 Copes and Nieves danced fast milonga on the top of a small table on *The Ed Sullivan Show.*[144]

PLATE 70

In a battle with gravity and space, they packed in hot cross-steps (*repiques cruzados*), ganchos, simple spins (*ruedas*), quick turns (*giros*), and showy kicks to the rear (*golpes para atrás*). Compacting the poetry and the heat of the dance while avoiding a bad fall, they danced with the bravery Borges associated with milonga. Before an audience of millions, they were illustrating lives lived for the tango.

In 1964 Copes and Nieves married in Las Vegas. Nine years later, in 1973, they divorced, but they kept on dancing professionally together until 2001.

TANGO ON CORRIENTES, 1977 In 1977 Copes and Nieves appeared in the Argentine movie *Argentina es así* (That's How Argentina Is). The shoot was on Corrientes, the great way of tango. Buses and cars move in the background. Nieves dances in a scintillating red dress enlivened with red fringes. It works because she made it. She was not only first lady of tango, she was also a woman who made her own costumes.

Nieves, compenetrada, echoes Copes. She returns every volley. They maintain a balance, upright and strong, "me in my column, he in his column, and a third column shimmering in between."[145] In a photograph you sense the three columns. From the waist up they are statues; from the waist down, limbs come alive in strong angles.

Then Copes turns. Nieves raises her right leg to ride his hip. Keeping her balance with the other leg, she follows his spin. They are dancing *calesita,* a mime of the carousel. They make it look easy. But move out of center, and the "columns" will fall. It works because Copes knows his partner's weight cold.

TANGO MÍO, 1985 In 1985, the same year they dazzled New York with *Tango Argentino,* Nieves and Copes appeared in *Tango mío,* a film for English television. They had been dancing together since 1955—thirty years—and they talk about this on camera. Nieves is radiant. She sums up their work: "Men and women dance tango 50/50, at least in the style that we do. Before, no. The man stood still while the woman pirouetted."

They demonstrate. Nieves crosses left over right, signature opening step. They call to each other with strong taps on the floor, dancing apart. Maria saunters inward. She places her feet in Juan Carlos's space. They embrace. He whirls and she whirls, she back-kicks he back-kicks. Legs flash and weave. Copes swivels his head from left to right, from right to left, as both turn in unison, inflecting a spiral with a strange countermotion. Making a strong leap, they come down together, ending their dance with one single sound.

They were at the peak of their form—in the words of Robert Duvall, "an impeccable Rolls-Royce without a speedometer."[146] How they won Paris, New York, and the world could be sensed in this flawless projection.

ULTIMATE TRIUMPH: *TANGO ARGENTINO*
> Later we discussed Tango Argentino and how it
> changed the world.
>
> —EVE BABITZ, *Tango, Two-Step, and the L.A. Night* (1999)

November 1983. The Argentine impresario Claudio Segovia persuades thirty-three of the finest tango singers, musicians, and dancers to fly to France for a week to represent their tradition at the Théâtre Châtelet in Paris's Festival d'Automne. He commandeers an Argentine military airplane. Because it makes several stops for the military, the flight to Paris takes thirty-six hours. Only one meal is served, by gruff *milicos* (soldiers) in uniform. Uneasily the cast notices that they are traveling with a very large companion: an Exocet missile in the front of the plane, being brought back to France for repairs. Finally they reach Charles de Gaulle airport.

When they return to Argentina, they fly Air France, getting VIP treatment. What happened?

Copes: "We were supposed to play the Théâtre Châtelet for a week but wound up playing a season. The first night, November 10, 1983, sold out. We thought, homesick Argentines from all over Europe. The second night, boom! Third night, boom! The fourth night the French started breaking down doors—for three thousand seats, all taken. The fifth night people were protesting outside with placards, chanting WE WANT IN! WE WANT IN! The house let them in. They sat in the aisles." The city of Picasso, Nijinsky, and Ravel had recognized one of the cultural events of the century. So, home on Air France—but the cast snapped back to reality when landing at Ezeiza airport: not even the specialized Argentine press, they discovered, was aware of their triumph.

Europe called them back. Their momentum renewed, this time they conquered Venice, Bologna, Milan, and Rome. Then in 1985 they came to New York.

On June 25 *Tango Argentino* opened for a week at the City Center Theater on West 56th Street. Excited critics lavished the dancers with praise. In October *Tango Argentino* opened again, this time on Broadway, at the Mark Hellinger Theater. A critical smash all over again, its run was extended until January 1986. The reasons for its success were clear: people savored the mixture of music and text, singing and dance, in what was self-evidently one of the richest offerings of national talent on the planet. The critic Sally Sommer remembered the musicians on stage, wearing glasses, ordinary guys who happened to have every arrastre and syncopation of tango at their fingertips.[147]

From the very first night it was also clear that the power of the show stemmed from seasoned, mature performers. Audiences were astonished to see middle-aged couples take over the stage like young zealots: "featured dancers are unabashedly middle aged."[148] Virulazo's portliness read like a beauty spot pasted on the middle of his motion: "Age and weight," wrote the theater critic John Simon, "are triumphantly overcome."[149] Dance critic Tobi Tobias felt the same way: "*Tango Argentino* presents a world in which mature people are perceived as sexually more interesting than the very young."[150]

Like light from a star, the steps of 1940s Buenos Aires at last lit up North America. In the musical selections, too, clarion calls from the past—Villoldo, Contursi, Mendizábal—mixed with modernity, Pugliese, and Piazzolla. Two warhorses, "Jalousie" and "La cumparsita," anchored the audience in the familiar.

Copes placed seven star couples, each performing alone, in seven separate episodes between interludes of song and music. Then, for the finale, he brought all the dancers together, turning the stage into a seething milonga. Each couple moved in their signature style.

Copes encouraged the dancers to face one another, as actual couples, rather than face toward the audience while dancing. A photograph from Copes's archive, of four couples dancing in Paris at the 1983 Festival d'Automne illustrates how richly this read (Plate 71). Above and to the left, on a dais, seated musicians "filter the past through a gauze of violins and bandoneóns."[151] Below, four couples interpret the tango in four different ways. To the left, Virulazo advances to the side of Elvira Santamaría in a move called *caminada de costado* (walk to the side). They clasp hands on high. To the right, Mónica and Luciano spin to the left in a giro; Mónica's legs flash spectacularly as they turn. They hold their hands less high. In the center, Copes and Nieves, in a private adagio, lock in going down toward the floor. The shape of their motion bears the name *el abanico* (the fan) because of the way it spreads out on the floor. At the far right, Elsa María Mayoral echoes the high curve of Elvira's right arm. Her partner, Héctor Mayoral, crosses his legs, preparing to tap his way around her (*taconeará alrededor de ella*). Summing up the vision, Copes

PLATE 71

says, "The point was liberation, the complete freedom of each couple."[152] Imagine the full impact in Paris, when, in addition to the spectacular dancing, Salgán played piano and Goyeneche shared his voice with the crowd.

The dancers in New York served North America the same fateful potency. We will look at a few of them.

VIRULAZO (JORGE MARTÍN ORCAIZAGUIRRE) AND ELVIRA SANTA-MARÍA Virulazo talked with Jane Boutwell of *The New Yorker:*

> My stage name was given to me by an Italian friend, many years ago, and it means scoring a hit in the game of bocce. Elvira and I became partners in 1961. We dance our version of the tango orillero, the real rustic tango that still lives in working-class social clubs. We hold our bodies further apart than many of the other couples and we bend slightly more at the knee.[153]

Virulazo and Elvira used their knees like a sword. Their pièce de résistance was a step called *metida* (putting feet into fray), which impressed *Ballet News:* "Virulazo, with serene dignity, skims the floor while engaging Elvira in teasing foot duels, as she moves backward in a series of small cross steps."[154] Virulazo kicked between Elvira's legs as she did this. Each kick was timed to the offbeat between steps. If he missed but one pulse, he would smash right on into her. But he didn't.[155]

They finished their tango with a touch of raw humor: ending a stride, Virulazo spanked Elvira. She smiled and cracked up.

GLORIA JULIA BARRAUD AND EDUARDO ARQUIMBAUD Dancing in New York to Troilo's "Milongueando en el 40" (Hanging Out in the 1940s), Barraud and Arquimbaud included a step that was known in the time of Villoldo, *la bicicleta* (the bicycle). Eduardo took Gloria's foot with his and made a circular motion. They pedaled across the stage, then followed this "take" with another, the mime of a horse on a merry-go-round (*calesita*). Their humor was sparkling. Gloria "called" with a hook (*gancho*), Eduardo "answered" with a counterhook, unhitching her leg with his, then bringing both down and guiding her forward.

Their dance turned percussive. They were tapping the floor with three piques, then dashing across stage and tapping the floor with three more. In their hands simple steps turned exciting. They rethought the sentada: taking a leap, Gloria landed with bent knees on Eduardo's right thigh. She kneeled there instead of sitting, rephrasing sentada, bringing the plane of action up high. Completing the pose, her right hand shot up while Eduardo's left hand went down, to rest at his waist. He looked at her and she looked at him. It was a personal moment.

NÉLIDA RODRÍGUEZ DE AURE AND NELSON ÁVILA By 1985, Nélida Rodríguez de Aure and Nelson Ávila had been dancing together for fifteen years. In 1970, asked to demonstrate different modes of tango—orillero, salón, fantasía—for Buenos Aires television, they had taken tango's lexicon and presented it to large audiences with their own seal of elegance. There is no better example than their corte at the finale of *Tango Argentino*: they bent to receive each other. Nélida's thigh shot between Nelson's legs, recalling maxixe. Their legs became angles, submitted to directional changes. The mirrored line of the left legs, the jut of the knees, the lean-back and lean-forward that tango received from the polka—all these contrasted, in their straightness, to the soft curves of the arms and the hands. The gravity of their faces, unsmiling and frozen, broadcast control: sexual lightning, caught in mid-zig or mid-zag. The New York dance critic Anna Kisselgoff caught this exactly: "Eroticism, which could become dangerous, is kept from crossing the line into realism by formal constraints."[156]

Nélida and Nelson are not only accomplished, they are brave. Nelson broke his elbow one month before going to New York. He was forced to wear a cast. Nothing daunted, they rehearsed for several weeks to make it look as if nothing had happened. Contingency met resilience.

GLORIA AND CARLOS RIVAROLA Gloria, wearing her famous cloche hat with towering egret feather (it picked up the tango rhythms of 1914 Paris like an antenna tuned to paradise), brought back with Carlos, resplendent in tux, the lushness and style of that era. They were vamping to "La cumparsita," the most famous of tangos. Their virtuosity came into focus in a remarkable sentada in which Gloria leaped onto Carlos's right thigh. She kneeled on her left leg and slithered the other forward. Both faces froze. Torsos were erect. An unbroken embrace completed an image of control.

ELSA MARÍA AND HÉCTOR MAYORAL Elsa María and Héctor Mayoral brought barrio fluency to the stage. Mayoral had learned to dance tango in Villa Urquiza, in practice sessions with Eduardo Rizzo, the brother of Carmencita Calderón.[157] For New York they translated Pugliese's "La yumba" into salón-style tango. They enchanted the *Times* critic Jennifer Dunning: "The tall, smiling Elsa María, and Mayoral, her genial partner, offer two of the evening's happiest moments in *Danzarín,* the revue's breakneck finale, as they dance head to head and Mayoral flips her into a slide."[158]

JUAN CARLOS COPES AND MARÍA NIEVES Critics declared them the best. María's ochos, for example, were nonpareil, as she trembled her waist (*contoneo de cintura*) while making fine pivots below. She and Juan Carlos would come to a halt, each looking into the eyes of the other. That stop with a look was a signature corte. Memorable too were their giros: María spun around Juan Carlos's frame. They made it look as if a shove (*envión*) by a spirit were making them spin without using their feet.

Copes and Nieves built up their sequences symphonically—a slow rhythmic intro, an adagio when violins took over, a furious finale when they got loose and let loose in a flurry of ganchos. (Double ganchos, they called them.) Copes would make Nieves spin, ganchoing her two times or more. So deep was their dance, so indestructible, that they were able to sustain arguments in front of an audience. María briefly flares, and Copes reacts, in the film *Tango mío,* but it happens in the twinkling of an eye. Their tangos could take anything, argument or accident, and still go on spinning.

MUTINY ON BROADWAY On opening night in New York, the cast of *Tango Argentino* awaited the critics' reaction in Luchow's restaurant. When the *Times* review arrived, one of the producers immediately read it, raced to Copes, and embraced him like a madman. The review was superb and featured a photograph of María and Juan Carlos. Copes was ecstatic— but cold, jealous faces surrounded him. He didn't notice; shortly he would.

The next day the other six couples called for a meeting with Segovia and Orezzoli. They brandished a document signed by all twelve stating that they no longer recognized Copes as choreographer. One by one they stood up and gave reasons why. Copes and Nieves were in the room, stunned with embarrassment. When Eduardo Arquimbaud started talking, Copes got up and walked out. María walked out as well. Copes went to an Argentine bar by himself, ordered a drink, and wept. He had tasted the humiliation that jealousy brings.[159]

The next day it occurred to him that some were hoping he would resign. So he showed up as if nothing had happened. Segovia and Orezzoli worked out a compromise: new program notes announced choreography "by Segovia, assisted by Juan Carlos Copes." The show ran for six more months. Copes had proven, as he did when he lost the Atlanta, that he was a man who could take it when fate tempered triumph and push came to shove.

THE GREAT BOOM IS TRIGGERED

Having seen, at long last, the real thing, the viewers of *Tango Argentino* were eager for more. They tangoed their way out of the Mark Hellinger Theatre.[160] "Something was missing," said Dunning, "a lobby sign-up table for tango lessons."[161]

It didn't take long for the "ecstatic reaction to furious feet"[162] to catch the attention of bona-fide and not-so-bona-fide teachers of Argentine tango. The play sparked a world boom in tango instruction that nearly twenty years later, in 2005, shows no sign of abating.

The boom brought old milongueros like Lampazo back into dancing. It also rerouted experts in jazz dance, like Kely and Facundo Posadas, into tango. It inspired films of the 1990s—*Scent of a Woman, True Lies, The Tango Lesson*—and films of the twenty-first century, including Jonathan Demme's *The Truth About Charlie* and Robert Duvall's *Assassination Tango*. It changed the life of Duvall, who started making pilgrimages to Buenos Aires, fell in love with an Argentine woman, and became North America's most famous tanguero. It pulled Nicole Nau and Ricardo Klapwijk out of Germany and Holland respectively in the 1990s and turned them into one of the hottest couples of the Buenos Aires dance world until they broke up in 2003.

Tango-tango, the real article from Buenos Aires, had impressed the whole world with its rich suite of moves. Although not a single black face appeared onstage in *Tango Argentino,* Afro-Argentine influence was felt nonetheless: many of the star couples had mastered canyengue, the early black mode of the tango; hence Virulazo and Elvira's playful duels of the feet, hence taconeo by Mayoral and María, hence taut syllabic structuring in Zotto's hot footwork, hence everyone's taste for offbeats, hipwork, and stops. El Negro Navarro, El Negro Santillán, La Parda Haydé, La Parda Ester, La Negra Martita, El Negro Lavandina, and many, many others took ghost curtain calls. It is time to restore this Afro-Argentine legacy.

THE AFRO-ARGENTINE ELEMENT

The presence of Afro-Argentines in the rise and development of one of
the world's great dance traditions remains to be fully assessed. I remember an afternoon in 2000 at the Estancia dos Adelas restaurant (now
closed) on Calle Ortiz in Buenos Aires. A waiter noted a photograph of
Kely and Facundo Posadas, arguably among the most distinguished couples now dancing tango in Buenos Aires, on the table by my plate. He
asked, "What country are they from?" It did not occur to him—because
Facundo was black—that they were as Argentine as he was, let alone that
one of their ancestors, Carlos Posadas, had contributed to the rise of the
music we could hear coming over a loudspeaker somewhere in Recoleta.

Why? We know "the answer": the alleged disappearance of Argentine
blacks in the wake of the war with Paraguay in the 1860s, a yellow fever
epidemic in Buenos Aires in 1871, infant mortality from poor living condi-
tions, and wave upon wave of Italian immigration. In the process, according to the standard commonplace, Argentina became the only white
nation in South America.[163] Argentine dance history refutes this.
Facundo Posadas, Anzuate, Margarita de Guillé, and other Afro-
Argentines are still dancing tango in 2005.

There were earlier protagonists. Witness Luis María Cantero, the Afro-
Argentine man we have met as El Negro Pavura (Black Dread). As an
adolescent, Cantero worked as a fruit-gatherer (vareador). When
Cachafaz opened an academy in 1912–13, at the corner of Blandengues
and Echeverría, he changed the boy's life. Together with other neighborhood vareadores, Cantero listened to the sounds pouring out of the establishment. They tried out the steps on the sidewalk. Later Cantero talked
himself inside. Then, accompanied by his sidekick the jockey Salustiano
Pintado, he continued learning tango in the Olimpo academy. In a few
short years he built himself into the champion tanguero of Lower
Belgrano.

By 1926 Cantero was running his own dancing studio, Le Dancing
Bleu. His friends in the racing world helped bring in trade. In 1927 the
newspaper Crítica organized a tango contest at the L'Aiglon ballroom at
200 Florida. El Negro Pavura was by far the best dancer. However, "the
crowd was stupefied when the judges gave the prize to one Buingas, who
moved in theatrical circles. Cantero's black skin was the reason."[164]

Word of this travesty reached the owner of Crítica, Don Natalio
Botana, who moved quickly to recognize El Negro Pavura as the actual

winner and awarded him one thousand pesos plus a gold medal.[165] The story ends more or less happily—but many black dancers were not lucky enough to be protected by powerful white friends or admirers. Nor were they recognized in print. Nevertheless they kept dancing, at the epicenter, decade by decade. Prominent were El Negro Pavura in the 1920s, El Negro Santillán in the 1920s and 1930s, and El Negro Lavandina and El Negro Carlos Anzuate at Club Nelson in the 1940s. From the 1950s into the 1970s, black dancers dramatically kept their culture in action—tango, candombe, Afro-Cuban, jazz dance—at the Shimmy Club in the Casa Suiza; this group included Tete Salas, Pocha La Madrid, El Negro Precinto, Facundo Posadas, and many, many others. At the same time, inspired Afro-Argentine dancers excelled at Sin Rumbo in Villa Urquiza: Marguerita de Guillé, Lidia "La Negrita" Rivero, Luis "El Negrito" Russo, Morenito y Olga, and Betti Pizarro. Betti Pizarro, strikingly handsome, danced an elegant tango de salón. She tangoed onstage in a Buenos Aires play called *La morocha*.[166]

The Posadases, Anzuate, and Margarita de Guillé remain prominent in the twenty-first century. In 2005 de Guillé was the godmother (*madrina*) of Sunderland club, one of the more famous of barrio milongas. She danced candombe all over town (Plate 72).

Behind the public rapture of famous white stylists—El Cachafaz, José Méndez, El Pibe Palermo, Petróleo—lay black inspiration. Some sharpened their moves by battling with virtuosi of color. Black tangoists taught two stars their very first steps: María Celeste, an Afro-Argentine, taught Cachafaz how to tango. Competition with El Negro Santillán and El Negro Pavura also had a bearing on the acuity of his dancing. And El Pibe Palermo, we recall, responded so brilliantly to training in the candombe-seasoned milonga imparted by his black mentor, Arturo Núñez, that his father is said to have shouted, "My son is turning black right in front of me!"

Méndez in the 1930s, though white, brought back black canyengue. He jousted continuously with El Negro Santillán, who himself partnered with two striking Afro-Argentines, La Parda

PLATE 72

Haydé and La Parda Ester. El Negro Lavandina and Petróleo, leaders of the 1940s revolution, both danced with black partners. Petróleo was first taught to tango by El Negro Navarro in 1928. Lavandina, himself a mulatto, could not have been more strategic in the shaping and polishing of new tango. Myriad intersections reveal the centrality of Afro-Argentine dancing. Blacks may have been a minority, but there is a truth above statistics. Copes and Nieves in *Tango Argentino* were the ultimate expression of African, Moorish, and European elements danced into creole coherence. Their erect Western torsos were brilliantly set off by the short Afro steps of canyengue and sparing Andalusian-like heel-taps.

TANGO AS ART: TOWARD AN AESTHETIC

The essence of culture consists of being true to oneself.

— JOHN M. CHERNOFF, *Hustling Is Not Stealing* (2003)

It's tanguero to pursue the city.

— ROBERTO J. SANTORO, *De tango y lo demás* (1964)

Buenos Aires is a city named for air. The founders meant breeze, but air can mean music, in this case a music that set the world dancing. The tangueros were inspired by their urban condition. In turn, the choreography illuminated the city to itself. Dazzling dance gifts from black and white gauchos, black and white sailors, white compadritos and compadritos of color, and Italian immigrants blended and fused in rich creole moments.[167] These swirling mixtures created milonga, canyengue, and tango.

The innovators were working-class. They lived on the margin. In shaping the tango, they discovered their own style of being. In an attempt to destroy this black-enhanced heritage (Ki-Kongo names appearing everywhere), upper-class writers exaggerated tango connections with prostitution and crime, knife fights and poverty. But the guys on the corner and the women in the academies believed in themselves. Tango was their will to full dignity.[168]

LET FOREVER BEGIN TONIGHT: THE MOVING WORK OF
ART CALLED TANGO

> Tango . . . makes them enjoy the last years
> of their lives with passion
>
> — EVE BABITZ, *Tango, Two-Step, and the L.A. Night* (1999)

In her greatest film, *Gilda* (1946), Rita Hayworth plays a songstress in Buenos Aires in 1945. She crosses the River Plate and sings the following words in a boîte in Montevideo:

> Amado mío.
> *Love me forever*
> *and let forever begin tonight.*

A businessman invites her to his table. He asks: "Let forever begin tonight—is that a date, Gilda?" He is hoping her poetics will lead to a relationship.

The song she sang was a bolero, not a tango. But the thought behind it was. Fleeing her evil husband, a thinly veiled Nazi, every word that she sang was a cry for liberation.

But how do we, as ordinary persons, realize what she promises, transcendent love? How do we build a love so strong that it will jump into the laughter and red wine, the tears and anguish, of lovers centuries beyond? Gardel's smile, itself immortal, leads back to the answer: tango.

Tango is the art history of love. It is the dance that teaches the world to love and to live in the idiom of Buenos Aires—the love of compadritos for *minas,* best friends, and honor, the love of gauchos for the beat of the *arrastre,* and myriad other loves, some blessed, some tragic.

To sing of love recaptures memory. To dance for love gathers more, particularly when the partners are lovers or married. On a night like that we see glittering couples, Juan Carlos and María, Miguel Ángel and Milena, Mingo and Ester, Gabriel and Natalia, Kely and Facundo, dancing eternally on film or on video. Time cannot touch the image they fashion. Forever *can* begin tonight.

Tango interprets affection in differing ways—close in and rhythmic in canyengue, suave in salón, over-the-top in fantasía.

To discover the steps of love and transcendence, follow tangueros to the dance. Rely on their comments to seek their aesthetic. If tango were sex only, the art would evaporate. You would have only clinical data. But all the best dancers combine art and sensuousness, exploring the consequences. Steps become brushstrokes. Pose becomes picture. Blends of dance elements burst into being, open-ended yet structured.

1. EMBRACE AND WAIT: THE START OF THE TANGO

> In tango there is a moment before the dance begins where the man very lightly touches the woman and she is so adept, she sort of can be knocked over with a feather as he touches her.
>
> — EVE BABITZ, *Tango, Two-Step, and the L.A. Night* (1999)

> Tango habitués do not start dancing when the music begins—perhaps they are resting or absorbing the melody.
>
> — OSCAR MORAN, *La pareja de tango: Filosofía y baile* (1999)

Tangueros pause as they start. In apart-dances, like disco or rock, couples swing into action at the very first beat. They cannot wait to get it on. Tangueros wait.

They take each other carefully into each other's arms and pose for a few moments on the dance floor, as if in deep thought. Only then do they move and become one with the music. Natalia Games explains: "We let a few measures go by—literally leave a few measures in the air [*dejamos unos compases al aire*]—to *hear* the music and enter into the climate of its theme."[169]

2. STERN FACE AND SEALED LIPS (CARA FEA)
Establishing their embrace, dancers set their expression, usually deadpan. It distantly relates to the admired detached expression of dancers among the Yoruba of Nigeria and Bakongo in Kongo. Lampazo called the effect *cara fea* (ugly face). It goes back to black compadritos and, before that, to candombe.

Unaware of the mask of black cool and its history, certain critics of tango have misread these signs of control. One called the tango as cold as a reptile, another as "an expressionless dance . . . for automatons."[170]

This rule of the milonga can be honored in the breach. Young couples sometimes smile at each other and old troupers do, too. But talking is normally taboo. Why? It dissipates the power of the dance.[171]

3. CIRCLING COUNTERCLOCKWISE: THE PATH OF THE SUN BECOMES THE PATH OF THE TANGO

> When I asked why [tango couples] circle counterclockwise they told me: because it's always been that way.
>
> —OSCAR MORAN, *La pareja de tango* (1999)

> The jazz composer, Thelonius Monk, frequently rose from his piano and proceeded to dance in a counterclockwise direction, his feet beating out intricate figures before he returned to the piano.
>
> —STERLING STUCKEY, *Slave Culture: Nationalist Theory and the Foundations of Black America* (1987)

Tango couples circle the dance floor counterclockwise. No one knows why, so they allege. But we saw the apart-steps of candombe pass into milonga, absorbed in the format of the Western embrace. The counterclockwise round takes place in candombe. Women and men wheel in a circle, leaning forward, leaning back.[172] Dancers, now couples, circle still in that direction, if no longer in strict conga lines.

The dance wheel continues in Kongo today. Elders define it as "the path of the sun" (*nzila ya ntangu*). Following the immortal track of the sun, so it is believed, imparts to the dancers longevity (*luzinga*).[173] In Argentina the path of the sun became the path of the tango.

Ntangu, "the sun," also means "hour, time, or season" in Ki-Kongo. It is one of many words that putatively converged in Buenos Aires, words like *tangana, tangalala,* and *matanga* in the formation of the creole term *tango*.

In Buenos Aires, we recall, Ki-Kongo was once spoken widely enough among blacks that an eighteenth-century missionary was able to compile a dictionary purely from words collected in that city. Out of this matrix emerged the key word *tango,* meaning "moving in time to a beat."

4. THE LEAD (LA MARCA)

> Tango can be discussed and we do talk about it but like everything genuine it conceals a secret.
>
> —JORGE LUIS BORGES, "La historia del Tango," *Obras completas* (1974)

Borges is right: part of the tango *is* secret. Strangers can't imagine how coded intelligence, igniting complex steps, passes from man to the woman, if they don't talk as they dance.

In Kongo full conversation normally is not used in the dancing court, so dance masters call with signs, shouts, drumbeats, or gestures when they want the chorus to respond with new steps:

The leader of the dance indicates new directions of the dance either by using hands, shouts, drumming, or gesture. *[Mfumu a makinu i intwadisi a makinu kanele vo mu moko, mu mpovo, mu ngoma, mu bimpampa.]*[174]

Signs and shouts trigger dance segments in candombe, too: an officiant brought the first section to a close with broom twirling. This signified not only "the end" but the purification of problems that might have arisen. A shout from the leader closed the second section. He closed the final free-for-all the same way.

The adoption of Western embrace position among blacks, from the waltz and other sources, transformed and compacted these means of expression. Now the man communicated by pressures of body and hand.

Call and response continued, among and within tightly embraced couples.[175] With body pressure the man calls for new moves. The woman replies, according to her knowledge and spirit.

Sometimes, but rarely, the woman calls and the man will respond. Carmencita Calderón remembers, dancing with El Cachafaz, that when she felt a corrida was appropriate, she would lead him on into it if he didn't first.[176]

Adriana Groisman's classic photograph, a woman on the floor of Grisel in Buenos Aires dancing tango with her man, renders a clear sexual contrast: strong arm and soft bottom (frontispiece). But at the same time we are looking into the heart of the *marca*. Flowing from his torso, the man's arm follows through to his hand, which curves around the side of her body. With arm, torso, hand, he leads as a block. Call and response becomes lead and response.

This kind of marking was present in canyengue. Dancing cheek to cheek, chest to chest, a man could indicate direction by shifting the weight of his body. In this early period, according to Juan Carlos Copes, the great Cachafaz sometimes even "marked" with his leg. This was confirmed by his famous partner, Carmencita Calderón.[177] Then came salón. *La marca,* for some, now meant the hand. Since the 1940s and the rise of modern tango, the lead has once again become bodily:

It is important that the man's torso begins the lead, so that the arms simply follow as extensions of the torso. The man rotates his torso, and his arms go with the movement as if the torso [and arms] were one unit.[178]

There is more. *La marca* is not a single method but a communicative series, nuanced by style and taste. Gabriel Angió, for example, signals "boleo" with his arm. Others, availing themselves of their own private code, subtly drum—*tac! tac!*—two or more fingers into the palm of the woman's hand or, as Copes once demonstrated, tap two fingers on the side of her body. For Angió, ocho is marked "from the center of my chest." With this pressure, he leads the woman "into the direction she will go." Mastering tango is mastering the making of signals.

La marca is part of the shared intimacy of tango, "not she and I but *us*," Copes says. It is a communicative drive, unseen and secret, that keeps tango moving in a state of excitement.

5. THE START OF THE DANCE (SALIDA) According to one veteran, Mingo Pugliese, there is no such thing as a basic in tango. *All* major steps, he says, form the basic. We know what he means: unlike a dance with just one or two moves, the figures of tango combine and recombine like a furious kaleidoscope.

Tango, however, like the *ginga* of Afro-Brazilian capoeira, *does* have a starting point, the *salida*, literally a stage entrance. The salida begins with a walk and ends with the man bringing his feet together while the woman crosses left over right. This opening moment can recur many times, stringing together like pearls further moments of the dance.

Before beginning the *salida*, in zero position, the couple stands quietly, taking up the embrace of the tango. Then comes the first move, the man opening up with a step to the side (*paso de costado*) with his left foot: *uno afuera* (step one [with the left] to the side), Lampazo called it.

The man moves his left foot forward, the right of the woman moving back (Plate 73). He continues, his left foot leading, her right going back. Their symmetry is superb, marking *the* classic image of tango (Plate 74).

The salida ends when the man closes both feet together and the woman crosses left over right.

Now starts the sequence that leads on to closure (*cierre*). The man starts forward, left foot leading, woman's right going back, creating again radiant symmetry.

Both turn together, at a 45-degree angle, to the left. They open their legs, then close them, completing another turn at a 90-degree angle. With the closure of feet, the *cierre* is done.

The man now moves *back* with his right leg, the woman advancing with her left.

This, then, is the rhythm of salida with cierre: close, open, move for-

PLATE 73　　　　　　　　　　　PLATE 74

ward; close, open, move out with a 45-degree turn to the left; open, close, turn at a 90-degree angle; close and move back, to start forward again with the man's left foot to the side.

The turns to the side break the flow of the dance, a tendency that grows stronger in the step called traspié.

6. THE DELIBERATE STUMBLE (TRASPIÉ) *Traspié* starts off with the first step of the salida, the step to the side of the lead's left foot. Continuing, the man moves forward, the woman retreats. Then comes a syncope: as the woman continues back, the man offbeats two steps to the side. He does this crossing left over right. *Pam-pam* goes the offbeat, doubling the time. At the completion of the sequence the man blocks his partner's foot, breaking her motion, preventing her from crossing her feet.

They continue. The man makes another traspié, that is, a counter-beat move, two steps on one note, crossing his feet or bringing his feet tight together.[179] This blocks, once again, the woman's crossover. She takes a simple step back.

7. SUDDEN HALTS, SUDDEN BREAKS (CORTES Y QUEBRADAS)

> Tony Droughon, an early hip-hop dance star, talking about
> b-boys ending a spin with a "freeze": "imagine, you're
> *spinning,* as fast as you can, and then you *stop,* in a beauti-
> ful position."
>
> —ROBERT FARRIS THOMPSON, "Hip-Hop 101," in William Eric
> Perkins, ed., *Droppin' Science* (1996)

Wheeling counterclockwise, cool and collected, leading and responding, completing the salida, optionally adding the offbeat traspié, the couple continues. The rich of mind, the more brilliantly trained, will inevitably swing into key moves of the black past—*cortes* (quick stops) and *quebradas* (breaks in the level of the body, with a twist of the hips).

Cortes and quebradas are more than moves. They are distillations of history. A young milonguero explains:

> Corte is synonymous with "freeze." The couple builds up momentum and
> suddenly stops. This heightens the pose. It gives it full impact. Any kind of
> gesture can be used. The woman freezes [*congela*] together with the man.[180]

Ending a phrase with a pictorial statement goes back to black roots. It is generally agreed that cortes and quebradas began with Afro-Argentines. The words *corte* and *quebrada* are cognate with the freeze and break of hip-hop and the stop (*cierre*) and the down-steps of mambo.

During the prehistory of the jazz dance, around 1833 in northern Louisiana, an observer watched blacks, performing a Kongo dance, stop "suddenly in a posture of surprise and pleasure."[181] In Kongo, sharp stops in the dance are called *télama nabyú* (standing abruptly) and, more to the point of linguistic impact on Argentina, *nzéngolo* (cut). In what appears to be a translation in meaning loaned from one language to another, an abrupt stop in tango is also called cut (*corte*).

Gabriel and Natalia perform two smoothly phrased cortes, with space between their bodies. They meet at the legs in the first cut, a reserved point of contact (Plate 75). One senses release in both upper bodies, a slight giving in, a slight pushing forward.

The other cut (Plate 76) is more elegant. Gabriel's chest is straight. In one frozen second, they stress the clear symmetry of their legs in full action. She moves into him. Their feet subtly meet in the center.

The *quebrada,* by contrast, is a pose where the man leans forward (*quiebre adelante*) or to the side (*quiebre al costado*) or back (*quiebre atrás*) while bending his legs. The woman will mirror this. Quebrada recalls the leans of the polka and the subtler Kongo leans of candombe.

Contrast quebrada with the end of the salida, at the point where the couple symmetrically moves back, at full standing height.

Quebrada transforms this: it loosens the torso and breaks up the symmetry. He's leaning forward. She's leaning back (Plate 77). He raises his left hand but angles his right shoulder down. The break with the ordinary is total: lightninglike limbs, angular elbows, and a woman's left foot that shoots back like an arrow. Penetration steps, like ghost forms of maxixe, appear: her knee parts his thighs, his leg shoots through hers.

All this is done with a reason: "*la quebrada* [the break] is so named because it breaks original posture to accentuate motion, heightening poses, making them flash and have savor."[182]

Quebradas are continuous in canyengue. The couple "gets down" and then stays there. Quebradas may trigger other steps from the past— sentada, ocho, lustrada. All build expression on Afro bent knees. You cannot seat a woman on your thigh unless you've lowered your leg and extended it. You cannot mime shining the shoes of your partner if your body's not "down."

PLATE 75   PLATE 76

8. SENTADA The man lowers his thigh. The woman, for one brilliant second, sits down on it, legs crossed or parallel. Or she sits on his thigh with both feet in the air. There is another elaboration where the woman rests lightly on the knee of the man, a pose documented by Santiago Stagnaro in his *Pierrot tango* in 1913 and continued by the great Vasco Aín in around 1940. Games and Angió illustrate: she rests on his hip as she moves through a turn (Plate 78).

In tango fantasía the woman takes a leap and lands with bent knees on the thigh of her partner. She is kneeling, not sitting, on his strongly extended limb. This is the forte of Gloria and Eduardo, thrilling their theater audiences.

In the 1937 Argentine film *Los muchachos de antes no usaban gomina* (Guys in the Old Days Didn't Gum Up Their Hair), a lithe brilliant tangoist (apparently José Méndez, but his name is not listed in the credits) guides his partner into a double sentada, one second on right thigh, one second on the other.

When short skirts came in in the 1940s, women preened their legs while being seated. One example: Angió surges forward with his right thigh prepared, and Games alights on it, crossing her legs (Plate 78). Giving him a faint, noncanonical smile, she instantly jumps down. A second example: Gabriel bends his left knee, and crosses over with flexed right. Natalia hops on his right and crosses her legs again, this time more frontally (Plate 79). Finally in a fast-moving segment of Zotto's exciting video *Perfume de amor,* Milena Plebs sits on the thigh of one dancer, then immediately on the thigh of another.

9. LUSTRADA (SHOE SHINE) *Lustrada,* which came in from the barrios, mimes shining shoes. It's a small trick effect (*pequeño truco*) that tangueros may use. In the first example, the man surreptitiously polishes his right shoe on the back of his left leg, like a soldier before a full field inspection (Plate 80). This prized piece of humor especially associates with orillero dancers like Pepito Avellaneda.

The step can turn bluesy, a danced double entendre, as when Games

PLATE 78   PLATE 79

shines her shoe up Angió's leg (Plate 81), from ankle to knee. A mime of
work begins to suggest an erotic situation.

10. A MILONGA RUN (CORRIDA PARA MILONGA) AND THE LITTLE
SNAKE (LA VIBORITA) Another strong move that comes down from the
past is the *corrida* (run), with a grapevinelike milonga step, *la viborita*.
This was a step that Pepito Avellaneda loved to show off. It was a step that
El Negro Lavandina taught Margarita de Guillé. The gist is quite simple:
while the woman moves backward, the man makes tiny figure-eight patterns, relentlessly advancing, zigging and zagging. This pivot-run pattern
is based on the ocho, the step discussed next.

Angió is excited as he zigzags his way toward Games. This lightninglike
pattern got affectionately nicknamed "the little snake" (*la viborita*). But
he not only zigzags, he sprints, to the spirited beat of milonga (Plate 82).

11. OCHO

Tango is structured by ochos. If I turn with my hips, making a torsion, my hips take a different direction. I step.
Making the torsion makes me pivot my foot. The pivot is
a consequence of the torsion.

PLATE 80   PLATE 81

According to legend, ocho comes from the blacks,
dancing in the street in Carnival comparsas [winding and
turning] and leaving figure-eight patterns in the dust of the
roads.

— MILENA PLEBS (June 7, 2004)

Ocho is exciting. Woman comes into her own. She breaks from her
partner in an independent motion: she steps and pivots, steps and pivots, creating a figure-eight pattern. She does this going forward and back,
in front of his body.[183] "There is torsion in ocho," adds Copes, "while
she faces the man with her torso, her hips and her legs take another
direction."[184]

The step got its name in the late nineteenth century, when women
danced in long skirts. The path of a woman, so it is said, left a figure-eight
pattern in the dirt floor of a cantina. The track named the motion.

Ocho appears in the earliest tangos. It was danced in the era of
milonga. Ocho in milonga is choppy and short (*cortadito*), in time with
the music. Later, in tango, ochos slide (*deslizan*) and float (*flotan*).[185]

Milonga reflects the influence of candombe and its creolized Kongo

PLATE 82

choreography, like dancing counter-clockwise with hands up like visors, shouting *e e e bariló*. Unsurprisingly, there are antecedents to ocho in the classical dancing of Kongo.

Solo dancers in Kongo twist (*zeka*) this way and that, forming figure-eight patterns. They do this to change the direction of the dance (*n'kini mieti zeka ngodi mu soba lusunga lwa makinu*). The figure-eight pattern is called *zinga ngodi* (literally, "enlacing two circles"). It is performed as a sign of balance (*kinenga*). But there is a deeper interpretation: dancing two circles represents "two ways of see-ing," "going deep in tradition and coming back."[186]

The same dance motion, with the same name, *ocho,* turns up in Kongo-Cuban palo dancing.[187] This double provenance strengthens the possibil-ity that we are looking at an ancient Kongo emblem of balance— between the sexes, between two worlds—which became creolized in Argentina into the most declarative step of the woman in tango.

Gabriel and Natalia demonstrate (Plates 83 and 84). In their version of old ocho, the man stays in place. The woman crosses one foot over the other in one direction, pivots, then crosses one foot over the other in the opposite direction and pivots. Making this action describes two full loops.

Abstracting this motion, the Argentine painter Juan Batalla, in a com-position called *El ocho,* 2004, centers eight small red circles within a big circle. Iron elements invade the emphasized circle. They represent the accompanying males.[188]

12. TACONEO TO PIQUE *Taconeo,* or heel-stamping, is a very old step. It goes back to heel-stamping gauchos, performing the dances called *gato* and *escondido*. Beyond that, it goes back to Moorish-tinged Spain. In the *tablao,* the master flamenquist stamps out loud fusillades, playing the floor as percussion.

It traces as well back to Kongo: a young man symbolically "seals" his love or his friendship, in front of a woman, by stamping once, then turning, then stamping and turning again. We witnessed this sequence at Diosso.

Distillations of such steps became tango. Carmencita Calderón taconeo'd her way across the whole of her career. She was famed for a walk combined with percussion, stamping her heel between steps. In a sense, she was "dribbling" the beat (*manteniendo control del balón*), like an Argentine soccer star, as opposed to English-derived "shoulder-charging."[189]

Other porteños played with percussion and scored innovations. Mayoral danced a circle of taconeos around Elsa María onstage in Paris in *Tango Argentino* (1983). Copes famously stamps out four beats to open a sequence of milonga.

Games and Angió, performing taconeo, begin from a quiet embrace. Then his left heel strikes the floor with a sharp-sounding noise (Plates 85 and 86).

Dancers in the 1940s evolved further tap steps. One was *picada,* described by Mingo Pugliese as a little hit (*una golpecita*) on the floor.[190] The other was *pique* (dribbling or bouncing), rebounding off the floor with the tip of the shoe.

PLATE 83   PLATE 84

Pique refers to bouncing a ball. That's how it works: the tip of the shoe no sooner strikes earth than it richochets back. Bounce and go on (*pico y voy*) is how Copes describes it.[191]

Games and Angió demonstrate pique (Plates 87 and 88). They rebound together, then come down together, in stylish figurations of silence and sound.

There is a beautiful variant where one foot strikes around the other with the tip of the shoe. The dancer taps in front, to each side, and behind the foot that is stationary. Then he shifts feet and repeats the whole process. Copes notates the series with mnemonic syllables: *pico, pico, pico, pam; pico, pico, pico, pam!*

13. TURNS (GIROS)

> *Light as a feather,*
> *she giro'd around him,*
> *her waist a wild call,*
> *in the midst of the speed.*

> — MARIO ÁRRAGA, *Poética del tango* (2004)

PLATE 85   PLATE 86

Decorate a decoration: the feeling is that there can never be enough of beauty, let alone too much.

—ZORA NEALE HURSTON, *The Sanctified Church* (1981)

Giro is Spanish for "turn." Spins are a marvel of tango. The woman turns around the man; he pivots at the center. They complement each other with bold shifting stances.

Dancers make spins for beauty, stringing pearls of bright motion along lines of flight.[192]

Spinning solo in place is common in Central Africa. Bakongo call it *bangumuka* (turn) or *nzyeta* (turn round). Bakongo believe that a turn "ties a knot" (*kanga kolo*) in the flow of the dance, providing punctuation and flair.[193] There are split-second turns in flamenco.

Bakongo turn solo; so do flamenquists. But tangueros are turning as couples. The man is the nucleus, while the woman turns around him. Giros of the 1940s were built, in part, on the early-twentieth-century *molinete* (spin to the left) and *contra-molinete* (spin to the right). But today's complex spins involve eight different parts (*ocho tiempos*), that is, eight different steps.

The man and the woman start, walking forward. The woman then

PLATE 87   PLATE 88

turns in four parts: a step going forward, a step around the side, a step going back, a step to the side. The sequence repeats, making a total of eight steps or moves.

Games goes around Angió counterclockwise, like a planet around the sun, except that the sun also dances. He follows her cycle with an inner rotation. This keeps his face facing hers. That inner rotation is a link to the past.

14. CAROUSEL (CALESITA)

> Calesitas are ideal for violin variations.
>
> —MARÍA DEL CARMEN SILINGO, *Tango-danza tradicional*

Calesita is a picture step, deft and balletic. It summons the image of a merry-go-round. Coming out of an ocho, the woman spins with the man, balanced on her left leg. She lifts up her right leg and, bending it, handsomely displays it against the side of the onturning man. She is miming a mount on a carousel. María Nieves remains forever the foremost exponent of this move.

15. THE PENCIL (LÁPIZ) In "the pencil" the man, with his left foot, traces a circle on the floor. As he completes it, his foot blocks hers. She makes a half-turn en route to this halt.

In the early days of the tango, men traced half-circles (*media lunas*) on the ground. Love of such figure-making continued.

Angió enters right. With the point of his left foot, he traces a counterclockwise circle. Games, caught in the motion, follows him closely. She stands for one second with her legs spread apart but keeps following the turn of his left foot until it blocks both her feet (Plates 89 and 90).

Angió's left foot is superb: subtly it levitates until only the point of the shoe is touching the floor. In that split-second we "see" a strong pencil (Plate 89).

16. THE DRAG/THE SWEEP (ARRASTRADA/BARRIDA) Penciling is doubled in the drag or the sweep step. But instead of tracing circles, the couple now marks out short lines. The man places his foot by the foot of the woman and carries it to another position. They sweep the area with magnetized feet.

They draw with their limbs as well as with their feet, legs angled like

PLATE 89   PLATE 90

the arms of a compass (Plates 91 and 92). The step is a consequence of a vital aspect of the revolution of the 1940s, namely the sharing of action between the man and the woman. Copes and Nieves, Zotto and Plebs, carried that trend to the highest point possible.

17. THE TURN OF THE SCREW (ENROSQUE)

> *They are excited, when dancing*
> *cheek to cheek plus* enrosque.
>
> — MARIO ÁRRAGA, *Poética del tango*

Enrosque is a specialized spin that came into being in around 1940 with Petróleo. The man spins on one foot while the other rests at the side of his ankle. The woman, meanwhile, revolves round the man, clockwise or counterclockwise.[194]

Enrosque takes its form from ballet. Games and Angió enact it (Plate 93). Starting in standard embrace position, Angió spins enrosque in a signature way: the tip of his right shoe rides the heel of his left. Games steps around him. There is light between their bodies. Their regard is

PLATE 91   PLATE 92

composed. Gabriel spins athletically, causing a crease to appear in his jacket. It traces the line of his torsion.

18. THE HOOK (GANCHO)

> Football and tango constitute the popular symbolic worlds of Buenos Aires.

— EDUARDO P. ARCHETTI, *Masculinities: Football, Polo and the Tango in Argentina* (1999)

> Poetic ability [is the] ability to take the measure of the world.

— MARTIN HEIDEGGER, *Poetry, Language, Thought* (1971)

Soccer (*fútbol*) is fabulously popular in Buenos Aires. It emerged as a national sport in the 1920s.[195] Many tangueros played soccer as youths, so it is hardly surprising that men would compare certain moves in the tango to an all-purpose feint in futbol called *amague*.

In an *amague* the player fakes going in one direction but immediately goes elsewhere, to confuse his opponent. Ganchos and boleos, analogously, break expectation. They baffle the uninitiated. There is a move in futbol called the *caño,* where the player shoots the ball between the legs of his opponent. Similarly, ganchos involve sudden penetrations of leg between legs. The move called boleo breaks straight from the knee, with an athletic back-kick.

Gancho (hook) probes and retracts, taking advantage of moments when the partner's legs are apart. Lightning-quick thrusts go between the two thighs but pull back, just as quickly as entered. It recalls bumbakana, but here the goal is to penetrate the thighs, not to strike them.

Ganchos are a plausible creolization of old Kongo dance games of sexual pursuit. Unsurprisingly, they go back to canyengue and milonga.[196] They are more than steps—they're invasions.

PLATE 93

Games starts striding. Her legs are wide open. Angió sees his chance. His foot angles in, a small guided missile that winds up between her thighs (Plate 94). She ganchos right back as he strides in a basic, finding the second to shoot her leg between his (Plate 95). What they're performing are *ganchos de frente* (face-to-face ganchos).

Ganchos laterales (ganchos done to the side) involve the woman kicking back, between the thighs of the man standing behind her.[197] This takes sharp timing.

Ganchos are physical. What makes them art is the abstracting of erotic energy. The woman inserts her leg suddenly and just as suddenly pulls it out, initiating a strong flick to the right and the left. A man and a woman dramatize belonging, each to the other, grazing their bodies at the speed of the mind.

19. BOLEO This brusque, virile move is hot, strong, and swift. It's a circular leg thrust, moving back lightning fast—a "whiplash" (*latigazo*), in tanguero idiom. It can be done by the man or the woman, solo or together.

PLATE 94   PLATE 95

One style of boleo consists of pressing both knees together and sketching, with one lifted foot, a horizontal circle, parallel to the floor, drenched with full energy.[198]

Watching Angió and Games performing boleo, we see two right legs shoot back in full action (Plate 96) and a staggered version, crossing right leg over left (Plate 97). There other styles as well.

The result is complex. There are three different angles of motion involved: heads turned in one direction, knees in another, and the whiplashing leg out in space. Beauty in contrast: vertical torso over lateral explosion, shooting out from bent knees. Inept tangueros make lazy, slack circles. Masters make one quick clear slash.

Copes and Nieves developed a variant where the woman, instead of flicking her foot, vibrates it back and forth quickly. They call this step the "hummingbird" (*paso colibrí*).

Boleos allegedly came in with Petróleo, but Mingo Pugliese maintains that they're older. Méndez was doing them back in the 1930s. Couples facing inward, in the wake of the *sobrepaso,* intensified boleos in mirrors of motion. As Carmen Silingo observes, "*Boleo* was born in the equaliza-

PLATE 96   PLATE 97

tion of the couple facing one another."[199] Likely sources go back even further: Boneo documented a back-kicking dancer among the Bakongo of
Buenos Aires around 1838 (Plate 19). Later, in the 1920s, Pedro Figari noted
in Montevideo similar back-kicks in Kongo-tinged candombe dancing.

20. FANTASÍA: THREE SAMPLES *Fantasía* turns tango into baroque
sculpture forms, as if Rodin were choreographer, ending the motion with
tableaux vivantes. Some say fantasía emerged in the 1940s, with dancers
like Todaro, to be deepened and confirmed in the 1950s by Copes and
Nieves and later Zotto and Plebs.

But intensity of pose has accompanied tango for a very long time. It
has ultimate roots in "sudden standing," the deliberate freezing of the
body among solo dancers in Kongo.

Making such poses, tangueros break free from embracing. They use
their free hands for making strong gestures. That is the key: the transitory
vaporization of the abrazo.

Aggression and submission brilliantly mix in a *tango de fantasía* by
Games and Angió (Plate 98). Taking a step back, Angió holds Games
firmly. He bends down her body, angling his shoulders as he does so.

But Games is not passive: she shoots a flexed leg between his two
limbs. Her other leg extends back at a very low angle. His left is flexed

and his right is extended. In this boldly staged threshold it is difficult to establish where aggression stops and submission begins.

From exaggerating *down* we move to exaggerating *up,* in a step called the fantasy bicycle (*bicicleta fantasía*) (Plate 99). Angió hooks his right foot with Games's left. With muscular ease, he lifts her straight up. His right leg is bent at an angle, as is hers. In this off-centered way he displays her. Once she is up, their two touching feet begin making circles, as if they were pedaling a bike in the sky.

A final example: a lateral spin of amazing velocity. This step, *la volada* (the short single flight), is athletically daring. The man lifts the woman, both feet off the ground, and spins her dramatically across a whole room. Her left leg extends in a frozen boleo while her right clamps his thigh. Her hair, like a flag, reacts to the wind and the force of the move (Plate 100).

CHAN-CHAN: THE LAST TWO NOTES OF THE TANGO Tango protects us from sameness. The milongas of Buenos Aires and Montevideo, Paris and Berlin, Tokyo and New York, provide fallout shelters against the hegemonic takeover of anglophone pop. Together with mambo and cumbia,

PLATE 98   PLATE 99

PLATE 100

reggetón and dance-hall, they help keep alternative cultures alive. They stave off the horror of turning on the radio and finding only one kind of music. Tango comes from the heart, like n'kwanga in Kongo. It moves on forever. I thank God for its sheer existence.

ENVOI: *EL TANGO* BY ROBERT COLESCOTT

Carlos Páez Vilaró's mural *Gardel* opened this book. Robert Colescott's acrylic on canvas *El Tango* (1995) closes it (Plate 101). This painting addresses the blackness of tango.

PLATE 101

Colescott is a visual stride pianist: he paints images and colors with sharp syncopation. Recalling Fats Waller, his means are hilarity and his taste is quite sure.[1]

Humor takes charge. A black man, outrageously masked as King Kong, shouts out to a white woman: "*Your* tango??" "Yes," she answers, "from Spain!" A man in a powder-blue shirt leans in to agree with her. Long-faced and mustachioed, he's Cesar Romero, famed "Latin lover" of the films of the 1940s.[2] He, too, is implicated: many Latinos are mestizo or mulatto or, if their ancestors came from Andalusia, share certain roots with western North Africa.

King Kong's argument with the lady and film star recalls the contrasting views of Vicente Rossi, the Uruguayan scholar who derived tango from blacks, and Carlos Vega, the musicologist from Argentina who argued that tango was essentially Iberian.

Colescott, like Borges, deeply respects tango's spirit. To personify its force, he places by Romero a tall standing woman of color. She is armed with a knife, to defend her tradition, and her body is daubed with ochre-like textures, as if she were emerging from a deep forest ritual. Her face is part mask and part mirror, alive with sequinlike accents. In her strange double visage, the painter suggests, "we read tango's hidden black mysticism."[3]

Cultural interplay makes tango swing, in darting responses to Africa, Europe, and creole Argentina. Colescott's sure touch is equally creolizing. There is homage to Goya: a naked white woman reclines at the bottom of the painting. Provocatively poised, she is clearly a *maja*, a fugitive from the style of the famed Spanish master. She represents sensuality, a force we encounter when we step into tango.[4]

Three black figures confront four white figures. Colescott's intimation seems clear: no matter what the statistics, blacks rule the roots of the tango. They are vividly present in tango today. His painting suggests what Alejandro Frigerio discovered, namely that the "disappearance theory" of blacks in Argentina is immediately challenged by black presence today in the dance and the music of that nation. From Frigerio's study:

one of the most notable stars of Argentine jazz is black
one of the leaders of the 1940's tango dance revolution was black
one of the finest milongueras of today is black
one of the finest dancers of contemporary milonga is black
the finest living tango musician is black
one of the best of Argentina's b-boys [so-called break dancers] is black[5]

To which one might add:

the fabled last partner of Petróleo was black
one of the finest Argentine interpreters of jazz dance, boogie, and
milonga is black.

If you follow the argument of this book you know who these artists are:

Oscar Alemán
El Negro Lavandina
Margarita de Guillé
Facundo Posadas
Horacio Salgán
Lucas Álvàrez[6]
La Negra Martita
Carlos Anzuate[7]

Colescott's *El Tango* spiritually represents these artists, and more. This
is especially true of the double-masked woman who centers the painting.
She is singing the notes of the tango. Her left hand rests on her heart,
source of memory and well-being, while her right hand ascends, a sign of
deep pleasure. *She* is the tango, masked black and white.[8]

NOTES

OVERTURE: GARDEL ON AVENIDA LIBERTADOR

1. Carlos Páez Vilaró kindly glossed every element of his mural during an afternoon interview at his residence in Punta del Este, Uruguay, on December 26, 2001.
2. Identifying the mounted jockey in his mural as Irineo Leguisamo, the famous racetrack contender of the 1920s and 1930s in Buenos Aires, Páez Vilaró burst into song. He sang the lyrics to "Leguisamo sólo" (Leguisamo Alone in the Stretch), which the Italian composer Modesto Papavero wrote in Leguisamo's honor in 1925. For more on Leguisamo and his career, see Jorge Larroca, *Entre cortes y apiladas* (Between Stopping and Riding High) (Buenos Aires: Ediciones Cruz del Sur, 1981), pp. 124–25, and Rodolfo Omar Zatti, *Gardel: Su gran pasión el turf* (Gardel: His Grand Passion, the Turf) (Buenos Aires: Corregidor, 1990).
3. Excerpted from Eduardo Romano, *Las letras del tango* (Tango as Literature) (Buenos Aires: Editorial Fundación Ross, 1995), p. 355.

PREFACE: MOVING WITH AN ARM AROUND LIFE

1. Eduardo Romano, ed., *Las letras del tango* (Tango as Literature) (Buenos Aires: Editorial Fundación Ross, 1995), pp. 275–76.
2. See Francis Bebey: "The first thing that attracts attention [in African music] is its vitality. [The] music is a challenge to human destiny; a refusal to accept the transience of this life." From his *African Music: A People's Art* (New York: Lawrence Hill & Co., 1975), p. 126.
3. Janny Scott, "Flirting with the Tango: It's Serious," *New York Times*, June 11, 1999, sec. E, p. 1.
4. But fortunately not anymore. See Juan Carlos Coria, *Pasado y presente de los*

negros en Buenos Aires (Past and Present of Buenos Aires Blacks) (Buenos Aires: Editorial Roca, 1997); and Dina V. Picotti, ed., *El negro en la Argentina* (Blacks in Argentina) (Buenos Aires: Editores de América Latina, 2001).

5. Three recent studies also are useful: Daniel Schavelzon, *Buenos Aires negra* (Black Buenos Aires) (Buenos Aires: Emece, 2003); Alejandro Solomianski, *Identidades secretas: La negritud argentina* (Secret Identities: Afro-Argentine Culture) (Buenos Aires: Beatriz Viterbo, 2003); and most especially Alejandro Frigerio, *Cultura negra en el cono sur* (Black Culture of the Southern Cone) (Buenos Aires: Universidad Católica Argentina, 2000).

6. Ricardo Rodríguez Molas, "Los afro-argentinos y el origen del tango" (Afro-Argentines and the Origin of Tango), in *Desmemoria* 7, no. 27 (2000), p. 89.

7. Sergio Pujol, *Historia del baile* (History of Dance) (Buenos Aires: Emecé, 1999), pp. 55–57.

8. Tomás Olivera Chirimini and Juan Antonio Varese, *El candombe: Sus orígenes, historia, proyecciones* (Candombe: Its Origins, History, and Influences) (Montevideo: Ediciones El Galeón, 1992), p. 7.

9. W. C. Handy, "Wyer Was Wrong," letter to the editor, *Downbeat,* May 21, 1952, p. 2. I thank John Szwed for bringing Handy's letter to my attention.

1. TANGO IN HOLLYWOOD

1. Interview with Robert Duvall and Luciana Pedraza, Buenos Aires, August 2000. In this chapter I am concentrating on Hollywood, with the exception of Verhoeven, Bertolucci, and Saura. For further details on tango in world film, see Pedro Ochoa's fine essay, "Tango and World Cinema" in *Doce ventanas al tango* (Buenos Aires: Fundación El Libro, 2001), pp. 159–74, and his superb *Tango y cine mundial* (Tango and World Cinema) (Buenos Aires: Ediciones del Jilguero, 2003).

2. From a Buenos Aires television special on the tango kindly shared with me by Alejandro Frigerio, winter 1999.

3. Lewis Lapham, editor of *Harper's,* was present at the White House dinner honoring the president of Argentina and saw Duvall dance. I am grateful to him for sharing this information during a long-distance telephone conversation in March 2000.

4. Rex Ingram, quoted in Liam O'Leary, *Rex Ingram: Master of the Silent Cinema* (London: BFI Publishers, 1993), p. 45.

5. John Storm Roberts, *The Latin Tinge: The Impact of Latin American Music on the United States* (Tivoli, N.Y.: Original Music, 1985), p. 45.

6. Lewis A. Erenberg, *Steppin' Out: New York Nightlife and the Transformation of American Culture, 1890–1930* (Chicago: University of Chicago Press, 1981), pp. 83–85 and fig. 7.

7. O'Leary, Ingram, p. 72. See Alfred Charles Richard, Jr., *The Hispanic Image on the Silver Screen: An Interpretative Filmography from Silents into Sound, 1898–1935* (New York: Greenwood Press, 1992), p. 235. See also Gayllyn Studlar, *This Mad Masquerade: Stardom and Masculinity in the Jazz Age* (New York: Columbia University Press, 1996), pp. 165–69.

8. Sergio Pujol, *Valentino en Buenos Aires* (Buenos Aires: Emece, 1994), p. 109. Pedro Ochoa, in *Doce ventanas al tango*, p. 162, says that *Four Horsemen* "should be taken as the clearest reflection of the first international boom of the tango," which he dates around 1913. Parisian tango influenced the rise of the tango-pirates of New York, whose spirit Valentino transposed to the screen.

9. From a conversation with Curtis Hanson, Los Angeles, August 1999.

10. Bernardo Bertolucci and Franco Arcalli, *Last Tango in Paris: The Screenplay* (New York: Delacorte Press, 1973), p. 184.

11. Norman Mailer, "A Transit to Narcissus," in Bertolucci and Arcalli, *Last Tango,* p. 210. For Pauline Kael's remarks, see her "Introduction" in the same volume, pp. 12 and 17.

12. Julie Taylor, "Tango," in George E. Marcus, *Rereading Cultural Anthropology* (Durham, N.C.: Duke University Press, 1992), p. 377.

13. Bertolucci and Arcalli, *Last Tango,* p. 185.

14. Ochoa, *Doce ventanas,* p. 165, adds: "No other music could . . . mark the climax of so intense a relationship." Ochoa shows how, in the wake of Bertolucci's prestige, the title *Last Tango* became a kind of international marketing concept for forgettable films, such as *Ultimo tango a Zagarolo, El último tango en Madrid,* and *Der Letzte Tango in Wien.* In addition, Sam Pillsbury's film *Zandalee* (1991) was vended by the Portuguese under the title *O Último Tango em Nova Orleans.*

15. Mailer, "Transit," p. 211. Mailer is puzzling out Schneider's character's motives for leaving Brando.

16. John Storm Roberts, *Latin Jazz: The First of the Fusions, 1880s to Today* (New York: Schirmer Books, 1999), p. 187. Juan Carlos Copes's remarks come from an interview in Buenos Aires, fall 1999.

17. Paul Verhoeven, personal communication, August 1999.

18. Ibid.

19. I thank Paul Verhoeven for sending me copies of both the original script in Dutch and an English translation of *Soldaat van Oranje.*

20. Ochoa, *Tango y cine mundial,* p. 211.

21. Juan Carlos Copes, personal conversation, Buenos Aires, summer 2000.

22. Marta Elena Savigliano, *Angora Matta: A Tango Opera* (Middletown, Conn.: Wesleyan University Press, 2003), p. 212.

23. The line that accompanies this moment is "I've been following you in the tango, Pablo. But to make a film, you have to follow me." Sally Potter, *The Tango Lesson* (London: Faber and Faber, 1997), p. 56.

24. Diego Curubeto, *Babilonia gaucha ataca de nuevo* (Buenos Aires: Editorial Sudamericana, 1998), p. 190. Luciano Monteagudo, writing in the Buenos Aires daily *Clarín* (November 20, 1997), p. 12, retitled her film *The Narcissism Lesson.* Pablo O. Scholz, *Clarín* (November 20, 1997), p. 7, applauded her taste in musical selections: Piazzolla, Manzi, Pugliese, di Sarli, Gardel, and Lepera.

25. Ochoa, *Tango y cine mundial,* p. 257.

26. Carol Fenelon brought this tango sequence to my attention.

27. In addition to Saura, equally laudatory in this regard are Leonard Schrader—*Naked Tango* (1990)—and Adam Boucher—*Tango: The Obsession* (1998). See Ochoa, *Tango y cine mundial,* for a thoughtful assessment of these two films.

2. TANGO AS TEXT

1. Jorge Gottling, *Tango: Melancólico testigo* (Buenos Aires: Corregidor, 1998), p. 14.
2. Ibid., pp. 21, 75, and 82.
3. Jorge Palacio, *El humor en el tango* (Buenos Aires: Corregidor, 1996), pp. 21–33. For the persistence of humor in tango, see Oscar Vásquez Lucio, *El tango en el humor gráfico y escrito* (Tango Humor in Cartoons and Writing) (Buenos Aires: Ediciones Club de Tango, 1996), pp. 83ff, and of course consult Borges's poem, "Alguien le dice al tango" (Someone Says to the Tango), in his *Para las seis cuerdas* (Buenos Aires: Emece, 1996), p. 37.
4. Ernesto Sábato, *Tango: Discusión y clave*, 2nd ed. (Tango: Code and Discussion) (Buenos Aires: Editorial Losada, 1997), p. 88.
5. As to Contursi and his impact, see Gabriel Ruiz de los Llanos, *Pascual Contursi* (Buenos Aires: Editorial del Nuevo Amnecer, 1993). See also Gaspar J. Astarita, *Pascual Contursi: Vida y obra* (Pascual Contursi: His Life and Work) (Buenos Aires: Ediciones la Campana, 1981). As for his brief career as a puppeteer, see Osvaldo Pelletieri, "Siempre Contursi," in various authors, *La historia del tango*, vol. 17, *Los poetas I* (Buenos Aires: Corregidor, 1981), pp. 3145–46. Contursi manned a small improvised puppet theater for the children of the neighborhood in a tenement near Calles Solís and Chile in the barrio of San Cristóbal.
6. I thank Pugliese's daughter, Beba Pugliese, for bringing to my attention her father's opinion of Celedonio Flores.
7. Sergio Pujol, *Discépolo: Una biografía argentina* (Discépolo: An Argentine Life) (Buenos Aires: Emecé, 1996), p. 9.
8. I am of course thinking of Harold Bloom's *Anxiety of Influence* (New York: Oxford, 1973).
9. Julie Taylor, *Paper Tangos* (Durham, N.C.: Duke University Press, 1998), p. 4.
10. David Frankel, the art critic, brings to my attention a spiritual overlap between this work and a beautiful song by Antonio Carlos Jobim, "Aguas de Março."
11. Raúl Alberto March, *Eladia Blázquez: Síntesis de la cancíon porteña* (Eladia Blázquez: Synthesis of Buenos Aires Song) (Buenos Aires: Corregidor, 1993), p. 12.
12. Ibid., p. 76.
13. Mario Árraga, *Poética del tango* (Tango Poetics) (Buenos Aires: Corregidor, 2004), p. 61.
14. Eugenio Mandrini, ed., *Poetas del tango* (The Poets of Tango) (Buenos Aires: Ediciones Colihué, 2000), p. 249.

3. THE CULTURAL PREPARATION

1. Sergio A. Pujol, *Gardel y la inmigración* (Gardel and Immigration) (Buenos Aires: Editorial Almagesto, 1991), p. 13. In spite of this permeability, Pujol continues, social tensions exist.
2. Carmen Bernard, *Historia de Buenos Aires* (History of Buenos Aires) (Buenos Aires: Fondo de Cultura Económica de Argentina, 1999), p. 355.
3. For more on chamamé, see Raúl Oscar Cerruti, *El chamamé* (Resistencia:

Editorial Norte Argentino, 1965); Marily Morales Segovia, *El chamamé* (Corrientes: Ediciones Daeunne, 1972); Ricardo R. Visconti Vallejos, *Historia del chamamé* (Buenos Aires: Corregidor, 1990); and Rubén Pérez Bagallo, *El chamamé* (Buenos Aires: Ediciones del Sol, 1996).

4. Silvia Peralta, ed., *Costumbres criollas* (Creole Customs) (Bahía Blanca, Argentina: Editorial Construcciones Sudamericana, 2003): "Red flags on his altar stand for innocently spilled blood . . . leaving a candle and a red ribbon [on his altar] accompanies a request for a miracle from Gauchito Gil" (p. 113). See also Félix Coluccio, *Devociones populares* (Popular Beliefs) (Buenos Aires: Corregidor, 2001), who gives another version for the dominance of red in the worship of Gauchito Gil—"he was a Federalist" (p. 114).

5. Ombúes dot the urban landscape of Buenos Aires. For a charming partial geography, see Leon Tenenbaum, "Ombúes ciudadanos" (Ombúes as Citizens of the City) in his *Buenos Aires: Un museo al aire libre* (Buenos Aires: An Open-Air Museum) (Buenos Aires: Corregidor, 1989), pp. 149–52.

6. Nicholas Shumway, *The Invention of Argentina* (Berkeley: University of California Press, 1991), p. 12.

7. Juan Carlos Martelli and Beatriz Spinosa, *El libro de la cocina criolla* (The Book of Creole Cooking) (Santiago del Estero: Sainte Claire Editora, 1991), pp. 12–13.

8. Ibid., p. 65. In addition, Monica Hoss de la Comte informs us, in her *La cocina argentina* (Argentine Cooking) (Buenos Aires: Maizal, 2000), p. 14, that locro derives from the Aymara word *luxru. Choclo,* green corn on the cob—the title of Villoldo's early classic tango—comes from the Quechua word *choccllo.*

9. Hoss de la Comte, *La cocina,* p. 26. She finds Moorish influence in the making of empanadas "brought from Spain [to the Americas] by Andalusians who for so many centuries had lived in contact with Arab [culture]." The connections between Andalusian and Moroccan cuisine are richly explored in Inés Elexpura, *La cocina de al-Andalus* (The Cuisine of Andalusia) (Madrid: Alianza Editorial, 1994).

10. Martelli and Spinosa, *El libro,* p. 26. For a charming exposition of matambre in Argentine cultural context, see Esteban Echeverría, "Apología del matambre," in his *Páginas literarias* (Literary Pages) (Buenos Aires: W. M. Jackson, n.d.), pp. 128–35.

11. This is but one recipe; there are many, many others. For the "galactic look," see the illustration on p. 45 in Hoss de la Comte, *La cocina.*

12. Betsy Cohen, *The Snow White Syndrome: All About Envy* (New York: Macmillan, 1987).

13. Samuel Oliver, *Pedro Figari* (Buenos Aires: Ediciones de Arte Gaglianone, 1984), plate 59, *Nostalgias del candombe.* Alejandro Frigerio brought to my attention the Buenos Aires custom of tying a protective red ribbon on a newborn.

14. Daniel Granada, *Supersticiones del Río de la Plata* (River Plate Superstitions) (Buenos Aires: Editorial Kraft, 1947), p. 260.

15. For context, read, for example, Titus Burkhardt, *Moorish Culture in Spain* (New York: McGraw-Hill, 1972).

16. Silvina Ocampo, *Autobiografía de Irene* (Buenos Aires: Editorial Sudamericana, 1975), p. 26.

17. Hoss de la Comte, *La cocina*, p. 70. Elexpuru, *La cocina*, p. 222.

18. Labelle Prussin, personal communication, September 4, 1998; André Borg, "L'Habitat a Tozeur" (Architecture in Tozeur), *Cahiers des arts et techniques de l'Afrique du Nord*, no. 5 (1959), pp. 91–107.

19. Oliver, *Pedro Figari*, plate 34, *El escondido* (1920s). For the full structure of the dance and its cycles of Andalusian-derived finger-snapping, hand-clapping, and stamping, see Antonio Cisneros Lugones, *Manual de danzas regionales del folklore argentino* (Manual of Argentine Regional Folk Dances) (Rosario: Editorial Ruiz, 1964), p. 22–23, and Carlos Vega and Aurora de Pietro, *Danzas argentinas* (Dances of Argentina) (Buenos Aires: Ediciones Culturales Argentinas, 1962), pp. 100–101.

20. *Exhibition of Paintings by Cesáreo Bernaldo de Quirós* (New York: Hispanic Society of America, 1932), p. 15.

21. The pampas' impact on the tangos of Agustín Bardi is discussed by Luis Adolfo Sierra, "Agustín Bardi," in various authors, *La historia de tango 4* (Buenos Aires: Corregidor, 1977), pp. 607–08.

22. Viejo Tanguero (pseud.), *El tango, su evolución y su historia* (Tango: Its Evolution and History) (1913; reprinted Buenos Aires: Club de Tango, 1995), pp. 12–13.

23. Sonia Ursini, *Horacio Salgán: La supervivencia de un artista en el tiempo* (Horacio Salgán: The Survival of an Artist in Time) (Buenos Aires: Corregidor, 1993), p. 144.

24. Philip D. Curtin, *The Atlantic Slave Trade: A Census* (Madison: University of Wisconsin Press, 1969), pp. 223, 241–42, 244–47, 260–62.

25. George Reid Andrews, *The Afro-Argentines of Buenos Aires* (Madison: University of Wisconsin Press, 1980), p. 27.

26. Curtin, *Atlantic Slave Trade*, p. 241.

27. The tentative identification of "Mondongo" as upriver mercenaries comes from a North Kongo oral tradition, as shared by Fu-Kiau Bunseki, November 2000.

28. The Libolo (Lubolo) belong to the Kimbundu cluster of northwestern Angola ethnicities. See George Peter Murdock, *Africa: Its Peoples and Their Culture History* (New York: McGraw-Hill, 1959), p. 292.

29. Robert Farris Thompson, *The Four Moments of the Sun* (Washington, D.C.: National Gallery of Art, 1981), p. 34.

30. Murdock, *Africa*, p. 292.

31. Fu-Kiau Bunseki, personal communication, July 2002.

32. Cited in J. Decapmaker, "Danses des Bakongo," *XVI Semaine Missiologique* (Louvain, 1938), p. 43.

33. Fu-Kiau Bunseki, personal communication, June 2002. See also Karl E. Laman, *Dictionnaire Ki-Kongo–Français* (Brussels, 1936) p. 7:175. Laman gives the ordinary meaning: twisting and grinding the hips in the dance.

34. Decapmaker, "Danses," p. 42.

35. Fu-Kiau Bunseki communication, June 2002.

36. J. Van Wing, "Les danses Bakongo," *Congo* 1, no. 2 (1937), p. 122.

37. Fu-Kiau Bunseki communication, June 2002.

38. Ibid.

39. Peter Forbath, *The River Congo* (New York: Harper and Row, 1977), p. 97.

40. John Thornton, "African Dimensions of the Stono Rebellion," *American Historical Review* 96, no. 4 (1991), pp. 364–67.

41. C. Daniel Dawson in conversation with the author, January 1999, New York.

42. Fu-Kiau Bunseki, personal communication, April 1999; Willie Ruff, interview by author, New Haven, Conn., September 2001. The derivation of "patting juba," the North American black thigh-slapping dance game, from the Kongo dance *zuba*, which is also focused on slapping thighs and chest, seems clear, art historically and etymologically. Note that the verb *zuba* literally means "to slap." See Laman, *Dictionnaire*, p. 2:832: "*nzuba*, a chief's dance in which women take part" and p. 1173: "*zuba*, to slap, to dance alone."

43. Christiane Falgayrettes, ed., *Objets interdits* (Forbidden Objects) (Paris: Musée Dapper, 1989), pp. 244–45.

44. Thompson, *Four Moments*, pp. 52–54.

45. Rubén Galloza, interview by author, Montevideo, August 1998.

46. Samba Jean, a Mu-Ladi scholar of Kongo dance and martial art, interview by author, July, 1990. I am grateful to Samba Jean for accompanying me to N'zieto village, southwest of Brazzaville, and for glossing the structure of the m'tela dance we witnessed there.

47. Van Wing, "Les danses," pp. 123ff. I thank Samba Jean for glossing dance terms in Ki-Kongo that Van Wing had documented.

48. I thank Kim Barkan for helping me film N'kwanga at Diosso, and Fu-Kiau Bunseki for glossing details of the dance.

49. Fu-Kiau Bunseki, interview by author, October 2002.

50. Laman, *Dictionnaire*, p. 2:870.

51. Ibid., p. 2:1161.

52. Ibid., p. 2:872. Laman refers to "sealing, as with stopper or plug."

53. Ibid., p. 2:916: "defame; malign, slander." Wyatt MacGaffey, personal communication, August 2002, suggests also *zonza*, "to quarrel, litigate, look for a fight."

54. Grey Gundaker, personal communication, July 2002, brought to my attention the possible convergence of *sosa* and *saucy* in the word history of *sass*.

55. Balu Balila, Mwanda village, Congo-Kinshasa, July 1985.

56. Richard and Sally Price, eds., *Stedman's Surinam: Life in an Eighteenth Century Slave Society* (Baltimore: Johns Hopkins University Press, 1992), pp. 276–77.

57. *Sangumuna* and *mwangisa* are actually synonyms, meaning "to scatter." Wyatt MacGaffey, personal communication, August 2002.

58. As Robin Kelley would say, they were "constructing a collective identity based on something other than work." See his *Race Rebels* (New York: Free Press, 1994), p. 169. The drawing of the Rio stevedores is illustrated in Peter Fryer, *Rhythms of Resistance* (Hanover, N.H.: University Press of New England, 2000), p. 46.

59. W. H. Hudson, *Far Away and Long Ago* (New York: E. P. Dutton, 1925) pp. 97–98.

60. Ricardo Rodríguez Molas, "La música y la danza de los negros en el Buenos Aires de los siglos XVIII and XIX," *Historia* 7 (1957), p. 111. The Bakongo make clear that they must dance with "[cultural] purity," and they were well aware that the "diversion and happiness" that their dances brought to the whites of Buenos Aires could be used as weapons toward their cause.

61. Glossed by Fu-Kiau Bunseki, August 2002.

62. Jorge Emilio Gallardo, ed., *Un testimonio sobre la esclavitud en Montevideo: La memoria de Lima Suárez Peña* (A Testimony of Slavery in Montevideo: The Memoir of Lima Suárez Peña) (Buenos Aires: Idea Viva, n.d.), p. 12.

63. I thank Fu-Kiau Bunseki for this translation.

64. Cited in George Reid Andrews, *Afro-Argentines*, p. 157.

65. Ibid.

66. Horacio Jorge Becco, *Negros y morenos en el cancionero rioplatense* (Blacks and Persons of Color in the Collection of Songs of the River Plate) (Buenos Aires: Sociedad Argentino de Americanistas, 1953), p. 8.

67. Ibid., p. 13.

68. Fu-Kiau Bunseki interview, January 2001.

69. Laman, *Dictionnaire*, p. 1:157.

70. Quoted in Robert Farris Thompson, "Hip-Hop 101," in William Eric Perkins, ed., *Droppin' Science: Critical Essays on Rap and Hip-Hop Culture* (Philadelphia: Temple University Press, 1996), p. 212.

71. A. Taullard, *Nuestro antiguo Buenos Aires* (Our Old Buenos Aires) (Buenos Aires: Prosser, 1927), pp. 355–56; Juan Pradere, *Juan Manuel de Rosas: Su iconografía* (The Iconography of Juan Manuel de Rosas) (Buenos Aires: Editorial Mente, 1970), p. 230: "Boneo's painting depicts the Kongo Angunga nation which c. 1838 was located on today's Santiago del Estero street around San Juan [street]."

72. Laman, *Dictionnaire*, p. 2:625.

73. Taullard, *Nuestro antiguo*, p. 349.

74. Andrews, *Afro-Argentines*, p. 163.

75. I thank Fu-Kiau Bunseki for bringing this Kongo proverb to my attention.

76. Marshall and Jean Stearns, *Jazz Dance: The Story of American Vernacular Dance* (New York: Schirmer, 1974), p. 22.

77. Melville J. Herskovits, *The Myth of the Negro Past* (Boston: Beacon Press, 1958), p. 63.

78. Cited in Luis Labrana and Ana Sebastián, *Tango: Una historia* (Buenos Aires: Corregidor, 1992), p. 20.

79. Ibid.

80. Source for *tshia-tshia* is Fu-Kiau Bunseki, personal communication, July 2001; for *sya-sya*, see Laman, *Dictionnaire*, p. 2:936. See also *sye-sye* in Laman with the same meaning, p. 2:938.

81. I am indebted to the late Rubén Galloza for sharing what his godfather, Silverio Veloz, told him: that he personally witnessed Figari sketching candombe dancers at Gaboto and San Salvador in black Montevideo. I also thank Lyneise Williams for bringing to my attention the related finding of Jacqueline Bartniz, *The Martinfierristas and Argentine Art of the Twenties*, vols. 1 and 2 (Ann Arbor, Mich.: University Microfilms, 1986), p. 166.

82. Lisa Lekis, *Folk Dances of Latin America* (New York: Scarecrow Press, 1958), p. 169.

83. Néstor Marconi, interview by author, Buenos Aires, January 1998.

84. Ventura R. Lynch, *Folklore Bonaerense* (Folklore of the Province of Buenos Aires) (Buenos Aires: Lajouane, 1953), pp. 48–49.

85. Ana Cara-Walker, *The Art of Creole Expression in Argentina* (Ann Arbor, Mich.: University Microfilms, 1983), p. 111.

86. Andrews, *Afro-Argentines*, p. 170.

87. José Hernández, *El gaucho Martín Fierro* (Buenos Aires: Ediciones Margus, 1997), p. 279.

88. For a list of black payadores, consult Juan Carlos Coria, *Pasado y presente de los negros en Buenos Aires* (Past and Present Among the Blacks of Buenos Aires) (Buenos Aires: Editorial J. A. Roca, 1997), pp. 97–106.

89. Marcos de Estrada, *Argentinos de origen africano* (Argentines of African Origin) (Buenos Aires: Editorial Universitaria de Buenos Aires, 1979), p. 176.

90. Marvin A. Lewis, "Higinio Cazón," in his *Afro-Argentine Discourse: Another Dimension of the Black Diaspora* (Columbia: University of Missouri Press, 1996), pp. 78–83. Lewis reminds us, at p. 81, that many gauchos were of African descent. Amalia Sánchez Sivori lists the name of a black payador, Ramón Barrera, who started out as a gaucho: see her *Diccionario de payadores* (Dictionary of Country Versifiers) (Buenos Aires: Editorial Plus Ultra, 1979), p. 47.

91. Beatriz Seibel, ed., *El cantar del payador* (The Song of the Country Minstrel) (Buenos Aires: Biblioteca de Cultura Popular, 1998), p. 45.

92. Ibid., p. 46.

93. Cara-Walker, *Creole Expression*, p. 300. She takes note of the cultural overlap between the playful insults in payada and the "dozens" in black North America.

94. For more on the life and death of Gabino Ezeiza, see Luis Soler Canas, "Gabino Ezeiza: Verdad y leyenda" (Gabino Ezeiza: Truth and Legend) in *Todo es historia* no. 2 (1967), pp. 65–77. See also Victor di Santo, "Gabino, la voz del pueblo" (Gabino, the Voice of the People), *Todo es historia* no. 387 (October 1999), pp. 20–23, and Alfredo de la Fuente, *El payador en la cultura nacional* (The Country Singer in National Culture) (Buenos Aires: Corregidor, 1986), pp. 63–73.

95. José Curbelo, "Los payadores negros en el Río de la Plata" (Black Country Versifiers of the River Plate), in Dina V. Picotti, ed., *El negro en la Argentina* (Buenos Aires: Editores de América Latina, 2001), pp. 209–14.

96. Ibid., p. 211.

97. Cara-Walker, *Creole Expression*, p. 114.

98. Fu-Kiau Bunseki, interview by author, November 1999.

99. Cara-Walker, *Creole Expression*, p. 113.

100. Andrews, *Afro-Argentines*, pp. 156–63.

101. Fu-Kiau Bunseki, personal communication, October 1998; Balu Balila, interview by author, Kinshasa, July 1995; Samba Jean, interviews by author, Brazzaville and N'Zieto, July 1990.

102. Oliver, *Figari*, p. 22.

103. For an excellent recent doctoral study of Figari and his art, see Lyneise Williams, *Awakening the Spirits: The Art of Pedro Figari* (Ph.D. diss., Yale University, New Haven, Conn., 2004).

104. For a clear description of this key *pericón* sequence, "while men are on their knees, women will turn and crown them," see Nilda de Castellón and Carlos Cárdenas, *Coreografía de danzas nativas argentinas* (Buenos Aires: Editorial Escolar, 1993) p. 3:132.

105. Oliver, *Figari*, pp. 40 and 46

106. Rubén Galloza, interview by author, Montevideo, August 1997.

107. Robert Farris Thompson, "Galloza's Afro-Atlantic Art," in Melody Capote and C. Daniel Dawson, *Candombe, Canyengue, and Consciousness: Afro-Uruguayan Culture in the Art of Rubén Galloza* (New York: Caribbean Culture Center, 1999), p. 3.

108. Lyneise Williams, personal communication, New Haven, Conn., July 2003.

109. Fu-Kiau Bunseki, personal communication, January 2004. Literally "a sign of union with the world of the spirit."

110. Rubén Galloza, quoted in Thompson, "Galloza's Afro-Atlantic Art," p. 3.

111. Dapper's 1668 print is illustrated in *Objets interdits* (Paris: Musée Dapper, 1989), p. 255. Figari's painting is found at Oliver, *Figari*, p. 63.

112. Oliver, *Figari*, p. 75.

113. Fu-Kiau Bunseki, interview by author, July 2000.

114. Ibid.

115. Alejandro Frigerio, *Cultura negra en el cono sur: Representaciones en conflicto* (Black Culture of the Southern Cone: Representations in Conflict) (Buenos Aires: Ediciones de la Universidad Católica Argentina, 2000), p. 48.

116. Gustavo Vilela, interview by author, Montevideo, summer 1997.

117. Maureen Warner-Lewis has spotted another Kongo precedent for deep back leans in jazz and tango dancing—an Nsundi dance, *lungondunga*, in which "in their exuberance the dancers may crouch down and bend their shoulders backwards until they are practically lying on the ground." See her remarkable *Central Africa in the Caribbean* (Kingston, Jamaica: University of West Indies Press, 2004), p. 243.

118. Lino Suárez Peña, *Un testimonio*, p. 7.

119. I witnessed timbula and the playful bumping of posteriors in North Kongo dancing in 1985 and 1990.

120. Frigerio, *Cultura negra en el cono sur*, p. 141.

121. Fu-Kiau Bunseki nuanced the meaning of the objects in the Benguela sala in a personal communication, December 2002.

4. HABANERA: THE CALL OF THE BLOOD

1. Bozidar Darko Sustersic, "Imaginería y patrimonio mueble" (The Patrimony of Images and Furniture), in *Las misiones jesuíticas del Guayra* (Jesuit Missions of the Guayra Region) (Buenos Aires: Manrique Zago, 1995), p. 161.

2. Oneyda Alvarenga, *Música popular brasileña* (Brazilian Popular Music) (Mexico City: Fondo de Cultura Económica, 1947), p. 239.

3. W. C. Handy, the blues composer, referred to the beat of the habanera as "the call of the blood"—black blood understood—in a letter to *Downbeat* titled "Wyer Was Wrong," May 21, 1952.

4. Cited in Alejo Carpentier, *La música en Cuba* (Music in Cuba) (Mexico City: Fondo de Cultura Económica, 1946), p. 110.

5. Ibid.

6. Ibid., pp. 112 and 113.

7. José García de Arboleya, *Manual de la Isla de Cuba* (Handbook on the Island of Cuba) (Havana: Imprenta del Tiempo, 1859), pp. 262–63.

8. Esteban Pichardo, *Diccionario provincial de voces cubanas* (Matanzas, Cuba: Imprenta de la Real Marina, 1836).

9. Félix Tanco, from a mid-nineteenth-century letter to Domingo Delmonte, cited in Jorge Castellanos and Isabel Castellanos, *Cultura afrocubana* (Miami: Ediciones Universal, 1994), p. 4:333. Tanco adds this detail: "Who can not realize that the bass patterns of the dancers of the country are echoes of the drum of the tangos? All is African."

10. Antonio Cisneros Lugones, *Manual de danzas regionales del folklore argentino* (Manual of Regional Folkloric Dances of Argentina) (Rosario, Argentina: Librería y Editorial Ruiz, 1969) p. 72.

11. J. E. Alexander, cited in Castellanos and Castellanos, *Cultura afrocubana,* p. 338.

12. Tamara Martin, "Contradanza y habanera en la identidad musical cubana" (Country Dance and Habanera in Cuban Musical Identity), *Revista de la Unión de Escritores y Artistas de Cuba* 7, no. 17 (1994), p. 93.

13. Jorge Novati and Inés Cuello, "Primeras noticias y documentos" (First Notices and Documents), in *Antología del tango rioplatense* (Buenos Aires: Instituto Nacional de Musicología Carlos Vega, 1980), p. 1:7.

14. Alejo Carpentier, *La música en cuba,* p. 52.

15. Fu-Kiau Bunseki, personal communication, February 2001.

16. Ibid.

17. Raúl Fernández, *Latin Jazz: The Perfect Combination* (San Francisco: Chronicle Books, 2002), pp. 18–19.

18. W. C. Handy, *The Father of the Blues* (New York: Macmillan, 1941), pp. 101–102.

19. Ibid.

20. John Szwed, personal communication, October 1999.

21. Ibid.

22. Emilio Grenet, *Popular Cuban Music* (Havana: Carasa & Co., 1939), p. 24.

23. Alejo Carpentier, *Ese músico que llevo adentro* (That Musician That I Carry in Me) (Havana: Editorial Letras Cubanas, 1980), p. 3:311.

24. Castor Pérez Diz, Andreu Navarro, and María Teresa Linares, *L'Havanera: Un cant popular* (Tarragona, Spain: Ediciones El Medol, 1995), p. 71.

25. "Habanera enbrujada" can be heard on Castor Pérez and Alfons Carrera's CD, *Duet: Vora la mar, a prop teu* (Duet: Next to the Sea, Right Beside You) (Barcelona: Audiovisuals de Sarria CD, reference no. 5.1641, 1998).

5. MILONGA: THE GREAT BUENOS AIRES CONVERSATION

1. Larry Rohter, "Brazil Cattle Region," *New York Times,* June 20, 2001, p. W1.

2. The milonga in Portuguese, originally published in Lauro Ayesterán, *El folklore musical uruguayo,* is cited in Roberto Selles, "La milonga," *La historia del tango,* vol. 12, *La milonga, el vals* (Buenos Aires: Corregidor, 1978), p. 2118.

3. Martin Lienhard, *O mar e o mato* (Salvador, Brazil: EDUFBA/CEAO, 1998), p. 91.

4. Ana Cristina Cara-Walker, *The Art of Creole Expression in Argentina* (Ann Arbor,

Mich.: University Microfilms, 1983), p. 226. Translation mine. There is a variant, allegedly dating from the 1860s, in Selles, "La milonga," p. 2096.

5. Borges discovered this gem: "In the suburbs of Buenos Aires I heard a milonga, composed by a convict in Tierra del Fuego, a convict by the name of Arnold. In that long milonga I ran across extraordinary verses." Cited in Cara-Walker, *Creole Expression*, pp. 354–55. Translation mine.

6. Jorge Luis Borges, "Milonga de jacinto chiclana," second-to-last stanza, *Para las seis cuerdas* (Song for Six Strings) (Buenos Aires: Emecé, 1965), n.p. Translation mine.

7. "Milonga de los morenos" (Milonga for Persons of Color), in ibid. Translation mine.

8. "El títere" (Fugitive from a Marionette Show), in ibid. Translation mine.

9. "Los compadritos muertos" (The Dead Hipsters), in ibid. Translation mine.

10. José Hernández, *El gaucho Martín Fierro*, I, verse 1142. Discussed in Selles, "La milonga," p. 2084.

11. Jorge Luis Borges, *El idioma de los argentinos* (The Argentine Idiom) (Buenos Aires: M. Gleizer, 1928), p. 136.

12. Ignacio H. Fotheringham, *Memorias* (Memoirs), p. 1:64; cited by Jorge Novati and Inés Cuello, "Primeras noticias y documentos," *Antología del tango rioplatense* (Buenos Aires: Instituto Nacional de Musicología Carlos Vega, 1980).

13. *Mbrekete pa* and *tshia-tshia* were identified as antecedents and glossed by Fu-Kiau Bunseki in an interview by the author, August 2000.

14. For the term *chan-chan* in Afro-Cuban musical discourse, see *Buena Vista Social Club* (Nonesuch CD, track 1) and *Cuban Son: Rhythmic Roots of the Sala Revolution* (Regnet CD 1046, track 14).

15. Kwabena Nketia, personal conversation, Los Angeles, January 1974. For other criteria see J. H. Nketia, *Drumming in Akan Communities of Ghana* (London: Thomas Nelson & Sons, 1963), pp. 168–69.

16. Fu-Kiau Bunseki, interview by author, January 2000.

17. I thank Chris Munnelly for the concept of the rogue comma.

18. Fu-Kiau interview, January 2000.

19. Néstor Marconi, interview by author, Buenos Aires, November 1998.

20. Ventura Lynch, *Folklore bonaerense* (Folklore from the Province of Buenos Aires) (1883; reprinted Buenos Aires: Lajouane, 1953), p. 49.

21. Ibid.

22. Alicia Dujovne Ortiz, "Sebastián Piana: Tangos livianos y milongas agudas" (Sebastián Piana: Light Tangos and Sharp Milongas), *Clarín* [Buenos Aires] (February 21, 1971).

23. For more on Piana, see "Murió Sebastián Piana" (Sebastián Piana Is Dead), á *Clarín* (July 18, 1994), pp. 34–35; Susanna Azzi, "Sebastian Piana," *Viva el tango* 8 (Winter 1997), pp. 18–31; Tomas Barna, "Sebastián Piana o la pureza criolla del tango y la milonga" (Sebastián Piana or the Creole Purity of the Tango and Milonga), *Club de Tango* 27 (November–December 1997), pp. 12–17; and Jorge Gottling, *Tango: Melancólico testigo* (Tango: Melancholy Witness) (Buenos Aires: Corregidor, 1998), pp. 87–91. Piana died at the age of ninety-one on July 17, 1994.

24. Fernando D'Addario, ed., *Letras de tango* (Buenos Aires: Editoral AC, 2003), pp. 110–11. Translation mine.

25. This milonga masterpiece is found on the CD *Aníbal Troilo, Roberto Grela y su Cuarteto Típico* (RCA Victor CD 74321 24418-2, track 2).
26. Juan Carlos Copes, interview by author, Buenos Aires, November 2000.
27. María Cieri, interview by author, Buenos Aires, November 2000.
28. Esmeraldo Emeterio de Santana, "Nação Angola," in *Encontro de naçoes de candomble: Anais do encontro realizado em Salvador, 1981* (Salvador da Bahia, Brazil: Centro de Estudos Afro-Orientais, 1984), pp. 35–36.
29. Carlos Anzuate, interview by author, Buenos Aires, September 2004.
30. Ibid.
31. "Enrique," Afro-Argentine, approximately fifty years of age, quoted in Alejandro Frigerio, *Cultura negra en el cono sur: Representaciones en conflicto* (Black Culture in the Southern Cone: Representations in Conflict) (Buenos Aires: Ediciones de la Universidad Católica Argentina, 2000), p. 47.
32. Ibid., pp. 47–48.
33. Translation of *e e e mbadi lo* by Fu-Kiau Bunseki, personal communication, April 1999. Translation of *e mbadi ona* from Karl E. Laman, *Dictionnaire Ki-Kongo–Français* (Farnsborough, England: Gregg reprint, 1964) p. 2:517.
34. Fu-Kiau interview, April 1999.
35. Facundo Posadas, personal communication, November 1999.
36. Ibid.
37. Oscar del Priore and Irene Amuchástegui, *Cien tangos fundamentales* (One Hundred Fundamental Tangos) (Buenos Aires: Aguilar, 1998), p. 274. Translation mine.
38. Facundo Posadas, personal communication, November 1999.
39. Ricardo Rodríguez Molas, "Los afroargentinos y el origen del tango" (Afro-Argentines and the Origin of Tango), *Desmemoria: Revista de historia* 7, no. 27 (2000), p. 89.
40. Norma del Carmen Soto Mayano de Baña, interview by author, December 2001, Buenos Aires.
41. Luis Bruni, "El Pibe Palermo: El último compadrito" (The Palermo Kid, Last of the Hipsters), manuscript, p. 1. Shared with me by Alejandro Frigerio.
42. Ibid.
43. See also Jorge Riva, "José María Baña: El Pibe Palermo," *Tango XXI* 6, no. 14 (March 1999), pp. 27–29. Includes photographs of Pibe dancing with Rosario Blanco, Carmencita Calderón, and his present partner, Norma.
44. Facundo Posadas, interview by author, Buenos Aires, November 2000.
45. Abel Bruno Versacci, telephone interview by author, Buenos Aires, November 1998.

6. DANCING ON THE EDGE: THE EARLY TANGO CALLED CANYENGUE

1. I thank C. Daniel Dawson for bringing to my attention Teresa Pereyra's painting in Buenos Aires in June 1998.
2. Fu-Kiau Bunseki, personal communication, January 1998.
3. Marta Antón, interview by author, Buenos Aires, June 2000.
4. Ibid.
5. Jorge Novati and Inés Cuello, "Primeras noticias y documentos" in *Antología*

del tango rioplatense (Buenos Aires: Instituto Nacional de Muscología Carlos Vega, 1980), p. 1:33. The authors date the appearance of the term *tango liso* to around 1907.

6. María Cieri, interview by author, Buenos Aires, January 1999.

7. Atilio Jorge Castelpoggi, *Buenos Aires mi amante* (Buenos Aires, My Lover) (Buenos Aires: Editorial Vinceguerra, 1991), p. 15.

8. Luis Luchi, *Poemas de las calles transversales* (Poems of the Cross-Streets) (Buenos Aires: Ediciones Salamanca, 1964), p. 38.

9. María Cieri, interview by author, Buenos Aires, January 2000.

10. Marshall Stearns and Jean Stearns, *Jazz Dance: The Story of American Vernacular Dance* (New York: Da Capo, 1994), p. 15.

11. Apropos of stylistic variation in canyengue, Gabriel Angió remarks, "What happens here is so personal. Look, I don't know anyone who has performed the same canyengue in front of me. Because if you watch Rodolfo [Cieri,] he doesn't stick his tail out [the way Lampazo does]. Rodolfo bends his knees. I have never in my life seen two persons dance canyengue the same way, so that you could define it as one single style." From a conversation with Gabriel Angió, Buenos Aires, September 2001. Mingo Pugliese, in another interview in Buenos Aires, November 2002, talks about variation in canyengue form through the decades. For instance, he remembers José Méndez dancing canyengue faster than today, and without the chest-on-chest quality characterizing the Cieri/Antón style of performance.

12. Francisco Canaro, *Mis memorias: Mis bodas de oro con el tango* (My Memoirs: My Golden Anniversary with the Tango) (Buenos Aires: Corregidor, 1999), p. 72.

13. Oscar Zucchi, *El tango, el bandoneón y sus intérpretes* (The Tango, the Bandoneón and Their Interpreters) (Buenos Aires: Corregidor, 2001) p. 2:423.

14. Mingo Pugliese brought Petróleo's statement to my attention in a conversation in Buenos Aires in October 2001.

15. Rodolfo and María Cieri, conversation, Buenos Aires, January 1999.

16. Beata Gulbinowicz, "Tango y cabaret en la Varsovia de entre guerras" (Tango and Cabaret in Warsaw Between the Wars), in Ramón Pelinski, ed., *El tango nómade: Ensayos sobre la diáspora del tango* (Nomadic Tango: Essays on the Diaspora of the Tango) (Buenos Aires: Corregidor, 2000), p. 318.

17. Mónica André Ogando, "Del burdel al salón: Una mirada sobre la evolución socio-coreográfica del tango para entender porqué es baile nuestro" (From Bordello to Salon: A Glance at the Socio-choreographic Evolution of the Tango in Order to Understand Why It Is Our [National] Dance," in Pedro Ochoa, *Doce ventanas al tango* (Buenos Aires: Fundación del Libro, 2001), p. 194.

18. Luis Alposta, *Con un cacho de nada* (With a Small Piece of Nothing) (Buenos Aires: Corregidor, 2001), p. 53.

19. Oscar Natale, *Buenos Aires, negros, y tango* (Buenos Aires, Blacks, and the Tango) (Buenos Aires: Peña Lillo Editor, 1984), p. 239. Natale is aware of the sharing, in black Cuba and Argentina, of the valences "winding down" and "weary" for canyengue in the popular speech of both countries.

20. Again I thank Mingo Pugliese for sharing this statement from a rich store of documented data on Petróleo.

21. El Gallego Manolo, interview by author, Buenos Aires, February 2002.

22. Ibid.

23. Ibid.

24. Rodolfo Cieri and María Cieri, interview by author, January 1999.

25. Andrés M. Carretero, *El compadrito y el tango* (The Hipster and the Tango) (Buenos Aires: Librería Plus Ultra, 1964), pp. 46–47.

26. Manuel Galvez, *Historia del arrabal* (Story of a Neighborhood) (Buenos Aires: Centro Editor de America Latina, 1980), p. 21.

27. Felipe de la Fuente, Jr., interview by author, March 2002.

28. Felipe de la Fuente, Sr., interview by author, Buenos Aires, November 1998.

29. For a brief discussion of his work, see "Ayer y hoy según la visión artística de Felipe de la Fuente" (Yesterday and Today According to the Artistic Vision of Felipe de la Fuente), *La Nación* [Buenos Aires], April 25, 1990, p. 8. In addition, there is a rich, full-page de la Fuente painting, *Verano porteño* (Buenos Aires in the Summer), in *45 años con el tango: Oswaldo Pugliese* (Buenos Aires: Editorial Candelario, 1969), p. 22.

7. TANGO AS MUSIC

1. Jorge López Anaya, *Historia del arte argentino* (Buenos Aires: Emecé, 1997), caption for plate 30.

2. Pablo Aslán, interview by author, Brooklyn, August 2004.

3. Pablo Aslán, interview by author, February 2005.

4. As a painter with a strong social conscience, Berni often genericized the faces of workers and musicians to accentuate their presence.

5. Michael S. O'Brien, e-mail to author, June 4, 2004. I thank Michael for sharing data collected in Buenos Aires from the tango violinist Damián Boletín, who played with Agri and Suárez.

6. Henry Edward Krehbiel, *Afro-American Folksongs* (Portland, Maine: Longwood Press, 1976), p. 93.

7. Hélio Orovio, *Diccionario de la música cubana* (Dictionary of Cuban Music) (Havana: Letras Cubanas, 1981).

8. Odilio Urfé, "Music and Dance in Cuba," in Moreno Fraginals, ed., *Africa in Latin America* (New York: UNESCO, 1984), p. 176.

9. Fu-Kiau Bunseki, interview by author, January 2000.

10. Jorge Novati and Inés Cuello, "Primeras noticias y documentos," in *Antología del tango rioplatense* (Buenos Aires: Instituto Nacional de Musicología Carlos Vega, 1980), p. 1:7.

11. See Arne Birkenstock and Helena Ruegg, *Tango: Geschichte und Geschichten* (Munich: Deutscher Taschenbuch Verlag, 1999). The success of "Milonga sentimental" prompted Piana and Manzi to compose many more.

12. Osvaldo Pugliese, quoted in Arturo Marcos Lozza, *Osvaldo Pugliese: ¡Al Colón!* (Buenos Aires: Editorial Cartago, 1985), p. 66.

13. Horacio Salgán, *Curso de tango* (Buenos Aires: private publication, 2001), pp. 86–87.

14. Michael S. O'Brien, e-mail to author, June 23, 2004.

15. Personal communications from Pablo Aslán, Brooklyn, July 2004; Pablo Ziegler, Buenos Aires, May 2003; and Néstor Marconi, Buenos Aires, November 1995.

16. Aslán communication.

17. Aníbal Troilo, las grandes orquestas del tango (BMT 608, CD 1, track 17, recorded 1943).

18. Diana Piazzolla, personal communication, June 2003.

19. Fu-Kiau Bunseki, interview by author, October 2000.

20. Salgán, Curso.

21. Fu-Kiau Bunseki, interview by author, November 2000.

22. Pugliese, quoted in Marcos Lozza, Pugliese, p. 66.

23. This escondido and gato appear on Herencia nativa (Native Heritage) CD (Editorial Escolar, EE 3, 1998, tracks 7 and 18).

24. Michael S. O'Brien, e-mail to author, June 4, 2004.

25. Alejandro Molinari, Roberto L. Martínez, and Natalio P. Etchegaray, Tango y sociedad (Tango and Society) (Buenos Aires: Foro Argentino de Cultura Urbana, 2003), p. 191.

26. Juan Maglio, Tango (Bandoneón CD, EBCD 126).

27. Juan Maglio: El bandoneón de "Pacho" (Bandoneón CD EBCD 36), track 5, "Emancipación."

28. Juan María Veniard in Antología del tango rioplatense (Buenos Aires: Instituto Nacional de Musicología Carlos Vega, 1980), p. 1:134. A photograph of Pacho's quartet, dated 1912, shows Luciano Ríos standing tall among his colleagues. See Rubén Pesce, "Principales protagonistas de la guardia vieja," La historia del tango, vol. 3, La guardia vieja (Buenos Aires: Corregidor, 1977), p. 432.

29. Ibid.

30. Pintín Castellanos, Entre cortes y quebradas (Montevideo: Colombino Hermanos, 1948), pp. 53–56.

31. Ubaldo de Lío, interview by author, July 2001. Novati and Cuello, "Primeras noticias," argue that Arolas realized marcato in 1910 with a version of "El choclo" that was "ninety per cent Italian, ten per cent creole."

32. Pablo Aslán, Cabarute (Lyrichord CD 7428, July 1995), liner notes.

33. Salgán, Curso, p. 23.

34. As documented by a photograph in Francisco Canaro's autobiography, Mis bodas de oro con el tango (Buenos Aires: Corregidor, 1999), p. 52.

35. Mónica Gloria Hoss de le Comtre, The Tango (Buenos Aires: Maizal, 2000), p. 17.

36. George Reid Andrews, The Afro-Argentines of Buenos Aires, 1800–1900 (Madison: University of Wisconsin Press, 1980), p. 4.

37. Horacio Ferrer, El libro de tango: Historias e imágenes (Buenos Aires: Ediciones Ossorio-Vargas, 1970), p. 2:211.

38. Ricardo A. Ostuni, "Tangueros de sangre negra: Carlos Posadas," Club de tango, no. 12, pp. 27–29.

39. Ibid.

40. Roberto Selles, "El Tango y sus dos primeras décadas, 1880–1900" in various authors, La historia del tango, vol. 2, Primera época (Buenos Aires: Corregidor, 1993) p. 177.

41. Novati and Cuello, "Primeras noticias," p. 5, n. 23.

42. Pesce, "Principales protagonistas" p. 451.

43. Novati and Cuello, "Primeras noticias," p. 5, n. 23.

44. Viejo Tanguero, "El tango, su evolución y su historia," *Crítica*, September 22, 1913, p. 10.

45. Ibid.

46. Roberto Selles, "El Negro Casimiro: El hombre que inventó el tango," in *Buenos Aires: Tango y lo demás*, no. 23 (1979), p. 11.

47. Enrique Horacio Puccia, *El Buenos Aires de Ángel G. Villoldo* (Buenos Aires: Corregidor, 1997), pp. 96–97.

48. Oscar Zucchi, *El tango, el bandoneón y sus intérpretes* (Buenos Aires: Corregidor, 2001), p. 2:434.

49. Facundo Posadas tells us that Guillermo Barbieri's son Alfredo became a famous comic in Argentine show business. Alfredo's daughter Carmen anchors a contemporary Argentine television program. Personal communication, March 2003.

50. Pablo Aslán, interview by author, New York, July 2004.

51. Donald Castro, "The Image of the Black in Argentina," *Afro-Hispanic Review* 7, no. 1 (1988), pp. 11–17.

52. Jorge Novati and Inés Cuello in *Antología del tango rioplatense*, p. 124. According to Juan María Veniard, the distinguished tanguero Vicente Greco was taught in 1903 "by the pioneer of the bandoneón in the tango, 'El Pardo' Sebastián Mejía."

53. Zucchi, *El tango, el bandoneón*, p. 1:101.

54. Ibid., p. 2:1122.

55. Luis J. Martín, *Los cafés del Parque de los Patricios* (Buenos Aires: Interjuntas, 1994), pp. 12–13.

56. Roberto Selles, "Joaquín Mora," *Diario Crónica* [Buenos Aires], December 8, 2002. Luis Adolfo Sierra, "Joaquín Mora: Perfiles de tango," *Viva el tango* no. 6 (Summer 1997), pp. 64–75. I thank Alejandro Frigerio for these references.

57. Blas Matamoro, "Raíces negras del tango," in various authors, *La historia del tango*, vol. 1, *Sus orígenes* (Buenos Aires: Corregidor, 1976), p. 73.

58. Néstor Marconi, interview by author, Buenos Aires, January 2003.

59. Blas Matamoro, *Historia del tango* (Buenos Aires: Centro Editor de América Latina, 1971), p. 19.

60. Roberto Daus, program notes for *Roberto Firpo y su orquesta típica 1916–1918* (Bandoneón CD EBCD 135).

61. Enrique Cadícamo, *Café de camareras* (Buenos Aires: Editorial Sudamericana, 1973), p. 239. Translation mine.

62. Philippe Lesage and Paulo César de Andrade, liner notes for *Argentine vals, tango et milonga 1907–1950* (Fremaux et Associés, CD FA 5004).

63. Liner notes for *Alma de Bohemio: Roberto Firpo y su cuarteto* (Bandoneón CD EB CD 8, 1989).

64. Lesage and Andrade, *Argentine vals*.

65. S. Nicolás Lefcovich, *Estudio de la discografía de Roberto Firpo* (Buenos Aires: S. Nicolás Lefcovich, 1997), p. 670.

66. Canaro, *Mis bodas de oro*, p. 72.

67. Ibid., p. 52.

68. Ibid.
69. *Francisco Canaro y su orquesta típica, 1941–1949* (Bandoneón, EB CD 108).
70. Ignacio Varchausky, interview by author, Buenos Aires, April 2004.
71. Ibid.
72. Pablo Aslán, interview by author, New York, June 2004.
73. Varchausky interview.
74. Enrique Cadícamo and Luís Adolfo Sierra, *La historia del tango*, vol. 7, *La época decareana* (Buenos Aires: Corregidor, 1977) p. 1064.
75. Jean Pierre Estival and Michel Plisson, liner notes for *Argentine Chamamé: Musique du Paraná* (Ocora CD C560052), p. 29, and Herschel Garfein, personal communication, April 2003.
76. Such playfulness continues in the violin work of Hermes Peressini.
77. Veniard, *Antología del tango rioplatense*, p. 135.
78. Ibid.
79. Peter Fryer, *Rhythms of Resistance: African Musical Heritage in Brazil* (Hanover, N.H.: Wesleyan University Press, 2000), p. 5.
80. Manuel Román, in Javier García Méndez and Arturo Penón, *The Bandoneón: A Tango History* (London, Ont.: Nightwood Editions, 1988), p. 44: "[Bandoneones] were devoted to religious music, to arias of operas, and to ballroom dances."
81. Ignacio Varchausky, interview by author, Buenos Aires, August 2003.
82. José di Giorgio, interview by author, Buenos Aires, June 2000.
83. Birkenstock and Ruegg, in *Tango*, sum up d'Arienzo in similar terms: "fast tempo, the rhythmized parlance of his pianist, Rodolfo Biagi, and the staccato handling of melodic instruments" (p. 164).
84. Facundo Posadas, personal communication, May 2003.
85. Oscar del Priore, *El tango: De Villoldo a Piazzolla* (Buenos Aires: Ediciones Manantial, 1999), p. 143.
86. Ibid.
87. Pablo Aslán, personal communication, July 2004.
88. Del Priore, *El tango*.
89. Gabriel Angió, interview by author, Buenos Aires, August 2000.
90. Antonio Canto, "Carlos di Sarli," in various authors, *La historia del tango*, vol. 15, *Di Sarli, Vardaro, Gobbi, Goñi* (Buenos Aires: Corregidor, 1980), p. 2688.
91. Juan Carlos Copes, interview by author, Buenos Aires, June 2003.
92. Federico Monjeau, "Notas sobre tango," *La mirada* [Buenos Aires], no. 1 (1990), p. 55.
93. The story of the funeral of José Oviedo was told to me by Kely Posadas in Buenos Aires, November 1999, and by Milena Plebs in Buenos Aires, November 2004.
94. Néstor Hernández, interview by author, Buenos Aires, November 1995.
95. The Posadas-Frigerio exchange is from an interview by the author in Buenos Aires, November 1998.
96. José Gobello, *Mujeres y hombres que hicieron el tango* (Buenos Aires: Centro Editor de Cultura Argentina, 2002), pp. 65–66, 85–86.
97. Ibid., p. 68.
98. Canto, "Carlos di Sarli," p. 15:2740.
99. José di Giorgio, interview by author, Buenos Aires, November 2002.

100. Gabriel Angió, interview by author, Buenos Aires, June 2002.
101. José di Giorgio, interview by author, Buenos Aires, January 2003.
102. Ibid.
103. Di Giorgio interview, July 2003.
104. Edmundo E. Eichelbaum, foreword, *Aníbal Troilo, La historia del tango* (Buenos Aires: Corregidor, 1980), p. 16:2870.
105. Juan Carlos Copes, interview by author, November 1998.
106. Marquitos Troilo, quoted in Federico Silva, *Informe sobre Troilo* (Buenos Aires: Plus Ultra, 1978), p. 24.
107. Silva, *Informe sobre Troilo*, p. 25.
108. S. Nicolás Lefcovich, *Estudio de la discografía de Aníbal Troilo "Pichuco"* (Buenos Aires: S. Nicolás Lefcovich, 1990), p. 12.
109. Blas Matamoro, *La ciudad del tango* (Buenos Aires: Galerna, 1969), p. 183.
110. Nuevo Quinteto Real (Warner Music Argentina CD 8577385944-2, track 4).
111. Emilio Fernández Cicco, *Noticias*, March 10, 2001, p. 52; Horacio Salgán, interviews by author, Buenos Aires, August and October 2002.
112. Salgán interview, October 2002.
113. Sonia Ursini, *Horacio Salgán: La supervivencia de un artista en el tiempo* (Buenos Aires: Corregidor, 1993), p. 20,
114. Facundo Posadas, interview by the author in Buenos Aires, April 2000.
115. Luis Adolfo Sierra, *Historia de la orquesta típica* (Buenos Aires: A. Pena Lillo, 1966), summarized their work: "orchestral flights in search of harmonic substance and effects of syncopation" (p. 202).
116. Fleouter's piece in *Le Monde* is quoted on p. 12 of Julio Nudler's liner notes for Salgán's CD set, Página/12 CD 1-2-3.
117. Ursini, *Salgán*, p. 141.
118. Ibid., p. 140. Translation mine.
119. Salgán, *Curso*, p. 20.
120. Karl E. Laman, *Dictionnaire Ki-Kongo–Français*, p. 1:205.
121. In an interview with Sonia Ursini—*Horacio Salgán*, pp. 147–48—the composer makes clear his intentions (1) to enrich tango's rhythmic power and (2) to introduce the bombo as an authentic national instrument.
122. For details, see Salgán, *Curso*, p. 21.
123. Salgán, quoted in *La maga*, February 14, 1996, p. 37.
124. Alan Lomax, conversation with the author in Philadelphia, November 1970.
125. Pablo Aslán, interview by author, New York, March 2003. See also José Judkovski, *El tango: Una historia con judíos* (Buenos Aires: Fundación IWO, 1988); Julio Nudler, *Tango judío: Del ghetto a la milonga* (Buenos Aires: Editorial Sudamericana, 1998); Lloica Czackis, "Tangele: The History of Yiddish Tango," in *Jewish Quarterly* 60, no. 1 (Spring 2003), pp. 45–53.
126. Herschel Garfein, interview by author, Brooklyn, February 2003.
127. Monjeau, "Notas sobre tango," p. 55.
128. Ibid., where Monjeau says "absence of heaviness . . . defines [Salgán's] rhythm."
129. S. Nicolás Levcovitch, *Estudio de la discografía de Julio de Caro* (Buenos Aires: Nicolás Levcovitch, 1997), p. 208.
130. Horacio Salgán, interview by author, Buenos Aires, November 2000.

131. Juan Álvarez, "Orígenes de la música argentina," *Revista de derecho, historia, y letras* (1908), p. 76.

132. Pugliese, quoted in Lozza, *Osvaldo Pugliese,* p. 64.

133. Ibid., p. 66.

134. Di Giorgio interview, January 2003.

135. Beba Pugliese, interview by author, October 2002.

136. Lozza, *Osvaldo Pugliese,* p. 58; Simon Collier, liner notes for *Osvaldo Pugliese in the 1940's* (Harlequin HQ CD 159), p. 4; Beba Pugliese, interview by author, Buenos Aires, October 2002.

137. See Osvaldo Pugliese, *Recorded Live at the Teatro Colón* (EMI 7 2435 222 2732).

138. Beba Pugliese interview.

139. Nélida Rouchetto, "Osvaldo Pugliese, su trayectoria" in *La historia del tango,* p. 14:2512.

140. Beba Pugliese interview.

141. Pablo de Santis, *Rico tipo y las chicas de Divito* (Buenos Aires: Espasa Humor Gráfico, 1994), p. 71.

142. Juan Carlos Copes, interview by author, August 2002.

143. Hilda Guerra, ed., *2 × 4 = Tango* (Buenos Aires: Grupo Editor de Buenos Aires, 1980), p. 119.

144. Beba Pugliese interview.

145. Pugliese, cited in various authors, *La historia del tango,* vol. 14, *Osvaldo Pugliese* (Buenos Aires: Corregidor, 1979), p. 2512; Beba Pugliese interview.

146. The classical Ki-Kongo phrase *kalunga ngwe* was creolized in Buenos Aires into *calunga güe.* See also Laman, *Dictionnaire,* 2:1134, on the word *yimba* or *yimbila,* "to sing out." The candombe phrase *oyeye yumba* appears in an Argentine film of the 1940s, sung by Bernaldo Kondon, one of many sources Pugliese would have been aware of.

147. Fu-Kiau Bunseki, interview, October 2000.

148. Laman, *Dictionnaire,* p. 1:430; Zoe Strother, letter to author, summer 2000; Beba Pugliese interview.

149. Beba Pugliese interview.

150. Copes interview.

151. Beba Pugliese interview.

152. Myriam Copes, interview by author, Villa Sarmiento, October 2002.

153. I thank both Myriam Copes and Ignacio Varchausky for copies of the San Pugliese prayer card.

154. Listen to *Beba Pugliese en vivo en Almagro* (Melopea CD MPV 1160, 1999). As to María Carla Novelli, see "La nieta de Pugliese tocará en Japón," *Clarín,* May 9, 2003, p. 2, "Espectáculos" section.

155. Diana Piazzolla, personal communication, Buenos Aires, March 2002.

156. See Alberto Speratti's book of interviews, *Con Piazzolla* (Buenos Aires: Editorial Galerna, 1969); a biography, *Astor,* by his daughter, Diana (Buenos Aires: Emecé, 1987); more interviews in Natalio Gorín, ed., *Astor Piazzolla: A manera de memorias* (Buenos Aires: Editorial Atlántida, 1991); *Piazzolla: La música límite,* a brilliant study by Carlos Kuri (Buenos Aires: Corregidor, 1992); Oscar López Ruiz's

Piazzolla loco, loco, loco (Buenos Aires: Ediciones de la Urraca, 1994); Mitsumasa Saito, *Astor Piazzolla: El luchador del tango* (Tokyo, 1998); Juan José Canavessi, *Astor Piazzolla: Lo que su música inspira* (Buenos Aires: Vinciguerra, 2001); and the finest study to date, María Susana Azzi and Simon Collier, *Le Gran Tango: The Life and Music of Astor Piazzolla* (New York: Oxford, 2000).

157. Diego Urcola (Argentine musician), in conversation with Maxine Gordon, New York, February 2003.

158. As a memento of this experience, Dizzy Gillespie later recorded a jazz piece called "Tangorine." See Gillespie, *To Be or Not to Bop* (Garden City, N.Y.: Doubleday, 1979).

159. Dominic Frasca, "The Influence of Jazz in Astor Piazzolla's Music," unpublished ms. (1991), p. 1. Thanks to Frank Tirro for bringing this gem to my attention.

160. See Kuri, *Piazzolla: La música límite*, p. 186.

161. The drawing is now in the possession of Astor's son, Daniel.

162. Diana Piazzolla, interview by author, Buenos Aires, March 2003.

163. There are many versions of this meeting. See, for example, Oscar López Ruiz, *Piazzolla loco,* where he claims that the apartment belonged to none other than the great cultural icon, the editor of *Sur*, Victoria Ocampo (p. 25).

164. For a brief note on Alberto Ginastera, see Vicente Gesualdo, *Breve historia de la música en la Argentina* (Buenos Aires: Claridad, 1998), pp. 354–55.

165. Azzi and Collier, *Le Gran Tango*, p. 32.

166. Carter Harman, *A Popular History of Music* (New York: Dell, 1956), p. 257.

167. Azzi and Collier, *Le Gran Tango*, p. 37.

168. Ibid., pp. 49–51.

169. Frasca, "Influence of Jazz," citing Piazzolla in an interview with Michael North, "The Tango Destroyer," *L.A. Weekly,* May 1, 1989.

170. Astor Piazzolla, quoted in Kuri, *Piazzolla: La música límite*, p. 61.

171. Liner notes, *Astor Piazzolla: Octeto Buenos Aires* (ANS CD 15276).

172. Azzi and Collier, *Le Gran Tango*, p. 120.

173. Paul Griffiths, liner notes for *Bartók: Divertimento. Dance Suite* (Grammophon CD 445 835-2, 1995), p. 1.

174. Herschel Garfein, interview by author, Brooklyn, April 2003.

175. Frasca, "Influence of Jazz," p. 5.

176. Ibid., p. 6.

177. Ibid., pp. 6 and 7.

178. See Ben Ratliff, "A Musical Dispute of the 60's," *New York Times,* February 15, 2003, p. B16.

179. Pablo Aslán, personal communication, July 2004.

180. Astor Piazzolla, in Gorin, ed., *Astor Piazzolla: A manera de memorias,* p. 39.

181. I thank Alicia Jamieson Churchill for enlightening me on this matter, March 11, 2003.

182. Diana Piazzolla, interview by author, Buenos Aires, March 2002.

183. Ibid.

184. Pablo Ziegler, personal communication, Buenos Aires, May 31, 2003.

185. Pablo Ziegler, interview by author, New York, May 2003.

186. Ibid.

187. Larry Rohter, "Tango Is In Again," *New York Times,* March 8, 2003, p. B21.

188. Ziegler interview.

189. Ignacio Varchausky, personal communication, March 15, 2004.

190. *Canaro* (Bandoneón EBCD 129). I thank Pablo Aslán for bringing this important CD to my attention.

191. Ferrer, *El libro de tango,* p. 3:894 (Ríos) and p. 3:1027 (Thompson).

192. Lisa Lekis, *Folk Dances of Latin America* (New York: Scarecrow Press, 1958), p. 172.

193. Luis Rodríguez Abella, "El tango argentino: Sus comienzos y su evolución," *Club de tango* no. 46 (January–February 2001), pp. 46–47.

194. Ben Ratliff, conversation with author, New York, May 2001.

195. Ben Ratliff, "Lincoln Center Jazz Orchestra Looks to Link Jazz and Tango," *New York Times on the Web,* May 15, 2001, p. 2.

196. Gabriel Plaza, "Marsalis descubrió que ama el tango," *La Nación,* May 6, 2001, sec. 4, p. 5.

8. TANGO AS DANCE

1. Simarra's "gaucho" gear is amazing: note the enormous spurs (they can't be dancing—she might get hurt) and transparent cloth with rich floral appliqué. Such spurs apparently derive from Arabized Spain. See Luisa J. Cossi, *Danzas de estrado, bailecitos de tierra y atuendos del gaucho y la paisana* (Buenos Aires: Centro de Estudios Internacionales, 2001), p. 30.

2. Gabriel Angió, interview by author, Buenos Aires, January 2000.

3. This is my theory.

4. See "The Dance of the Closing of Lorea Market, 1909," in Margarita Gutman, ed., *Buenos Aires 1910: Memoria del porvenir* (Buenos Aires: Artes Gráficas Corin Luna, 1999), p. 161. See also the two male dancers tangoing their way down a street in La Boca in 1926, heads facing forward, leader's left hand and follower's right hand in front, in Simon Collier et al., *Tango* (New York: Thames and Hudson, 1995), p. 118.

5. Mingo and Ester Pugliese, interview by author, Buenos Aires, June 2003.

6. See Horacio A. Ferrer, *El tango: Su historia y evolución* (Buenos Aires: A. Peña Lillo, 1960), p. 13.

7. Another observer praised Agbeke for the "correct freezing of her glance." See Robert Farris Thompson, *African Art in Motion* (Los Angeles: University of California Press, 1974), pp. 260 and 259.

8. Original text in Ki-Kongo given by Fu-Kiau Bunseki in an interview on October 2003: "*N'kini kazibulanga n'nwa mu moka bu kena va mbasi a makinu ko. Kadi kasidi mu nitu ko. Fwiti dimba mu mayembo ma kimpeeve.*"

9. Jorge Novati and Inés Cuello in *Antología del tango rioplatense* (Buenos Aires: Instituto Nacional de Musicología Carlos Vega, 1980) pp. 1:7–8.

10. Ibid.

11. Gabriel Angió, interview by author, New Haven, Conn., October 2003.

12. José Gobello, *Breve historia crítica del tango* (Buenos Aires: Corregidor, 1999), p. 16.

13. Domingo F. Casadevall, *Buenos Aires. Arrabal. Sainete. Tango* (Buenos Aires: Compañía General Fabril, 1968), p. 22.
14. See José Hernández et al., *La pampa* (Buenos Aires: Emecé, 1946), photograph facing p. 77.
15. For more on gaucho athleticism, see Benjamin D. Martínez, *Folklore litoral* (Buenos Aires: J. Lajouane & Co., 1924), p. 109ff.
16. Sally Sommer, interview by author, July 2003.
17. See Charles and Angeliki Keil, *Polka Happiness* (Philadelphia: Temple University Press, 1992), p. 10.
18. Ibid., p. 9.
19. See Hector Arico, *Danzas tradicionales argentinas* (Buenos Aires: Talleres Gráfico Vilko, 2002), p. 116, and Rubén Pérez Bugallo, *El chamamé* (Buenos Aires: Ediciones del Sol, 1996), p. 226.
20. Pablo Ziegler, interview by author, Buenos Aires, May 30, 2003.
21. Ricardo Visconti Vallejos, *Historia del chamamé* (Buenos Aires: Corregidor, 1990), p. 146.
22. Bugallo, *El chamamé*, p. 227.
23. Quoted in Ricardo Ostuni, *Viaje al corazón del tango* (Buenos Aires: Ediciones Lumière, 2000), p. 20.
24. See Peter Fryer, *Rhythms of Resistance* (Hanover, N.H.: Wesleyan University Press, 2000), p. 154.
25. See Jorge Miguel Couselo, "El tango en el cine," in *Buenos Aires tango: Revista bimestral* no. 1 (1970), p. 19.
26. PBT stands for *pebete*, "a kind of bread" and also "a young guy."
27. See Keita Fodeba, *Les hommes de la danse* (Lausanne: Éditions Clairefontaine, 1954), p. 78.
28. Nicole Nau-Klapwijk, *Tango: Un baile bien porteño* (Buenos Aires: Corregidor, 2000), p. 48.
29. Antonio Pau, *Música y poesía del tango* (Buenos Aires: Editorial Trotta, 2001), p. 39.
30. Nau-Klapwijk, *Tango*.
31. There were doubtless more women dancing at this time.
32. Ricardo García Blaya, quoted in "The History of the Tango," *Economist*, December 22, 2001–January 4, 2002, p. 38.
33. Pau, *Música y poesía del tango*, p. 40.
34. My first introduction to all this was a long conversation with the distinguished Rio ethnomusicologist Luis Heitor Correa de Azevedo in Paris in March 1958. He was the first to point out to me how polka lay behind the rise of both maxixe and tango.
35. José le Pera, *Carlos Gardel: Sus amigos. Su última gira* (Buenos Aires: Corregidor, 1991), p. 98.
36. Pau, *Música y poesía del tango*, p. 40.
37. Ibid.
38. See Oscar del Priore, *El tango de Villoldo a Piazzolla* (Buenos Aires: Crisis, 1975), p. 19, on "the oldest figures." On "marking" the ocho and the presence of corridas and lustradas in the earliest tangos, see Enrique Cadícamo, *Café de camareras*

(Buenos Aires: Editorial Sudamericana, 1973), pp. 46 and 160. Arrastradas and balanceos are mentioned in Sergio Pujol, *Historia del baile: De la milonga a la disco* (Buenos Aires: Emecé, 1999), p. 28.

39. This step adds mime to the "get-down" position of canyengue.

40. El Profesor Silva, *El arte de aprender a bailar* (Buenos Aires: 1930), p. 16.

41. Nau-Klapwijk, *Tango*, p. 218.

42. Mingo Pugliese, interview by author, Buenos Aires, January 2001.

43. Eddie Palmieri, conversation with author, New Haven, Conn., April 2002.

44. Mingo Pugliese, interview by author, Buenos Aires. June 2002.

45. Natalia Games, interview by author, Buenos Aires, July 2003.

46. Le Pera, *Carlos Gardel*, p. 100. The artist's name is given with variations: "Arturo de Nava" in certain citations, but "Navas" in the libretto to the play, *Justicia criolla*, in which he appeared. I settle on "Arturo de Navas" as an arbitrary midpoint in the range of the name-changing. See José Gobello, *Mujeres y hombres que hicieron el tango* (Buenos Aires: Centro Editor de Cultura Argentina, 2002), p. 61.

47. Le Pera, *Carlos Gardel.*

48. Ibid.

49. *Caras y caretas,* February 7, 1903.

50. I thank Juan Carlos Copes for this observation, which was independently voiced by Gabriel Angió.

51. Nau-Klapwijk, *Tango*, p. 219.

52. See Karl E. Laman, *Dictionnaire Ki-Kongo–Français: betama,* "to bend low," "get down" "to crouch ready for battle" (p. 1:33) and *bindakana,* "that which is is crossed or enlaced," (p. 2:41).

53. Fu-Kiau Bunseki, interviews by author, July 2001 and October 2003.

54. The smartness of the dancing reminds Mingo Pugliese of the style of the great tango dancer Vasco Aín, who was active at this time.

55. Gabriel Angió, interview by author, August 3, 2003.

56. Milena Plebs, interview by author, Buenos Aires, April 2004.

57. Nicolas Slonimsky, *Music of Latin America* (New York: Thomas Y. Crowell, 1945), p. 114.

58. See Juan Averna, *Los olvidados bailarines de tango* (Buenos Aires: Printex, 2001), pp. 33, 38.

59. Oneyda Alvarenga, *Música popular brasileña* (Mexico City: Fondo de Cultura Económica, 1947), p. 239.

60. Zeca Ligiero, interview by author, New Haven, Conn., September 2001.

61. Anne Bernays and Justin Kaplan, *Back Then: Two Lives in 1950's New York* (New York: William Morrow, 2002), p. 69.

62. Estela Canto, cited in various authors, *La historia del tango,* vol. 2, *Primera época* (Buenos Aires: Corregidor; 1977), p. 272.

63. Nardo Zalko, *Paris/Buenos Aires: Un siglo de tango* (Buenos Aires: Corregidor, 2001), p. 62.

64. Sem, *Les possédées* (April 1912; Buenos Aires: Academia Porteña del Lunfardo, 1997), p. 29.

65. Marjorie Howard, quoted in Jody Blake, *Le tumulte noir* (University Park: Pennsylvania State University Press, 1999), p. 46.

66. See Luis Aliposta, *El tango en Japón* (Buenos Aires: Corregidor, 1987), pp. 31–44.
67. See Mingo Pugliese, *Boletín de tango* no. 14 (pp. 5–6), 1998.
68. Quoted in Pujol, *Historia del baile*, p. 71.
69. Ibid.
70. Nau-Klapwijk, *Tango*, p. 115.
71. Francisco García Jiménez, *Estampas de tango* (Buenos Aires: 1968).
72. See Roberto L. Martínez et al., *De la vigüela al fueye* (Buenos Aires: Corregidor, 2000), p. 169.
73. *Tapadas* are tango equivalents of the "carving contests" of jazz.
74. Irene Amuchástegui, "El Cachafaz fue, lejos, el más grande de todos," *Clarín*, July 2, 1997, "Espectáculos" sec., p. 20. Compare Pujol, *Historia del baile*, p. 172, who describes Cachafaz as "half-tough guy, half-aristocrat" (*medio compadrito, medio aristócrata*).
75. Amuchástegui, "El Chachafaz."
76. Le Pera, *Carlos Gardel*, p. 98.
77. Pujol, *Historia del baile*, facing p. 160.
78. According to Eduardo Arquimbaud, Calderón's father was a dancer and lifted his hand the same way. He may be a source for the "look." Interview by author, Buenos Aires, August 2003.
79. Pujol takes note of this signature: "his characteristic way of taking the woman's right hand by the end of her fingers." See *Historia del baile*, p. 174.
80. María Nieves Rego, interview by author, Belgrano, August 2003.
81. See Sally Banes, *Terpsichore in Sneakers: Post-Modern Dance* (Hanover, N.H.: Wesleyan University Press, 1987), p. xiii.
82. Juan Carlos Copes, interview by author, Buenos Aires, August 2003.
83. Juan Carlos Copes, interview by author, New York, winter 2001.
84. Mingo Pugliese, "Geschichte und Aktualität des Tangotanzes [History and Actuality of Tango Dances]: An Encounter with Mingo Pugliese," interview by Anne Hess, part 2: *Boletín del tango*, no. 16 (1998), p. 12.
85. Alejandro Frigerio, sharing a story told by Palermo, his grandmother's former suitor.
86. El Vasco Aín, quoted in Manuel Castello, *Los bailes de pareja* (Palma de Mallorca: Olaneta, 1997), p. 86.
87. Nicanor Lima, *El tango argentino de salón: Método de baile teórico y práctico* (Buenos Aires, 1916).
88. I watched Miguel Ángel Zotto dance canyengue in the apartment of Kely and Facundo Posadas in Buenos Aires in 2001.
89. I am grateful to Mingo Pugliese for this photograph and its tentative dating.
90. Petróleo, cited in the tango website of Gabriel Angió, Buenos Aires, 2002.
91. Mingo Pugliese, interview by author, Buenos Aires, June 2003.
92. Mingo Pugliese, "Geschichte und Aktualität," p. 12.
93. Sally Sommer, conversation with author, November 11, 2003.
94. María Susana Azzi, *Antropología del tango* (Buenos Aires: Ediciones de Olavarría, 1991), p. 41.
95. Mingo Pugliese, "The Mingo Pugliese Chronicles," *Planet Tango* website, 1999, p. 1.
96. Azzi, *Antropología del tango*, pp. 40–41.

97. Ibid.
98. I thank Mingo Pugliese for bringing these films to my attention and for many details in the life history of José Méndez.
99. Averna, *Los olvidados bailarines de tango*, p. 39.
100. Pugliese, "Mingo Pugliese Chronicles," 1997, p. 1.
101. Pugliese, "Geschichte und Aktualität," pp. 6–7.
102. Eduardo Aruimbaud, interview by author, Buenos Aires, June 2002.
103. See also Pujol, *Historia del baile*, pp. 195–96: "Different dancers were gradually changing the code. Thus just as José Orradre is recognized as the first man to transform the opening move of the woman with a backward cross-step, so Petróleo invents the *giro enroscado*, an elegant spin inspired by ballet."
104. Lili Palmer, "Petróleo: The Great Innovator of the 1940's," 2002 website, p. 1.
105. Petróleo, cited in the tango website of Gabriel Angió, Buenos Aires, 2001.
106. "Palabra de Tango: Mingo Pugliese," *Cabal*, Buenos Aires, July–August 2001, p. 22.
107. Ernesto Lopardo, interview by author, Buenos Aires, June 2004.
108. Mingo Pugliese, as recalled in a conversation in Buenos Aires with the author, January 2001, but stated earlier in his conversation with Anne Hess in Buenos Aires in 1998.
109. Mingo Pugliese, "Geschichle und Aktualität des Tangotanzes," interview by Anne Hess, part 3, *Boletín del tango* no. 21 (1998), p. 14, and part 1, *Boletín del tango* no. 14 (1998), p. 11.
110. Atilio de Guillé died in 2001.
111. Betti Pizarro died in 2002.
112. See Ángel Battelini, *A los amigos milongueros* (Buenos Aires: Printex, 1995), pp. 27, 52–53, 64, 82–83.
113. Carlos Anzuate, interview by author, Buenos Aires, August 2003.
114. Roberto Tonet, interview by author, Buenos Aires, June 2000.
115. Lampazo, interview by author, Buenos Aires, November 1995. Mingo Pugliese also believes Arturito invented milonga traspié.
116. Mingo Pugliese, conversation with author, Buenos Aires, June 2002.
117. Averna, *Los olvidados bailarines de tango*, p. 43.
118. The phrase "language of rotation" was coined by Sally Potter in *The Tango Lesson* (London: Faber and Faber, 1997), p. 17.
119. Gabriel Angió, interview by author, Buenos Aires, August 2003.
120. Nau-Klapwijk, *Tango*, p. 50.
121. Averna, *Los olvidados bailarines de tango*, p. 31.
122. Ester Pugliese, interview by author, Buenos Aires, June 2002.
123. Juan Carlos Liberti, interview by author, Buenos Aires, September 2003.
124. Mingo Pugliese, interview by author, Buenos Aires, December 2003.
125. Fernando Noy, "La esencia del tango en un sólo cuerpo," *El pianota urbano* 108 (February 2001), p. 1.
126. See Juan Carlos Copes, "Confesiones del último malevo," *Gente*, October 26, 1995, p. 98.
127. Ibid.
128. Juan Carlos Copes, interview by author, Buenos Aires, April 2002. See also Mariano del Mazo, *Juan Carlos Copes* (Buenos Aires: Corregidor, 2001), p. 33.

129. Mingo Pugliese, interview by author, Buenos Aires, June 2003.
130. Juan Carlos Copes, interview by author, Buenos Aires, August 2003; Carlos Anzuate, interview by author, Buenos Aires, August 22, 2003; Del Mazo, *Juan Carlos Copes*, p. 42.
131. María Nieves, interview by author, Buenos Aires, August 2003.
132. Ibid.
133. Del Mazo, *Juan Carlos Copes*, p. 48.
134. Dena Kleiman, "It Takes Two Who Tango," *New York Times*, October 8, 1985.
135. Nieves interview.
136. Nieves, quoted by Jane Boutwell in "The Tango," *New Yorker*, October 28, 1985.
137. Copes interview, August 2003.
138. Copes, quoted in Boutwell, "Tango."
139. See del Mazo, Juan Carlos Copes, p. 57.
140. Copes, quoted in Boutwell, "Tango."
141. Copes interview, January 2002.
142. *Milonga* (Patty Records LP P-102, 1960).
143. *Copes* is pronounced "cope-is."
144. They actually tried the stunt earlier, at the Club Flamboyán, Puerto Rico, in 1959, where the table slowly collapsed as they danced. The management loved it, thinking the accident was part of the show. Nieves interview.
145. Nieves interview.
146. Robert Duvall, interview by author, Buenos Aires, June 1998.
147. Sally Sommer, interview by author, New York City, June 2000.
148. Kleiman, "It Takes Two."
149. John Simon, "Theater: Tango Argentino," *New York*, October 28, 1985, p. 98.
150. Tobi Tobias, "Some Like It Hot," *New York*, October 28, 1985, p. 54.
151. Luis Nordan, "Buenos Aires," *New York Times*, June 15, 2003, p. 31.
152. Copes interview, June 2003.
153. Boutwell, "Tango."
154. *Ballet News* 7, no. 7 (January 1986), p. 14.
155. Boutwell, "Tango."
156. Anna Kisselgoff, "The Tango Whirls with Passion," *New York Times*, October 20, 1985.
157. Averna, *Los olvidados bailarines de tango*, p. 33.
158. Jennifer Dunning, "Stage: Tango Argentino at the Mark Hellinger," *New York Times*, October 10, 1985.
159. Del Mazo, *Juan Carlos Copes*, pp. 110–20.
160. William A. Raidy, "Tango Argentino exhilarates aficionados," *Newark Star-Ledger*, October 10, 1985, p. 80.
161. Dunning, "Tango Argentino."
162. Ibid.
163. For a rebuttal of all this, see Lucía Dominga Molina and Mario Luis López, "Afro-Argentinians: 'Forgotten' and 'Disappeared'—Yet Still Present," in Sheila S. Walker, ed., *African Roots/American Cultures* (London: Rowman & Littlefield, 2001), pp. 332–47.
164. Averna, *Los olvidados bailarines de tango*, pp. 48–50.
165. Ibid.

166. Black dancers at Sin Rumbo were glossed by Margarita de Guillé, in interview by author, Buenos Aires, December 30, 2003. For photographs of Betti Pizarro, Atilio and Margarita de Guillé, Kely and Facundo Posadas, et al., in action, see Battelini, *A los amigos milongueros*.

167. As to the contribution of compadritos of color, see Alfredo Luis Sancini, *El tango en los barrios del sur* (Buenos Aires: Fundación del Libertador, 1997), p. 7.

168. See John M. Chernoff, *Hustling Is Not Stealing: Stories of an African Bar Girl* (Chicago: University of Chicago Press, 2003), p 43. Chernoff talks about the will of the people to be true to themselves.

169. Natalia Games, interview by author, Buenos Aires, December 2003.

170. Ezequiel Martínez Estrada, *Radiografía de la pampa* (Buenos Aires: Editorial Losada, 1942), p. 220.

171. Compare the Kongo saying: "The dancing court is not a spot for speaking with someone—that is taboo" [*mbasi makinu ka bendo kia mokisa ko—kiina*]. Fu-Kiau Bunseki, interview by author, January 2004.

172. Andrews, *Afro-Argentines*, p. 163.

173. Fu-Kiau Bunseki, conversation with author, January 2004.

174. Ibid.

175. See María del Carmen Silingo, *Tango-danza tradicional, método: Curso de primer nivel* (Buenos Aires: Editorial Plus Ultra, 1995), where she defines the use of the hand as "the call of the dancer to his partner at the beginning of each movement" (p. 8).

176. Carmencita Calderón, interview by author, Buenos Aires, April 2004.

177. Author interviews with Juan Carlos Copes, March 2004, and with Carmencita Calderón, April 2004, both in Buenos Aires.

178. Mauricio Castro, *Tango: The Structure of the Dance* (Buenos Aires: Cesarini Hermanos Editores, 2000), p. 21. See also Nau-Kapwijk, *Tango*, p. 190.

179. Gabriel Angió, interview by author, Buenos Aires, April 2004.

180. Gabriel Angió, interview by author, Buenos Aires, December 2003.

181. Dena Epstein, *Sinful Tunes and Spirituals: Black Folk Music to the Civil War* (Urbana: University of Illinois Press, 1977), p. 43.

182. Gabriel Angió, interview by author, Buenos Aires, March 2004.

183. Nau-Klapwijk, *Tango*, p. 218.

184. Juan Carlos Copes, interview by author, Buenos Aires, March 2004.

185. Natalia Games, interview by author, Buenos Aires, August 2003.

186. Fu-Kiau Bunseki, interview by author, January 2004.

187. Felipe García Villamil, interview by author, Los Angeles, June 1999.

188. Juan Batalla, interview by author, Buenos Aires, April 2004.

189. Eduardo P. Archetti, *Masculinities: Football, Polo, and the Tango in Argentina* (New York: Oxford University Press, 1999), pp. 63 and 67.

190. Mingo Pugliese, interview by author, Buenos Aires, December 2003.

191. Copes interview.

192. See Castro, *Structure of the Dance*, pp. 37–40, for more on turns (*giros*).

193. Robert Farris Thompson, *When Saints Go Marching In: Kongo Louisiana, Kongo New Orleans* (forthcoming in 2005).

194. Angió interview, April 2004.

195. Archetti, *Masculinities,* pp. 58–59.
196. Silingo, *Tango-danza,* p. 46.
197. Ibid., pp. 45–46.
198. Angió interview, December 2003.
199. Silingo, *Tango-danza,* p. 40.

ENVOI: *EL TANGO* BY ROBERT COLESCOTT

1. David A. Jasen and Gene Jones, *Black Bottom Stomp* (New York: Routledge, 2002), pp. 72 and 102.
2. In an interview at the home of the painter in Tucson, Arizona, on March 31, 2002, Robert Colescott generously identified all the figures in the painting and talked about what they meant or suggested.
3. Ibid.
4. Long-distance interview with Robert Colescott, January 24, 2005.
5. Alejandro Frigerio, *"Negros" y "blancos" en Buenos Aires: Representando nuestras categorías* ("Blacks" and "Whites" in Buenos Aires: A Study of Our [Racial] Categories). Lecture given at the conference "Black Buenos Aires: Memories, Representations, and Customs of the Afro Community" in the Centro de Museos de Buenos Aires, November 14–15 2002, pp. 2–3.
6. Ibid., p. 3.
7. From the author's own notes.
8. Colescott, long-distance interview.

ACKNOWLEDGMENTS

Acknowledgments begin with Erroll McDonald, my editor at Pantheon. Erroll spotted this book, trapped in another volume, endlessly in progress. He made a suggestion. This book resulted.

My strongest intellectual debt is to Alejandro Frigerio, a leading scholar of the Afro-Argentine experience and a peerless colleague. Alejandro led me to Sin Rumbo, Sunderland, Almagro, and other milongas, as the ballrooms of the tango world are called (not to be confused with milonga, the name of a dance). Thanks to his hospitality and that of his wife, María Julia Carozzi, herself an accomplished scholar of tango and a charming intellectual who knows how to laugh, I heard Goyeneche sing tango. I watched Ricardo and Nicole Nau-Klapwijk fierily dance it, the same night at Café Homero in June 1990. As the nineties continued, I kept going back to Buenos Aires, year after year, hopelessly in love with the tango, prime emblem of the culture of the capital. Alejandro was always there for me, glossing key terms, suggesting new milongas, writing into my notebook terms and observations.

We worked together taping the interviews with tangueros and milongueros that form the backbone of this book. It was a pleasurable collaboration, deepened by the frequent presence of María and their enchanting daughter, Rocío.

In Montevideo, in January 1997, Beatriz Santos took me with her to view candombe-drumming comparsa groups parading down Calle Isla de Flores, in the Barrio Sur, the Harlem of the city. Later, at home, her husband played guitar to illustrate points about tango. Rubén Galloza, the late painter laureate of the Barrio Sur, shared many insights. Galloza knew why Pedro Figari, famed Uruguayan painter, was able to document black gestures so accurately, and he shared this intelligence with me.

The first tanguero in Buenos Aires who became my friend was the late and great Lampazo. He introduced me to Portalea, a magnificent stylist of the tango dance floor.

Lampazo also made certain that I met Gabriel Angió—"*ese pibe es maravilloso, tenés que conocerlo*" (that guy's incredible—you've got to know him)—and his brilliant partner, Natalia Games. Through Lampazo I also met Margarita de Guillé and Facundo and Kely Posadas, leading dancers of tango and milonga. The Posadases, in turn, made sure I met—and saw in action—María and Rodolfo Cieri, key dancers of tango-canyengue, and introduced me to a black star of tango, Carlos Anzuate, whose milonga dancing is nonpareil. Anzuate, in turn, made sure that I met the surviving half-brother of one of the greatest black tango dancers of the century, Félix Luján, better known as El Negro Lavandina. Kely and Facundo arranged for my first meeting with the star of *Tango x 2*, Miguel Ángel Zotto. Finally, Kely and Facundo led me to the famous Casa Suiza basement, where as late as the 1970s candombe was danced after midnight by Buenos Aires blacks. Equally memorable were evenings with Mingo and Ester Pugliese and El Pibe Palermo. Mingo danced out his points about history and nuance in the restaurant of the Guido Palace Hotel, as buses whizzed by outside and clients looked on in awe. Pibe on two occasions danced out *his* arguments right in the middle of the Hereford restaurant (now closed) on Calle Presidente Ortiz.

I treasure the night I finally met the premier dancer of the tango, Juan Carlos Copes, and his charming wife, Myriam. He confirmed the presence of black candombe elements in the dance called milonga and demonstrated, curling right foot over left ankle, how one might dance to melody, as opposed to rhythm, in the tango. Myriam opened up Juan Carlos's well-organized archive to me. María Nieves, Copes's fabulous former partner, spent hours with me patiently outlining her life and art from the 1940s to now. Equally delightful to interview was Milena Plebs, surely one of the most elegant of the women of tango.

The late Antonio Agri shared his rich knowledge of the tango violin. Néstor Marconi found time between concerts to teach me the lore of bandoneón and to write, in musical notation, points about phrasing in my notebook. He was a window into composition and melody, especially when he talked about milonga. I learned a lot about modern tango piano in two conversations with Pablo Ziegler and specifics about music structure and the history of tango music in six sessions with Pablo Aslán, a leading tango musician and composer of New York.

Adolfo Nanclares, who was then working for President Raúl Alfonsín, gave me in 1988 a copy of Hermenegildo Sábat's print *The Endless Tango* (1987). That gift triggered another passion, the study of Argentine art about tango. I started interviewing porteño painters who turned out to be *macanudos* (great guys). Sábat, again and again, shared books, paintings, family, and lore. Rafael de la Fuente explained his take on tango hipsters and where he had hung out in his youth. Guillermo Kuitca posed for my camera to show how he dipped first one bare foot, then the other, into gleaming black acrylic, to tango his way across the canvas. My understanding was deepened by conversation with the tango surrealist Juan Carlos Liberti and two remarkable artists named Juan Batalla and Dany Barreto. The latter two friends personally guided me through a medley of altars to Gauchito Gil, a popular saint linked to candombe black dance, in the province of Corrientes in the winter of 2003.

The surest translator of tango into visual art is Sábat. Filmmakers and city planners turn to him as an authority. His book on the tango is a classic in the field. His tango mural in a downtown Buenos Aires subway station is a national landmark.

Many of these pages were prepared in Buenos Aires, where Claudia Manieri, of the Guido Palace Hotel, ministered to the needs of a restless writer. Paul Verhoeven generously found time in a busy film schedule to set me straight on the tango in his classic film, *Soldier of Orange*. Robert Duvall, the movie actor, speaking fluent Spanish, talked about his relation to tango in the Hereford Restaurant in Buenos Aires. John Szwed and Frank Tirro listened to jazz-tango mixtures in the work of Piazzolla, sharing their insights as historians of jazz. So did Herschel Garfein, a brilliant young composer, who talked about structure in payada, habanera, milonga, and tango. Sasha Mandl, a world-class violinist, pored over works by key tango composers and talked about quality and impact. Pablo Aslán read my chapter on tango music two times and made many useful criticisms, as did Michael O'Brien in Buenos Aires.

Zoe Strother dipped into her incomparable field knowledge of Pende culture and came up with cognates for Kongo dance terms with a bearing on the earliest days of black tango. Wyatt MacGaffey patiently sat down in Louisville and read and critiqued vernacular citations in the section on Kongo classical dance. So did John Janzen in Kansas. I thank them both.

When I wrote all this up in New Haven, Junellen Sullivan, then my administrative assistant, and Karen McGovern, my present assistant, played Saint George to the dragons of interruption, staying fax, phone, and e-mail interruptions. So did Trish Cawley. John Loge helped make my computer do what it was supposed to do.

My son, Clark, generously edited every chapter and every verse. His wife, Laura Watt, was there for me too, critiquing paintings of tango, sharing the insights of a gifted young painter. Laura's enthusiasm for the paintings of Pedro Figari reaffirmed mine. My daughter, Alicia, and her husband, Ian, also looked at paintings and made me see more. Ian's shot of Carlos Páez Vilaró's giant mural, *Gardel,* on Avenida Libertador in Buenos Aires, became my favorite photograph of the city. My daughter was invaluable to me on two field trips to Buenos Aires. And Caitlin, Alicia and Ian's daughter—my granddaughter—took lessons from Lampazo in Villa Urquiza. She pridefully diagrammed, into my notebook, how the move called the ocho unfolds in pivots. She does it better than Madonna.

Lyneise Williams found, time and again, obscure articles about black Montevideo and the early days of tango. David Doris brought in, with matching *simpatía,* numerous recondite texts hidden from my notice. Bárbaro Ruiz Martínez checked Afro-Cuban usages of the term *canyengue* and shared what he learned. Janet Stanley of the National Museum of African Art activated her biblio-computer on my behalf. So did John Gray, the prince of Afro-Atlantic historiography.

Sally Sommer, a brilliant colleague in jazz dance aesthetics, glossed videos and paintings of tango dancers and made them light up, finding patterns within patterns. I remember a similarly intense evening in New York, when Juan Carlos Copes talked about milonga almost until dawn, even though he had performed earlier that evening on the stage of the George Gershwin Theatre.

Fu-Kiau Bunseki Lumanisa, Samba Jean, and Balu Balila were doctors to the sections on the Kongo roots of tango, milonga, and candombe. So was Felipe García Villamil, a leading priest of the Kongo religion in Cuba, now practicing in Los Angeles, California. C. Daniel Dawson was a prince in the night on the phone. He listened patiently to pages-in-preparation, always helping to clear the diction.

I salute tango scholars, whose works ground my own. I learned about tango from a woman's point of view while reading Julie Taylor's *Paper Tangos* and María Savigliano's *Tango and the Political Economy of Passion* and *Angora Matta: A Tango Opera.* Savigliano is an Argentine scholar who lives and works in the U.S. I was comparably instructed in tango machismo by Eduardo Archetti's *Masculinities: Football, Polo, and the Tango in Argentina.* Then there is the late Simon Collier's indispensable *The Life, Music, and Times of Carlos Gardel,* María Susana Azzi's classic *Antropología del tango,* and the superb collaboration of Azzi with Collier, *Le Gran Tango: The Life and Music of Astor Piazzolla.*

There are books on jazz and the blues, but nothing compares with the passion and precision that Argentine and Uruguayan scholars devote to writing about tango. Classics in this field are many, but especially inspiring were Oscar del Priore's *El tango: De Villoldo a Piazzolla y después;* Tomás de Lara and Inés Leonilda Roncetti de Panti's, *El tema del tango en la literatura argentina;* Sergio Pujol's *Jazz al sur* and *Historia del baile;* Alejandro Frigerio's *Cultura negra en el cono sur;* and Vicente Rossi's *Cosas de negros.* We add to that list an important work by American scholar George Reid Andrews, *The Afro-Argentines of Buenos Aires 1800–1900.* Finally, I am specially indebted to key works by Argentine experts on tango: Carlos Vega, Horacio Salas, José Gobello, Jorge Novati and Inés Cuello, Estela dos Santos, and Horacio Ferrer.

Parts of these chapters were written on the tables of Jean-Michel Gamme and Jean-Pierre Vuillermet's Union League Cafe in New Haven. I was equally welcome to write at Caffe Adulis, where the three Eritrean brother-owners—Sahle, Ficre, and Gideon Ghebreyesus—even went so far as to twist dials to cast extra light on my table. Similar courtesies were extended by Jeff Horton at Scoozie's Restaurant and John Clark at Zinc. All of these restaurants are in New Haven.

Chris Munnelly backed this whole project since 1995. He generously found time to help out on field trips to Punta del Este, in Uruguay; Trinidad, in Paraguay; and Villa Urquiza in Buenos Aires. I thank him for spectacular colleagueship.

Finally, I thank the tangueros and milongueros who patiently sat down for long interviews about the meaning and aesthetics of their art. The ultimate custodian of the clarity of this text is David Frankel, who edited this book and protected its spirit, just as he did with an earlier book I wrote on black altars. *Che, macanudos y macanudas, mil gracias.*

ROBERT FARRIS THOMPSON
February 14, 2005
New Haven

INDEX

Photograph of Milena Plebs and José Oviedo by Alejandra Quiroz: plate 50.

Ricardo Sanguinetti: plate 3.

Clark Thompson: plate 46.

Courtesy of Robert Farris Thompson: plates 26, 37, 38, 48, and 68.

Photo by Robert Farris Thompson: plates 5, 10, 12, 30, 32, 39, 40, and 72.

Courtesy of the archives of *Todo Es Historia:* plate 31.